SCHOOLS AND SOCIETIES

SCHOOLS AND SOCIETIES

Second Edition

STEVEN BRINT

STANFORD SOCIAL SCIENCES
An imprint of Stanford University Press
Stanford, California 2006

Stanford University Press
Stanford, California

First edition published by Pine Forge Press, © 1998.

Printed in the United States of America on acid-free, archival-quality paper

Library of Congress Cataloging-in-Publication Data

Brint, Steven G.
Schools and societies / Steven Brint — 2nd ed.
p.   cm.
  Includes bibliographical references and index.
  ISBN 0-8047-5505-1 (cloth : alk. paper) —ISBN 0-8047-5073-4 (pbk. : alk. paper)
   1. Educational sociology—United States.   2. Schools—United States—Sociological aspects.   I. Title.

LC191.4.B75   2006
306.43—dc22

2006004024

Typeset by G&S Typesetters in 10/13.5 Minion

Last figure below indicates year of this printing:
15   14   13   12   11   10   09   08   07   06

CONTENTS

PREFACE

The daily papers in the United States are full of stories about national testing, multicultural curricula, bilingual education, vouchers, values teaching, the virtues and vices of "conceptual math," teacher qualifications, and a host of other school-related issues. The intensity of the debate about these issues suggests that Americans are unusually preoccupied with their schools. Hovering over these debates is an abiding concern about whether children are learning the things they will need to know to succeed in an information-rich, global economy—and, more to the point, whether one's own children will get the education they need.

What many people do not appreciate is how often school issues are at the center of public passions in other countries as well. A government in Canada decides to lower teacher qualifications to bring more teachers into the schools and a full-fledged national crisis ensues. A political party in France calls for stricter controls on subsidies to Catholic schools and dormant, but centuries-old divisions in French society spring to life again. A report on bullying in Japanese primary schools becomes a national *cause célèbre*. Other social institutions may be as important as schools, but often it is schooling that people around the world seem to care about.

The power of schooling to excite public passions is not as surprising as it first seems. Most days of the year, hundreds of millions of parents turn over temporary custody of their children to these public houses of instruction. Parents naturally hope this will be time well spent. In particular, the hopes parents entertain for their children's later life success are caught up in the power of schools to equip children with skills and attitudes that will help them. Collectively, too, citizens hold high expectations of schooling. Perhaps outside of the legal system, no other social institution is as thoroughly implicated in collective concerns about national identity, inter-group relations, and future progress.

This book is based on a new approach to understanding schools as social institutions. It moves away from the now rather tired debates between functionalists and conflict theorists over whether schools serve the whole of society or primarily the interest of elites. The forms of schooling we have today originated as means to address the interests of social classes and status groups in intergenerational reproduction, and they have been significantly advanced by the nation-building interests of state elites. However, as these forms developed they began to serve purposes that were legitimated, at least, in societal terms. These purposes include transmitting school knowledge, helping to socialize the young, and selecting motivated and able people to move ahead in the educational structure and, ultimately, in the occupational fields connected to it.

The book is intended to do more than summarize the existing sociological literature on schooling. It is intended to bring that literature into a more coherent focus than has been available so far. Indeed, my ambition from the beginning was to write something more than a textbook. Stanford University Press's interest in publishing this revised and updated second edition suggests that the scholarly community has found something of value in the book, over and above its utility as an aid to classroom instruction. I hope *Schools and Societies* will continue to be read by scholars and students as a synthetic book about schooling that provides a framework that can be adapted for thinking about social institutions generally. I believe the second edition represents a significant step forward toward this goal.

The book offers a new way of thinking about some key issues in the sociology of schooling. Here are just a few examples: It classifies the systems of schooling in the industrialized world in a way that reveals how different systems influence the life chances and outlooks of the students who participate in them. It provides the first broadly comparative treatment of schooling in the developing world. It offers a new way of thinking about the divisions of class, race and ethnicity, and gender as they influence educational outcomes. And it provides the first overview of how the school reform measures proposed over the past 25 years have worked out in practice.

Although *Schools and Societies* is intended to be something more than a textbook, it is, of course, also a textbook. It has been used in many universities as a primary text in sociology of education and social foundations of education courses. It is designed to be used in upper-division undergraduate classes and graduate-level classes. It can be used also as a supplementary text in courses on social institutions, socialization, and social stratification. Instructors who use the book as a primary text will find that they have ample room to supplement it with readings of their own choosing, either to enrich and highlight materials covered in the book or to provide alternative interpretations of school processes and outcomes discussed in the book.

We are living at a time when all state institutions are under unusual stress. Trends toward the privatization of schooling are all around us, including large increases in parental support for tutoring, private elementary and secondary schooling, home schooling, and a variety of choice programs, including charter and magnet schools. It is a good time to assess how public schooling, one of the most important state institutions, has developed historically and comparatively.

We are also living at a time when the first signs of a global culture are emerging. If we can avoid conflict between ideological or political-economic systems, the next generation of adults will be in closer touch with people in many countries around the world. Studies of schooling have not, by and large, caught up to the emergence of global society. If we choose to broaden our scope of vision, we will see that we have a rich canvas of schooling organizations from which to gain insight about our own and other societies. I have written this book partly in the hope that it will encourage the next generation of educators, social scientists, and engaged citizens to think about schooling from a perspective more appropriate to the world that is emerging. I hope that the book also conveys the intellectual excitement of using the tools of sociology to look at schools from this global comparative perspective.

ACKNOWLEDGMENTS

When Wendy Griswold asked whether I would be interested in working on this book, I had just finished a lengthy study of the professions. I thought this book would make a good transition project and would not take long to write. But the gaps in my understanding of schooling quickly ended any plans I had for fast work of this book.

The finished work seems to me to have been worth the extra time and effort it required. My first thank you, therefore, goes to Wendy for that fateful telephone call—and for her encouragement and collegiality. My second thank you goes to Steve Rutter, the publisher of the series in which this book first appeared. Because of his attentiveness and good spirits, Steve helped to make writing the book a pleasurable experience in unexpected ways. I am especially grateful to Norris Pope of Stanford University Press for his strong conviction about the merits of this book. I am also grateful to Kate Wahl for shepherding the book through the publication process at the press.

Many scholars have commented on chapter drafts or sections of chapters. They have helped me to sharpen the arguments and saved me from errors. I would like to thank Jutta Allmendinger, David Baker, Burton Clark, Jaap Dronkers, Susan Eckstein, Bruce Fuller, Patricia Aljberg Graham, Floyd Hammack, Mark Hanson, Mazen Hashem, Barbara Heyns, Michael Hout, Dan Lortie, Doug McDowell, Christine Musselin, Caroline Persell, Rob Read, James Rosenbaum, Jack Schuster, Lennart Svensson, David Tyack, Roger Voothroyd, and Pamela Barnhouse Walters for comments that helped to improve the quality of the book. Fred Muskal read the entire manuscript of the first edition in draft form and provided particularly helpful comments. I would also like to thank Clifford Adelman, David Cohen, Kevin Dougherty, Adam Gamoran, Elizabeth Hansot, Michael Hout, Jerome Karabel, Paul Kingston, John Meyer, Thomas Mortenson, Gary Natriello, Lois Peak, George Psacharopoulos, Brian Rowan, Alex Star, Lennart Svensson, and David Swartz for sending along data or bibliographic information that helped.

David Boyns worked as my research assistant during most of the period in which I drafted the manuscript. In addition to tracking down source material, he provided sharp comments on several chapter drafts and a good, critical mind on which to try out ideas.

Becky Smith edited the manuscript of the first edition with an eye to improving its clarity and accessibility.

I first studied the sociology of schooling during several years in the late 1970s and early 1980s when I was in daily contact with a group of talented colleagues at the Huron Institute in Cambridge, Massachusetts. I would like to thank Kevin Dougherty, David Karen, Katherine McClelland, David Swartz, and Jerome Karabel for their many contributions to the social construction of a sociologist.

My wife, Michele Renee Salzman, helped with compositional problems on many occasions and provided sustaining encouragement on all occasions. She is my spring for all seasons of the year. I would like to rededicate this book with love to our children, Juliana and Ben, in the hope that they will continue to become well-educated people: knowledgeable, open to the world, principled, wise, and active.

SCHOOLS AND SOCIETIES

1   SCHOOLS AS SOCIAL INSTITUTIONS

The words "education" and "schooling" are sometimes used interchangeably, but they are not the same. Education, learning about the particular ways of a group, occurs willy-nilly throughout life at home, in peer play, at religious ceremonies, at work. These informal processes of learning occur in every distinct social group. Young Ponapean Islanders in the South Pacific, for example, learn from parents or neighbors that the quietness of a man is like the fierceness of a barracuda, and they also learn how to shape bark to make a watertight canoe. American children also learn most of the things that equip them to survive in their society—from how to act if approached by a stranger to how to operate kitchen appliances—from the people around them in the course of daily life. The same is true of important parts of education in every group and every society: much of what individuals find it necessary to learn for survival and acceptance is taught outside of schools.

As the title *Schools and Societies* suggests, this book is not about education. Instead, it is about schooling, which is the more organized form of education that takes place in schools, and about the consequences of this organized form of education for individuals and for societies. Although schooling is in some ways more limited than education, it has great influence on the members of society. We are on strong ground to limit our scope to the study of schooling, because so much organized social effort goes into the formal education found in schools. It is also much easier to compare what happens in schools in different countries than it is to discuss the truly inexhaustible subject of what happens in educational processes generally.

A related distinction is the one between two academic disciplines: the philosophy of education and the sociology of schooling. The philosophy of education concerns itself primarily with how education ought to be organized and the ends that it ought to serve. Sociology concerns itself with what schools are actually like, with why schools are the way they are, and with the consequences of what happens in schools.

In making this distinction, I do not intend to imply a criticism of philosophy. Asking good questions about what schooling ought ideally to be can make existing forms of social life more visible and clear. For example, the philosopher's idea that liberal education ought to provide a way of experiencing universal themes, such as the qualities of mature judgment, provides a good vantage point for sociological investigations about how changing national interests and cultural traditions help to shape the actually existing humanities curriculum. Both modes of thought have a legitimate place in the universe of academic study, but sociology is primarily concerned with what actually exists and how it came to be.

Mark Twain's Education on the Mississippi

In *Life on the Mississippi*, the American writer Mark Twain provides a memorable reminiscence of his apprenticeship as a Mississippi riverboat captain. Twain's portrait reminds us of the difficulty of learning hard subjects and about what is gained and lost in the educational process. It also raises good sociological questions: Why are so few teachers as effective as Mr. Bixby? And why have schools displaced on-the-job apprenticeships in so many fields?

Like many adventurous boys in the 1830s, young Sam Clemens (Twain's original name) longed to pilot one of the magnificent steamboats that carried the vast assembly of humanity from roustabouts to fine ladies and their cargo up and down the great Mississippi. Clemens managed to apprentice himself to a veteran pilot, a Mr. Bixby, in return for $500 to be paid out of his first wages as a pilot. Twain recalls the easy confidence with which he began his ordeal of learning the river. "I supposed that all a pilot had to do was keep his boat in the river, and I did not consider that could be much of a trick, since it was so wide."

This easy confidence did not last the morning. Bixby began his lessons by pointing out some landmarks on the river where the water changed depth.

> Presently he turned on me and said: "What's the name of the first point above New Orleans?"
>
> I was gratified to be able to answer promptly, and I did. I said I didn't know.
>
> "Don't know? Well, you're a smart one!" said Mr. Bixby. "What's the name of the next point?"
>
> Once more I didn't know.
>
> "Well, this beats anything. Tell me the name of any point or place I told you."
>
> I studied for a while and decided that I couldn't.
>
> ". . . You—you don't know?" mimicking my drawling manner of speech. "What do you know?"
>
> "I—I—nothing for certain."
>
> "By the great Caesar's ghost, I believe you! You're the stupidest dunderhead I ever saw or ever heard of, so help me Moses! The idea of you being a pilot—you! Why, you don't know enough to pilot a cow down the lane."

Thus begins the education of the young Mark Twain on the Mississippi River. Soon Clemens's notebook "fairly bristles" with the names of towns, "points," bars, islands, bends, and reaches on the river, for the only way to get to be a pilot is to "get the entire river by heart." When he has finally completed his apprenticeship on the river, Twain reflects on what he has gained and lost in the effort:

> Now when I had mastered the language of this water, and had come to know every trifling feature that bordered the great river as familiarly as I knew the letters of the alphabet, I had made a valuable acquisition. But I had lost something

too. All the grace, the beauty, the poetry, had gone out of the majestic river! A day came when I began to cease from noting the glories and the charms which the moon and the sun and the twilight wrought on the river's face; another day came when I ceased altogether to note them. All the value any feature of it had for me now was the amount of usefulness it could furnish toward compassing the safe piloting of a steamboat. (Twain [1896] 1972:31, 48–9)

THE SOCIETAL IMPORTANCE OF SCHOOLING

Schooling is very highly valued by governments and their citizens. One indicator is that schooling takes up a large amount of young people's time. If we assume that the average young person spends six hours in school five days a week and nine months a year for at least 12 years, the total number of hours in school between the ages of 6 and 18 is almost 13,000. For the increasing number of people who complete a college degree, that figure climbs to over 17,000 hours of schooling. People who graduate from college will have spent, on average, one out of six of their waking hours in school from their sixth through their twenty-first year—and that does not count homework!

As Figure 1.1 shows, children spend more time in school than they do watching television and playing with friends during the course of an average week. Moreover, school hours are more important as socializing agents for most children, given the amount of attention school requires and the highly involving competitions and group interactions that occur there. Judging simply in terms of the amount of time they take up, schools are also substantially more important than other community socializing institutions, such as churches and recreational activities (see Figure 1.1). Even those who attend religious services every week, for example, spend only approximately one-tenth the time in their churches, synagogues, or mosques between the ages of 6 and 18 than they do in their schools.

Another indicator of the importance that modern societies place on schooling is the amount of money they are willing to spend on it. Indeed, the most fundamental thing to be said about schooling in the contemporary world is that it involves substantial expenditure. Citizens devote relatively large amounts of their hard-earned money to build schools, to maintain school grounds, to purchase equipment and materials, and to pay the salaries of teachers and staffs.

The contemporary education "industry" is impressively large. In the United States, expenditures on schooling from kindergarten to college account for approximately 7 percent of the gross domestic product (GDP). More than $725 billion is spent on education each year in the United States (OECD 2004:219). This amount is not as much as Americans spend on health care, but nearly twice as much as the construction industry's share of the GDP, more than five times the share of either the food products or auto industries, and ten times the share of radio and television broadcasting (U.S. Bureau of the Census 2003:439).

Another good measure of a society's commitment to schooling is the number of people working in schools. Schoolteachers are by far the largest occupation classified as professional by the U.S. Bureau of the Census, numbering more than 5.5 million in 2002. College instructors and professors accounted for another million, pushing the total number of

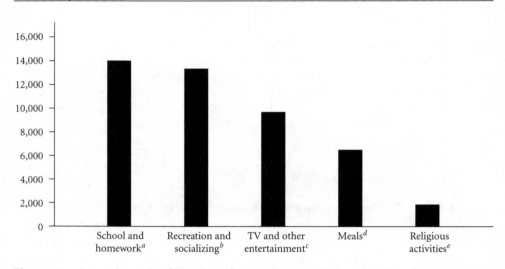

Figure 1.1 Approximate Total Number of Hours Spent on Various Activities for an Average
American Child, Ages 6–18

[a]School and homework: Calculated as 6 hours of school and 1 hour of homework per school day.

[b]Recreation and socializing: Calculated as 2.5 hours per day during the school year and 6.5 hours per day during summer vacation.

[c]TV and other entertainment: Calculated as 2.5 hours per day.

[d]Meals: Calculated as 1.5 hours per day.

[e]Religious activities: Calculated as 2 hours per week (churchgoers only).

teachers in the United States well past 6.5 million. Another 849,000 people worked in educational administration. The United States now has three teachers for every nurse, three for every engineer, seven teachers for every lawyer, and eight teachers for every doctor (ibid.:399).

Expenditures on schooling are similarly high throughout the developed world. As Table 1.1 indicates, in the richer industrial societies spending on education at all levels typically accounts for between 5 and 8 percent of the GDP. The United States is on the high side (along with Korea, Australia, Canada, and several Scandinavian countries); Greece, Ireland, and the Czech Republic are on the low side (OECD 2004:219–21). People in developing countries may place even more faith in schooling as a road to economic and social progress, but they have fewer resources to devote to it. In developing countries, expenditures on schooling typically average between 2 and 3 percent of GDP. But they sometimes reach up to one-quarter or more of the government's total budget (Kurian 2001).

Why does virtually every country on the planet want to invest such large amounts of money in schooling? The answer is complex. Schooling was at one time limited to an elite, no more than the top 2 or 3 percent of the population, and it was run by private academies or by church officials. In Europe, the shift to schooling for the masses began in the late 1700s led by kings who wanted to build a stronger loyalty to the state among poorer populations, particularly those living in the hinterlands (Bendix 1968:243–8). In the United States, the shift to mass schooling began a short time later, in the early 1800s, and was linked to an evangelical enthusiasm for building civic virtue in the new democracy. Later, it became linked to the effort of the Protestant mainstream to Americanize new immigrants. In a het-

TABLE 1.1
*Educational expenditures as a percentage of GDP,
selected countries, 2001*

Country	Educational spending as a percentage of GDP
Korea	8.2
United States	7.3
Denmark	7.1
Sweden	6.5
Canada	6.1
Australia	6.0
France	6.0
Mexico	5.9
United Kingdom	5.5
Germany	5.3
Italy	5.3
Hungary	5.2
Japan	4.6
Czech Republic	4.6
Ireland	4.5
Greece	4.1

SOURCE: Organization for Economic Cooperation and Development (OECD 2004:229).

erogeneous society, composed of many ethnic and religious groups, schools were the closest approximation to an American established church. They taught Protestant-entrepreneurial values—such as temperance and industriousness—that were generalized into a creed, as "the American way of life" (Berthoft 1971:438).

Today, schooling is often thought to be an all-purpose panacea. More and better education is seen as the best solution to the common problems that ail most societies. Does a society have too many poor people? Does it have an epidemic of drug use? Does it have too many children who suffer at the hands of abusive parents? The first solution that many people think of is to try to change attitudes and behaviors through more education in public schools (Graham 1993).

Most important, schooling has become strongly associated with interests of the nation-state in the development of a trained workforce and well-disciplined citizenry. Most people believe that education is the route to a better life. Economists who study human capital (that is, the productive skills and experience of human beings) argue that improved education contributes not only to the economic value of individuals but also to a country's overall prosperity. Economists have even quantified the economic value of education, arguing that an increase of one year in the average education of a population is associated with an increase of between 3 and 6 percent of total economic output (OECD 2004). In the developing world, schooling is associated with economic progress to such a degree that governments have often spent more on schools than is economically prudent.

Schooling seems to have other benefits as well. More highly educated people are healthier. They read more books and newspapers than other people, and are more likely to be informed about current events. They participate more actively in the political and civic life of their communities; they are more cosmopolitan and tolerant in their social attitudes; and they express higher levels of trust and happiness. What's more, educated people show these attributes, even when social backgrounds and current incomes are statistically controlled to isolate the effects of education alone (Davis 1982; Hyman and Wright 1979; Kingston et al. 2003). Cognitive ability may lie behind some of these "education effects," but it does not explain them all.

Elementary and secondary schooling is primarily an activity of the state. In the West, the state wrested control of education from churches in the eighteenth and nineteenth centuries. It is supported by taxes and provided free of charge to children. Some number of years of attendance is usually compulsory. This amount may vary from 5 or 6 years in many developing countries to 10 or 11 years in most of the industrialized world. Indeed, although they were confronted by religious and ethnic opposition, nation-building states were able in the end to control the provision of primary and secondary schooling in every country but the Netherlands, where religious divisions prevailed. Today, primary and secondary schooling is primarily a publicly controlled activity in every country but the Netherlands (where financing, however, is public). The private sector is comparatively large in countries like Korea and Japan, because of private supplemental schools that children attend after regular school.

Higher education is a different matter. Here public and private alternatives very often coexist. Korea, the United States, Japan, and Australia have quite high private expenditures for college- and university-level education—half or more of all spending in these countries is private. Most of this spending comes in the form of tuition fees. By contrast, low tuition fees have remained a distinctive feature of Western European countries, even during the current period of enthusiasm for market-oriented public policies. Germany and most Scandinavian societies provide higher education almost exclusively through public institutions and public funding (OECD 2004:230). Table 1.2 shows the mix of public and private enrollment at all school levels for 11 developed countries.

Given the preponderance of governmental control of schooling today and the nearly universal attendance of young people through age 14, it is remarkable to think that education in Western Europe and the United States before the late eighteenth century was almost entirely private or church run. It is even more remarkable that formal schooling, even in the elementary and early secondary school years, was limited to only a small upper crust instead of covering 100 percent of the age group.

THINKING SOCIOLOGICALLY

As befits the social expenditure devoted to it, schooling is a much-thought-about and highly organized activity. In this respect, it contrasts sharply with the haphazard character of most other kinds of education. However, the organization of schools has also been criticized for serving the needs of society (or society's elites) to the detriment of individuals. Neither the level of planning nor the criticisms are surprising once we appreciate that schools are powerful institutions. They are society's major means of shaping its young and of sorting them for future roles.

TABLE 1.2
*Relative proportion of public spending on educational
institutions by level, selected countries, 2001*

| | PERCENT OF SPENDING FROM PUBLIC SOURCES | |
Country	Higher education	Primary/ secondary education[a]
Denmark	98	98
Germany	91	81[b]
Sweden	88	100
France	86	93
Czech Republic	85	92
Italy	78	98
Netherlands	78	95
Hungary	78	93
Spain	76	93
United Kingdom	71	86
Canada	59	92
Australia	51	84
Japan	43	91
United States	34	93
Korea	16	76

SOURCE: Organization for Economic Cooperation and Development
(OECD 2004:242–3).

[a] Includes post-secondary nontertiary education (e.g., vocational-
technical institutes).

[b] Includes "dual system" of apprenticeship training financed, in part, by
private industry.

The Logic of Curriculum

As educational organizations, schools have many advantages as compared to less formal
processes of education in everyday life. These advantages have to do with schools' selectivity and sequencing of curricular materials, their efforts to maintain strong boundaries
between what they do and do not allow into the classroom, and their sustained focus on
learning.

1. *Selectivity.* Schools are highly selective about what they teach. Overt commercialism,
   popular fashions, popular music, street language, and racial and ethnic prejudices
   are among the things usually selected out. Language and literature, math and science, history, social studies, and a few other subjects are nearly always selected in.
   To some degree, communities choose what they want to allow into the relatively
   purified environment of the schools, but these decisions must be made on the
   grounds of intellectual merit. Sometimes these choices become part of political conflict in communities. Should sex education be taught? Should world history take a
   global perspective or a national perspective? Because schools emphasize intellectual
   merit, however, these conflicts only very rarely permit purely popular elements to
   infiltrate the classroom environment.

2. *Boundaries.* Schools make efforts to maintain strong boundaries in relation to the
   outside world. Teachers and administrators defend the curriculum and classroom

against many undesirable features of the environment outside of the school. In school, for example, older children don't learn how to creatively torment younger children, although they may learn this skill in their neighborhood gangs. They do not learn how to swear or give free rein to prejudice. High- and low-status identities that exist outside of the school are in principle, if not always in fact, treated with indifference within its confines. It doesn't matter whether a student is rich or poor, Protestant or Catholic, male or female. The controlling identity is supposed to be the student identity. What happens in the academic environment of the school is all that is meant to count.

3. *Focus.* Everyday life is full of learning, but it is episodic. Learning occurs as a by-product of other activities, such as getting the chores done, fooling around with friends, or talking about the day. Only in schools is a focus on learning sustained and continuous. Because the focus is on learning, classrooms involve plenty of explanation, many examples to help students to understand new material, and lots of repetition! The attention of the classroom may waver from learning, but it does not waver for very long in most classrooms.

4. *Sequencing.* The curriculum of the classroom, as compared to the curriculum of everyday life, is sequenced for efficient learning. It is organized in a progressive way. Features that are fairly fundamental and accessible to the young must be mastered first. Later lessons build on earlier learning. Building on prior knowledge makes lessons more easily comprehensible and allows teachers to monitor student progress in learning elementary tasks before more complex tasks are attempted.

Through these four features of content organization, schools are intended to provide students with opportunities to escape from the limitations of the social groups into which they are born. Most education that occurs outside of schools simply reproduces the skills, worldviews, and customs of a particular group. In contrast, schools *at their best* provide a kind of magic carpet that can allow students to escape from the confines of their own particular group and make contact with a broader environment. We cannot be too idealistic about this, of course. Schools are far from perfect learning environments. Teachers and other students are cursed regularly in school corridors, and some schools have violence and bullying problems. But at least we can say that the great majority of schools are organized to limit and minimize these intrusions.

The Underside of Schooling

Not everyone sees the basic principles of school organization in such a positive light. Among social critics, schools are often described as threatening and dispiriting places, where the young are subjected to a regime based on equal parts academic fear and mind-numbing boredom.[1] Needless to say, theirs is a picture of schooling that compares unfavorably with the free-flowing, creative, and nonthreatening character of more informal educational processes. Here is what one critic, John Holt (1964), had to say about American schools:

To a very great degree, school is a place where children learn to be stupid. . . . Infants are not stupid. Children of one, two, or even three throw the whole of themselves into everything they do. They embrace life, and devour it; it is why they learn so fast, and are such good company. Listlessness, boredom, apathy—these all come later. Children come to school curious; within a few years most of that curiosity is dead, or at least silent. Open a first grade or third grade to questions and you will be deluged; fifth graders say nothing. (p. 157)

Schools are relatively "purified" and elevated environments, but they are quite clearly also hierarchical, rule-bound, strictly disciplined, relatively impersonal, and continuously graded environments. Schools are, in these respects, the first performance-based bureaucracies that most people encounter. A clear chain of command descends from school board to superintendent to principals to teachers with students at the bottom of the chain. The rights and obligations of students, teachers, and administrators are strictly regulated by formal administrative rules and by informal rules of decorum, whose violation elicits sharp censures. The personal interests and needs of students, who may be considered little more than immature workers, are typically of less interest to teachers than their success at mastering their lessons and conforming to classroom rules. Testing is a continuous vexation felt in many a brow, palm, and bladder.

Moreover, in most schools, relatively little about classroom life is spontaneous or charged with emotion. John Goodlad's (1984) research group studied 1,000 American classrooms in the late 1970s and early 1980s. He summed up the results of his investigation as follows:

> The physical environment of most of the classrooms [was] devoid of amenities likely to provide comfort, unattractive or at least aesthetically bland, and cramped for space. They lacked decoration in the form of wall hangings, prints of good paintings, contrasting colors on walls, doors, and cupboards. . . . The picture is of increasing drabness as one moves upward through the grades. [The] relationship between teachers and classes of students was almost completely devoid of outward evidences of affect. Shared laughter, overt enthusiasm, or angry outbursts were rarely observed. . . . I wonder about the impact of the flat, neutral emotional ambience of most of the classes we studied. Boredom is a disease of epidemic proportions. (226–7, 229–30, 242)

Holt's (1964) judgment, shared by generations of critics, was that schools "make children stupid" by making them fearful of their performance and bored by the ways in which they are expected to learn. However, those who are more sympathetic to the practices of the schools see the same characteristics deplored by Holt—discipline, rules, and tests—as precisely the characteristics that allow immature students to learn difficult lessons with some measure of efficiency and success.

The evidence is mixed on this point, which may be why the argument has persisted for 250 years. Most students adapt relatively easily to a structured environment and do not find school particularly alienating. This is especially true for students whose home life has a consistent level of order and whose parents are supportive of the educational mission of the schools (Entwisle, Alexander, and Olson 1997; Ho and Willms 1996). Indeed, for some students, schools provide a relatively engaging and supportive refuge from the vicissitudes of an unstable home life, where fostering and nurturing behaviors are less in evidence.

Moreover, both teacher morale and student learning appear to be enhanced in schools that are relatively structured. Teacher morale, for example, is associated with high levels of confidence in the support for them provided by principals and with clear rules about teachers' rights and responsibilities (Moeller 1964; Liu and Meyer 2005). Higher levels of student learning are associated with good order in classrooms (Coleman and Hoffer 1987); with the amount of time spent on task rather than in free-form or classroom management activities (Edmonds 1979); even with the amount and difficulty of the material covered during a term, provided that it is age appropriate (Dreeben and Gamoran 1986).

The Management of Motivation

Even so, the management of motivation in performance-oriented bureaucracies is never an easy task, and it is particularly difficult when the people from whom performance is required are children or young adults who are surrounded by others of their own age. Children are naturally full of energy, and they have limited attention spans. Some intelligent children (as judged by the staff) receive more than their share of attention in school, placing others in their shadows. Similarly, some children are able to resist the promptings of emotion and exuberance better than their classmates and are often appreciated by teachers for their restraint. Those who do not stand out or stand out negatively are inclined to withdraw interest from the school and may encourage others to do so as well. Some students—in some schools, a large number—are unable or unwilling to adapt to the school environment and are chronically unhappy in it.

The task of stimulating and channeling motivation is naturally difficult under these circumstances. It is made more difficult because some of the most effective devices used in motivating adult workers, such as wages and salaries, are not available to school authorities. Teachers and schools consequently work in an emotional terrain studded, figuratively speaking, with land mines of potential student resistance.

In their efforts to stimulate and motivate children, schools rely on organizational blueprints and strategies that go well beyond simple classroom discipline and whatever rapport may develop between teachers and students. These blueprints and strategies are foundations of the social order of the school. By social order, I mean the norms of conduct, orientation, and identity into which children are inserted and with which they must learn to comply, if they want to avoid the school disciplinarian. Elements of the social order of schooling include the organization of space and time, the use of rituals both to differentiate and integrate students, the creation of status hierarchies, and the use of standardized membership categories. Some elements of this social order are not formally organized; instead, they emerge through the joint activity of teachers and students in the everyday life of the classroom. Looking with fresh eyes at these everyday features of schooling can help to prepare us for thinking in a more analytical way about how schools operate as institutions.

Structure: The organization of time and space. In schools, space and time are organized both to control students and to allow for psychologically useful intervals of separation between staff and students. The physical spaces into which children are allowed are strictly delimited, and the school day is cut up to avoid leaving students much time away from the eye of watchful authorities. Certain physical spaces, the teachers' lounge, for example, are designated for staff alone to regroup and let off steam during class breaks. Certain time periods, such as recess and lunch, are designed to let children group spontaneously and release pent-up energy. Movement between activities is strictly regulated. Bells organize access to classroom space during the day. Access to certain other school spaces, such as the principal's office or the nurse's office, is restricted to students, who must be directed to them by their teachers.

Structure: Rituals. Schools also rely on rituals for shaping and motivating students. Rituals are focused gatherings that channel group attention and involvement in a particular direction and generate collective enthusiasm for the school. Rituals fall into two categories. Differentiating rituals highlight those who best conform to school ideals. These differentiating rituals include tests, performances, and award ceremonies. The difficulty with differentiating rituals is that although they affirm the hierarchical divisions of the school and may increase motivation among some students, they may also decrease motivation among those students whose loyalty to the school is already weak. Integrating rituals, which allow for collective identification with the school, balance differentiating rituals. Integrating rituals focus attention on emblems of the school or activities that allow for the participation of large numbers of students. These integrating rituals include pep rallies and sporting events, dances and other school-sponsored social activities, academic and extramural competitions with other schools, and the celebration of school traditions or school heroes that build sentimental attachments to the school (Bernstein 1975, chap. 2).

Structure: Multiple status hierarchies. Students are integrated into the life of the school also because school authorities allow students to explore many different paths to gaining status. In general, loyalty to the school is easier to retain where many roads to status are available than where only the academic road exists. This is why schools affirm their primary purpose through tests and awards to scholars but also encourage the emergence of non-academic hierarchies based on good looks and popularity, athletic ability, musical and dramatic gifts, and participation in student government. One reason why high school is often a more pleasant experience for students than middle school is that high schools generally offer more extracurricular activities and thus more routes to status. Indeed, in the majority of American secondary schools, the most athletic and the most popular students are far more admired by their classmates than are the top scholars (Coleman 1961; Tye 1985).

Even the nonconformist student underground sustains a kind of loyalty to the school. Membership and status in this counterculture make school at least bearable for some students, however rebellious their stance against school authorities. Many intelligent administrators take the position that the student underground is a valuable part of the life of the school, even though these administrators may themselves be a frequent object of its scorn.

Structure: Standardized membership categories. In general, things would go much worse if schools simply bestowed benefits on the quick-witted and motivated few while blasting the confidence of the majority. Indeed, many individual differences in performance are obscured by broad standardized membership categories that allow students with highly unequal achievements to be treated more or less equally. The category "high school graduate," for example, is treated as a meaningful element of the American social structure, even though high school graduates include some people who know a great deal and some who can barely read and write. Similar ambiguities emerge from other widely used educational categories, such as "history course," "four units of credit," and "credentialed teacher." Some history courses are tough; others are easy. Some units of credit are demanding; others are not. Some formally certified teachers know how to inspire and connect; others are inept.

These categories are treated as standard by schools, and precisely because they are treated as standard, they support the schooling enterprise (Meyer and Rowan 1978). If high school graduates were seriously compared to one another, or credentialed teachers were examined closely for evidence of equal competence, profound doubts about the system might very well arise. Insofar as people assume that the categories mean something, they do mean something and the business of schooling goes along with great success, churning out graduates, credit hours, majors, and teachers. (We should not push this argument too far. No doubt, if performance and school categories managed to be completely unconnected, public support of schooling would suffer.)

The existence of these standardized membership categories also contributes to the ability of schools to maintain motivation. It is easier to maintain motivation where legitimacy is allocated in large measure by membership in a category rather than by differences in individual performance. If students were only those who succeed at a high proficiency level, a great many young people would drop out of school and pursue activities in which they had a better chance of feeling accepted and appreciated.

Emergent elements: The community life of schools. Emergent properties of everyday interaction in school also help to maintain the social order of schools. In the classrooms of the young, where children remain together throughout the day, a community life usually emerges, a village-like atmosphere that provides pleasure to those who are villagers, however temporarily. Running jokes, pleasing forms of recognition ("our little detective," "our speedy weaver"), even absorbing forms of half-serious conflict ("the king of the boys vs. the queen of the girls") create an atmosphere of community. Myths and legends about previous students and teachers also abound, especially about those defined as odd or unsavory by the majority. Sometimes, stories about these characters of school folklore remain long after the original parties have left the school. These myths and legends also help to define a moral order of the school by characterizing the boundaries between the normal and the deviant as defined by the student body. In larger schools, as children move past the primary grades and experience for the first time the continuous breakup of relationships in their hour-by-hour movement through classrooms and subject matters, this kind of community-like atmosphere fades.

Recurring temporal patterns also knit together the classroom community. The energy and attention of teachers and students alike follow the rhythms of the school day, week, and year as if traveling on the current of a powerful river. Two former teachers, Ann Lieberman and Lynne Miller (1987), perceptively describe the American variant of these school rhythms. A daily routine exists: taking attendance, continuing from yesterday, introducing today's material, winding down, and making assignments. Days are punctuated by interruptions, with some settling down required after each interruption. Mondays are often hard for everyone, and Fridays are hard at least for students who are already thinking of the weekend.

In the annual rhythm, fall is a time of promise, with a downward spiral from the excitement of the new school year through Thanksgiving, and a brief resurgence between Thanksgiving and Christmas. For most, January is brief. February is very long, and the promise of summer stirs first in March. The final weeks are filled with activities, and then the patterns learned and shared are rudely put to an end on a Friday in June. These rhythms are elements of school organization that help define the behavior of all who are involved.

SOCIOLOGICAL THEORIES OF SCHOOLING

As you may have already sensed, the underlying coherence of schools makes them an eminently suitable subject for sociology. Sociologists are trained to analyze the relationships that define the workings of organizations and institutions; the social and historical context in which these relationships develop; and the actual behaviors of people in concrete settings, as opposed to the idealized accounts that people sometimes give of their behavior.

Theories of Schooling and Society

Theories of the causes and consequences of schooling were once divided between "structural-functional" and social power (or "conflict") theories. The first emphasized society-level interests and the construction of an institutional order to serve those interests; the second emphasized elite interests and the unequal distribution of resources between social classes. In this book, I will argue that the choice between these two approaches is a false one. Both can help us to develop a good sociological understanding of schooling; and neither has proven entirely sufficient on its own.

Structural-functionalist theories. This approach emphasized the capacity of institutions to reduce the randomness of human action and to channel human action along specified lines (through "structures") to meet socially approved ends (or "functions"). A student, for example, might feel like breaking out into dance on top of his desk during a lesson, but he probably would not do it, because schools channel action along other lines—ostensibly in the direction of learning course materials. They also back up their efforts to channel action with incentives (like grades) and sanctions (like detentions).

Talcott Parsons (1951), a leader of the structural-functional school, described the elementary structural characteristics of any social institution as consisting of the following:

- Institutions have responsibility for a particular socially defined *collectivity* (or collectivities) whose members are defined as eligible to participate. In the case of schools, the collectivity consists of groups of age-defined children, living in some proximity to one another, and treated as students; and the staff, the teachers, who are hired to instruct them.

- Personnel in an institution are organized into *status-roles*. Status refers to privileges and responsibilities within a hierarchy of authority. Roles refer to expected behaviors, which can be monitored and controlled by others higher up in the hierarchy.

In schools, students, teachers, and administrators are the key status-roles. Each one has a defined position, privileges, and responsibilities, and each one has a set of behavioral expectations associated with their activities. Teachers, for example, inject their unique personalities into their roles, but all teachers will be expected to spend time introducing and explaining new material, writing important information on the board, correcting mistakes, asking questions related to lessons, and so on.

- The practices in institutions are strongly influenced by *norms*, or the rules and conventions that regulate behavior. Norms can relate to what is not allowed to happen in the institution (e.g., What kinds of teasing and taunting are impermissible?). Or they can related to what is expected to occur in the institution (e.g., How much time is supposed to be spent on reading as compared to math?). Institutions reward action in accord with norms, and when norms are broken, sanctions come into play—ranging from expulsion at one extreme to a raised eyebrow at the other.

- Institutions are legitimated by *values*, or the ultimate purposes to which the institution is committed. In the case of schools, these values include the effective transmission of school knowledge and codes of "good conduct." Authorities often appeal to values to legitimate their actions, to resolve conflicts, and to rechannel action.

Schools, like other institutions, are seen by structural-functionalists as serving important society-wide purposes. Parsons (1959) argued that schools in modern industrial societies are charged with socializing students into the culture of achievement and for aiding in the selection of students for demanding positions in the occupational structure. No society, Parsons argued, fully succeeds in removing family advantages from the process of adult status attainment, but schools contribute to "achievement-based" mobility by rewarding academically able, conformist students from lower-status backgrounds. Parsons and his colleagues recognized that the values and norms of the schools were not simply accepted by all. Some students fail to meet the schools' performance demands, and may come to reject these demands, leading to dropout and delinquency. Other students identify much more strongly with the culture of peer popularity than with the culture of school achievement, leading to tensions between the two ranking systems. (Nevertheless, for Parsons both hierarchies are desirable; socially capable adults—winners in the popularity realm—are necessary for leadership and performance roles, while intellectually capable adults—winners in the academic realm—are necessary for technical roles.)

John W. Meyer and Brian Rowan (1977, 1978) offered what became an influential revision of the structural-functional theory of schooling. It emphasized that institutions are rooted more in widely recognized cultural categories than in shared societal values—and that they are important not so much because they reduce randomness and meet social purposes, but because they provide legitimacy. For Meyer and Rowan, a school may or may not educate students effectively, but if it faithfully mirrors the organization of other schools, it will be accorded legitimacy in the eyes of the public. It can use that legitimacy to muster the resources it needs to survive. This approach leads to the surprising conclusion that schools do not need to succeed in educating students (at least not very well) to succeed in gaining legitimacy from the public and other organizations in their environments. But, whether they educate well or not, they must conform to existing legitimating categories to succeed as organizations.

Social power theories. Meyer and Rowan's insights are provocative, but a weakness of their approach, shared by structural-functionalism, is that it de-emphasizes the power of elites (and later the state as an instrument of elite interests) to design institutions that reflect their own interests and ideals more closely than those of society at large (Lockwood 1956; M. Mann 1986). This weakness is the central focus of a leading alternative to structural-functionalism: social power (or "conflict") theory. The powerful are the designers of institutions for conflict theorists, and they are also the main beneficiaries of these designs.

In some respects, conflict theorists have the stronger side of the argument. It is clear that the interests of the powerful have been an important influence on schooling from the beginning. The first formal schools began because they served the needs of religious and political leaders for scribes. The first compulsory schools in Europe served the interests of rulers in creating loyal subjects, who would be willing to pay taxes and bear arms. Indeed, throughout the history of schooling, we can see the imprint of powerful groups creating and transforming schools. In the United States, the large business corporations provided the decisive models for the "one best system" of schooling that became popular during the Progressive Era—a system based on standardized school districts, strict hierarchies of authority, age-graded classrooms, and regular testing for performance evaluation (Tyack 1974). The influence of elites continues to shape schooling in the United States. For example, a few influential academics, business leaders, and politicians worked together to institute a regime of high-stakes testing in the United States in the 1980s. This change cannot accurately be described as reflecting the consensus of society as a whole. In fact, many students, teachers, and parents do not think high-stakes testing serves the interests of children, or that it leads to the development of higher-level thinking skills. In this case, like so many others, policy was shaped by a political coalition, not by "society."

Corporate and other elite groups are not the only source of influence on school policies. Members of well-organized social movements have sometimes had an impact as well. In the United States, for example, the implementation of multicultural curricula can be attributed to social movement activists of the 1960s and 1970s who demanded more attention to issues of race and gender in the school curriculum. In general, however, business leaders (and their allies) are better able to organize and implement plans for change, because they have better access to the levers of state power.

The social power approach also correctly emphasizes that the interests of the main actors in schools—students, teachers, and administrators—are not always in alignment. Teachers, for example, may feel that principals need to back them up in all discipline cases, while principals may worry about alienating the parents of a misbehaving student, particularly if those parents are influential in the community. Such conflicts of interest are common in schools (as in other institutions). These conflicts of interest must be taken in consideration, along with the smooth coordination and control of actors in status-roles emphasized by structural-functional theory.

Although we should be wary of all views that do not offer an analysis of the social power interests served by schooling, we are not well advised to adopt the opposite position either:

that the power of elites is all that matters in the organization of schooling. The most important elites in democratic-capitalist societies are business leaders and wealthy investors. Samuel Bowles and Herbert Gintis (1976) argued that schools serve the interests of business elites by creating a docile labor force, used to taking orders from authorities, and by legitimating a highly unequal distribution of wealth and income. For Bowles and Gintis, the widely accepted idea that schools are based on equality of opportunity and earned rewards provides a powerful legitimating ideology that masks the perpetuation of a system that is strongly skewed in favor of the privileged.

Few will dispute that schools in many communities fail to deliver on their promises to provide real channels of upward mobility for disadvantaged students. But are schools really decisively shaped in the most important ways by business elites? Well before the era of capitalism, schools fostered a degree of docility from students, and they have always supported the authority of teachers. How could they not, when students are admitted to learn and teachers are paid to teach? Schools have also attempted to foster qualities other than docility—including passionate engagement with learning and independent thinking. The efforts, which have always met with mixed success, precede capitalism by more than a millennium. It is true that schools have, throughout their history, helped to reproduce the advantages of the privileged few. This is far from unique to schooling in capitalist societies. Indeed, schooling before the age of capitalism was far more unequally distributed than it is today. The ancient Greek academies, so admired today for their probing discussions of philosophy and life, were designed to train the sons of the aristocracy to rule by developing their strength of mind and rhetorical skills. Schools today are in many respects *less* authoritarian and *more* egalitarian than those of the precapitalist era. Moreover, they do not sort primarily for business occupations. Instead, they seem designed mainly to search for talent for the intellectual and professional occupations. This is clear both from the subjects taught in primary and secondary schools (history, literature, science, math), and those that are usually not taught (business management, the history of entrepreneurship).

A Weberian alternative. A somewhat more complex view than that provided by Bowles and Gintis is, therefore, required. More persuasive theories of schooling emphasize the multiple interests that human beings have pursued through schooling. One particularly useful theory of schooling is that of Randall Collins (1977). Collins argued that schools have been devised to serve three distinct human interests: (1) to allow students to acquire practical skills that yield advantages in occupational guilds and labor markets, (2) to affirm membership in a status group through transmission of esoteric knowledge, and (3) to allow students to acquire credentials that provide access to offices in large organizations (and thereby limit eligibility for these positions). In Collins's theory, the main action shifts away from the shaping of schools by "society" or "wealthy elites" to the pursuit of formal education by individuals who are attached to the various strata and classes in society. Collins explicitly links his conception of the interests served by schooling to Max Weber's famous triad of power resources: market power (class), cultural power (status), and political power (party).

One of the appealing features of Collins's theory is that different types of schooling are shown to have distinctive qualities related to the interests they serve. Practical skills schools typically offer "stripped down" curricula oriented to the efficient transmission of occupational skills with few frills attached. Competence is demonstrated by performance, rather than by passing long sequences of courses. Flight schools provide a good example today; as soon as a person can clearly demonstrate that he or she knows how to fly, the work of the school is done. Schooling for status group membership, by contrast, is always "impractical" in the sense that it focuses on subjects that have little direct value on the labor market. In ancient China, these subjects were calligraphy, literature, and poetry; in ancient Greece, philosophy and mathematics; in eighteenth-century England, classical languages and literature. These curricula develop cultivated persons who can be recognized by other members of a status group as one of their own. The emphasis is on refinement and esoteric knowledge, whether religious or secular. Finally, Collins shows that schooling for access to bureaucratic positions is highly legalistic, and based on a strict accountancy of course units, course sequences, and degree requirements. Exams play an important role in allocating people to tiers in the system. Unlike practical skills schooling, competence is demonstrated through persistence and series of formal evaluations. This type of schooling leads to the production of occupational specialists, who can be expected to demonstrate loyalty to their organizational superiors.

Collins's theory points us in the right direction, but it is not the last word on schooling as a social institution. First, it is important to understand the relative autonomy of institutions—their efforts to seal themselves off from their environments at least as much as they are influenced by their environments. Institutions never *simply* serve powerful interests. They develop processes and interests of their own (for example, in the case of schools the nurturing of academic talent is one), which they very often pursue at some distance from the interests of the most powerful groups in society. (Think of how many children of alumni have been denied admission to selective colleges and universities because they lack a sufficient level of academic talent.) In addition, interests originally left out of the construction of the institution may effectively demand influence in the institution, once it is well established. Processes of accommodation to outside interests and (limited) democratization are particularly common in the case of public schools. Think of the shift from Eurocentric to multicultural curricula in American schools in the late twentieth century. It is very difficult for taxpayer-supported institutions to serve only the interests of the groups that were decisive in their founding.

Collins's analysis is overly "demand-driven." The consumers of education have all the power in his theory. The interests of the suppliers of schooling are barely discussed; Collins seems to assume that a response will always be forthcoming to demand for different types of schooling. As we have seen, however, elite groups do not simply respond to demand. They have often been the primary actors. They supplied early schools to train political leaders, scribes, and theologians, and they did so in ways that reproduced their group's culture and extended its influence. The compulsory and publicly funded character of primary and secondary schooling in the modern era means that the state has had a great impact on the type of schooling students receive. As we will see, states have sought to produce a disciplined and technically competent workforce, while appealing to democratic sentiments of the populace, and preserving some spheres of schooling for the training of elites.

A final limitation is that Collins's theory shows a tilt toward middle- and upper-class people who are able to use schooling to advance their interests. Unfortunately, compulsory public schooling is implicated in the reproduction of inequality as much as in status affirmation and the production of mobility opportunities. For this reason, it is important to focus on students who fall by the wayside, as well as those who stay the course.

In this book, I will retain an interest in the themes of structural-functionalism; I will investigate schools' persistent structures, their means of channeling action, and their larger social purposes (both overt and hidden). At the same time, I will incorporate themes from the social power tradition, including the Weberian tradition represented by Collins, to analyze such fundamental issues as: (1) the interests in society that give rise to schools; (2) the beneficiaries of schooling; (3) the sources of conflict within schools; (4) the sources of failure to realize institutional values; and (5) the sources of change in school structures and practices.

Advantages of a Comparative Perspective

Now that we have the beginnings of a theoretical perspective, we can think about how best to study the institutions of schooling. Sociological arguments and theories are built in large part on comparison. If we want to know whether the United States is particularly schooling-conscious, for example, we need to compare indicators of schooling-consciousness, such as per capita spending on schools, for this country and others. If we want to know whether the kind of training teachers have makes a difference in how well they teach, we need to compare otherwise similar teachers who have graduated from different kinds of training programs. If we want to know whether class size makes a difference in learning, we need to compare how much is learned, on average, in small and large classes.

This book is comparative in a broader way than most. Sociology is at its best when it has a truly global focus. From a scientific point of view, the most important reason for taking a global view of schooling is that it allows us to compare more varied data. It is hard to understand the forces playing on schools if we limit our experience to a country in which only a certain number of these forces are at work. For example, let's say a social scientist thought that countries with centralized national ministries for schooling have more equality because budgets and instructional materials tend to be standardized across the entire country. This question obviously could not be answered by looking at the United States alone, because American schooling operates within a system of decentralized, local control. The answer to this question would require a broader canvas of comparison.

Even those who are not scientifically inclined can learn from the experiences of other cultures. The value of global comparisons is not just that the practices of other peoples are intrinsically interesting, although they *are* intrinsically interesting. Nor do practical interests alone encourage us to look beyond our own shores, even though the world is, in some ways, growing more interconnected with every passing year. The truth is, even if we are interested only in our own society, we can't always know much about it without thinking about the experiences of others.

Very often, what seems to be a unique problem in the United States may, in fact, represent an example of a more general phenomenon. For example, many Americans think of the race problems in the United States as a uniquely American dilemma. However, comparative study suggests that African Americans in the United States may have comparable experiences to those of other very highly subordinated minorities, such as the Oriental Jews in Israel and the Burakamin in Japan (Ogbu 1978). Accepting this conceptual shift raises the further interesting issue of whether any other society has done a better job than the United States in integrating highly subordinate minorities through schooling, and, if so, how they have done it.

Conversely, what many people believe to be an established fact—say, the relationship between small classes and higher achievement scores—may turn out to be less general than we imagine. In many East Asian countries, classes of 40 or more are not uncommon, and class size appears to have little relation to achievement (White 1987). This fact raises the further interesting question of what goes into creating an atmosphere in which 40 children can concentrate effectively together.

By looking at the experience of other peoples, we can also test possibilities that we have contemplated for ourselves. Americans love to think about ways to improve their schools, but the ideas that are proposed often have only the charm of novelty without a supporting practical wisdom. Given the reforms that have been proposed in recent years, we should be able to profit from considering the experiences of societies that, like England, have instituted market-based voucher systems, or, like Germany, have maintained work-related apprenticeship programs for teenagers. To appreciate what it might mean to make standardized testing a still more important part of the school experience, we could look at East Asian societies, where achievement is high but adolescents are exposed en masse to the searing ritual of "exam hell" (Rohlen 1983) and are given to fervent prayerful offerings in the hopes of a high score (Zeng 1996).

Where Are the Best Schools in the World?

In 1991, *Newsweek* magazine devoted a special section to what it called the best schools in the world (The Best Schools 1991). It suggested sending children to Italy for kindergarten, to New Zealand to learn reading, and to the Netherlands to learn math. Once they are literate, children should, according to *Newsweek*, go on for science training in Japan where they will learn through hands-on techniques and wait to learn principles until after they learn practical applications. They should take foreign language instruction in the Netherlands where two foreign languages are required. For high school, children should be sent to Germany. The editors of the magazine lauded the multitrack system in Germany, where only the top third go on to academic study leading to the university, and the majority combine apprenticeship training with job-related academics. The United States is not completely absent from this list of bests in the world. *Newsweek* considered the United States to excel in arts education and in graduate training.

Articles like this are at least as interesting for what they tell us about contemporary educational ideals as for their specific recommendations. The preferences in this article reflect today's concerns about academic achievement. A different set of choices would almost certainly have been made in the 1960s, when well-to-do people like the editors of *Newsweek* thought schooling should also improve cross-cultural understanding and individual creativity.

Nevertheless, like comparative social science, the article does help to expand our horizons. It encourages us to value a wider range of international experience than we might otherwise be exposed to. It suggests ways the experiences of other countries might be relevant to improving our own institutions.

Careful readers, however, will also be wary of the methods by which this list of bests was chosen. Other journalists, with different sources, might well have chosen different schools and different practices. For example, according to international achievement tests, mathematics teaching is apparently about as effective in Hungary now as it is in Japan. It is also important to remember that the practices of other countries can seldom be imported wholesale into American education. For example, foreign language teaching in the Netherlands is effective partly because students in this small country near the center of Europe will inevitably be called on to speak other languages. By contrast, American students grow up speaking English, the language of international business and science, and are consequently relatively insulated from pressures to learn new languages.

THREE LEVELS OF ANALYSIS

Sociological analysis can be compared to photography: like skilled camera work, it requires facility in the use of a number of lenses. In particular, sociologists must work with the equivalent of wide-angle lenses when they are concerned with very large-scale social changes. They must work with middle-horizon lenses when they are concerned with the everyday operation of institutions, as they exist at a given point in time. And they must master the close-up, telephoto lens to examine the workings of institutions as they exist in small-group and face-to-face interactions. In the analysis of social institutions like schooling, each of these levels is important.[2]

The broadest perspective can be termed the *macro-historical* level of analysis; the second, the *meso-institutional level* of analysis; and the third, the *micro-interactional* level. These levels are not always easy to distinguish, because actions at the higher levels are part of the context in which patterns at the lower levels develop. Nevertheless, they are sufficiently distinct to be discussed separately. Table 1.3 summarizes the major concerns of sociologists of schooling at each of these three levels.

The Macro-Historical Level

To understand the social institutions we inhabit, we need to know how they came into being. The macro-historical level of analysis is critical for understanding the development of the current purposes and activities of schools.

Schools have developed for many different reasons, but the most important are to teach the culture of a status group, to cement political loyalties to a ruler, and to prepare young people either for public life or for an occupational craft. In the West, the ancestors of our contemporary primary, secondary, and tertiary schools developed for very different reasons

TABLE 1.3
Levels of sociological analysis of schooling

Level of analysis	Major concerns
MACRO-HISTORICAL	
Development of school structures and purposes	Origins of school purposes and structures in comparative perspective
	Historical change in school purposes and structures in comparative perspective
	Consequences of school purposes and structures for society and particular groups in society
MESO-INSTITUTIONAL	
Operation of schools as social institutions in particular times and places	Organizational structures and practices for channeling energy and attention
	Environmental influences on schooling
	Interests and relationships of major categories of actors
	Consequences of institution for learning, socialization, and social selection
MICRO-INTERACTIONAL	
Staging and interaction processes involved in classroom activities	Structural influences on interaction within schools
	Methods used to develop learning communities
	Interaction-based successes and failures in instructional activities
	Consequences of school interactions for learning, socialization, and social selection

and at very different times. Compulsory primary schools were invented in the early eighteenth century by modernizing kings and emperors, who wanted to teach the rudiments of literacy to their subjects while building an identification among young people in the hinterlands (most of whom had weak attachments to the state) with the language and national heroes of the political center. The predecessors of our secondary schools have an ancient pedigree in private Greek academies, where teaching of philosophy and rhetoric was explicitly rooted in the life conditions and ideals of an aristocracy interested in preparing its sons for public life. The predecessors of today's universities developed during the Middle Ages. They carried on traditions of secular and sacred learning, but were most important for educating young men who intended to enter a handful of "learned professions" connected to the church: medicine, law, the clergy, and university teaching itself.

We can see clearly at this level of analysis that institutions of schooling have always been stamped by the interests and ideals of particular groups and organizations. The interests of kings and emperors were connected to the origins of primary schooling; the interests of the governing classes of the ancient world were connected to the origins of the Greek academies; and the interests of the church and the ruling classes of European feudalism were connected to the founding of universities. The historically developed ideologies of these classes and institutions are very often decisive for the organization of schools. Imagine how different schooling would be if the ideals of the medieval craft guilds had somehow come to dominate public secondary schooling rather than the liberal arts tradition of the Greco-Roman aristocracy. We would likely have quite a bit more vocational education than we do.

Schools sometimes change when new classes or new organizational interests gain power. For example, state-controlled primary and secondary education arose in early modern Europe when the Protestant Reformation disrupted the Catholic Church's control, and nation-states expanded into this newly freed institutional space (Durkheim [1938] 1977). Schools also change when new connections are made between existing schools, when new populations enter schools, and when new market incentives develop. For example, vocational education became a part of secondary schooling in the United States around the turn of the century, at a time when new populations (mainly from immigrant families) were entering secondary schools for the first time. Those who were already involved in the secondary schools had a market interest in preserving the value of the high school degree, and others had an interest in gaining access to these valuable degrees. In the end, a compromise was worked out: academic education for those headed for higher levels in the academic and class structure and vocational education for the majority of the new entrants (Powell et al. 1985; Labaree 1988). Class interests were surely involved here, but so were market incentives, demographic changes, and newly strengthened connections between primary and secondary schools.

Thus, as we look at the multicolored threads that make up the fabric of educational history, we see a smaller number of golden threads: influences that stand out more strongly than the others. The connection between state power and democratic ideology has been particularly important in our own century as a force in the development of schooling throughout the world. (It was important as early as the 1820s in the highly democratic United States.) Our contemporary systems of schooling reflect the working out of connections between new and surviving forms of schooling; the gradual expansion of student aspirations from lower to higher levels as the previously normal attainment levels no longer satisfy ambitions for upward mobility; the differentiation of curricular tracks to satisfy markets for educated labor; and the creation of standardized models of schooling that flow from the center to the peripheries of power.

Exactly how these forces are manifested in any given country depends on how much power is held by the coalitions that support existing forms of schooling and how conflicts among educators, political parties, and other interests are resolved. The structure of schooling is, therefore, not exactly the same throughout the world. As we will see in Chapters 2 and 3, people's life experiences are very strongly influenced by differences in these structural forms. The status pride of pre-World War II British university graduates was distinctly related to the small numbers of secondary school students who had the chance to enter universities. These small numbers were an outcome supported by the state's alliance with the elite graduates of Oxford and Cambridge. The feverish effort of Japanese students approaching the end of their high school years is shaped by the decisive importance of secondary school-leaving examinations for later life success in Japan.

The historical development of schooling demonstrates the futility of talking about schooling as functionally connected to the needs of society as a whole. Even today, schools serve the interests of some groups better than others. Students from highly educated and well-to-do families tend to do much better in school than students from less advantaged families. Those whose interests are not fully satisfied by the dominant form of schooling may have incentives to develop their own schools, as in the case of Christian academies, home schools, and charter schools today. These alternative schools, developed to affirm the status culture or improve the opportunities of "underserved" groups, may join the field of organizational competitors in the next round of historical development. Indeed, from a macro-historical perspective, one of the most important changes of the last two decades is the growing "privatization" of schooling, all the more remarkable for an institutional sphere that was more or less exclusively state-controlled and financed for 150 years. Privatization has taken many forms, from the rise of multibillion dollar tutoring industries in many countries to the creation of alternative school structures, either partly or wholly outside the state system (Davies, Quirke, and Aurini 2005).

Macro-historical analysis is challenging because it requires looking at institutions not simply in terms of their origins and development but also in comparative perspective. Other societies, with different traditions and different coalitions of power, are a natural context from which to better understand one's own social institutions and their development.

The Meso-Institutional Level

Most sociological work on schooling is conducted at the middle horizon, or institutional, level of analysis. At the institutional level, sociologists stop the historical clock and focus on schools, as they exist at a given point in time. Institutional analysis is important because it shows us how schools are organized and what kinds of forces they respond to in their environments. It can also help us to understand why schools do not work as well as they might.

Institutions can be defined as arrangements developed to perform particular sets of tasks or to regulate particular activities by limiting the number of ways these tasks and activities are accomplished. Sociologists sometimes distinguish institutions from organizations. Institutions provide categories and rules that apply across a wide range of organizations performing the same general tasks. Thus, "Middletown Elementary School" is a specific school organization, but it shares many structural similarities with other elementary schools, such as similar categories of personnel—principals, teachers, and students—and a similar organization of the school day. These are among the institutional features of schooling. Institutions reduce randomness by encouraging conformity across a wide variety of organizations performing the same general tasks. Marriage, for example, is an institution that regulates sexuality and child rearing by organizing action along a limited set of socially prescribed paths. Schools in contemporary societies are institutions that (1) transmit school knowledge to the young, (2) attempt to shape conduct and values, and (3) sort students for positions in the class and occupational structure.

Schools are organized to channel energy and attention along lines approved by authorities; they are situated, however, in a larger social environment from which they cannot be fully insulated. They are composed of nominally cooperating categories of primary actors whose interests are, however, rarely in complete harmony. Institutional analysis, therefore, can be divided into three parts: (1) analysis of the organizing structures and practices through which action is channeled; (2) analysis of power and influence in the broader environment as it influences the institution; and (3) analysis of the roles and interests of key actors.

1. *Analysis of structures and practices for the channeling of action.* The structures and practices of school life are strongly influenced by the larger purposes schools have come to serve. In the contemporary world, these purposes have mainly to do with the transmission of subject matter material the schools want students to know (i.e., cultural transmission), the values and behaviors they want students to express (i.e., socialization), and the identification of academic "winners" and "losers" (i.e., social selection). Energy and attention are focused on these purposes (with some "down time," of course, for less regulated interaction in lunchrooms and corridors and on playgrounds).

   Schools are highly formalized, even regimented, settings, less so than armies, but more so than, say, fraternities or sororities or even many workplaces. The school hierarchy is designed, above all, to enforce rules and settle conflicts about what should be occurring in the classroom. School and classroom rules also direct energy and attention by defining approved activities. Teachers in classrooms are central to the flow of student energy and attention during class periods. They initiate and direct most of what happens in the classroom. Students may resist teacher-centered initiatives, but the cost of resistance can be steep.

   Much of the institutional channeling of energy and attention occurs through language, backed by rewards and punishments. But not all of it does. Some of this channeling also occurs in the physical and temporal markers that escape notice because they become part of everyday routine. Spaces are defined, time is divided, instructional groups are formed, and routines are developed—and these are part of the means of producing schooling. Students may learn to follow the teacher's directions as one way of producing schooling, but their minds and bodies are also propelled into different physical spaces by bells that demarcate the beginning and ending of classes, and by class schedules that divide time and create a particular mix of students and teachers in particular physical spaces.

2. *Analysis of influences in the external environment.* Although schools, like all institutions, attempt to insulate themselves from their environments, the activities and effectiveness of schools are nevertheless greatly influenced by the environments in which they are situated. These environments include both the structure of relationships among schools at different levels, and their ties to outside groups.

   The flows of students between levels of schooling constitute one important feature of the schooling environment. Thus, in the developing world, many students do not complete primary school. In the developed world, primary school is now a universal feeder to secondary schools, but students may be split at the secondary level between students who are expected to move on in the educational system and those who are expected to move out to the labor market. In other cases, the great majority of students experience an academic secondary education. In addition, at any given time, a certain range of alternative schooling types exists in the environment, and these forms are at least potentially organizational competitors. If two-year colleges do not exist in a society, they are not an option for secondary school graduates. If they do exist, they may compete for students with four-year colleges, trades schools, and the labor market. Analysis of competition and market share must therefore be a part of our study of the relations among schools.

Schools are connected not just to one another but also to a broad range of other groups and organizations in society. For example, the organization of public schools closely follows the laws and policies of the state under whose jurisdiction they lie. Schools are influenced also by local communities; and by employing organizations through the labor market. Schools are also connected to educational organizations, such as textbook publishers and professional associations of educators. We can see how much the external environment matters simply by comparing schools in wealthy and poor neighborhoods. We are likely to see quite a bit more conformity in wealthy neighborhoods, and students who are more engaged in their schooling. Most kids will arrive on time for their classes, and at least pretend to be paying attention during class. The story can be very different in poor neighborhoods. The level of attention will likely be lower in most classes. More swearing will be heard in the corridors, and some teachers will act in a harsh way toward students. Misbehavior (by the school's norms) will be common, and some students will call it a day after lunch. Why? Students in poor neighborhoods tend to be less invested in schooling for a variety of reasons. One reason is that schools are not as rewarding to them as to students from affluent backgrounds.

Different environmental influences will attract more or less attention from sociologists depending upon the particular issue under consideration. For example, the quality of teaching in public schools is highly dependent on the quality of teacher training institutions. It makes sense to pay close attention to admissions requirements and curriculum of teacher training institutions if we are interested in the quality of teachers in a society. On the other hand, if we are interested in the amount of uniformity that exists in schooling, we will want to pay more attention to the degree of centralized control exercised by the state. When schools are under the jurisdiction of a central government (as they are in Sweden and Japan and were, until recently, in Italy and France), many features of public schooling will be uniform throughout the country: the level of expenditures per student, the course materials studied, and the kinds of training that teachers must have. In decentralized systems like the United States, where schooling is a state and local responsibility, quite a bit more inequality and variation will likely exist. If we are interested in comparing levels of student engagement and achievement between schools, we will want to pay close attention to the socioeconomic composition of the community from which the school draws its students.

3. *Analysis of the interests of the major actors in the institution.* The three major categories of actors within schools are students, teachers, and administrators. In the broader community, parents are a fourth important set of actors. These actors are involved in an enterprise that can be described as at least largely cooperative. Institutional structures and practices that are operating as intended ensure a working

accommodation, if not a true consensus. Observers from Mars would no doubt be impressed in the similarities of schooling around the world. Classes form at regular times and follow similar routines, including solving problems, presenting projects, and taking exams. Administrators work with teachers to solve behavior problems in classrooms, and teachers work with students to transmit curricular materials. However, the relationships between the major actors are not entirely cooperative. This is because the major actors have at least slightly different interests in schooling. Students and their parents are mainly the carriers of popular aspirations (including demands for practical education) and normative expectations about effort; teachers are mainly the carriers of school knowledge and educational standards; and administrators are mainly the carriers of the existing rules of school organization resource distribution. Administrators are also subject to political pressures that few teachers experience.

When differences of interest exist, some degree of tension or even outright conflict can be expected. Teachers, for example, may want students to work harder than students want to work if left to their own devices. Teachers may challenge resource allocations of administrators, if they feel that their classrooms are underfunded; and administrators may attempt to enforce unpopular rules.

Some of the most important studies of schooling have been based on looking for departures from the ideals that are intended to animate interaction in institutions. These studies have shown, for example, that teachers sometimes typecast students as academically mediocre simply on the basis of their dress, cleanliness, and language before they really know much about their academic abilities (Rist 1970). These studies have explored the role of teacher expectations in producing high and low levels of student performance (Rosenthal and Jacobsen 1968). They have also shown how informal "treaties" lowering performance standards can develop between teachers hoping for popularity and students interested in reducing work requirements (Powell, Farrar, and Cohen 1985).

The Micro-Interactional Level of Analysis

Virtually every situation in school involves encounters between people. The micro-interactional level of analysis is concerned with what happens in these encounters. Analysis of this immediate experience of schooling is critically important for showing how all the possibilities of schooling—mastery of course materials, dutiful compliance, confusion, disengagement, active hostility—are set into motion. The important elements are what people bring into their encounters, the way they present themselves to one another, and the way those presentations are interpreted and acted upon.

The context of interaction is as important as the process of interaction itself. To use a theatrical metaphor, the staging, scenery, costumes, and props are as important as the lines exchanged between the actors. The staging represents the preexisting understandings that influence the action on the stage. In the classroom, the staging includes the experiences and motives that students, teachers, and administrators bring with them to the classroom; the definition of the situation that prevails in their encounters; and the numbers and kinds of other actors who share the classroom stage. For example, the kinds of interactions that take place vary greatly between classrooms in which large numbers of disengaged students are gathered together and those in which small numbers of highly engaged students are present.

Although the staging of interaction is important, much of the best microlevel work focuses on the gestures and spoken lines of the actors, the process of face-to-face interaction itself. Sociologists use videotape, transcripts, and their own observation to hone in on how people represent themselves to others through their dress, language, and behavior; how others interpret those representations; and the responses people develop in light of those interpretations. This three-step process—expression, interpretation, and response—occurs simultaneously on both sides of every interaction. Conversations can be thought of as many bits of interaction strung together, and relationships can be thought of as strings of interactions across time.

For example, if a young man wants to project an image of toughness, he may sport a buzz cut, beard stubble, mirrored sunglasses, tattoos, and torn shirt, and he may work out to maintain an impressive physique. He may speak little and, when he does, primarily in short bursts laced with obscenities. Most people will interpret this display as characteristic of a street tough and will want to steer as clear as possible. The young man's friends, however, may interpret the same representations as the essence of a stand-up kind of person unwilling to let the world take advantage of him. And the young man's mother might interpret his symbolic actions as a stage on the road to adulthood. The young man, meanwhile, is making interpretations of these other people's symbolic representations and is responding to them in light of his understandings. He may choose to practice his tough guy persona on his mother—or respond appreciatively to her maternal support.

By showing how both successes and failures of classroom life can arise from the way in which actors interpret and respond to the symbolic expressions of others, micro-interactional analysis can add to our understanding of some of the most basic issues of mass schooling. Micro-analysis can be particularly important for showing how effective teachers manage their authority and construct learning communities and for revealing some of the less obvious causes of static and distortion in the teacher-student interchange.

Authority is a basic requirement of classroom life because neither order nor learning is possible without it. However, the management of authority requires considerable skill. Writing in the 1930s, Willard Waller catalogued the various means by which the adults of his time represented themselves as respect-worthy figures (the Old Soldier, the Mother, the Favorite Aunt, the Man about Town) and the repertoire of social control procedures (from raised eyebrows and withering comments to suspensions and expulsions) that teachers of his time used to maintain their control over classroom life (Waller 1932). Since Waller's time, problems in the management of authority have received more attention, particularly as these problems relate to issues of fairness and flexibility. Microlevel analysis has helped to document how teacher expectations may influence students' behavior (Rosenthal and Jacobsen 1968) and how teachers interpret social class and ethnic cultural cues to identify "good" and "bad" students (Rist 1970; Erickson 1975). It has also helped to show how a language of community can be used by educators to include disadvantaged people symbolically and to gain allies, and how, by contrast, a language of technical expertise can be used to de-authorize others, as when teachers use jargon to de-authorize parents as specialists on their children's behavior (Mehan 1993).

Once teachers have established their authority, they must construct a successful community of learners. In the United States, the most effective teachers combine clear task leadership with strong projections of personality and character. They maintain high and challenging standards but also work on maintaining rapport. The expectations of students and teachers can, however, vary greatly from culture to culture. Therefore, different kinds of teachers are effective in different societies. In Japan, teachers expect students to work patiently through their errors and to accept that errors are an important part of learning to be overcome through hard work. The idea that students have greater or lesser abilities is practically irrelevant. Japanese students, in turn, expect their teachers to be technically skilled performers, rather than, for example, encouraging helpers or subject matter specialists (Stevenson and Stigler 1992). As long as these expectations are mutually met, the educational connection is successful.

Throughout the world, confusion and misunderstanding are as much a part of the classroom life as clarity and comprehension. Many of these breakdowns come from disengaged teachers, who have lost sight of the value of instruction, or unmotivated students, who do not feel the value of actively participating in the hard work of learning. Other breakdowns may be due to students' limitations in comprehending the material presented, or teachers' limitations in presenting it well. Clearly, however, breakdowns also occur even when both students and teachers have accepted the legitimacy of classroom effort and are trying to approach their work in a serious way. Take the following example from England of how students in one school were labeled as either "dull" or "intelligent." In this study, working-class children were more likely to ask very basic questions of their teachers and to ask why they needed to learn the material. Middle-class children may have had the same questions but were more likely simply to absorb the material, assuming that eventually they would understand why they were being asked to learn it. Teachers tended to see the first type of students as dull and the second as intelligent. However, another equally valid interpretation would be that the middle-class students had learned to be passive and deferential; that they were, in a sense, less engaged in active learning (Keddie 1971). Many such studies help us to understand why interaction in the classroom so often fails to accomplish as much as it might.

THE SCIENTIFIC AND HUMANISTIC FACES OF SOCIOLOGY

Sociology is an unusual discipline in that it presents both a scientific and a humanistic face to the world. It is both a set of propositions about human social relations and a way of understanding and appreciating the world around us. Sociologists who identify themselves primarily with the scientific side of the discipline have developed a number of propositions to explain patterns in human social relations. They have also developed a large number of empirically based generalizations about the causes of social phenomena. For example, we will see that a variety of factors are well established as important influences on student learning, including parental expectations, the composition of peer groups, the level of teacher qualifications, and the amount of time devoted during the school day and year to learning. We would not be able to draw conclusions about which influences are most important without rigorous scientific studies.

Because of their rigorous methods, sociologists are sometimes in a position to suggest ways to improve our institutions of schooling. For example, by looking at different kinds of teaching under experimental conditions, researchers have developed a clearer sense of the behaviors used by effective and less effective teachers. Similarly, we now have considerable evidence that smaller classrooms and smaller schools can at times help to build a sense of community among students, which, in turn, helps to create a stronger commitment to schoolwork (see, e.g., Finn and Achilles 1990). When educators and policymakers take findings like these seriously, they can lead to improvements in how well schools work.

But the discipline has something else to offer in addition to scientific principles and policy advice. Max Weber ([1921] 1978), one of the greatest of the "founding fathers" of sociology, thought that the discipline's major contribution would lie in its capacity to enrich human judgment. Sociology allows us to see into the character of our institutions and the consequences they have for our lives. It can also help us to see the forces at play in the actions of others and the ways our own actions may be influenced by a specific set of socially conditioned understandings. Looked at in the right way, sociology offers nothing less than a new way of seeing the world and our places in it.

It is not surprising, therefore, that sociology includes a gallery of institutional landscapes and human portraits, and not only data files for testing hypotheses and producing mathematical formulas. The pictures in this gallery can be jarring, because the opportunities and constraints of the social structure often give rise to false hopes and draining struggles. We see, for example, some educational reformers who are buoyed by public acclaim for their efforts to improve schooling, but are unable to demonstrate that the changes they champion actually work. We see intensely people-oriented teachers who are led by the uncertainties of teaching to build walls around their classrooms, depriving themselves of the human contact they prize so highly. And we see the rebels among working-class adolescents who, through their acute sense of moral superiority to the rule-followers among their peers, prepare themselves for lives of numbing labor.

Some of the portraits are vivid spots of color on a relatively colorless canvas. Many of these portraits involve the transforming power of human cooperation and human connections: the electrical charge of a class that is humming along on all cylinders, the graceful gesture of a young person who stands up in support of a fellow student who seems to be faltering, or perhaps that rare occasion when a teacher interprets a sullen young person as going through a stage on the road to maturity at the same time the young person begins to see the teacher as a trustworthy ally. Although we will be dismayed by the pictures in the sociological gallery as often as we are reassured by them, we do not have to look hard to see a discipline fully engaged in understanding human relationships in all their complexity.

ORGANIZATION OF *SCHOOLS AND SOCIETIES*

The remainder of this book will take up issues that are important to anyone interested in schooling. You will see the guiding influence of the theoretical framework outlined in this chapter, a perspective that combines an interest in both social organization and social power. You will see an effort to address issues of schooling at the macro-historical, meso-institutional, and micro-interactional levels of analysis. You will see the adoption of a global comparative perspective on schooling, and a willingness to draw on both the scientific and humanistic foundations of sociology.

Chapters 2 and 3 provide an overview of schooling in the industrialized and developing worlds. These are the chapters most concerned with the macro-historical level of analysis. In these chapters, I discuss the rise of schooling and the forms schooling has taken in several societies. I also discuss the major issues facing schools in rich and poor societies.

Chapters 4 through 7 examine the major contemporary social purposes of schools: the transmission of school knowledge, the socialization of personality and conduct, and the sorting of students for positions in the class and occupational structure. These chapters rely primarily on macro-historical analyses to examine the development of these purposes, and on studies at the meso-institutional level to illuminate the current issues surrounding them.

Chapter 8 takes up issues related to the teaching and learning of school knowledge. This is the chapter in which the micro-interactional level of analysis plays the largest role. Chapter 8 examines the forces outside and inside of classrooms that influence the interaction of teachers and students and the successful transmission of school knowledge.

Part of the interest of sociology derives from what it can tell us about how to improve our institutions. Chapter 9 looks at recent school reform programs in the United States. It brings together evidence about the effectiveness of such reforms as educational vouchers, magnet schools, business partnerships with schools, and community outreach programs. Accountability reforms will be a special focus of Chapter 9, because these reforms are the most influential of the recent efforts to make schools work better. The chapter concludes by discussing the ingredients that go into making good schools.

SCHOOLING IN THE INDUSTRIALIZED WORLD

historical context
comparison between US. & Germany
Table 2.1

This chapter will examine the structure of schooling in the industrialized societies. By industrialized societies, I mean those in which most people are employed in manufacturing and services industries, rather than in mining and agriculture. Because of the higher productivity of industrialized economies and their domination of world markets for finished goods and business services, people living in industrialized countries have higher average incomes and living standards than people living in developing countries. The industrialized world includes the United States and Canada, the United Kingdom, all of the countries of Western Europe and Scandinavia, the most developed countries of the old Soviet bloc in Central Europe (such as Hungary and the Czech Republic), Israel, Japan, Australia, New Zealand, and several of the emerging industrial powers of the Pacific Rim, including South Korea, Taiwan, Hong Kong, and Singapore.

A sharp distinction between the industrialized and the developing world can be misleading. Life in the inner-city ghettoes of the United States and in the peripheral zones surrounding cities like Rome and Paris can be just as poverty-stricken, crowded, and chaotic as life in any Third World country. Meanwhile, urban centers and industrialized regions as modern as any places on earth can be found in China and India, which are still considered developing countries by many, because of their high rates of rural poverty.

Nevertheless, the situation of the average citizen of industrialized and developing countries remains different enough for the contrast to continue to matter. For the past 60 years, most citizens in industrialized countries have been able to count on economic growth and security from the devastations of war on home soil. Most have also had the advantage of stable and responsive political systems. These advantages have allowed for a steadiness and regularity in the development of schooling that is not as common in the developing world—and particularly not in the rural areas in which most people live.

More than 250 years ago, a few European governments began the experiment of creating mass educational systems out of what had been a patchwork of sites for teaching basic literacy and job-related skills to the children of workers and peasants, and the masterworks of culture to the upper classes. Many rulers, fearing rebellion, were slow to see the advantages of schooling for the masses. But educators and policymakers throughout the industrialized world have now had more than 100 years to develop schooling as an institution for the masses. One of the most important tools for creating this social machinery was the introduction of national examinations to help decide the educational fates of children at key transition points. Examinations encouraged discipline and focused attention, but they came at a price. The educational functions of the school became subtly subordinated to its selective functions. Sociologists have been sensitive to the workings of this "social machinery" for a long time, as the 1927 comments of Pitrim Sorokin indicate: "Up to the last few years, the school was regarded primarily as an educational institution. Its social function was seen in 'pouring' into a student a definite amount of knowledge, and, to some extent, in shaping his behavior. . . . At the present moment it is certain that the school . . . is at the same time a piece of social machinery, which tests the abilities of the individuals, which sifts them, selects them, and decides their prospective social position" (Sorokin [1927] 1959:188). Our starting point, then, must be to see that we are discussing, throughout the developed world, huge training and sorting machines.

Schooling can be understood as a fundamental part of the economic development and regulatory apparatus of the state, well supported by taxpayers because of its capacity to create productive workers and "good citizens." It is a highly organized (and, therefore, frequently effective) government activity. School districts and schools themselves have the advantages of highly developed bureaucratic organization, with the stability and clarity that organization brings. Indeed, some parallels with military organization exist: children are expected to show discipline in the classroom; teachers keep them moving briskly through their paces; and we even call some classroom exercises "drills."

Industrialized countries also have professionalized teaching "forces." Teachers are generally well educated (nearly all have college-level or higher degrees). They have studied methods of instruction and been required to demonstrate at least minimal competence in the classroom through practice teaching. They continue with in-service and other professional development programs during their careers.

Most students from industrialized countries are well prepared to learn when they come to school thanks to familial support for learning, exposure to learning media, and preschool experiences. They stay in school much longer than students in developing countries (by as much, on average, as six to eight years more). Living in modern, fast-paced, demanding societies serves these students well in schooling. Most adapt quickly to the performance expectations of the school. Some excel and others attempt to comply with expectations that they keep their grades up. Students in the industrialized world consequently score much higher than students from developing countries in international assessments of mathematics and reading. (See Chapter 4.)

We can appreciate the many similarities in school organization and social context that we find in the industrialized world, but it also makes sense to think about differences in the design of schooling systems, and what consequences these differences have for students. I ask several questions in this chapter: Just how did these huge "machines" for educating and processing children come into being? In what ways are they similar to one another? In what important respects do they differ? Do the differences affect students' experiences of schooling? And, if so, how do they affect these experiences?

I will show that important features of schooling do vary among the industrial societies—and that these differences have consequences for students' experience of schooling. Consider, for example, schooling in three countries: the United States, Germany, and Japan.

In the United States, most children will receive much the same instruction through the end of high school. Some 85–90 percent of the age group will eventually finish high school (NCES 2001a). Of those who finish high school, the great majority, as many as three out of four graduates, will go off to one of more than 4,000 two-year or four-year colleges and universities. Schoolwork will not be so demanding for most students that it takes up all their time. Students will have considerable time for socializing with friends, for participation in extracurricular activities, and, later, for part-time work. College entrance tests will not keep anyone out of higher education, though they will be an important factor in determining admission into a small number of highly selective colleges and universities. The anxiety these tests create will generally last for only a short time before and after the exam. Most students will want to continue past high school to get the kind of degree that may give them a leg up in the job market, but it will not generally be considered a life-or-death matter if one drops out before completing a degree. Many people return to college later in life to finish degrees or to "retool."

Contrast this relatively open structure and the easygoing attitude it fosters, with the systems of two other wealthy industrial democracies. In Germany, children are divided at an early age into three types of schools. This placement will, in the great majority of cases, have a decisive influence on the child's future life trajectory. The bottom track does not lead students in the direction of higher education, and the middle track leads, for most, to technical colleges with short degree programs. Even graduating from the top track allows entry to college only if the student has passed a demanding secondary school-leaving examination, known as the *Abitur*. Upper secondary school in Germany is a serious business. The *Abitur* is normally taken at the end of 13 years of education, a longer period than in most other countries. The level of knowledge demanded is high. Preparation for the examinations therefore looms very large in the upper secondary student's life in Germany, leaving not much time for extracurricular activities (Eckstein and Noah 1993:62). In Germany, even those who leave formal schooling at the end of the compulsory period are busy with school in their teenage years. Nearly all will attend continuation school part-time while participating in state-supported apprenticeships in a business or industry. Between school and work, they are adults at a time when American teenagers are still at the beginning of their period of deciding what they want to do with their lives.

In Japan, the intensity of schooling is greater still, though the structure involves less overt tracking than in Germany. The great majority of Japanese teenagers take academic rather than vocational studies; a vocational track exists only for the bottom fifth. School is long and intense with as many as 45 students in a classroom and demanding, fact-laden drills a staple of instruction in the upper grades. Extracurricular activities are not discouraged, but students have less time to devote to them than American teenagers. After school, most take additional classes at *juku*, and nearly all also attend these supplementary schools on Saturdays. And no wonder: performance in school matters greatly for later life success. High schools accept students on the basis of examination scores, and, later, scores on secondary school-leaving tests determine who will be admitted to the universities and in what fields they will be admitted. The rigid pecking order of high schools, universities, and subject fields, in turn, determines who will be eligible for the more desirable jobs in Japanese companies and government agencies. Under the circumstances, it is not surprising that a popular saying among Japanese teenagers is: "Fail with five, pass with four"—the five and the four referring to hours of sleep after nighttime study.

I will begin by discussing the historical setting in which contemporary patterns of schooling developed, focusing on the key difference between systems founded for purposes of elite preparation and those founded on the ideals of "democratic uplift." In the second part of the chapter, I will develop a typology of schooling systems, using Germany and the United States as polar cases, and England, France, and Sweden as examples of intermediate types. I will also discuss the Japanese system to show that culture and high-stakes testing counts in the performance of schooling systems. The Japanese structure is not too different from the American, but performance differences have been notable.

The organizational structures of schooling would not be very important to sociologists unless they were connected to variation in important outcomes of schooling. In this chapter, I will show that understanding differences in structural designs unlocks much of what is important in the relation of schools to their societies. Differences in schooling structures matter both for the life chances of students and for aspects of students' consciousness. In the last section of the chapter, I will discuss the forces and interests that have shaped the schooling systems of the industrialized world. I will also show that these systems are beginning to resemble one another much more than in the past under the influence of such transnational organizations at the European Union (EU) and the Organization for Economic Cooperation and Development (OECD).

SCHOOLING IN COMPARATIVE-HISTORICAL CONTEXT

The expansion of public schooling has been unfolding for more than two centuries. This expansion began first in the core countries of Western Europe and North America, and later spread throughout the rest of the world. It is best thought of as a governmental response to increasing social and economic demand for higher levels of educational qualification, supported by the growth of white collar occupations in industrializing societies. These responses, however, began from two distinct starting points: In Europe, the assumption was that schooling beyond the primary level was for elite preparation. By contrast, in the United States (and the other English-speaking democracies of the New World), the assumption was that schooling served "public purposes"—notably the development of a character structure fit for a self-governing republic—and was therefore a general good that should be widely provided.

These two different starting points left an important imprint on the direction that system-building efforts took. The premises of *elite preparation* encouraged more highly structured tracking at the secondary level, as well as relatively restricted access to higher education. The premises of *democratic uplift* encouraged predominantly academic schooling, more flexible and limited tracking at the secondary level, and wider access to higher education.

The Premises of Elite Preparation

European princes made the first efforts to extend the right of primary schooling to the masses in the early 1700s. In a few cases, "enlightened" monarchs, hoping to elevate the cultural level of their subjects, were responsible for these initiatives. This was true, for example, in the case of Frederick IV of Denmark, who created the first mass public schooling in the 1720s. More often, however, the motives of princes were profoundly conservative, as in the case of the compulsory schooling legislation of the leaders of Prussia (a once independent country that is now part of Germany).

Prussia, dominated by the landed Junker class and its spirit of military service and bureaucratic efficiency, provided the world with the basic organizational structure of modern schooling, including teacher-training institutes, age-graded classrooms, common curricular standards, and examination-based assessments for promotion. The Prussian teacher has been described as the military commander of the classroom. (Indeed, many European powers thought that Prussian successes on the battlefield started in the drilling of students in primary schools.) Some advanced efforts of instruction, based on drawing out the natural curiosity of children, were adopted in Prussia in the early 1800s, but Prussian educators sought mainly to teach basic literacy and to instill a sense of loyalty to the Emperor (Bendix 1968:244–5). Efforts to strengthen patriotism, through stories of national heroes and national achievements, became important throughout Europe in the nineteenth century, as leaders recognized that the children of the working classes might some day be needed by their kings and ministers for fighting in wars under the banner of the nation-state. In later years, motives for maintaining and expanding public schools were mixed in complex ways, with interests in labor force development becoming more important over time.

The adoption of compulsory public schooling occurred more quickly in some European countries than others. In the early-adopting states, like Prussia and France, free and compulsory public schooling was introduced in the early 1800s. In these countries, political leaders maintained autonomy from both the church and the landed upper classes and had at their service a highly professional civil service bureaucracy. In late-adopting states, like England, free and compulsory public schooling became law only near the end of the 1800s. In these countries, the state was very closely aligned with the upper classes, and the upper classes were content to allow the church to provide rudimentary schooling for the working classes and the poor (Cubberly 1922, chaps. 22–4). Neither early adopters nor late adopters expected children of the industrial working class or the rural peasantry to go beyond a few years of primary schooling.

The sons of landowners, wealthy merchants, and professionals monopolized the upper levels of schooling. Indeed, the secondary schools and universities were among the institutions most closely associated with preservation of the culture of the old aristocratic ruling class. They had their origins as institutions for the training of sons of the nobility (who took their primary education from private tutors). Secondary schools slowly developed as a means of preparing the next generation of the elite for a university education. Although radical ideas of extending access to secondary schooling were entertained by European politicians from the 1840s on, these ideas were resisted by most politicians as encouraging unsuitable instruction for the laboring poor (Cross Commission 1888, quoted in Archer 1979:742). In the representative view of Jules Ferry, a progressive Education minister in the French Third Republic, confraternity and true democracy required a first mixing of the rich and the poor on the grounds of the school, but such a democracy did not require mixing to extend beyond the basic primary level (Ferry, quoted in Archer 1979:643). Fee requirements and entrance examinations that built on the culture of the leisured classes prevented all but a small number of working-class students from pursuing the academic degrees that were necessary for admission to universities. Only exceptionally talented and motivated working-class children were sponsored into the elite (Turner 1960).

Strong vested interests naturally developed around the preservation of a very rigorous secondary and higher education requiring extensive knowledge of esoteric works. Secondary school teachers and university professors were strongly committed to maintaining educational quality and selectivity (Husén 1965; Heidenheimer 1973). Together with their allies in government, they successfully resisted efforts, often led by socialist or labor parties, to expand access to academic secondary and higher education. Even in a country like Sweden, which was governed by the leftist Social Democratic Party for most of the twentieth century, public education did not shift in the direction of untracked secondary schools until the early 1960s, and even then the shift was strongly resisted by secondary school teachers and university professors whose values were shaped by the elitist assumptions of their institutions (Heidenheimer 1973).

The Premises of Democratic Uplift

Public schooling in the United States originates in a markedly different social and political context. In the colonial United States, literacy was taught primarily in the home or in neighborhood "dame schools." Laws providing for public schooling were on the books as early as the mid-1600s, but this public schooling came to be associated exclusively with the poor. In most places, public schools fell into disuse or disrepute. Schools that taught more advanced subjects or occupational skills required fees. Apprenticeships, rather than formal schooling, were a popular means of learning trades and professions (Edwards and Richey 1963, chaps. 1–3).

Interest in publicly supported education for all children increased following the American Revolution, however, and this interest typically built on ideas about the requirements for good citizenship in a republic. Nearly all the leaders of the American Revolution were advocates of free and compulsory public schooling for the primary grades, agreeing with New York Governor George Clinton that the state would gain advantages to morals, religion, liberty, and good government from "the general diffusion of knowledge" (quoted in Welter 1962:24).

The 1830s and 1840s were a period of mobilization for the common school movement. Early leaders of the movement, such as Henry Barnard of New York, visited Prussia to examine their public school systems firsthand. The most urbanized states took the lead in the development of public schooling, particularly Massachusetts and New York. Communities developed public schooling in a piecemeal fashion, and a wide variety of funding arrangements were tried, including partial public support to supplement fees. Struggles were fought with taxpayers over finance and with churches over control of the curriculum, but by the 1840s, free and compulsory public primary schools were well institutionalized in New England and the Mid-Atlantic states. The spread of public primary schooling to the western and southern United States occurred mainly in the 1850s, although attendance remained spotty and facilities primitive in many communities (Edwards and Richey 1963, chaps. 9–10).

Public secondary schooling got an early start in the United States. The first public high schools were established in Massachusetts in the 1820s and spread to other cities in the next decades. Very few attended these public schools, because admission was usually by examination. Private, fee-requiring academies remained more popular. Nevertheless, by the latter decades of the nineteenth century American educators (and also educators in other English-speaking democracies of the New World) were arguing that all children had a right to secondary schooling, sentiments that would not be common in Europe for more than a half century.

What explains this difference? First, no well-entrenched aristocratic or quasi-aristocratic groups existed in the English-speaking democracies to guard the universities and secondary schools as bastions of a status-linked high culture. (This kind of defense in the United States was limited to a small segment of the system: the elite private preparatory schools and "Ivy League" colleges.) The enfranchised groups were overwhelmingly small-property owners. The interests of this small-property-owning class, particularly when joined to the evangelical force of Protestant idealism, greatly encouraged the use of state power for purposes of creating a virtuous citizenry. The populism of Andrew Jackson's presidency helped to extend this spirit in a more democratic direction by advancing the idea of education as the right of all in a democracy. The pragmatic spirit of the small-property-owning classes, storekeepers and farmers, also supported the use of schooling as a means of teaching economically useful subjects.

Horace Mann, the leader of the *common school movement* in Massachusetts, is a major figure in the development of public schools in the United States. Mann's speeches expressed the view that the current generation is but the temporary keeper of the property and civilization of the country. Because the succeeding generations must be saved from poverty and vice and prepared for the adequate performance of their social and civic duties, those who refuse to enlighten the intellect of the rising generation are guilty of "degrading" the human race (quoted in Cremin 1957:75–7).

The goals of democratic uplift, advanced by educators like Mann, were often explicitly mixed with fears about the customs of new immigrants. Both primary and secondary schools were used for socializing (sometimes known as "Americanizing") the more ambitious of the immigrant newcomers along the lines of the civic and moral ideals favored by the country's Protestant and conservative upper classes. Indeed, compulsory schooling laws were enacted earliest in states with numerically dominant Anglo-Protestant majorities (Meyer, Tyack et al. 1979; Benavot and Riddle 1988).

Economic arguments also played a role in the popularity of public schooling in the United States. Americans looked at mathematics teaching, for example, simultaneously as a way of creating a more rational citizenry and as of practical value in commerce (Cohen

1982). The ideals of civic virtue and economic pragmatism mixed easily in the minds of many eighteenth- and nineteenth-century Americans. The first public high schools, for example, dating from the 1830s, were meant to create well-disciplined (but not overly cultivated) elites of young people for managerial and commercial occupations (Labaree 1988). The idea of using schooling for practical occupational purposes extended even to higher education beginning as early as the 1860s with the passage of the first Morrill Act. This Act created *land-grant* universities intended to provide practical training in mechanical sciences and agriculture for young people from all walks of life. No European university system of the time could have contemplated a similar act. The intellectual elite that dominated the European university systems would not have considered the possibility of extending higher education to the sons of farmers and factory workers.

The Rising Demand for Schooling

Those responsible for the development of schooling in the industrial world began from these two distinct starting points, but they subsequently encountered the same great source of change, namely, the increasing social demand for schooling.

Occupational change contributed to increased interest in secondary and, later, higher education. In industrial societies during the first half of the twentieth century, lower-level white-collar administrative jobs increased, while farm and industrial blue-collar jobs decreased. This occupational change was accompanied by expansion of secondary school enrollments, as employers began to look for more qualified workers for the new white-collar positions (Trow 1961). More recently, the great change has been the growth of professional and managerial jobs. This new occupational upgrading has been accompanied, in turn, by the growth of higher education enrollments, as employers began to hire still more qualified workers for the new positions involving relatively sophisticated problem-solving skills and more specialized intellectual training. The secondary schools were at first charged with preparing elites for higher education; they were, in Trow's terms, "elite preparatory institutions." But they became "mass terminal institutions" during the era of rapid growth in white-collar occupations, and they later became "mass preparatory institutions" during the era of rapid growth in professional and managerial occupations.

Occupational change is probably not the most important factor behind the rising demand for schooling, however. The sociologist John Meyer and his associates (Meyer, Ramirez et al. 1979) showed that school enrollments around the world, in industrial and nonindustrial societies alike, have increased much faster than can be explained simply by occupational changes. At any given level in the schooling system, from primary to higher education, an S-shaped enrollment curve can be traced. At first, enrollments increase slowly. Once they reach a takeoff point, however, they increase rapidly, leveling off only once near-universal enrollment has been achieved. Figure 2.1 provides a graphic representation of the growth of enrollments over time in secondary schooling and higher education.

Thus, an even more important force than occupational change has been changing public attitudes about how much schooling is "enough." The popular desire for more schooling can be stimulated by many factors other than changing occupational requirements.

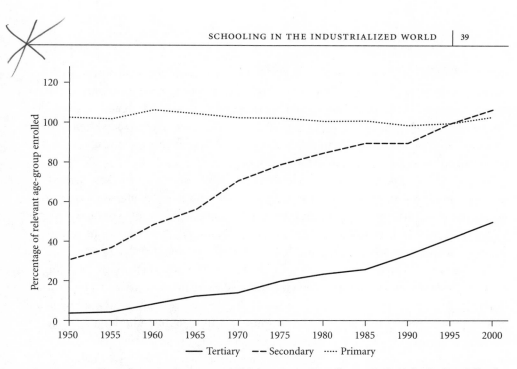

Figure 2.1. Elementary, Secondary, and Tertiary Gross Enrollment Ratios[1] for Industrialized
Countries,[2] 1950–2000

SOURCE: Schofer and Meyer (2005). Additional data provided by Evan Schofer.

NOTES: [1]Gross enrollment ratios = total enrollments divided by the total number of people in the relevant range (as determined by government definitions). Gross enrollments are multiplied by 100 to yield the percentages reported in the table. Gross enrollment ratios can exceed 100 due to errors in the numerator.

[2]N of countries varies in these graphs by year from a low of 31 to a high of 36.

Some families may see additional schooling as providing important social benefits, such as the prospect of mixing with a higher class of people. Others may see it as providing opportunities for economic advancement. These families will pursue strategies that allow them to invest more heavily in schooling, even at the expense of immediate consumption. When enough families begin to make the sacrifices necessary for their children to receive more schooling, higher aspirations become a defensive necessity even for families that are not unusually ambitious. Simply maintaining the family's reputation in the community may require more schooling for the younger generation than the older generation received.

Governments have built on popular aspirations for more education. They have been particularly interested in developing curricula attuned to changes in the labor market. The role of state policy in expanding and directing schooling for manpower development purposes was evident as early as the 1850s in the United States and the 1870s in Japan. It has been an important influence everywhere in the industrialized world since World War II. Indeed, John Meyer and his associates have argued that the S-curve pattern of rising educational attainments throughout the world reflects the interests of both national leaders and ordinary citizens in embracing a global cultural belief that associates educational attainment with higher levels of development and prosperity (Meyer et al. 1979, "World Education Revolution": 52).

The form and rate of educational expansion has, however, varied considerably across countries. Highly centralized governments, such as Japan and the former Soviet Union, were able to make large-scale changes far more quickly than changes could be made in de-centralized systems. Fully developed public schooling systems were operating in Japan within a few years of the Meiji Restoration in 1868 and in Russia within a few years of the Bolshevik Revolution in 1917 (Cummings 2003). Public schooling expanded more slowly in most of Europe, because of the resistance of the state bureaucracy and the upper classes, who claimed secondary education as their own.

Very often, social demand for education was directed by state policymakers toward the development of vocational secondary schools. The state and industry played an active role in creating vocational schools in the German-speaking world and in some of the Scandina-vian countries in the later 1800s. In these countries, the state took a paternalistic role in re-lation to the working classes, trying to help them prepare for their fates in the emerging in-dustrial system. The new technical and vocational schools provided job-related training to many adolescents who, government officials assumed, were not destined to continue their studies beyond the minimum level. This state activism was typically supported by labor unions and socialist parties, because of their interest in using public education to reinforce identification with the working class and, by extension, with the parties who claimed to rep-resent that class. By contrast, governments in countries like England and France, which were dominated by the philosophy of laissez-faire individualism, left children and young adults to their own devices in the labor market following the end of primary schooling.

Throughout Europe, restrictive policies prevented much change in the supply of places in upper secondary schools and universities until after World War II. In the 1930s, for ex-ample, fewer than 5 percent of French students attended secondary schools (Neave 1985). The French began, very hesitantly, to reform their schooling system in the 1940s and 1950s to allow more students to attend and complete secondary schooling. Policymakers in other countries were still slower to adapt to changing occupational structures and labor market conditions. In England and Sweden, for example, policymakers contained social demand for schooling in highly restrictive structures through the early and mid-1960s. Thus, in the first decades following World War II, policymakers in most European countries added vo-cational tracks in secondary schools to prepare the majority of students for jobs rather than for higher levels of schooling.

Examination systems often grow in importance when educational systems shift from a focus on reproducing "cultivated" status groups to a focus on providing qualifications for positions in large organizations. Max Weber (1917) first recognized this relationship in his studies of state bureaucracy in ancient China, and Randall Collins (1979) extended Weber's insight as a general principle of educational stratification. During the first decades of sec-ondary school expansion in Europe, rigorous secondary school-leaving examinations very frequently kept the proportion of students going on to higher education at a low level. Over the past two decades, the European countries have adjusted their examination systems to permit a larger pool of students to go on to higher education. In England, for example, the once famously difficult school-leaving examinations were adjusted a decade ago to increase the pool of students eligible for higher education and to reduce the high levels of school leaving at age 16. These changes have had the desired effects: between 1986 and 1996, the proportion of 18-year-olds qualified for higher education jumped by 50 percent. And school leaving at age 16 dropped by even more than 50 percent. Still more dramatic changes in examination pass rates have occurred in France and several Scandinavian countries.

Thus, governments have played an important role in slowing and hastening changes in educational attainment. All governments have tools at their disposal to retard, encourage, and channel demand for higher levels of schooling. These tools include the use of fee requirements, the tracking of students into academic or vocational programs through examination results and teacher recommendations, changing the length of degree requirements, and the creation of credentials and qualifications to signal levels of human capital development and thereby to influence employers' hiring decisions.

Nevertheless, pressures for expansion have led to a similar march of enrollments throughout the industrial world. First, primary enrollments reached saturation in the early and mid-twentieth century. (The United States was not the only leader here. At the turn of the twentieth century, four years before primary education became compulsory by law, Japanese primary schools had reached the saturation level of 100 percent enrolled.) Next, secondary enrollments climbed. These enrollments have now reached the saturation level in the industrialized societies, although some societies, such as England and the United States, continue to have high drop out rates. And, finally, beginning in the 1960s, the proportion of the age group enrolled in post-secondary education also grew.

Indeed, the rapid expansion of higher education is a worldwide phenomenon, extending beyond the countries with already high levels of secondary school completion. This expansion must therefore reflect not only the inflationary push of credential seekers, but the broader influence of a model of society in which science, democratic participation, and national development all figure prominently. This model has been embraced by policymakers around the world. In it, people who have obtained university knowledge are considered desirable for a wide variety of social positions, and many more young people than before are seen as candidates for higher education (Schofer and Meyer 2005).

Participation in post-secondary education grew rapidly in nearly every industrialized country in the 1990s, a pattern that has continued and even accelerated in the 2000s (OECD 2004:276). This rapid growth was accompanied by less difficult examination requirements and, in some cases, by a reduction in secondary school course loads. Today, in the developed world, half of young people enter universities or other institutions offering university-level qualifications. In some countries, participation rates exceed 80 percent of the age cohort (OECD 2005:249). Of course, not all who attend complete degree programs. On average, about one-third of young people in the industrialized world attain university degrees. The completion rate varies considerably, however, between a high of 45 percent in two outlying countries, Australia and Finland, and lows of 20 percent in several German-speaking countries (OECD 2004:272–6).

The differentiation of students' occupational fates consequently now occurs later in life. Where children were once commonly divided into separate tracks by age 10 or 11, they now study similar curricula until age 15 or 16. Most systems now begin occupational streaming in upper secondary school. Short-cycle programs of one or two years connected to specific occupations have also been introduced in higher education, along the lines of American community college programs. Most systems also provide many more options for students to change courses of study and to prepare for critical examinations. Thus, we have seen a proliferation of occupational streams and options for most students in Europe at ages 15 or 16, and for students in the United States by age 18.[1]

Even so, some important differences between countries remain. Comparisons between several national systems can bring out the importance of inherited institutional structures, deep-seated social divisions, and distinctive policy choices as these forces interact with common pressures to expand schooling and to rationalize it in relation to the market demand for educated labor.

SIX SCHOOLING SYSTEMS

For comparative purposes, we need discuss preprimary and primary education only briefly. Today, all industrial societies have what amounts to universal schooling through age 15 or 16. Major efforts are being made to extend schooling earlier in the life cycle, both because of the prevalence of women's employment and because preschool has been shown to improve children's learning readiness. If both preschool and university completion become commonplace, educational life expectancy will soon be 17 or 18 years for the majority of students in the industrialized world, compared to the 10–12 years that were typical only a little more than a generation ago. All these societies offer reasonably similar curricula for primary school students, emphasizing the "three R's" combined with quite a bit of character and citizenship training. (See Chapter 4.)

One important structural difference at the primary level remains, however. Some countries have relatively powerful government ministries of education; others organize public education in a more thoroughly decentralized way. Sweden and Japan remain as examples of systems that are more centralized than others (although they too have encouraged greater autonomy of municipalities in recent years). Standardized national curricula, funding patterns, and personnel requirements are characteristic of centralized systems. In other countries, financing, administration, and planning are decentralized either at the regional level, as in Germany and Canada, or at the state and local levels, as in the United States. Most other European systems combine centralized funding and goal-setting with decentralized decision-making about allocation of funds and choices of textbooks and teaching methods (Eurydice 2002:32–5).

By contrast, Americans favor not only local control but also decentralized financing of schools on the grounds that such schools will be more responsive to the particular interests and concerns of the communities in which they are located. For example, communities that prize diversity may be able to express those values more clearly in their classrooms than if they operated under the dictates of a national ministry of education. It also seems unfair to many people to penalize communities that want to spend more on schooling by making them conform to a central bureaucracy's formulas for funding all schools equally.

Local financing does have drawbacks, however. It fosters high levels of inequality between communities in school resources and staffing. Centralized financed systems spend essentially the same amount on every student; public school children in wealthy areas receive no more than students in impoverished areas. By contrast, in locally controlled systems, such as in the United States, per student expenditures can vary significantly, because the tax base to support schools differs greatly among communities.[2] Not long ago, the richest districts of the state of Texas, for example, spent as much as nine times as much on their students as did the poorest districts in the state (Kozol 1987:223). Today, states often attempt to compensate for inequities in local funding bases, but not all states make this effort and even those that do are not completely successful. It remains common within the United States for affluent suburbs to spend more than twice as much per student as the impoverished central cities they surround (Condron and Roscigno 2003).[3]

Although this important difference at the primary level should be kept in mind, the major contrasts among schooling systems in industrial societies are found not at the primary or even at the lower secondary school level (grades 7 through 9), but at the upper secondary school level (grades 10 through 12, corresponding to American high school years—in some countries, also including grades 13 and 14). These are the grades in which students begin to approach either higher education or the job market. Major differences are also found in the structure of what the Europeans call "tertiary" education and Americans call "post-secondary" or higher education.

A few key structural differences help to unlock students' opportunities in the six systems, and the characteristic attitudes that develop among students concerning their educational experiences:

- The age at which students are separated into higher- and lower-track schools
- The proportion of students enrolled in academic and vocational curricula in upper secondary schools
- The extent to which vocational curricula are strongly or weakly tied to good jobs in the labor market and to post-secondary opportunities
- The proportion of students completing university-level education
- The extent to which a separate set of highly selective elite institutions are directly connected to the top corporate and government jobs[4]

United States and Germany: Schooling Opposites

Among the more populous countries in the industrial world, no schooling systems are as different as those in the United States and Germany. The differences between the two are significant from bottom to top. The Americans offer academic schooling, rather than separate academic and vocational tracks, through high school and send large numbers of students on to higher education. They have one of the highest college graduation rates in the developed world. By contrast, the Germans divide children at an early age, provide for vocational apprenticeships for a near majority at the upper secondary level, and graduate only about half the proportion of young people from university-level education as the Americans do.

Germany. German schoolchildren are divided at the age of 10 among three distinct kinds of schools stratified by academic prestige (Lehmann 1994). The *Hauptschule* is designed for children who, it is assumed, will eventually work in blue-collar, crafts, and lower-level service jobs. The *Realschule* is designed for children who are expected eventually to work in routine white-collar and technical jobs. The *Gymnasium* alone is for academic study leading to the university and eventually to the more intellectually demanding professions and to executive management. Some German regions (Länder) have adopted integrated schools, *Gesamtschule*, but continue to track students within the school.

At the end of the lower secondary years, students receive certificates that allow them to continue schooling or to move into vocational training. Three options exist: most students from *Gymnasium* continue their general education studies in preparation for the *Abitur* and the university; most students from *Hauptschule* and *Realschule* move into the *dual system* of vocational training, the former more often into training for trades and the latter more often into training for business occupations (Brauns and Steinmann 1997). From an American perspective, the most distinctive part of German schooling is the dual system. In this system, students spend part of their time working in apprenticeships to learn a trade and part of their time in "continuation schools" funded by the state. This system has helped to produce high skill levels among German workers. The German system has even become a model for some business-oriented reformers in the United States, who feel that it would serve the interests of many American high school students better than the general education curriculum currently emphasized in American high schools.

A passing mark on the *Abitur* signals successful completion of secondary school and provides the necessary admission ticket to higher education. The elite quarter of German students who pass the examination are entitled to enroll in any German university and (with a few exceptions) in any field of study they desire. In this sense, higher education institutions differentiate among students hardly at all. Students who make it through academic training in secondary school are considered to have demonstrated their maturity for higher-level study. This situation contrasts markedly with the American system, which is much more open but makes no such confident assumptions about the readiness of students for higher-level study (Teichler 1985; Lehmann 1994).

As in much of Europe, higher education in Germany is publicly supported and attendance essentially free for those admitted. Even so, less than one-quarter of young people enter one of only 325 institutions of higher learning in the country (OECD 1996:279). More than half of these are technical colleges, or *Fachhochschulen*, with shorter degree programs, similar to American community colleges.[5] These technical colleges have been a center of growth in recent years. Until recently, the first university degree was intended to take four years, but most students took five years or more to finish it. Less than 15 percent of the age group received their university diplomas. (Because university students began their studies later in Germany than in the United States, it can be argued that the university diploma has been more like an American master's degree than like an American bachelor's degree. This makes the 15 percent figure look rather more impressive.)

In Germany, university education is strongly oriented to the arts and sciences, and all German universities are considered equal to one another. Thus, tracking in German secondary schooling is compatible with and supports a relatively undifferentiated structure of higher education. Efforts to standardize higher education throughout Europe, under the guidelines of the 2000 Bologna Agreement, have recently led to the introduction of three-year university degrees in Germany. These have been resisted by the German professorate to a greater degree than in other EU countries, because universities in Germany are not widely accepted as mass institutions.

The United States. Consider the contrasts between the German and American public schools. At the time when German students are being separated into entirely different schools based on their likely occupational fates, American students remain in "comprehensive" schools studying the same curriculum. Few secondary school students are formally tracked, and the great majority take academic courses (though of differing rigor levels), combined perhaps with one or two vocational "electives." Vocational courses are weakly connected to jobs, and many wage incentives exist for high school graduates to continue their schooling in two- or four-year colleges. No high school graduates are barred by their course of study from continuing schooling after high school. Even colleges are liberal arts oriented at the lower division level, due to the tradition of general education distribution requirements. About two-fifths of American college students choose liberal arts or science majors, remaining out of the occupational preparation stream for two more years through graduation. The remaining 60 percent begin occupational studies in their junior year of college (Brint et al. 2005).

From the beginning of the American republic, weak state control over higher education made it relatively easy for a wide variety of groups to open colleges. American higher education now includes institutions ranging from religious colleges of a few hundred students to public universities of 50,000 or more. Altogether, there are some 2,400 four-year colleges and universities and another 1,600 two-year colleges, 10 times as many institutions for a population only 3.5 times as large as the German population. Each of the institutions competes for new students, thereby encouraging college attendance. Clearly, American society provides lots of entrepreneurial opportunities—not only in higher education, but in business and religion as well. (In fact, some have argued that the diversity of religious organizations—and the "market competition" it engenders—is one reason why religiosity is also higher in the United States than elsewhere.)

Until recently a higher proportion of American students went on to higher education than anywhere else in the world. Through the mid-1990s, about 40 percent of high school students entered four-year colleges and universities, and another 25 percent entered two-year community colleges. Not everyone survived, of course, but about one out of three 18-year-olds eventually graduated with a bachelor's degree. Considering the time and expense required to obtain a bachelor's degree, this was an impressive achievement. The United States remains one of the leaders in the production of college graduates, but it is no longer far ahead of other countries.

In the United States, students can study a rich array of practical, job-related subjects in college, as well as liberal arts and sciences courses. Students often wait until college to begin to make serious decisions about their work lives. In marked contrast to Germany, where the situation is exactly reversed, the largely untracked structure of American secondary schooling feeds into to a highly stratified system of higher education. The American system pushes the hard decisions about career preparation—and, consequently, the differentiation of life fates—back into the college years for the majority of students who go on to college (Allmendinger 1989).

The adult population of the United States continues to be among the most highly educated in the world, but over the last decade, social scientists have pointed to signs of declining productivity in American higher education relative to other systems. Some European systems now produce a higher proportion of university graduates than the United States from among their new cohorts of young adults and a much lower proportion of dropouts. As I will discuss further in Chapter 6, both the growing income gap between rich and poor and the increasing cost of college education have contributed to declines in the relative productivity of the U.S. system.

The U.S. and German systems are not alone at the poles of schooling possibilities in the contemporary industrial world. The Canadian and most of the East Asian schooling systems resemble the American system in many ways; they too have a comprehensive and academically oriented upper secondary level and a relatively large proportion of high school graduates continuing into higher education (OECD 2004). Correspondingly, the Austrians and the Swiss, who are geographically and culturally close to the Germans, have created structures of schooling that are very similar to the German system and, in fact, produce an even smaller proportion of university graduates (ibid.).

The German "Dual System" of Vocational Training

In Germany, tracking begins at age 10 and schooling opportunities are limited for those in the lower tracks. Yet, oddly enough, German workers at all levels enjoy greater income equity than the workers in most industrial societies, including the United States. One important reason for this equity is Germany's dual system. The system is dual because it combines further schooling and on-site apprenticeship training for a near-majority of German youths above the age of 15.

Compulsory schooling ends in Germany at age 15. Not long ago, some 60 percent of German youths moved into the dual system at the end of compulsory schooling, but today the proportion is under half. Most of these apprenticeship programs run for two or three years. They include training for a great variety of occupations, from auto mechanics to banking, though the great majority is in the skilled blue-collar occupations. A typical week includes three or four days of work with a company and one or two days in a local vocational school. Some companies operate on-site schools. The schools emphasize practical skills but include academic material related to these practical skills. McKernan (1994) reported on one lesson involving a procedure for bending metal. While the students were learning this procedure, the teacher was also writing on the board the formulas related to the stress capabilities of the metal. Classroom learning also includes continued exposure to subjects that would be found in an American high school—languages, math, and social studies.

Apprenticeship students are paid an allowance equivalent to 20 to 25 percent of the full wage paid to a journeyman worker. An allowance of less than $1000 per month is not much to live on, but it is adequate for the large proportion of apprenticeship students who continue to live in their parents' home.

Training under the dual system is meant to be broad, and students in the course of their training usually rotate through a number of jobs. Even so, the upward mobility of German workers with apprenticeship credentials is more limited than in many other industrial countries. The relatively restricted mobility of German workers is compensated by the high wages that prevail in German industry. Many argue that these wages reflect the high levels of skill typical of workers trained in the dual system.

The high skill levels might also help to explain the historically strong popularity of the system with German employers. All the major industrial and commercial firms take part in the apprenticeship system, even though they have no direct financial incentive for doing so. Companies support apprenticeship training through dues they pay to one of two national business associations. Apprentices are not required to stay with the companies that train them, and indeed most leave their companies within a year of leaving the apprenticeship program (Maurice, Sellier, and Silvestre 1986). In recent years, the system has come under criticism by employers and some social scientists, primarily for its lack of flexibility (Blossfeld 1992). But it has also found proponents, even in the United States, where some argue that secondary education is failing a large minority of students who are not academically inclined and would like better preparation for skilled work.

England and France: Modernizing Class-Divided Systems

Policymakers in England and France have made concerted efforts, beginning in the 1970s and 1980s, to modernize systems that were once strongly divided by social class. Children from the working classes were channeled into lower level schools, eventually leading to vocational training options, while children from middle classes were far more likely to move into higher level schools and then on to universities. In England, the goal of policymakers has been to keep students in school beyond the minimum school-leaving age and to expand the numbers of students in higher education. In France, the goal of policymakers has been to increase pass rates for secondary school-leaving examinations and to build higher education enrollments, largely through the expansion of occupational training options in higher education. In the process, the once highly decentralized English system has become more centralized, while the once highly centralized French system has become more decentralized (Deer 2002).

England. English schooling was renowned not long ago for the upper-class ambiance of its elite secondary schools and ancient universities and for the "11-plus" examination that divided children among three separate institutional tracks at that tender age on the basis of examination results (grammar schools for high-scoring kids, technical schools for those in the middle, and secondary modern schools for lower-scoring kids). It is no wonder that stereotypes of English schooling emphasized the aristocratic character of higher education, dominated by the universities at Oxford and Cambridge, and the desire of most working-class students to leave schooling as soon as they possibly could.

Indeed, the majority of students—some 60 percent in the 1960s and 1970s—dropped out of school at the minimum school-leaving age and went off on their own to seek employment. This was by some measure the highest rate of school leaving among the wealthier European countries. Only the most promising students remained to study in the sixth form (grades 11 and 12) for the demanding General Certificate of Education advanced-level (A-level) exams (Eckstein and Noah 1993:48–50). Those who passed two of these difficult exams were qualified to enter the universities, but less than one in five adolescents made it that far (ibid.:173–4), and not many more than 10 percent completed university-level degrees.

Paul Willis's study of the "counter-school culture" of working-class students attending a secondary modern school in the midlands of England provides a flavor of the discontent, which developed in response to class segregation and the boys' antipathy to what they saw as the false promises of the schools:

> "The lads" specialize in a caged resentment which always stops just short of outright confrontation. Settled in class, as near a group as they can manage, there is a continuous scraping of chairs, a bad tempered "tut-tutting" at the simplest request, and a continuous fidgeting about which explores every permutation of sitting or lying on a chair. During private study, some openly show disdain by apparently trying to go to sleep with their head sideways down on the desk, some have their backs to the desk gazing out of the window, or even vacantly at the wall. There is an aimless air of insubordination ready with spurious justification and impossible to nail down. . . . Comics, newspapers and nudes under half-lifted desks melt into elusive textbooks. A continuous hum of talk flows around injunctions not to, like the inevitable tide over barely dried sand, and everywhere there are rolled-back eyeballs and exaggerated mouthings of conspiratorial secrets. (Willis 1979:13)

Educational policy during the last generation has been intended to expand the educational attainment of students from middle- and working-class backgrounds—to reduce the number of "lads" and to increase the number of grads. Yet, the formerly class-divided structure of English schooling has created unique problems for policymakers. In their efforts to bring the system into alignment with schooling in other industrial societies, English policymakers have been forced in two directions. For those who could be induced to stay in school beyond age 16, they pushed in the direction of American-style expansion of higher education opportunities. For those who could not be induced to stay in school, they began to expand in the direction of German-style apprenticeship and job training.

Beginning in the mid-1960s, the tripartite structure and the 11-plus exam were replaced with untracked comprehensive schools. In the 1980s, the government introduced a national curriculum to set standards for a unified primary and lower secondary education, rather than a class-divided system.

During Margaret Thatcher's administration in the late 1970s and early 1980s, the government also introduced the further education (FE) colleges to reduce the amount of school-leaving at age 16. These colleges provided vocational and academic options for 16- and 17-year-olds. Not unlike American community colleges, the FE sector now enrolls an increasing number of adults and part-time students. The government also introduced new qualifications to encourage students to remain in school after age 16. These National Vocational Qualifications (NVQ) consisted of modules of coursework and practical experience; some 6000 were introduced between 1979 and 1986. The new vocational qualifications were taken up by employers as desirable credentials for jobs that did not require secondary school completion. In 1991, the government introduced the General National Vocational Qualifications (GNVQ) as a "bridge" between vocational training and traditional academic qualifications. The GNVQ provided national curricula in more than a dozen occupational fields and were marketed to employers as providing a mix of academic and practical skills that would be transferable across firms and industries (Brauns and Steinmann 1997). During the same period, the government changed the secondary school-leaving examination to allow students with a wider range of coursework to take and pass the examination.

Changes in higher education were equally extensive. The government established a three-year bachelor's degree and integrated the two tiers of higher education—polytechnics and universities—into a unified structure of higher education. Instead of government funds being allocated to universities on the basis of traditional criteria of academic prestige, new performance measures were introduced to allow newer universities to compete to improve their standing (Thompson, Tyler, and Howlett 1995). Each of these steps can be interpreted as an effort to catch up with the rest of Europe, beginning from an unpromising starting point.

The changes resulting from these policies have been dramatic, although the shadow of the old system remains. Today, the school-leaving group is well under 30 percent (DFES 2004). This remains a high proportion by the standards of most European countries, but it is nothing like the 60 percent who left school at age 16 in the 1960s and 1970s. The government now issues youth credits to all 16- and 17-year-old school leavers. These credits provide access to apprenticeship and training programs in a variety of different forms. Some of these forms involve part-time school attendance and provide qualifications for jobs in the middle of the occupational structure. Others provide qualifications for lower-level jobs.

The FE sector enrolls a third of all 16- and 17-year-olds and an even larger number of adults. Some 500 FE colleges, equivalent to grades 11 and 12 in the United States, offer a mix of technical, vocational, and academic courses. Many students pursue vocational qualifications for middle-level jobs and move directly into the labor market. However, approximately one-quarter of 18-year-olds who enroll in higher education come from the FE sector. Some adults also eventually enroll in higher education after attending the FE colleges.

Higher education has also been thoroughly transformed in recent years. The proportion of the age group attending college doubled in the six years between 1988 and 1994 alone from just over 15 percent to nearly one-third (OECD 1996:333). Today, only a handful of countries have a higher proportion of college graduates at the typical age of graduation. Thus, a system that was once among the most restrictive in Europe has become one of the more open in a matter of two decades. The English accomplished this feat by standardizing the three-year bachelor's degree (a very short degree program), by broadening opportunities to take the examinations needed for college entry by expanding the number of courses that count as qualifying, and by expanding the path to higher education from the FE sector.

Each of these changes has motivated more students to aspire to stay in school for the bachelor's degree.

English higher education has remained highly stratified in prestige, however, with the ancient universities of Oxford and Cambridge in the top rank, the University of London following not far behind (and even more prestigious in some science and medical fields). The "redbrick universities" founded in the 1950s and 1960s and, especially, the polytechnics lag behind in prestige and resources. Admission to Oxford and Cambridge is by competitive examination. Like elite higher education elsewhere in the advanced world, these ancient universities, once known for their aristocratic undergraduates and classical courses of study, have become largely upper middle class, integrated by gender, and increasingly science oriented in the years since World War II (Soares 1999). At the same time, the performance measures introduced by the Thatcher government have allowed some highly entrepreneurial universities, such as the University of Warwick, to move up in the rankings (Clark 2004).

France. The French were among the first to provide nationwide primary education. In 1830, French educational minister François Guizot introduced plans, which had already been discussed at the time of Napoleon, to develop a national system of basic education, highly centralized, broad in content, rigorous, and—in the spirit of the French Revolution—completely separate from organized religion. (The rigor of this education cannot be doubted. Until the 1980s, about half of all schoolchildren repeated at least one grade.)

Secondary school, however, remained the preserve of the elite. "[A] sharp line was drawn between primary education, which was for all young people, and secondary education, which was for the select few" (Cummings 2003:19). As late as the 1930s, only 4 percent of French youth were admitted to the *lycées*, the French secondary schools. These students were almost exclusively from upper-middle- or upper-class families (Neave 1985). The French began a long process of democratizing secondary schooling after World War II by adding a common curriculum in lower secondary schools and by reducing the amount of grade repetition (which nevertheless remains high by American standards).

By the late 1950s, French Prime Minister Charles de Gaulle and his planners began to make inroads in democratizing secondary education. However, even in 1965, after more than a decade of reform effort, only one-fifth of French students studied in the *lycées*, and just half of those were able to pass the *baccalaureate* examination, which alone permitted admission to universities. The *baccalaureate* was widely considered one of the most demanding examinations in Europe (Eckstein and Noah 1993). The majority of students took vocational courses or general education courses (*cours complémentaire*), which led to nonuniversity qualifications.

This situation changed radically in 1985, when the French minister of education, Jean-Pierre Chevènement, influenced by experts forecasting the need for more students who had passed the *baccalaureate*, created two new types of *baccalaureate* exams and raised the expected secondary school completion rate to 80 percent of the age group (de Meulemeester 2003). The road to the *baccalaureate*, which once led exclusively through the academic *lycées*, thus became three roads. Almost half of successful candidates now come either from technical (30 percent) or vocational (18 percent) programs (Ministère de L'Éducation Nationale 2005). Combined with larger age cohorts, the new options have led to 7 times as many 17- and 18-year-olds taking the baccalaureate examination as did in 1970. Even with pass rates that have remained relatively constant in recent years at 60 to 65 percent (rather than the desired 80 percent), the proportion eligible for higher education shot up from 300,000 in 1970 to 2.1 million in 2000 (ibid.).

Today, only a few French students begin occupational studies at the end of lower secondary school. Instead, at age 16, those remaining in school (more than 80 percent of the age group) are divided by academic achievement into academic and occupational streams. They are assigned to different schools, academic *lycées* and *lycées professionels*, respectively. Teachers' evaluations are primary in this process, although parents may appeal teachers' recommendations (OECD 1996:275–6). The majority (nearly 60 percent) pursues technical and vocational training at the *lycées professionels*. Students can prepare for a wide variety of occupational specializations in these schools. Well over 200 types of vocational certification can be obtained on completion of studies. At the lowest level, these schools emphasize work orientation for future semiskilled workers. At the highest level, there are specialized courses for future technicians and junior managers; and in the middle, highly specialized courses for apprentice skilled workers. The curriculum at every level of the *lycée professionel* is oriented toward work-related skills and knowledge (Holmes and MacLean 1989:59).

As planners hoped, higher education credentials have become increasingly important in the labor market, and more than 60 percent of students in the age group now enroll in some form of tertiary education. Many study in "short-cycle programs" of two years that are not considered university level, or drop out before completing the work for their diplomas in general university studies. However, three, four, and five-year degree programs also exist and provide valuable qualifications for many occupations and professions. Thus, occupational streaming now cuts across institutional lines; occupational programs in secondary school frequently lead to more occupational training in post-secondary education.

Thanks to the relaxation of examination requirements and the introduction of shorter degree programs and vocational qualifications in higher education, the expansion of French higher education has been nothing short of spectacular; over the last decade, the completion rate has nearly doubled. The opening of access to higher education for students from vocational and technical secondary schools and the adoption of the three-year degree program are two important causes for this huge increase (Deer 2002). Indeed, France has one of the highest post-secondary completion rates in the world; 55 percent of students attain some form of post-secondary credentials. This figure includes both those who receive "short-cycle" credentials, roughly equivalent to those offered in American community colleges (18 percent of the age group), and those who receive "long-cycle," or university-level, credentials (37 percent of the age group). The comparable figure for the United States is 40 percent—including the 8 percent who receive short-cycle associate's degrees and the 32 percent who receive bachelor's degrees (UNESCO 2005, Table 29).

With the advent of mass higher education, a new internal stratification has developed between scientific and nonscientific specialties. The humanities no longer represent the foundation for high educational status, as they did during the period of restricted admission. In the new era, scientific and engineering disciplines have the highest prestige and also attract more male students and more students from high socioeconomic backgrounds (Eurydice 2003; Neave 1985).

The top 10 percent of upper secondary school students compete for a rarer prize than university admission. Following an extra year or two of preparation, these students take the demanding *concours* examination, which alone allows for admission to the *grandes écoles*. The most prestigious of the *grandes écoles* were established during the reign of Napoleon as a way of training leadership for the civil service. Today, there are more than 200 *grandes écoles*, each one designed to train students for specific fields, such as engineering, business, or public administration. The state civil service continues to absorb a large proportion of the best students (Bourdieu 1996). Admission to the most selective of the *grandes écoles* is even more important in French society than Ivy League colleges are in American society. Graduation from one of the leading *grandes écoles* more or less guarantees a life in one of the command posts of French society (Suleiman 1978; Bourdieu 1996).

Competition for admission to the *grandes écoles* has always been fierce (one of the greatest of sociologists, Emile Durkheim, failed twice before gaining admission to the *École Normale Supériere*). Among French sociologists, there has been a strong suspicion that social background contributed to shaping teachers' evaluations of their students. Pierre Bourdieu's study of the distribution of evaluative comments in a girls' preparatory school tended to confirm this suspicion, albeit with limited data:

> The taxonomy of adjectives . . . is organized according to the hierarchy of "inferior" [lower-class] qualities—servility, vulgarity, clumsiness, slowness, poverty, etc.; "medium" [lower-middle-class] qualities—pettiness, narrowness, mediocrity, accuracy, conscientiousness, etc.; and "superior" qualities—sincerity, expansiveness, richness, facility, expertise, finesse, ingenuity, intelligence, culture, etc. . . . The most favorable epithets appear more and more frequently as the social origins of the pupils rise. . . . Parisian origins constitute an extra advantage. (Bourdieu 1988:202, 198; *sentences reorganized for clarity*)

The creation of a mass system of higher education in France led, perhaps inevitably, to increased demand for admission to the *grandes écoles.* The number of students competing for spaces in the *grandes écoles* has nearly doubled since 1980. (Something similar has occurred in the United States; as the bachelor's degree has become a less lofty qualification in the job market, the number of applications for places in Ivy League and other selective institutions has steadily grown, and the number of students taking advanced placement tests has more than doubled in a decade. See College Board 2005.)

Sweden: A Traditional Multitrack System with High "Educational Life Expectancy"

The Swedish system illustrates the most common way that European policymakers accommodated inherited structures of elite secondary and higher education to the increasing social demand for equality of educational opportunity and marketable educational credentials. The Swedish government provides strictly equal schooling in the primary and lower secondary school grades. In the upper secondary school years, schooling is divided into multiple tracks, most of which are vocational. Until recently, most students in vocational programs did not attend university. But that has now changed. All programs provide eligibility for higher education, and some 80 percent of students at some point take university classes, though many are interested in taking only a few courses to "top off" their upper secondary qualifications (OECD 2005).

Swedish policymakers abandoned a highly class-divided system of primary and secondary schooling in the 1950s and 1960s under the leadership of Social Democratic reformers. At the primary and lower secondary level, Sweden is now among the most egalitarian of all industrialized societies, making special efforts to provide equal schooling for the major ethnic minority, the Saami people, and for rural students (Swedish Institute 1996). Highly egalitarian policies are possible because of national-level control of curriculum, teacher recruitment and pay, and per student expenditures.

Until the 1970s, the Swedes divided post-compulsory education between separate vocational and academic schools. Reforms of the 1970s led to the creation of comprehensive upper secondary schools, the *gymnasieskola*. Students begin upper secondary education somewhat later than elsewhere in the industrial world (at age 16 or 17) and can continue in upper secondary school (depending on course of study) through age 20. Today, there are 17 national study programs, only 2 of which are academic (social sciences and natural sciences). The vocational programs require more hours for completion, and at least 15 percent of the time must be spent at work places (Swedish Institute 2004). The 15 national vocational programs range from child care, vehicle repair, and construction to graphic media, hotel management, and business administration (Swedish Institute 2004). Core subjects are common to all programs: Swedish, English, civics, religious studies, math, natural science, physical education, health, and art. About half of Swedish upper secondary students enroll in vocational programs; the other half in academic programs. Students can also design individualized courses of study, if they wish.

Sweden has in recent years opened access to higher education, and it now has one of the highest post-secondary entry rates in the world. Some 80 percent of Swedish young people attend university at one time or another (OECD 2005:249). Cost of attending university is nominal, and the Swedish government has encouraged a philosophy of lifelong learning and continuous skill improvement. The government has supported this philosophy with subsidies to encourage university attendance for workers over age 25. Many Swedish university students return to university after a few years working (or in military service), seeking additional course work or degrees that will be valuable to them in their jobs. Through the 1980s, higher education graduation rates in Sweden were no higher than the European norm. Since that time, however, university completion rates have increased dramatically. Women's participation has been an important force everywhere, but it has been particularly important in Scandinavian countries, where women constitute 60 percent or more of post-secondary enrollments (Eurydice 2002:102).

Thus, the pattern of adjustment in Sweden has gone through several stages: first the elimination of tracking in elementary and lower secondary schools and the introduction of preschools; next, the elimination of separate tiers in upper secondary schooling and the creation of comprehensive schools with vocational and academic tracks; and, finally, the encouragement of vocational students to continue their studies in post-secondary institutions.

By 2000, one-third of young adults (age 30 to 34) in Sweden had post-secondary qualifications, significantly higher than the European norm of one-quarter (ibid.:111). Average "educational life expectancy" in Sweden is more than 20 years, well above average for the industrialized world (OECD 2005). Preschool attendance is nearly universal, secondary schooling is long, and the great majority of students have at least some post-secondary education. Similar, and indeed often more pronounced patterns are found in other Scandinavian countries, such as Finland, Iceland, and Norway.

As in Germany, Swedish universities do not offer a separate elite track. Instead, they are modeled along the lines of the German universities. They are regarded as equal in standing and are expected to admit any qualified student for whom a place is available.[6] Recently, a few private universities, such as the Chalmers Institute of Technology, have challenged the monopoly of the state on higher education. They have emphasized business and technology and a more corporate model of teaching and learning (Clark 2004, chap. 5).

Schooling in the Former Soviet Union

One of the more unusual cases in the industrial world's taxonomy of schooling systems no longer exists. For students of the sociology of schooling, the interest of the old Soviet Union lies in the purposes schooling served in that society, and the tensions that existed between a class-oriented ideology and the industrial interests of the state.

After the revolution of 1917, Soviet leaders quickly modernized Russia's backwards educational institutions. Thousands of new primary and secondary schools opened in a matter of years, and teachers were trained under the strict dictates of "the workers' state." In the Soviet Union, experience with manual labor was included as part of the curriculum throughout the elementary years, and both the brightest and least motivated students were expected to become competent at industrial arts (Bronfenbrenner 1970). Efforts were also made to socialize children into the norms of collective life. Most children's games in the old Soviet Union emphasized cooperative activity, rather than competitive activity. Teachers encouraged competition, but this competition was rarely between individuals, as it is in the United States. Instead, students sitting in a particular row of desks would compete with other groups formed in the same way. In this way, students were encouraged to develop norms of shared contribution to group performance (ibid.).

The structure of Soviet schooling, however, was not much different from that of other European systems. Tracking began at age 14 and competitive examinations were used to allocate access to higher education and the elite positions that were connected to graduation from higher education. Ironically, for most of the 70-year history of the Soviet Union, schooling provided relatively little opportunity for children from the industrial working class and the peasantry. Indeed, schooling was more thoroughly dominated at the upper levels by the leading classes than were the schooling systems of most bourgeois democracies. Competitive examinations for admission to higher education favored children whose parents had higher levels of formal education (Dobson 1977; Kerblay 1983).

This *de facto* preference appeared to many Soviets to violate principles of the workers' state, and it led to episodic attempts to reform the system so that children from working-class and peasant backgrounds would have greater chances of success. The major example of ideologically determined preference was the Soviet "class affirmative action" era of 1927–31. During this period, Joseph Stalin changed admission policies in higher education to give preference to candidates from working-class and peasant backgrounds. Many scholars have interpreted the policy as an effort by Stalin not just to actualize Soviet egalitarian ideas but, more important, to build a cadre of extreme loyalists among the new men who were favored by the policies (Fitzpatrick 1979; Bailes 1979). After just a few years, Stalin's experiment foundered on complaints of educators and managers about the quality of the new cohorts of university graduates, and competitive testing was reinstituted. Other episodes of class affirmative action occurred under Nikita Khrushchev in 1958–64 and again under Leonid Brezhnev in 1969–70.

Thus, educational policy in the old Soviet Union oscillated between overriding concerns with talent discovery and social efficiency and overriding concerns with equality. Efficiency concerns, which promoted greater reliance on testing, favored students from more privileged backgrounds; equality concerns favored the lower classes somewhat. In spite of the Soviet Union's proletarian ideology, talent discovery and efficiency concerns came first for all but 12 of the 70 years of Soviet rule.

Japan: A Test-Based System

The leaders of the Meiji Revolution of 1868 immediately declared that every child should be literate and attend school regularly. They looked to Europe and the United States for models. Amazingly, as many as 25,000 new schools were founded in just a few years following the Charter Oath of 1872 (Cummings 2003:94–5). These schools looked very much like their American counterparts:

> A typical school had an external wall around a playing field, with the school prominently visible from the front gate. . . . The new elementary school was a two-storey frame building of brick construction with plaster and with hard wood floors. Students were expected to proceed down the pathway from the front gate to the front entrance of the school, and put on their slippers. Proceeding down the hall, there were two classrooms on each side and at the back there was one room for the principal and a second for the teachers, and on the first floor there were additional classrooms. Rather than allow the children to sit on mats (as earlier schools had), the classrooms provided wooden desks for each child (ibid.:95).

The elementary schools were "beacons of modernity, with their European architecture, their expectation that children sit on chairs at desks, and that all young people regardless of class or gender should study together in a common classroom" (ibid.:96).

The Japanese also adopted the American preference for academic education for the majority. Elementary schools provided courses covering "subjects as diverse as physical and moral education and science and world geography" (ibid.). Schooling in Japan remains academic in orientation, both at the elementary and secondary levels. Today, about 10 percent drop out during upper secondary school, another 10–15 percent take terminal vocational degrees, and more than 70 percent go on to some form of post-secondary education, though only about 40 percent to universities. Three-quarters of students who attend university complete their degrees. Like the United States, Japan has one of the higher university-level graduation rates in the world.

To be sure, some structural differences between the American and Japanese systems do exist: First, the system is centrally controlled; curriculum, teacher salaries, and per student expenditures are all equalized across communities. The Japanese also have small, but highly separate vocational tracks for students who have done poorly in their early years of study, or prefer to work with their hands. These vocational tracks have strong links to employers (Rosenbaum and Kariya 1989). Since 1994, a controversial new "integrated" academic-vocational track has been introduced into Japanese secondary education. As in France, the Japanese also maintain an elite system of top-ranked public universities, the most important of which is Tokyo University, for training future corporate and government leaders. In the United States, highly selective private universities play a somewhat analogous role, but elite recruitment is not as tightly focused on a small handful of institutions (Kanaga 1994).

Although the Japanese schooling structure is comparable in many respects to the American structure, student achievement (as measured by standardized test scores) is significantly higher, especially in the fields of science and mathematics. Here we can see that culture matters. Japanese families materially support and morally enforce expectations that children will work hard and achieve good marks in school. Family pride is very much connected to the school performance of children, especially male children. School is therefore a central interest in Japanese families, and nonworking mothers often buy their children's textbooks so that they can know exactly what their children are studying (White 1987). The large family expenditures on education—some one-third of total family spending—are perhaps the best indicator of the motivational push provided by the Japanese family for educational achievement (Shields 1992).

Boys are encouraged more than girls. Women attend college at the same rate as men, but the majority enrolls in two-year occupational training colleges, originally modeled on American junior colleges. More than 80 percent of these two-year college students in Japan are women. In spite of reforms intended to increase women's participation in four-year colleges, only 40 percent of four-year college students are women (compared to nearly 60 percent in most of the industrialized world). Many academically talented female students continue to gravitate to traditionally female fields (Nagasawa 2005).

Even with strong family support for achievement, the effort of Japanese students would not be as high if academic performance mattered less in determining life opportunities. In East Asia, competitive examinations have a long history as a precondition to training for state service. It is therefore not surprising that testing has played an exceptionally important role in Japan (and in other East Asian societies). For many decades, upper secondary schools have been ranked by their success in placing graduating students into prestigious universities. These rankings have caused parents to want their children to attend the "better" secondary schools. Students take tests for admission to these preferred high schools, thereby beginning a long period of pressure to do well on admissions tests. For university admissions, students take two types of tests: first, the national achievement test, administered to all students applying for university admissions; and, second, each university's individual admissions test. Test performance is closely connected to college and university admissions. The prestige of the university attended and the field of study are, in turn, tightly connected to the jobs students can obtain after graduation. Particular universities are closely associated with particular firms, and even where they are not, they are closely associated with higher and lower levels in Japanese organizational life.

As Thomas Rohlen wrote, Japan has built a well-oiled "educational machine" for harnessing effort:

> A simple but powerful formula . . . has dominated Japanese secondary education ever since the establishment of middle schools: the difficulty of a school's entrance exams is the crucial measure of its students' talent. Employers choose to allow this criterion of school reputation, rather than an individual's grades or subjects studied, to guide their selection of personnel for managerial jobs. Entrance exams thus become the route to success. (Rohlen 1983:58–9)

It is no wonder that Japanese students refer to the period of intense preparation for the testing that will so strongly influence their life fate as "exam hell."[7]

Japan has been the major influence on schooling organization throughout the rest of East Asia. Hong Kong has, however, adopted what may be the strictest system of elimination through examination. In Hong Kong, only the top 2 percent finish a university education, and exam-based competition starts unusually early. Entrance into good primary schools is exam based. Another exam is necessary for entry to secondary school. Still another determines qualification for entry into "sixth form" (or university preparation). For every thousand primary students in the early 1990s, only 130 were allowed entry into sixth form and only 22 went on to graduate from university. By the time a child has finished his or her education at the highest level, they would have had to pass as many as seven highly demanding examinations (Morris, McClelland, and Ping Man 1997).

SCHOOL STRUCTURES, OPPORTUNITIES, AND CONSCIOUSNESS

Now that we have taken a tour of six schooling systems, we are in a position to ask whether and how differences in school structures matter for students. The two big questions we will want to answer are whether differences in structure affect the "life chances" of students from different social backgrounds and whether they affect the consciousness of students.

School Structures and Life Chances

Sociologists know that certain kinds of school structures can be highly detrimental to the life chances of working-class and low-income students. Systems that separate children early in life have consistently been found to lower the probabilities that working- and lower-class students will continue schooling through secondary school or enter college (Halsey, Heath, and Ridge 1980; Husén 1965; OECD 2000). Very rigorous secondary school-leaving examinations (or college entrance examinations) also reduce the intake of students from lower socioeconomic backgrounds into higher education. For this reason, it is not surprising that when the Scottish shifted their rigorous "A-level" examinations to an exam that tested students only on course materials all had encountered, pass rates soared, particularly among students from lower socioeconomic backgrounds (Gamoran 1996). The connection between very challenging tests and elite intake is strong, whether one looks at the French *concours* exam (Bourdieu 1988), the English A-levels (Halsey, Heath, and Ridge 1980), or the earliest versions of the SAT exam in the United States (Lehman 1999).

However, structures of schooling are clearly not the only influence on the prospects of attainment for either upper- or lower-class groups. Dynamic economies produce more opportunities and more equal conditions in society also create more equal conditions in educational attainment (Jonsson 1993). Societies may compensate for very unequal schooling structures by improving opportunities for less advantaged groups in other ways. The early branching system in Germany is not as detrimental to the life chances of working-class students as it would be in the absence of the excellent skills produced by their dual system of vocational training. Nor is a simple expansion of educational opportunity always a recipe for greater equality. If more students attend college than can be absorbed by the occupational structure, the main result will be lower incomes for college graduates and sometimes also alienation among graduates who cannot find jobs (Barbagli 1982; Dore 1975; Freeman 1976).

These complexities require us to develop a sophisticated view of the relationship between schooling structures and students' life chances. Life chances are most directly influenced by developments in the world of work. Although some school structures are undoubtedly connected to the perpetuation of social inequalities, societies can also develop compensating devices to make up in the world of work what is denied in the world of schooling. Moreover, the rapid expansion of places in higher education will not necessarily solve problems of inequality; in most cases, it will displace these problems to higher levels in the system.

Structural differences between systems may be at least as important for the distinctive mobility paths they create as for their system-level effects on students' life chances. The German system, as we have seen, creates strong links between apprenticeships and skilled blue-collar jobs; the French and Japanese system creates strong links between elite higher education institutions and corporate or government management. Similarly, in the United States strong network ties exist between leading media firms, law firms, financial institutions, diplomatic and intelligence posts, and graduates of a handful of private colleges and universities (Useem and Karabel 1986; Karabel 2005). Employers and new recruits are linked by family connections, private school attendance, and even by specific forms of social recognition at school (such as shared membership in an eating club or secret society). Studies of how school structures affect life chances should, therefore, continue to focus not just on such matters as the difference that early branching and college placement tests make for the reproduction of social inequalities but also on the personalities and networks that link specific school sites and specific job sites. (I will have more to say about the links between schooling, social mobility, and inequality in Chapters 6 and 7.)

School Structures and Consciousness

In some ways, students throughout the industrial world are now participants in a global youth culture. Blue jeans, rock music, cell phones, shopping malls, and the adventures of increasing independence are great attractions nearly everywhere. However, underneath these familiar activities lie some important national differences in students' outlooks on the world, and these differences are very much related to the design of schooling in different countries.

You may already have pictures in your mind of national student types based on stereotypes from books or movies: the cultivated Briton; the hard-driving Japanese; the optimistic American. Some writers argue that national types are best explained as products of a unique national character or of particular historical experiences. However, differences in institutional structure are probably the immediate source of many national differences in adolescents' personality and outlook. Indeed, differences in schooling structures may be connected to such diverse features of consciousness as the perception of status boundaries, the willingness to concentrate intensively, the extent of "opportunity consciousness" versus class consciousness, and even to levels of confidence about the future. (We have to use the cautious word "may" because the cross-national evidence is not yet completely convincing about some of these outcomes.)

How might school structures be related to something as seemingly unrelated as where people draw status lines? The answer is that lines of institutional demarcation are also lines of social distinction. In Germany and Sweden, where all universities are considered similarly prestigious, the distinction between the university and nonuniversity educated is what matters. In the United States, where colleges and universities are extremely numerous and diverse, status is connected instead to the selectivity of the college (and, to a lesser extent, field of study). Similarly, in societies like France, Japan, and England, which have very strongly delineated elite tracks, a major status distinction divides graduates of the elite universities from everyone else.

The kinds of testing and job linkage structures that develop in schooling systems also have an impact on student attitudes. The extraordinary discipline of Japanese secondary school students makes sense because exams figure decisively in admission to higher education and higher education figures decisively in one's later career. The high investment of Japanese parents in the education of their children is, of course, another factor that encourages this intensity. But this, too, is connected to the strong ties between schooling success and adult status. Surely, the cultivation and air of superiority that once marked British sixth formers (those in the final two years of preparation for university) were connected to the fact that fewer than 20 percent passed the advanced-level qualifying exams that allowed for university admission. By contrast, the lesser importance of college admissions tests in the United States and the loose connection of schooling to jobs work together to blunt academic competitiveness in secondary school. In such a system, interests in popular culture and peer group friendships tend to fill the space unoccupied by academic pursuits (Clark 1983).

Not surprisingly, more inclusive systems tend to give rise to higher levels of "opportunity consciousness" than class-consciousness (Brint and Karabel 1989:220–5). Few American students experience obvious blocks to their educational mobility, such as separate vocational tracks or life-defining tests. The sense that the future remains open is pervasive in such a system. The more restricted systems give rise to a sharper sense of what is possible for people of a certain social class. In much of Europe, at least until recently, the vertical vision of the upwardly mobile was not as common as in the United States, and a sense of identification with one's own social class somewhat more common. (It seems likely that the vast expansion of higher education in Europe will lead to more vertical vision and a loosening of class identifications.)

A sense of the possibility of upward mobility through schooling does not necessarily translate into a firm confidence about the future, however. People are never more anxious than at the stage of life in which their fate is undecided. For the majority of students, the American system pushes fateful decisions far out into late adolescence and early adulthood. In systems where differentiation occurs earlier, students' expectations are shaped and stabilized earlier (Buchman and Dalton 2002).

EXPLAINING THE VARIETY OF SCHOOLING STRUCTURES

Explanations for variation in institutional structure move in one of two directions: (1) the systems approach or (2) the comparative historical approach. Some sociologists think of institutions as composed of parts that vary together as a system. For these sociologists, changes in one part of the system encourage other adjustments until a new equilibrium is reached. Other sociologists reject the systems metaphor and focus instead on the social context, institutional inheritances, and policy decisions that give rise to distinctive institutional designs. The comparative historical approach provides a much better guide in the case of school sructures, but the system approach merits some discussion. Its plausibility is suggested by the common use of the term "system" to describe the organization of schooling.

The Systems Approach

It is possible to think of schooling as a system of interrelated parts, albeit much more loosely connected than, say, an automobile engine's parts. These schooling parts would include, for example, the organization of tiers and tracks, the amount of screening that occurs due to standardized testing, and the strength of linkages between schools and jobs.

The parts of schooling systems seem to some researchers to bear a logical connection to one another. For instance, compared to more open systems, more restrictive systems might seem logically to be built on clearer distinctions between tiers and more testing to determine who will be selected into higher tiers (Clark 1983; Eckstein and Noah 1993). Indeed, as I have shown, policymakers can influence the flow of students through levels of schooling by introducing occupational options and qualifications, by changing the requirements for key examinations, and by adjusting the length of time necessary to obtain degrees.

However, the coordination of structural elements is far from perfect. High academic standards in secondary school would seem logically to go with low rates of university enrollment. But the Japanese have both high standards and relatively high enrollments in university-level education. Conversely, the Swedish system produces comparatively few uni-

TABLE 2.1
Differences in schooling structures in six industrialized countries

PRIMARY AND LOWER SECONDARY SCHOOLING

	Tracking in separate institutions	Equity in per capita spending
Japan	No	Yes
France	No	Yes
Sweden	No	Yes
United States	No	No
United Kingdom	No	No
Germany	Yes (Age 10)	No

UPPER SECONDARY SCHOOLING

	Percentage completing by normative age, 2002	Percentage of students in vocational programs, 2003	Secondary school-leaving examination
Japan	90–95	20–25	
Sweden	90–95	50–55	
France	85–90	55–60	
Germany	80–85	60–65	
United States	75–80	—[a]	
United Kingdom	70–75	65–70	

POST-SECONDARY EDUCATION

	Net entry into university-level studies (as percent of cohort), 2003[b]	Percentage of young adults (age 30–34) with tertiary qualification, 2000[c]	University equality esteem	Strength of linkage between elite universities and elite positions
Sweden	75–80	30–35	Yes	Weak
United States	45–50 (est.)[d]	35–40	No	Strong
United Kingdom	45–50	25–30	No	Strong
Japan	40–45	40–45 (est.)[e]	No	Very Strong
France	35–40	25–30	No	Very Strong
Germany	35–40	25–30	Yes	Weak

Sources for Quantitative Data: Eurydice (2002:111); National Center for Education Statistics (NCES 2003:216); Organization for Economic Cooperation and Development (OECD 2002:42); OECD (2004:279, 280); OECD (2005:247, 249); United States Census Bureau (2001).

[a]All students in the United States are officially in "general" or "academic" tracks. However, some students take a significant number of vocational courses during their secondary school years.

[b]This figure refers to "tertiary, type A" curricula in the OECD classification of educational levels and does not include short-cycle "tertiary, type B" curricula. In the United States, "tertiary, type A" is equivalent to four-year college curricula, while "tertiary, type B" is equivalent to two-year community college curricula. When enrollments in type A and type B curricula are combined, the country percentages are as follows: Sweden (87 percent); the United Kingdom (78 percent); France (73 percent); Japan (73 percent); the United States (63 percent); and Germany (52 percent). See OECD (2005:249).

[c]In this column, tertiary qualification includes "tertiary, type A," "tertiary, type B," and higher-level research degrees. Figures are not available for "tertiary, type A" only.

[d]In OECD statistical digests, U.S. figures are reported combining two-year and four-year participation. The estimate for four-year college graduates is based on an assumption of 25 percent of entering two-year college students transferring to four-year institutions. See Dougherty and Kienzl (2006). Of the total post-secondary enrollment in the United States in 2000, two-year college students constituted nearly 40 percent. See NCES (2003:216).

[e]The figures in this column are drawn from the Eurydice database. Japan is not part of this database. The figure is estimated from OECD data for adults age 25 to 34 in 2000. See OECD (2002:42).

versity graduates, even though it de-emphasizes testing and provides financial aid to all students who need it. As these examples indicate, we will be misled if we imagine that a strong "systems logic" forces the key parts of schooling systems to vary together. (See Table 2.1.)

If systems logic will not take us very far, what, then, can help to explain these differences in institutional design? In my view, we should focus instead on how political decisions about schooling have been made in the two generations since the end of World War II and, no less important, the social and organizational context in which these decisions have been made. To develop explanations for structural differences in schooling, we need good comparative political sociology combined with good comparative public policy analysis.

The Comparative-Historical Approach

There can be no simple answers to the question of how popular aspirations have interacted with state interests and inherited structures to create distinctive national systems of schooling. Good answers are possible, however, if we keep in mind the following essential elements: (1) the two starting points from which contemporary systems developed; (2) the strong social demand for more education that all countries have experienced; and (3) the institutional legacies, social divisions, adaptations of external models, and government investment and policy decisions that have shaped this demand into one of a handful of structural designs.

The politics of expansion. I have argued that changes in schooling systems since World War II have been, above all, the result of government efforts to accommodate a rising social demand for formal education and to channel this demand in the direction of advancing national economic development goals. The major decisions have been whether to adopt the American model of general and academic secondary education for most students and relatively open access to higher education, or to retain traditional European tracking structures and, especially, more restricted access to university-level education. Most governments at first compromised between these two models by increasing access and equalizing curricula at lower levels while pushing differentiated curricula back later in the secondary school years (Heidenheimer, Heclo, and Adams 1983). Indeed, among the industrial societies, only the English-speaking democracies (the United States, Canada, Australia, and New Zealand) and some East Asian countries (such as Japan and Korea) enrolled a majority of upper secondary school students in academic curricula. Elsewhere, the majority of upper secondary students enrolled in vocational programs (Eurydice 2002:86). More recently, European governments have introduced opportunities for vocational students to obtain post-secondary credentials, thereby greatly expanding their higher education systems.

Expansive tendencies in the U.S. system were already well established before World War II. Substantially more students graduated from upper secondary school and attended college in the United States than anywhere else in the world. In particular, the large number of colleges and universities already established in the United States before the war encouraged competition for students and consequently high levels of college going. American policy-makers reinforced these expansive pressures by adopting social reform goals in the 1960s aimed at improving the opportunities of minorities and women. These commitments led to the creation of relatively generous financial aid programs and affirmative action policies aimed at increasing rather than limiting college enrollments. Few strong ties existed between educational credentials and particular jobs. This competitive situation stimulated a constant interest in higher-level qualifications and high levels of job switching.

The conditions prevailing in Germany following World War II provide a sharp contrast to those in the United States. In Germany, decentralization and a divided reform movement permitted conservatives to contain the rising social demand for schooling within a highly tracked structure. The Germans lacked a crusader who could push reform to the top of the agenda against the fears of conservatives about the quality of academic schooling and the fears of the well-organized left that a reformed system would lead to the more complete subordination of workers. In the more conservative German regions, the idea of common secondary schooling for all students never gained a hearing (Heidenheimer 1973). Most teenagers enrolled in the dual system of vocational training. The success of the dual system reduced pressures for expansion at higher levels of the system. The German example suggests that high wages and skills in industry are correlated with reduced demand for higher education, whereas low wages and skills in industry are correlated with high demand for higher education credentials (Maurice, Sellier, and Silvestre 1986).

Germany remains distinctive, but it is becoming less distinctive. Even the Germans have increased access to academic study in secondary school and to higher education, albeit to a lesser degree than other European polities. The lowest of the three tracks of secondary schooling, the *Hauptschule*, has become increasingly unpopular and difficult to support. This track may fade out in the end. Moreover, in recent years, a debate has arisen in Germany about the costs and flexibility of the dual system, and some corporate and political leaders are now pushing for a complete or partial dismantling of the system (see, e.g., Blossfeld 1992). These efforts could push German schooling in the direction of later differentiation and more credential-based job competition.

In the mid-1960s, with the election of a Labour government, the British belatedly abandoned their system of highly tracked lower secondary schooling. However, they maintained a higher education system very nearly as restrictive as the one in Germany. Social factors largely explain this halfway move in the case of England. Class divisions were stronger in England than virtually anywhere elsewhere in Europe, and school institutions strongly reinforced these divisions. The secondary school-leaving exams were difficult to pass for students who did not come from highly cultivated backgrounds, and no provisions were made for more general or vocational training in secondary schools. Not surprisingly, working-class students abandoned the system as early as they could, and higher education remained an elite preserve.

Since the 1970s, the English have engaged in a self-conscious policy of modernization, which has greatly reduced this legacy of class division without yet entirely eliminating it. The transformation of English secondary and higher education is the most recent illustration of the importance of centralized control. In the 1960s, local education authorities (LEAs) were given leeway to decide about replacing their tripartite systems of secondary schooling with comprehensives and to experiment in other ways with schooling. Although most LEAs adopted the comprehensive structure as a reform, some maintained the old tripartite system. The Thatcher government consulted with the LEAs, but simultaneously moved to centralize control over educational policymaking. The result has been a complete overhaul of English secondary schooling and higher education since the 1970s: the introduction of the FE college sector and youth credits and apprenticeships for school leavers, the creation of a unified higher education system, changed examination requirements, and a weakening of the influence of Oxford and Cambridge over academic culture in England.

Faced with less serious social cleavages, most European governments adapted more quickly than the English to increased social demand for schooling while continuing at first to accommodate the quality concerns of academic elites. Most did so by democratizing lower levels of schooling while introducing highly differentiated occupational streaming in the upper secondary schools and, later, in post-secondary education.

This does not mean that reform necessarily came easily. One of the leaders of the Swedish reform movement, Torsten Husén (1965), has described the ebb and flow of a decade of debate over whether to abandon the German-style early-tracking system in Sweden. Similarly, parliamentary discord in the Fourth Republic ruined the efforts of reformers to democratize secondary schooling in France. Reform did not come until a new leader, Charles de Gaulle, had a substantial enough majority to subdue his legislature (Monchalban 1994). Nevertheless, once the battles were won in centralized polities, they tended not to be fought again. Moreover, reform led to greater standardization and equalization of instruction in the lower grades, something that does not exist to this day in the highly education-conscious United States.

In recent years, higher education enrollments have been allowed to trend upward in Europe in response to the perception of an increasing labor market demand for advanced credentials. This has often required adjusting requirements for secondary school-leaving examinations to allow students from technical and vocational programs to take the exams, and the creation of new post-secondary curricula in vocational fields. At the same time, the value of the leading university degrees has been preserved, both through limiting admission to high-demand fields (such as medicine) through *numerus clausus* mechanisms and by maintaining high levels of selectivity in elite institutions. In these ways, modern educational systems have managed to satisfy both social demand for increased educational opportunity and upper-class interests in the production and reproduction of an elite stratum.

External models, inherited traditions, and social divisions. Specific national responses have been influenced by widely supported institutional legacies, such as the German dual system of vocational training, the French *grandes écoles*, and the large and diverse population of colleges and universities in the United States. The U.S. system of mass secondary and, later, mass higher education exercised a pervasive influence throughout the developed world. More specific innovations have frequently been adopted by neighboring countries, as indicated, for example, in the borrowing of the British three-year degree by the French (and later the EU); in the borrowing of the Japanese examination system by the Koreans and other East Asian governments; and in the borrowing of the German "dual system" by Austria and Switzerland.

The postwar history of schooling in France and Japan illustrates the importance of external models and inherited structures. The French borrowed from the British the three-year university degree and mechanisms to increase pass rates on secondary school-leaving exams. They have transformed higher education, without revolutionizing it, by maintaining the *grandes écoles* at the pinnacle of the system. In Japan, the external models were at first voluntarily adopted following initial contact with the West and later enforced by the American occupation in the years after World War II. The American occupation encouraged more opportunities at the secondary school level through a common curriculum. These external models were adapted to preexisting institutional preferences: in particular, the Japanese continued to favor a few imperial universities to train top elites for industry and government, and they relied from the beginning on examination-based social selection for access to prestigious secondary schools, rather than the American model of neighborhood-based "comprehensive" schools.

Choices about the shape of schooling systems have also been influenced at times by social factors, such as the strength of class divisions in England. Internal social cleavages have been an important influence in both France and Japan as well. In France, North African immigrants remain largely outside the higher education structure, and only the beginnings of affirmative action policies have been considered as mechanisms for increasing participation of immigrant groups in higher and elite education institutions. The sharp gender divisions in Japanese society have largely kept women out of the competition for the most desirable spaces in higher education and the occupational elite. They have also encouraged the unique development of two-year colleges oriented particularly to the training of women. In England, exceptionally strong class divisions limited the prospects of educational reform longer than in most of Europe.

Finally, school designs have been influenced by several distinct political forces: for example, in all countries, by the degree of centralized control over public education; in most Western European countries by welfare state traditions of strong state planning to connect schooling and work; in low-income countries like those in Eastern Europe, by low levels of investment in education.

Within these structures of opportunity and constraint, policymakers have been able to influence the flow of students through the system by building new types of schools, introducing new occupational curricula and qualification levels, changing examination requirements, and altering the length of degree programs.

Educational ministries in all industrial countries are interested in coordinating school studies with the occupational needs of their economies. In general, they tend to consider the workforce of the future as requiring higher levels of schooling. These similarities reflect a universal recognition of the state's interest in an educated citizenry and in the connection of schooling to labor market circumstances. They also reflect the revolution in expectations that has been one of the fruits of industrialism and affluence. Under the pressure of these common forces of change, the schooling systems of industrial societies may tend to converge still more in the future. International organizations, such as the Organization for Economic Cooperation and Development and the European Union, have facilitated this convergence by disseminating policy and statistical information among member states and by promoting a common set of educational policies. We can see the coordination of transnational policy elites in recent educational policies that have encouraged both decentralization of decision-making and greater accountability through international testing programs. Coordination is also notable at the post-secondary level. The Bologna Agreement, negotiated in 2000 as part of the integration of the European Union, will lead to higher levels of post-secondary degree completion throughout Europe by standardizing the three-year degree, along the lines pioneered by the English and the French, as the dominant higher-education degree program throughout the EU.

CONCLUSION

Industrialized societies produce higher levels of educational attainment than developing societies. Schooling is more organized and teachers are better prepared. The commonalities among schools in the industrialized world can mask some important continuing differences. Schooling structures in industrialized societies are designed differently and produce different mobility paths and different outlooks among students.

The American educational structure, like a giant missile staging system, has historically offered a strong boost upward for most students. The great majority of students studies general or academic subjects until they reach college. The upward propulsion carries large numbers into higher education, where for the first time consequential forms of differentiation begin. The German system, by contrast, resembles a branching system of train tracks that split a short time after the train leaves its originating station. Trains on the separate tracks carry approximately equal numbers of children destined for different kinds of work. Between these two extremes are systems that differentiate students later than the Germans but earlier than the Americans. Systems like those in France and Sweden start off looking like the American common schooling system, but place most students into vocational courses of study by age 16. These systems at first limited entry into higher education to the academically oriented minority, but some systems, like the French, now encourage students from upper secondary vocational tracks to move into higher level university training programs.

The size of the academic and vocational layers in differentiated systems can vary substantially. Some, such as the Japanese and American systems, push children along together through age 16, and then separate them into a relatively narrow vocational track, a bulging middle track for students engaged in general academic curricula, and a thin layer of elite training. Most systems, however, direct a majority of students into programs leading to vocational qualifications. Until recently, the vast majority of vocational students moved directly into the labor market upon completion of upper secondary school programs (or before). Since the mid-1980s, most governments in the industrialized world have encouraged movement from vocational programs into post-secondary and university-level higher education.

Contemporary differences in schooling structure do not result from any deep-seated patterns of national character or culture. Rather, they help to produce aspects of national character. Status identifications, for example, are associated with the most prominent lines of school differentiation. Undifferentiated higher education systems create status lines based on occupational expertise, rather than aristocratic elitism. By contrast, those systems in which elite tracks are sharply differentiated produce status systems strongly marked by elitism. Other characteristic expressions of "national culture" from the extent of class and opportunity consciousness to the extent of intensity or carefree confidence are, I have argued, also connected to structures of schooling.

These structures are largely the result of political decisions made by elites beginning from two different starting points and in response to the common pressure of increased social demand for schooling. The two different starting points are the premises of democratic uplift and elite preparation. These premises reflect different class and ideological circumstances at the beginning of the age of mass schooling. In the United States, the dominance of the small-property-owning class supported premises of democratic uplift. In Europe, the dominance of propertied and cultivated elites in a more class-divided society supported the premises of elite preparation. These two starting points led to radically different levels of enrollment at higher levels of schooling in the nineteenth and early twentieth centuries. Beginning from these two distinct starting points, all governments have been influenced by a gradually rising social demand for higher levels of educational opportunity. In response to this demand, governments have been inclined to supply more education in the hope of fostering economic and technological development.

Modern educational systems have not followed a single standard design model. Instead, they have shown the influence of political forces (such as degree of centralization), social forces (such as the strength of class and gender divisions), and institutional legacies (such as the prestige of elite universities). Policymakers have worked to develop systems within a context shaped by these forces.

This chapter has emphasized the differences that continue to distinguish national schooling systems in the industrialized world. Nevertheless, it is important to recognize that schooling systems are gradually becoming more alike over time. Virtually all industrialized countries, for example, require attendance of children for at least 10 years between the ages of 6 and 16. Most have, in addition, made efforts to democratize secondary schooling and higher education so as to provide greater opportunities for students from less advantaged social backgrounds. The concern for access has helped to make higher education a fast-growing sector throughout the industrial world.

Chapter 3 will show that the governments of developing countries have many of the same interests and objectives, but their schooling systems face a different set of circumstances, most notably, greater physical insecurity and economic need among students, and many fewer resources with which to provide schooling and for all.

3 | SCHOOLING IN THE DEVELOPING WORLD

colonial legacy
continuing problems
theory of under development.
Dependency theory.

The developing world includes most of the Southern Hemisphere: Latin America and the Caribbean; the war-torn lands of Southeast Asia (and, at least for the time being, also some fast-developing countries in East Asia, such as Thailand and Malaysia); islands like Papua New Guinea in the southern Pacific Ocean; the southern Asia peninsula that includes India, Pakistan, and Bangladesh; the Arab countries of the Middle East; and virtually all of Africa.

Some people living in industrialized societies envy the rich folk knowledge of rural people in these less developed parts of the world. They feel that this folk knowledge expresses the more cohesive and communally oriented way of life of developing societies and that it is connected to the real needs of people who interact in a simpler and more satisfying way with their environments. These sentiments echo those of the French philosopher Jean-Jacques Rousseau ([1754] 1964). Writing in the mid-1700s, Rousseau criticized the unnaturalness of urban, commercial civilization and exalted the greater sense of integration of societies untouched by the corrupting influence of urban civilization.

However popular these views may be on a few college campuses in the industrial world (and among supporters of Green parties in Europe), the leaders of less developed countries have consistently rejected them—and for compelling reasons. Most inhabitants of imagined idyllic villages actually live in destitute conditions, lacking the amenities of the modern world from indoor plumbing to DVDs. The historian Daniel Kevles sums up this reality well:

> Stripped of the gauzy romanticism of myth, the pre-industrial village was for most people a place of exhausting and unremitting subsistence labor, harnessing men, women, and children to the mind-numbing tasks of farm and household. It subjected most of its inhabitants to local prejudices, enforced ignorance, and arbitrary power, while leaving them vulnerable to devastating diseases and early death. (Kevles 1995:4)

Under the circumstances, it is little wonder that *modernization* has been the great rallying cry of people in less developed countries. Modernization refers to the cluster of social processes—economic development, improved communications and transportation, the creation of progress-oriented mentalities—that are both the cause and the effect of movement from poverty-stricken traditional societies to prosperous industrial societies. The leaders of the world's less developed countries have consistently seen schooling for the masses as a symbol of progress and modernity and a means of economic development. In the words of Sékou Touré, the leader of the independence movement in Guinea:

> Man's social behavior and economic activities are directly conditioned by the quality of his education. It is in order to free the youth of this country from all the social evils inherited from the past that [we] are anxious to develop educational facilities and allocate an important share of [the] budget to educational purposes. (Touré 1965:125)

The hopes of leaders like Touré have not been completely realized in the developing world. This chapter considers schooling in the developing world in the context of the aspirations of modernizing leaders and the obdurate problems they face. The chapter concentrates on three major topics: (1) how the schooling systems in the developing world have been influenced by colonialism, postcolonial politics, and indebtedness; (2) the successes and failures of schooling in the contemporary developing world; and (3) the complicated relationship between schooling and economic development. Some other important topics, such as patterns of teaching and learning in the developing world, will be discussed in later chapters of the book.

BACKGROUND OF SCHOOLING IN DEVELOPING SOCIETIES

To understand schooling in the contemporary developing world, it is necessary to understand something of the impact of colonialism, the hopes inspired by nationalist movements, and the specific problems that hamper development: poverty, traditionalism, and physical insecurity. In recent years, these problems have become less pronounced in some countries but have worsened in some others. In the latter countries, very high levels of indebtedness have limited the ability of governments to improve public schooling.

The Colonial Legacy

Nearly all developing countries were once colonies—that is, they were under the direct administrative rule of one or another of the European powers. The Americas broke free from European rule in the late eighteenth and early nineteenth centuries, but most countries in Africa, the Near East, and Asia won their independence only in the past 60 years. Between 1945 and 1968, 66 countries gained political independence from colonial rule. Thus, most of the developing world consists of rather new states.

Colonial rulers were mainly interested in raw materials, cheap labor, and acquiescent subjects. Schooling for the masses was sometimes considered helpful for these purposes, but it was a comparatively low priority. Racism played a major role in shaping the attitudes of the colonizers to the colonized. In the absence of strong official support, Christian missionaries sometimes introduced formal education as a way of evangelizing the indigenous populations. Some improvements occurred after World War II, perhaps as a reaction to the genocidal racism of the Nazis, but they remained in line with colonial, rather than native, interests. Little technical or agricultural schooling was provided, and schooling was infused with the content and ethos of the colonial powers. It also continued to be racially segregated and unbalanced. At the higher levels, schools enrolled the children of virtually all of the rulers but less than 1 percent of the ruled. For example, of the 25,000 secondary students in Kenya in the years before independence, only 8,000 were Africans (Eshiwani 1985).

It is not surprising that the outlooks of rural people in this period were inwardly turned and parochial. When the political scientist Daniel Lerner (1958) asked poor farmers in Turkey to comment on the policies of the government, the farmers looked at him with blank, amused, or quizzical expressions. It was impossible for them to put themselves in the role of distant authorities, or to understand why they might want to.

But colonialism did provide fertile ground for the nationalist movements that fought for independence. Typically, nationalist sentiment emerged first among the country's native-born elites, who had been exposed to high-quality elementary and secondary schooling and usually to higher education abroad. These were the people who colonial administrators depended on to help manage the native population and to support colonial government and business enterprise. Nearly all of the leaders of the nationalist struggle in the Third World—Gandhi, Nehru, Sukarno, Nkrumah, Mohammed V, U Nu, Jinna, Ben Bella, Keita, Azikiwe, Nasser, Kenyatta, Nyerere, Bourguiba, Lee, Sékou Touré—came from the gentry and professional classes and studied at the most important universities in England and France, such as the London School of Economics and the Sorbonne (von der Mehden 1969:72–90). Anti-colonial ideas and sentiments, cultivated in discussions at universities, were among the unintended exports of the Western metropoles to their colonies in the rest of the world.

Continuing Problems

Measured in historic terms, life in most of the Third World today is improving at an encouraging pace. People now live longer on average than before, are more likely to have enough food to avoid hunger, and are more often literate (UNHDP 2004). Nevertheless, modernizing leaders in these countries continue to be faced with resistant problems related to poverty, traditionalism, and physical insecurity. In sub-Saharan Africa and some other countries, such as Bangladesh and Haiti, these problems remain acute. "An unprecedented number of countries saw development slide backwards in the 1990s" (ibid.:132). In 46 countries, people are actually poorer today than in 1990, and human development indicators (such as literacy, school attendance, and life expectancy) declined in 20 countries between 1990 and 2000 (ibid.).

Poverty. Some 80 percent of the world's population is located in the developing world, but owns less than one-fifth of its total wealth (Kurian 2001). Virtually every economic and social indicator—trade, living standards, health, schooling, and political stability—shows dramatic gaps along the North-South global divide.

Basic literacy, for example, is nearly universal in the developed world, but still well under 50 percent in parts of sub-Saharan Africa (and occasionally below 20 percent for rural women). In industrial societies, completion of primary education is essentially universal; in the poorest countries primary completion rates are typically below 40 percent (UNHDP 2004). Perhaps most noteworthy of all: public expenditures on schooling per inhabitant are on average 20 times lower in the developing world than in the industrialized world. In some developing countries, school textbooks must be shared by as many as 20 students (UNESCO 1994:36), and, at an extreme, the student to teacher ratio can be as high as 75:1. (The ratio, which includes all instructional staff, is less than 20:1 in the United States.)

In every respect, the material conditions of schooling in developing countries are worse than the material conditions of schooling in the industrial world. In low-income developing countries, and particularly in rural areas, primary school students may attend an open-air school or study in a shabbily constructed building that lacks such basic educational resources as maps, globes, science equipment, and library books. The teachers in these schools have less formal education on average than high school graduates in the United States. Students may share their classrooms with more than 50 other children, a good many of whom are chronically undernourished, parasite ridden, and hungry. A team of Indian social scientists described one rural school in a poor province as follows:

> The children huddle in two rooms on sacking brought from home. The second room is very dark. There is no teaching equipment whatsoever. . . . Children write on their slate, or play. The playground is full of mud and slime. . . . There is no toilet. . . . The only teaching aid available in all schools is a stick to beat the children. (PROBE 1999:40–43)

Poverty of this magnitude is invariably a scourge of schooling. The differences are well illustrated by a study by Uday Desai (1991) of the factors statistically associated with school dropout in an Indian village. Living in a slum and not having educational supplies in the home were two factors, both obvious enough. But two other factors also stood out: not having bathroom facilities in the house and living far from a source of drinking water. In rich countries, we tend to forget how much simple physical energy may be necessary to cope with the basic demands of life. Parents of poorly nourished children are often unwilling to allow their children to attend school. This simple fact is an important explanation of low enrollment rates in the poorest regions of the world.

Even the better-off countries of the developing world have large pockets of extreme poverty, but the degree of poverty in the Third World varies considerably from region to region and country to country. The developing countries of Asia, Latin America and the Caribbean, and the Arab states are, in general, not as impoverished as sub-Saharan Africa or the rural areas of the South Asia peninsula that includes India, Pakistan, and Bangladesh. Indeed, it is frequently better to think of the wealth of countries of the world in terms of a continuum rather than a sharp break between rich and poor. Book ownership is one such graded measure on this continuum. In the industrialized countries, every inhabitant owns on average five books. In the better-off developing countries, such as Chile and Ukraine, every 5 to 10 inhabitants will own one book. In the very poorest countries, such as Chad and Niger, people outnumber books by 50 or more to 1 (UNESCO 1994:32).

Traditionalism. Poverty is also associated with another impediment to development: traditional outlooks, which revere "the way things have always been." The sociologist Edward Shils noted that the timeless ways of the past weighed heavily on the ambitious plans of leaders of the new states:

> Fealty to rulers, respect for the aged, bravery in war, obligations to one's kin, responsiveness to the transcendent powers which make and destroy men's lives—these are [the] virtues [of

traditional societies]. . . . The freedom of the individual, economic progress, a concern for national unity and dignity, and an interest in the larger world have little place in the outlook. (Shils [1962] 1975:496)

Certain groups in Third World countries suffer particularly from these traditional outlooks. Women (particularly rural women) are acutely disadvantaged in many developing countries, because their role is socially defined to be central in the private sphere of the family, but entirely secondary in the public sphere (Alrabaa 1985; Robertson 1985). In most of the Third World, rural populations are far more resistant to changing ancient ways than are urban groups. (People living in rural areas also do not see schooling as having much utility for their lives, which may be the more important factor.)

Often the schooling gaps between these more traditionally oriented groups and other members of the society are extreme: UNESCO estimates that of the 800 million adult illiterates in the world, two-thirds are women. In extreme cases, half of women may be illiterate compared to one quarter of men (UNESCO 2005). Urban-rural differences are frequently severe. Not long ago in Colombia only 20 percent of rural children finished primary school compared with 60 percent of urban children. Even the average male in rural areas of sub-Saharan African countries, such as Angola, Burkina Faso, Mali, and Niger, has fewer than five years of schooling (ibid.).

Poverty and traditionalism create the basis for a half-hidden, half-open conflict between schools and families. Children are valuable workers on family farms. This is especially true where farms are large enough to require the work of many but budgets are too tight for the employment of hired labor. Compulsory schooling may be entirely ineffective in the face of these opposing economic incentives. Researchers have attributed a good part of high elementary school dropout rates characteristic of many developing countries to precisely these factors. Not long ago, minors in Paraguay, for example, contributed on average one-quarter of the family income, and in rural Indonesia boys could earn as much as 40 percent of the family income as agricultural laborers (UNDP 1994). Even in cities, young children can be important auxiliary earners for their families, or they may be turned loose at young ages to fend for themselves. In the mid-1990s, UNICEF estimated that 100 million children worldwide, equivalent to about a third of the American population, lived at least for brief periods on the streets (UNICEF 2000).

Another factor contributing to high dropout rates is the disconnection between the experience of school life and the experience of home and community life. In her reminiscence of an early visit to rural Mexico, anthropologist Nancy Hornberger suggests several bases for alienation from schooling:

In the mountains outside of San Cristobal, Mexico, [I wondered] what the Tzotzeil-speaking children think and feel as they sat in the freezing cold morning fog, on unfamiliar school room chairs, listening to a language no one spoke in their homes, required to attend school by an unknown and distant state. (Hornberger 1987:210)

Although success in school may be supported in the expressed values of the village community, such success in fact exposes students to social and psychological tensions. Successful students in a village near Mount Kilimanjaro in Tanzania were labeled by peers (and sometimes by their families) as "disrespectful" and caught up in "European ways." The cross-pressures led many to avoid studying, both at home and in public, and also to experience repeated bouts of illness (Stambach 1998).

Physical insecurity. Sheer physical security is also far more likely to be an issue in the Third World than in industrial societies. Physical insecurity can come from war, rebellion, famine, malnutrition, or epidemic. In Cambodia, for example, school enrollments were greatly reduced for some 20 years as an indirect result of the state terrorism of the Pol Pot regime (Kingdom of Cambodia 1994). The situation is not very different in other countries suffering from the devastation of years of civil war, ethnic conflict, or war with nearby neighbors. In the 1990s, 46 countries were involved in wars, mainly civil wars, including half of the world's poorest countries. This violence has brought devastation and cultural stagnation to Afghanistan, Algeria, Angola, Haiti, Mozambique, Somalia, Sudan, and Zimbabwe, among other countries in the developing world (UNDP 2003:2). AIDS has become a mass killer in sub-Saharan Africa, reducing average life expectancy to 47 years. Life expectancy is already under 40 in countries, like South Africa, with highest rates of infection. Life expectancy is slowly being reduced to nineteenth-century levels (World AIDS Conference 2002).

Children and young adults cannot concentrate on school lessons where they fear for their lives, or see little hope for the future because of constant warfare or disease. Two U.S.-trained anthropologists, Adel Assal and Edwin Farrell (1992), described the disruptive effects of the civil war in Lebanon during the late 1980s: "[Many students] spoke of the constant sound of guns and bombs. They related experiences of schools closing during bombardments and children manifesting physical symptoms such as stomach aches" (278). Because of the constant movement of the population to avoid unsafe areas, many students were transients, and some of the best teachers left, often for other countries. The numbing effects of war showed up most often among the older children. As students got older, school became more meaningless. With the passing of play at adolescence, many of these young people seemed to be more lost than they were as children. Boredom appeared to be the state that came with the perception that their lives were being wasted (ibid.:286). If boredom can be defined as an irritated state of disinterest, this finding makes sense. Interestingly, the same kind of effects can be seen in U.S. inner-city schools surrounded by threats of instability and violence.

Low enrollments and high dropout rates are typical of countries in which the problems of physical insecurity are acute. Indeed, several countries hard hit by war—Afghanistan, Ethiopia, Mozambique, and Somalia—experienced negative rates of enrollment growth in the 1980s (Lockheed, Verspoor, and Associates 1990:24). The lowest "school life expectancy" rate is in Afghanistan, a country that has experienced more than two decades of nearly constant fighting. Children attend school for an average of two years in Afghanistan. Thinking about the impact of violence and disease in the Third World, I am reminded of the historian Marc Bloch's conclusions about the end of the European Dark Age and the beginning of sustained European development in the tenth and eleventh centuries:

> However much may be learnt from the study of the last [barbarian] invasions [in Europe], we should not allow their lessons to overshadow the still more important fact of their cessa-

tion. Till then these ravages had in truth formed the main fabric of history in the West as in the rest of the world. Thenceforward the West would almost alone be free from them. . . . This extraordinary immunity was one of the fundamental factors of European civilization in the deepest sense, in the exact sense of the word. (Bloch 1961:56)

EDUCATION, POLITICS, AND SOCIETY

The structure of schooling in the developing world has gone through two phases. During the first 30 years following World War II—the immediate postcolonial period for most of the Third World—the basic outlines of and rationale for a Western model of schooling were widely accepted. Nevertheless, quite a bit of variation in organization and accepted practices existed. Some of this variation arose from differences in preexisting traditions or commitments to different development philosophies. In addition, the kinds of regimes that held power frequently made a decisive difference. Leftist intellectuals in power built on existing traditions to push mass schooling forward as energetically as they could. In other countries, the landowners and military men who held the reins of power (either throughout the period or at least for many years) tended to be wary of the costs and the potential control problems associated with a more educated population. They were usually more restrictive than expansionist in their thinking about schooling.

By contrast, the second postcolonial generation (from the mid-1970s to the present) has been marked by the declining influence of the politics of ideological passion and by increasing adherence to a new standard model of schooling designed for efficiency and equity under conditions of constrained governmental resources. This new model has been energetically promoted by international donor agencies, particularly by the World Bank. Although this model has become popular throughout the developing world, the poorest and most war-torn governments have lacked the resources and the capacity to do much more than aspire to conformity.

The First Postcolonial Generation

Certain commonalities in Third World schooling have existed since the first days of independence, because leaders in the developing world from the start emulated features of the modern and progressive schooling systems of the West. The sociologist Alex Inkeles (Inkeles and Sirowy 1983) marveled at the pervasive diffusion of a standard set of concepts, institutions, and practices that define schooling throughout the world. Even in remote and isolated villages, he observed, schools, teachers, and curricula are organized and act in remarkably familiar ways. We perhaps take for granted this sort of standardization in a railroad system or an airline, he wrote, but "that such consistency should apply as well in a realm which would seem to permit endless diversity [is] notable" (Inkeles and Sirowy 1983:304).

The following are some of the structures and practices that conform to a standard pattern throughout the world:

- Public responsibility for schooling is a well-institutionalized principle, and this responsibility is generally administered by a central ministry of education with a formal inspectorate to oversee the conduct of education throughout the country.

- Schooling systems in every country establish an articulated ladder consisting of preschool, primary, secondary, and higher education.
- Attendance is compulsory for several years throughout the world.
- Teachers nearly everywhere are formally prepared and certified.
- The administrative hierarchy of superintendents, principals (or headmasters), and staff is commonplace.
- The length of the school day and the school year are standard within a relatively narrow range across the world.
- The subjects taught in the formal curriculum had a surprisingly high level of consistency worldwide. Primary school curriculum everywhere consisted of approximately 50 percent of the time spent on language skills and mathematics, with language skills receiving the most attention. Science, social studies, and arts were given approximately equal time during the week—about half as much time was spent on each of them as on mathematics (Benavot and Kamens 1989; Lockheed et al. 1990).
- Formal testing is used throughout the world to measure how well students have learned curricular materials.

Inkeles's study of the world's schooling systems circa 1980 found a marked convergent tendency over time in nearly half of the 30 elements of school structure and practice he investigated and a slower and more moderate convergence in four others (Inkeles and Sirowy 1983:326–7).

Why were elements of the Western model adopted so widely in the postcolonial world? Some analysts would describe this outcome as one face of Western *hegemony* (cultural domination by the Western powers). This interpretation is certainly plausible, but it is by no means self-evident. Emulation is not the same thing as domination, and it can become a means to greater autonomy. As John W. Meyer and his colleagues (Meyer, Nagel, and Snyder 1993) observed in relation to a study of educational adaptation in Botswana, "It is not obvious that the interests of [Western] agencies gain or that Botswana's interests lose in the transactions involved" (467). Like the early promoters of mass public schooling in the West, leaders of the new states envisioned societies made up of individuals who were entitled to have access to literate culture and who could be socialized for active and enlightened citizenship. They also saw schools as contributing to national economic development. From these premises, some common lines of educational action followed. At the same time, it is clear that Western agencies and experts helped to disseminate forms of organization and practices that became part of the standard model of schooling.

Varieties of schooling in the postcolonial Third World. Although a number of premises and practices were rather widely shared from the beginning, schooling in the developing world remained diverse in other respects. One reason for variation was that, after independence, governments often adopted distinctive practices of their former colonizers. These were familiar and accepted parts of the school environment for the first postcolonial generation. Thus, secondary school examinations in English-speaking Africa were modeled on the British O-level examinations, and only Anglophonic Africa had the distinctive British institution of the sixth form as a prelude to examinations (Foster 1985). In former French colonies, high rates of grade repeating were common, just as they had always been in France (ibid.). Some scholars have noted that students' levels of educational aspiration were higher in former British colonies of Africa as compared to former French colonies, and they argued that this discrepancy reflected the somewhat greater support for native schooling typical of British administrators influenced by missionary initiatives (ibid.).

Governmental policies on vocational education also varied, because some governments evaluated vocational education positively in relation to development goals, whereas others did not. The communist and socialist countries of the developing world, with their ideological commitment to manual labor, were the most strongly wedded to rapid expansion of vocational education (Carnoy and Samoff 1990). In some nonsocialist countries, such as Ghana and Zaire, vocational education was considered the quickest route to developing a modern, technically trained workforce. In other countries, however, vocational education had little appeal because it offended the status aspirations of upwardly mobile young people and their parents. Vocational education was particularly unpopular where national leaders had attended European universities and where upper-class social mores disdained manual labor. Even in countries like Ghana, which championed vocational preparation, implementation was often weak or nonexistent because of the desire for higher-status academic curricula (Foster 1965). Many countries overproduced secondary school graduates in the post-independence period because the demand for academic schooling exceeded the development of white-collar and professional jobs in the economy. Both Egypt and India, for example, produced far more secondary school and university graduates than they could employ, and both, as an unintended consequence, became exporters of high-talent manpower to other countries (Harbison and Myers 1964:183).

Countries in the developing world also differed in their levels of tolerance for nontraditional forms of control. In Kenya, for example, the government tacitly supported the *harambee* (or self-help) schools, which ran parallel with the official system and were meant to provide an alternative to government-funded schools. In most places, however, governments sought to bring all educational institutions under their control.

The Harambee Schools of Kenya

To this day, in the east African country of Kenya, a large number of secondary schools are operated under community authority rather than under government authority. These *harambee* (or self-help) schools are unlike educational institutions anywhere else in the world. Whole communities pay for them through donations and self-assessments. They are operated under the authority of local religious or other community organizations. Some are assisted by the government, but most are independent except insofar as curricula and other standards must be approved by the Ministry of Education.

The harambee schools grew out of traditions of community organization in Kenya. Residents in an area would join together to provide private, voluntary financial assistance, materials, or labor for a project. Neighbors, for example, might contribute a few shillings toward the construction of a borehole, a cattle dip, or some other facility from which all could benefit (Widner 1992:61–2). When Jomo Kenyatta took power following Kenyan independence in 1963, he institutionalized the harambee system as part of his nation-building effort.

School projects quickly became central to the harambee movement. In most communities, clan elders, church leaders, primary school committees, and local notables became the focal points in efforts to raise funds for a harambee secondary school. The school committees used local materials and voluntary (usually female) labor to get the schools started. They collected donations and sometimes enforced levies on households and local traders. They hired headmasters to administer the schools and continued to contribute through donations and self-imposed levies for the continuation of the schools.

The harambee schools have fostered community pride and have frequently been more responsive to community concerns than would be true of bureaucratic governmental organizations. At the same time, however, they have also been subject to abuse not only by intriguing politicians but also by private speculators and nonaccountable headmasters. Businessmen have occasionally operated harambee schools as educational franchises, hiring cheap instructional labor and using fees for their own enrichment. Headmasters have sometimes diminished community enthusiasm for the schools by refusing to spend sufficient time listening to questions and explaining their actions (Anderson 1975). More recently, community overreach has become a serious problem. Expensive projects proliferated in the early 1980s, and often remained half finished because of the financial burdens the projects placed on poorer residents (Widner 1992).

Although high educational standards were maintained in some of the harambee schools, they soon became a distinctly lower tier of secondary schooling in Kenya. Just a decade after independence, the harambee schools were attracting only the marginal secondary school students. Those who did well on the primary school-leaving examinations were allowed to enroll instead in the national schools or, at a step lower, in government-maintained schools (Dore 1975:69–70). As a result, harambee school graduates often have trouble finding good jobs. One response has been the development of harambee technical institutes, but they have enrolled only a few thousand students each year (Eshiwani 1985).

If there is a lesson in the harambee experience, it has to do with the difficulty of maintaining the spirit of *gemeinschaft* (community) in a modernizing society. Started in the spirit of traditional community, harambee schools quickly became a means of supplying the social demand for more schooling in a way that did not directly cost the government. They just as quickly fell to the bottom of the Kenyan secondary schooling system, and they also fell prey to a host of modern problems—from the intrigues of party politics to the speculations of unscrupulous business people to the unresponsiveness of hired bureaucratic officials. That they have nonetheless persisted is testimony to the adaptive powers of peasant communities to more modern conditions and to the ability of modernizing politicians to find new purposes for old traditions.

Populist and authoritarian leaders. The greatest differences in the educational policies of the new states stemmed from the social and ideological character of the regimes that held power. Mass-mobilizing populist leaders and status quo-oriented authoritarian leaders are no longer familiar political types to people in the industrialized world, where the institutions of market-oriented democracy hold sway, but they loomed large in the early postcolonial developing world.

Mass-mobilizing leaders are those who make direct and regular appeals to the aspirations of the poor for a better life and attempt to stimulate the energy of the people for the purposes of nation building and economic modernization. Mass-mobilizing leaders have run a gamut from those committed to revolutionizing society completely to those who are content to make relatively modest changes in the life chances of the poor. The ideals that inspire mass mobilization clearly vary, but they create three distinctive types of leaders:

- Anti-colonial and nationalist leaders operating in competitive democracies. For example, leaders like Mahatma Gandhi of India were motivated primarily by anti-colonial sentiments and favored democratic forms of nation building.

- Militant leftist leaders controlling dominant-party or single-party states. These include socialists such as Gamal Nasser in Egypt, Julius Nyerere in Tanzania, and Jomo Kenyatta in Kenya, and communist heads of single-party states like Mao Tsetung of China and Fidel Castro of Cuba.

- Religious militants, like the ayatollahs of Iran, who are now important in parts of the Islamic world.

Status quo-oriented leaders are those whose highest priority is to maintain social order and stability. These status quo-oriented leaders are also of three main types: representatives of traditional dynastic families, civilian dictators, and military leaders. Even today, traditional ruling families, such as the Al-Aziz as-Sa'ud in Saudi Arabia and the as-Sabah in Kuwait, dominate many of the oil-producing Arab states of the Middle East. Dynastic families also played an important role elsewhere in the developing world, particularly in Latin America and Africa, though they did not manage to hold on to direct state power for long. By contrast, civilian dictators and military men have repeatedly come to power in the Third World when elite interests have been challenged by popular unrest. In Africa, for example, most countries have experienced episodes of military rule, and in about half of the countries military rule has been longer than civilian rule.

The schooling policies of these types of leaders reflect their ideology. The most radical mass-mobilizing governments—those in China, Cuba, Tanzania, Mozambique, and Nicaragua under the Sandinistas—made extraordinary efforts to bring about social and political transformation through schooling. They mounted intensive literacy campaigns, set up thousands of adult education centers, insisted on the combination of vocational and academic schooling (including requirements that urban students work in the countryside), and restricted higher levels of schooling to concentrate on the schooling of the poor. They have usually engaged in highly charged campaigns of political resocialization to create "new socialist men" (and women) (Carnoy and Samoff 1990).

The literacy campaigns were among the most ambitious accomplishments of mass-mobilizing socialist and communist leaders. The first mass literacy campaign was mounted by the Chinese in the mid-1950s at a time when some 85 percent of their largely rural population was illiterate. The Chinese did not achieve universal literacy, but they did, by official estimates, cut illiteracy by two-thirds (Arnove 1986). In Cuba, shortly after the revolution, Fidel Castro closed the schools and sent 250,000 teachers and university students to the countryside with instructions to achieve a fully literate population in nine months. Cuba was already highly literate. The official estimate was that the campaign cut illiteracy from 21 percent to just below 4 percent. (Some scholars have argued that the costs of training were so high and the level of new literacy achieved so modest that the Cuban literacy campaign cannot be classified as the rousing success the revolutionaries claimed. See Fagen 1969:54–5.) Nicaragua under the Sandinistas also launched a literacy campaign (Arnove 1986). Official numbers of people educated by these campaigns are widely disputed, but the campaigns clearly made a difference. These efforts show that if goals are highly specific, methods sharply focused, and the population sufficiently motivated, major cultural changes can occur in a very short time.

Socialist and communist leaders have been justly criticized for their failures to bring freedom and prosperity to their countries. But they did have some successes. Their schooling policies often equalized opportunities between advantaged and disadvantaged groups. During the period of the Cultural Revolution (1964–72) in China, for example, the large gaps in educational attainment between urban and rural children, and between boys and girls, narrowed appreciably (Hannum 1999). (Equalization had significant costs for intellectuals and professionals, who were sent into the countryside to work and to learn from the peasantry. Some intellectuals have recalled studying in their huts by flashlight, terrified of being caught with a book.)

Most mass-mobilizing leaders have had more modest goals, and they have often had to live with the compromises inherent in democratic government as well. The desire to improve economic opportunities for the poor has, however, been a constant among mass-mobilizing populist leaders whether socialist or not. As the economists Frederick Harbison and Charles Myers (1964) put it, mass-mobilizing nationalist leaders were invariably interested in "massive and immediate expansion" of schooling (179). Mass-mobilizing leaders in the early postcolonial years spent more on schooling as a proportion of gross national product (GNP) than would have been predicted simply by looking at the wealth of their countries or the levels of enrollment they inherited (Garms 1968).

The policies of status quo-oriented authoritarian leaders provide a striking contrast. Dynastic rulers invariably have wanted to preserve traditional society as much as possible and to allow modernization to take place slowly if at all. They have been aligned with the largest religious organizations, the largest landowners, national and international business elites, and the military. They are invariably quite distant from the aspirations of the poor. Civilian dictators supported by the military (such as the Duvalier family in Haiti, the Kim family in South Korea, and the Mobuto family in Zimbabwe) have also aligned themselves with the interests of national economic elites. The United States supported many of these civilian dictators during the Cold War, because of their favorable attitudes toward multinational firms and their strong commitments to suppressing communist and socialist movements.

By contrast, military men have frequently come to power promising reform and modernization. They have sometimes acted decisively on these promises, as, for example, in Peru in the mid- and late 1960s (Stepan 1978) and, to a lesser extent, in Ethiopia after 1974 (Liebenow 1987). More often, however, after short-lived efforts to build support through reform measures, they have shown themselves to be far more interested in control and stability than in social reform. Whereas most mass-mobilizing leaders in the developing world saw schooling as an investment in national development, authoritarian leaders tended to highlight the costs of educating the populace and to fear the independence of educational institutions. They restricted educational funding and, when they feared unrest, they also repressed academic freedom.

The consequences of authoritarian rule are well illustrated by the history of South American schooling during periods of military rule. Studies of educational expenditures in these countries from the 1950s and 1960s showed that under equivalent conditions, military leaders spent less on social welfare than civilian regimes did. Military regimes were marked, in particular, by rapid increases in social spending to establish legitimacy, followed by equally rapid returns to the status quo (Schmitter 1971). The patterns have been more complicated in Africa, where military governments often succeeded dynastic leaders who were even less interested in schooling for the masses (Odeotola 1982). Nevertheless, a leading student of military government in Africa concludes that studies suggest "better development under civilians than under military rule" (Liebenow 1987:153–4). As in Latin America, some military regimes had a reforming disposition at the time they assumed power, but lost it over time.

More recent evidence further confirms the relationship between authoritarian rule and restrictions on schooling for the poor and working classes. When military leaders came to power in Brazil, Uruguay, Argentina, and Chile in the 1960s and 1970s, they closed down public schools in many urban working-class districts, fired teachers thought to be hostile to the regime, and reopened schools only gradually when loyalists could be recruited to teach and administer them (Hanson 1996). In Brazil, Argentina, and Chile, university enrollments were restricted, radical students expelled, dissenting faculty silenced or fired, and university autonomy in matters of self-governance strictly curtailed (Levy 1986).

One consequence of status quo-oriented leadership has been to shift the benefits of schooling away from the poor and in the direction of the well-to-do—more precisely, to those among the well-to-do who were politically conservative or disengaged. These regimes characteristically had a negligent attitude toward the poor and cultivated the wealthier classes so that they could stay in power. In countries such as Argentina, Brazil, Chile, and Uruguay before the movement toward democracy of the late 1980s, children from the most poorly educated families had no more than a 5 percent chance of entering a university, but children whose parents had university educations had a 50 percent chance or more of admission. Because higher education was well supported by the state in the form of free tuition and other benefits, but loans for living expenses were hard to obtain, the state ended up providing larger subsidies for the schooling of the affluent than for the schooling of the poor (Schiefelbein 1985:196).

The "Golden Life" of Latin American University Students

Until recently, the image of the university student in South America was very much like the image of the college student in the United States during the 1920s, when few attended and those who did usually came from upper- and upper-middle-class families. South American universities were seen as places of cosmopolitanism and hedonism in the midst of highly inegalitarian social orders.

The image reflected the unusual circumstances of university students in Latin America, who have traditionally been treated with extraordinary largesse by the state and unusual deference by the larger society. University attendance was (and in most countries still is) free or almost free of charge. In addition, university students sometimes had an astonishing package of fringe benefits: access to subsidized transportation, housing, and food, free health insurance, sports facilities (in some cases likened to country clubs), equipment, free language courses, textbooks, and tickets to many cultural events (Schiefelbein 1985:204). The rest of society paid its respect to university graduates by addressing them with special titles in everyday life: doctor, *ingeniero* (engineer), *abogado* (lawyer), and *licentiado* (graduate, including the connotation of knowledgeability). Graduates were also traditionally privileged to gather in guilds and unions to lobby those in power for the purpose of limiting certain income-producing activities to only those with specific diplomas (Schiefelbein 1985:205).

The "golden life" of university students might have seemed less unjust to many if the universities had been open to students from all social backgrounds. In fact, however, children from high social status families were overrepresented in Latin America more than virtually anywhere else in the world. Part-time employment in university towns, scholarships, and loans were not widely available, making higher education too expensive for working-class and poor families. Those loans that were available required collateral that was out of reach of most families. In addition, entrance examinations in Latin American universities were closely tied to class-linked cultural knowledge.

The golden life is no longer. With the coming of the new democratic regimes of the 1980s and the new spirit of freedom, colleges and universities became open-admissions institutions in many countries: Anyone with a high school degree could attend free of charge. In Argentina, in the 1990s, nearly 40 percent of college-age people were enrolled in higher education (UNDP 1994). In addition, the World Bank and other international agencies have repeatedly called for reduced state support for higher education in Latin America, the introduction of income-weighted tuition, and scholarships and loans for low-income students. Some countries, such as Colombia, have begun to introduce modest tuitions, and other countries, such as Argentina, Chile, and Brazil, have debated the possibility of introducing tuition.

Memories of the golden life remain important, even when the conditions to support it no longer exist. With higher enrollments, underemployment and low wages have become common among university graduates, particularly among graduates in nontechnical fields (Winkler 1990). In spite of rapidly declining rates of economic return, students continue to enroll in large numbers in fields like law and humanities. Why? In part, it is because the technical fields require mathematical and scientific backgrounds that are generally lacking among secondary school graduates. But socially conditioned expectations related to the golden life may also be important. Students may continue to expect the traditional deference accorded graduates and the cachet of being established in a profession, while paying little attention to the growing likelihood that they will be underemployed.

The Second Postcolonial Generation

In the second postcolonial generation, two distinct trends in schooling, leading in opposite directions, have been evident. On the one hand, schooling systems in the developing world are becoming more similar to one another. Some of this convergence is based on the declining politics of passion and the rise of incremental technocratic planning. Most of the change, however, is based on the models of school policy promulgated by the World Bank and other donor agencies. On the other hand, countries in the developing world are becoming less similar in their economic and social circumstances, leading to decided improvements in schooling in some countries and stagnating or even deteriorating conditions in others.

The waning of left and right. Today, both mass-mobilizing and status quo-oriented leaders are on the wane in the developing world. Communism and socialism no longer represent inspiring political ideals for many policymakers, charismatic anti-colonial leaders have become national symbols rather than active forces, and state bureaucracies in the developing world have begun to operate much like state bureaucracies elsewhere. Altogether, the politics of passion has greatly subsided.

Insofar as mass-mobilizing leaders can still be found in the developing world, the fundamentalist leaders of the few Islamic states are arguably the most important examples. (Anti-globalization activists are also important, but none, with the arguable exception of Hugo Chavez of Venezuela, have thus far gained state power.) It is, of course, tempting to see these leaders as status quo-oriented authoritarians than as mass mobilizers, because they strenuously resist change in matters of religious doctrine. Yet in regard to schools, Islamist leaders have often acted more like mass mobilizers. Overall, government expenditures for public schooling as a percentage of GDP tend to be higher in countries like Iran and Libya than elsewhere in the developing world, and literacy rates are also a little higher (UNDP 2003). Like previous mass-mobilizing leaders, leaders of Islamic states have wanted to use schooling to support the cultural development of the masses and nationalist sentiment. They have, however, also insisted on orthodoxy in fields touching on morality and politics, not unlike the communist mass mobilizers of the Cold War era.

Status quo-oriented authoritarian governments in the Third World are also yielding, although not yet completely. In the 1980s, civilian governments took over in all countries in Latin America previously ruled by the military. These new civilian governments have seemingly consolidated the power of democracy, and in the process expanded opportunities for schooling. Some military governments in Asia, such as South Korea, have also given way to civilian control. Military regimes still control large parts of Africa, but democratic forces are making a few inroads. The most brutal and corrupt of the military regimes in Africa, that of Idi Amin in Uganda, for example, gave way to civilian control (Diamond, Linz, and Lipset 1986).

With the development of democratic regimes, incremental, expert planning has become the norm in the developing world. The premises of this planning, however, have been set by external policy analysts, and particularly by analysts and policymakers associated with the World Bank.

The role of the World Bank. Those who have tried to explain the remarkable similarities among schools throughout the world have usually emphasized the role of models drawn from the experience of mass schooling in the West and promoted by international agencies and international schooling experts. These well-promoted models provide a kind of cultural grid for the rest of the world (Meyer, Ramirez, et al. 1979; Meyer, Ramirez, and Soysal 1992).

Such an analysis helps to explain why so much similarity existed from the beginning in Third World schooling systems, but it does not explain very well why these systems have changed over time. In fact, the "standard model" of the first postcolonial generation has changed significantly over the past quarter century. The new elements include an increasing consensus about what kinds of resources and practices are necessary to improve learning, more reliance on private funds to support schooling, a decreasing emphasis on vocational education, and a widely accepted methodology for evaluating schooling policies. These new elements are largely the product of the research and advocacy of the World Bank.

The World Bank, located in Washington, D.C., is an institution financed by the wealthiest industrial countries for the purpose of providing loans and advice to the developing world. Not only have the educational researchers of the World Bank accumulated large amounts of data about the developing world, they have also analyzed it in a rigorous way and come to conclusions about what works and what does not work in Third World schooling. Sociologists know that successful agents of change combine knowledge, a commitment to action, and access to the levers of power (Etzioni 1968). Many efforts to improve schools have the first two ingredients in this recipe, but only rarely the crucial third. This is the great advantage of the World Bank's reform efforts: it not only has knowledge and commitment, it also has the clout to follow through effectively. In a developing world that is more and more loan dependent, its research findings are broadly comparable to the ideology of early nationalist leaders, and its power of the purse broadly comparable to the popular support enjoyed by the first generation of nationalist leaders.

World Bank researchers do not see eye to eye on every issue, but they have developed a coherent framework for analyzing how schooling funds should be spent given a country's available resources. This framework combines a concern for the efficient use of resources with a concern for equity in the distribution of resources between advantaged and disadvantaged groups. The policy approach might be called "back to basics" at the primary level combined with "let the market decide" at the post-primary level. The World Bank has concluded that most educational policymaking has been a disaster, with too much funding of higher education relative to primary schooling, too much funding of vocational education relative to general education, and too little private investment in schooling relative to public investment. It argues that developing countries have had the best results where the following criteria are met:

- Schooling budgets are allocated largely to primary schooling, especially when primary schooling is not yet universal.

- Resources for the unschooled are freed by reducing the length of compulsory schooling.

- Private schools are tolerated as a way to reduce the pressure on hard-pressed public resources.

- General education, which is more flexible and less costly, is emphasized over vocational education.

- Social demand—giving people the schooling they want and will pay for—is emphasized above the level of primary schooling (and in the poorest countries, also at the level of primary schooling).

- Subsidies to higher education are returned to the lower levels of society in the form of special scholarships for the poor.

- Wage differentials between graduates of different schooling levels are maintained so as to provide incentives for further human capital development among those who are able to finish primary school (Psacharopoulos 1986).

The World Bank has also expressed consistent views over the past decades about what kind of learning should be taking place in classrooms and how that learning can be enhanced. It has taken a stand against vocational education as an ineffective and costly substitute for sound general education. In the view of World Bank researchers, vocational education is an inefficient and ineffective means of economic development. The major contribution of formal schooling to agricultural development has been through the provision of literacy and numeracy rather than through the development of practical or agricultural curricula in the schools (Psacharopoulos 1987). Quality in learning, according to the World Bank's researchers, can be achieved through trained teachers, adequate instructional materials (especially textbooks), increased time on academic tasks, exams to monitor progress, and provision of basic nutritional requirements (where possible) through school lunch programs (Lockheed et al. 1990). Attractive buildings and new equipment, curricular reforms, even smaller class sizes are not considered to be as important to educational progress (Gannicott and Throsby 1992). According to a World Bank-sponsored study, structured class time; active, hands-on learning; and parental involvement can help to improve literacy learning, even if "class size is allowed to float up a little" (Fuller et al. 1999).

Unlike most advocacy groups, the World Bank has the leverage to bring its vision of good schooling into practice at least into the official policy documents that serve as models for practice.[1] For the most part, the power of the World Bank is indirect. It recommends and advocates, but it is rarely so heavy-handed as to insist on conformity with its recommendations as a precondition to the provision of loans. Nevertheless, in their hopes of gaining World Bank approval, leaders must take its recommendations into account. This implicit power is supported by the direct contribution donor agencies make to schooling in the developing world. The World Bank is the largest external donor for educational projects, with annual lending commitments of more than $2.35 billion (World Bank 2005a). This is only a small proportion of the total government spending on public schooling, but its loss would nevertheless be greatly missed.

The leverage of the World Bank is based on the reliance of Third World economies on development loans, and their high levels of indebtedness. A basic principle of power is that the more one party depends on another for external resources to survive, the more likely that party is to conform to the wishes of the resource provider (Pfeffer and Salancik 1978). Thus, countries badly in need of development loans are more likely to conform to the recommendations of donor agencies than those less in need. Those countries less in need of World Bank development funds—many in East Asia fit this criterion, as do an increasing number in South America—are in a position to go their own way in schooling policy. Many countries in the developing world are deeply in debt, however. In the most impoverished countries of sub-Saharan Africa, debt obligations are more than 100 percent of GDP (UNCTAD 2004). These countries may spend twice as much on debt service as they do on health and schooling. It is not surprising that they take the recommendations of the World Bank and other donor agencies seriously.

The World Bank's school policy recommendations, based on years of study, seem eminently sensible, but room exists for debate. For example, the World Bank consistently argued for freeing resources devoted to higher education for support of lower levels; the governments of some developing countries feel that students simply would not have enough money to attend universities without substantial subsidization. Many African universities were known to have good academic standards. Should they become much smaller and havens for the wealthy? Without substantial state subsidization, they probably would have. The World Bank's position makes sense given the scarcity of resources available to many African governments, but an argument can be made on the other side. Indeed, in a recent policy document, the World Bank changed course, arguing that developing countries must begin to invest in their post-secondary educational systems, if they hope to compete effectively in the global economy (Hopper 2002).

A single, dominating model can reduce variation not only in useful ways (by reducing the amount of wasted effort) but also in potentially problematic ways (by discouraging new ideas and adaptive responses). One size does not necessarily fit all. We can see this in the diversity of reactions to a new World Bank policy advocating decentralized school management. This seems like an eminently sensible idea—decentralization should ideally create more initiative and accountability at the local level—but it has met resistance in places like Indonesia. Studies of implementation in Indonesia have attributed inaction to traditions of deference to authority and related definitions of teachers as "dutiful civil servants." "Western notions of local autonomy . . . are both puzzling and distasteful to many Indonesians. For the Javanese, at least, such notions conflict with their perception of a unified source of power and authority and are thus difficult to accept" (Devas 1997:365).

Much as in population genetics, variations in social systems can be important for the new directions they suggest, or for their more suitable fit to particular circumstances. Industrialized societies, after all, have developed a number of quite different working structures of schooling. These provide a useful range of possibilities to consider, as well as solutions that

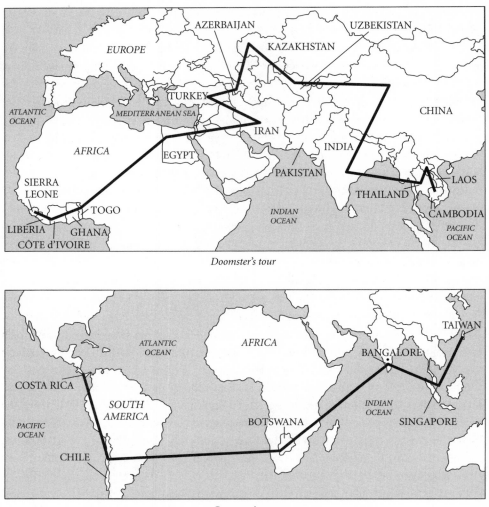

Doomster's tour

Cornucopian tour

Figure 3.1   Two Views of the Developing World
source: Adapted from Kennedy (1996).

may be better adjusted to national history and social context than any single model, in all likelihood, could be.

Diverging economic trends. The Third World now includes both a large number of economic success stories and a number of economic disaster areas. It also includes a middle range of countries, making more gradual or mixed progress in reaching development goals. Figure 3.1 shows historian Paul Kennedy's (1996) two versions of a tour through the contemporary developing world. One is a "cornucopian tour" through the "success belt." The other is a "doomster's tour" through the "disaster belt."

As economic circumstances have diverged in the developing world, so have some schooling circumstances. The high-income countries in the developing world—countries like Argentina, Taiwan, and Kuwait—now enroll virtually all children in first grade, graduate

85 percent or more from primary school, and send at least two-thirds on to secondary school. They may enroll 20 to 25 percent of the relevant age group in college, a higher proportion than some industrialized societies (UNESCO 2005). By contrast, few students in the least developed countries have the family support to stay in school for long—sometimes even to attend at all. Because of governmental budgetary constraints, secondary schools and colleges cannot accommodate everyone even if students did have the wherewithal to continue. The poorest developing countries, therefore, allow natural attrition, combined with primary school-leaving examinations, to limit the number of students continuing on to secondary school. Records are not very reliable, but published reports suggest that primary completion rates under 40 percent are typical in the least developed countries. Secondary enrollment rates are reported as high as 30 percent and as low as 10 percent. Tertiary enrollment is invariably below 5 percent and more often 1 percent or less. Even these figures overestimate enrollments in the very poorest countries. In Mali, less than one-quarter of all children in the relevant age group are enrolled in primary school, only about 5 percent are enrolled in secondary schooling, and less than 1 percent are enrolled in higher education (World Bank 2005b).

In the poorest countries, the amount of actual time spent on learning is also much lower. A careful study of actual school time in Haiti in 1984 showed that the official version of the school year was far from fully realized in practice. The school day often began late, teachers were frequently absent on Tuesday and Friday market days, and 48 public holidays were celebrated instead of the official 28. With unofficial school closings and delayed openings, the functional school year was only 70 days, 40 percent of the international standard. In a study of 15 village schools in India, two-thirds of the teachers were absent at the time of the investigators' unexpected visits, and the substitute teachers did little more than keep a semblance of order among the pupils (Dreze and Sen 1995:125). In Malawi, the school year is 192 days—higher than the international standard—but one-third of those days are during the rainy season, when the roads are impassable and students cannot go to school. One study of class time in a poor region of rural Peru found that only 6 percent of the total time that students were at school was devoted to academic instruction. The rest of the time was spent on recreation periods and sports competitions, waiting during adult meetings, time lost to teacher absences, housekeeping activities, and unsupervised desk work. Some social scientists see a correspondence between the way schools are organized and the roles students will play in later life:

> As can be seen in the descriptions of planting, watering, cleaning, cooking, child care, long walks and so on, Quechua children are expected to handle many practical, physical jobs themselves; correspondingly, they are apparently not expected to handle intellectual jobs, even with the teacher's help. (Hornberger 1987:216)

The deterioration of schooling in low-income countries. Overall, one sees significant progress in educational development. Most countries in the world are approaching universal completion of primary school, and about 80 percent now go on to lower secondary schooling (UNESCO 2005). Enrollment rates of 35 to 60 percent in upper secondary schools are most common, and some developing countries with very committed governments do significantly better than that.

However, schooling in low-income countries has not just stagnated; in some cases, it has deteriorated. Indeed, the greatest force currently aligned against the standard model is declining economic and population conditions in the poorest regions of the developing world—and particularly in sub-Saharan Africa (World Bank 1988; UNHDP 2004). As economies idle, debt burdens accumulate, and populations continue to grow, the state finds it more and more difficult to keep its institutions operating effectively. Those parts of the world that remain outside the standard model promulgated by the World Bank do so more often because of deficient resources and disorganization than because of ideas or traditions opposed to the World Bank's recommendations.

The United Nations has identified 50 countries as "least developed." Three-quarters of these countries are in sub-Saharan Africa. Here participation in lower secondary schooling is uncommon, and participation in upper secondary schooling rare. One of the most discouraging features of the current global situation is the declining capacity of states in these poorest countries. The average income in the richest 20 countries is now 37 times that of the poorest. This ratio has doubled in the past 40 years, mainly because of lack of growth in the poorest countries (World Bank 2003:2). For every dollar in development aid, three dollars may go back to the West in the form of debt-service payments (UNCTAD 2004). Since 1980, deterioration of enrollments and schooling quality has been a fact of life in many of the countries of sub-Saharan Africa. School enrollments have fallen as a proportion of school-age populations. Per pupil expenditures on schooling have fallen at every level, and much of what remains has been misallocated. Even the capacity to monitor what is happening has been lost in some countries:

> In sub-Saharan Africa, we are losing track of enrollments, of whether teachers are even getting paid, and of textual and other available materials. Is there any ministry in sub-Saharan Africa that can say that it knows more about what textbooks are currently available than it did 20 years ago? (Heyneman 1993:513)

Some deterioration in expenditures on schooling has also occurred in rural areas in the countries of South Asia (which include India, Pakistan, and Bangladesh), although enrollments have not declined. Rural areas in these countries are the other large center of concentrated poverty in the world. Because governments can no longer support free, public schooling, in some countries of sub-Saharan Africa and South Asia, families are now required to pay at least token fees for use of the public schooling system from primary school on.

Privatization. Privatization of public schooling is a worldwide trend, as governments seek to cope with huge social demands on limited budgets. Several South American countries have experimented with more comprehensive forms of privatization, through provision of subsidies to private schools (as in Argentina), or vouchers to parents to use at either public or private schools (as in Chile and Colombia). The private school share of enrollment is consequently larger in South America than in the rest of the developing world.

The most comprehensive experiment occurred in Chile in the 1980s and 1990s. Vouchers were given to parents and could be used at private or public schools. Many students from all classes shifted to private schools, but the higher the income level of the family the more likely they were to use vouchers for private schooling. Three-quarters of families in the top income quintile enrolled children in private schools, compared to one-quarter of families from the bottom two quintiles. Costs of transportation and limits on information about private schools led to less participation of the poor. The economist Martin Carnoy concluded: "Higher income groups take advantage of private alternatives . . . and (have the) ability to access schools where average achievement is higher" (Carnoy 1998:336).

Studies have come to mixed conclusions about whether private school subsidies and voucher programs led to educational improvements in the South American countries that have experimented with them. In a study of 10 South American countries, students in private schools consistently performed better than students in public schools. However, when researchers statistically controlled for both individual socioeconomic status and the higher status of peers found in private schools, the private school effect across the 10 countries averaged zero. Students in a few countries showed small positive effects for attending private schools, and others showed small negative effects (Somers, McEwan, and Willms 2004).

SCHOOLING AND ECONOMIC DEVELOPMENT

For social scientists and planners, one of the most important issues has been the role of formal education as a factor in economic development. Students of schooling and economic development have posed several key questions: How much is an educated labor force associated with economic development? Is mass schooling a necessary precondition for economic development? Is it more a consequence of development than a cause? Or is it a contingent factor important in some cases and not in others?

These questions have been debated by development scholars for more than a generation. Until recently, two major theoretical perspectives existed concerning the role of schooling in economic development. One is usually known as *dependency theory*; the other, as *human capital theory*. These are being challenged and at least partially replaced today by *theories of state-led development*, which emphasize contingencies and view human capital development as one important factor among others. The recent successes of several high-performing Asian economies lend empirical support to the theories of state-led development.

Dependency Theories

In the 1960s and 1970s, many social theorists argued that the Third World suffers because the developed world continues to exploit it even in the absence of colonial structures. Developing countries thus remain dependent on the industrial societies.

One version of dependency theory, the "world system" theory of Immanuel Wallerstein (1974), argued that countries in the world are connected by the functions they perform in the world economy. *Periphery states*—most of the former colonies of the Third World—supply raw materials to *core states*—the industrial societies where those materials are refined, combined, and assembled into products. Those products may be sold in home markets or in global markets, including in the countries where the raw materials originated. For example, large quantities of sugar cane are harvested in some tropical countries and imported to the United States, where they are turned into sugar and combined with other ingredients to be resold to the rest of the world as candy bars and other products. The "raw material states" of the periphery are poor and backward; the "complex operations states" of the core are wealthier and forward looking.

Exports do not always improve the situation of periphery states, because most profits are restricted to the local landowning elites and the merchants (who, if foreign nationals, remit profits to the home country). Export earnings therefore provide precious little capital for diversifying local economies. A relatively few people may gain wealth from their roles as overseers and middlemen in world economic transactions, but most of the population remains rural and is engaged in small-scale farming either for subsistence or for local markets. Others are employed as cheap hired labor for multinational agribusiness, mining, or sweatshop industry.

Semiperiphery states lie between these two poles. They export some raw materials to the core states but also produce some products for regional or global consumption. They are economically not as advanced as the core, but they are also not as poor as the periphery. World system theorists would consider countries like Chile and Thailand to be semiperipheral.

Dependency theorists place little faith in schooling as a force in economic development. They argue that low levels of school funding and enrollment are closely connected to the country's location in the world division of labor. International business most needs the Third World to supply cheap labor for extracting raw materials and producing some commercial products. Even nationalistic governments that wish to develop their schooling systems usually do not have enough money to do so effectively. Dependency theorists conclude that resources spent on schooling serve not disadvantaged groups and the poor but rather landowners and local and international business people seeking large pools of cheap but competent labor (R. Clark 1992).

It is difficult to avoid seeing one obvious flaw in dependency theory: for national and multinational business, expanding markets in developing countries are at least as important a goal as employing cheap labor. In fact, larger markets for the goods and services in which developed countries specialize will not evolve unless the people of Third World countries accumulate more disposable income. Dependency theorists have also not been able to explain why some countries move into the core of the world capitalist economy from the semiperiphery and others into the semiperiphery from the periphery. Nor have these theories been able to account for the different levels of development among countries that have very similar populations and natural resources.

The evidence indicates that rapid population growth, ethnic and class hostilities, and the corruption of officials have scuttled the development hopes of many Third World countries more thoroughly than the profit seeking of international business ever could. For example, the devastations brought by civil war and tyranny have kept Cambodia stagnant while nearby Thailand, a very similar society, develops rapidly. Conversely, far-sighted economic policies, useful strategic alliances, and determined and cohesive leadership have promoted development in countries where world system or dependency theory would not have expected it. No better explanation exists for why the Czech Republic, for example, should be poised on the edge of economic prosperity while many of its next-door neighbors in the former Soviet bloc continue to flounder.

Human Capital Theories

The overwhelming majority of development scholars in the West subscribed to human capital theory, the leading rival to dependency theories throughout the 1960s and 1970s. Human capital theory assumes that economic development is possible for any country that is fully developed and uses its human resources. Education is at the center of human capital theory, because it is based on the importance of a well-trained workforce for economic development.

In a well-known book, *Education, Manpower, and Economic Growth* (1964), the economists Frederick Harbison and Charles Myers laid out what was by that time the conventional wisdom among development scholars who accepted human capital theory:

> The builders of economies are elites of various kinds who organize and lead the march toward progress. Their effectiveness as prime movers depends not only on their own development but on the knowledge, skills, and capabilities of those whom they lead as well. Thus, in a very real sense, the wealth of a nation and its potential for growth stem from the power to develop and effectively utilize the innate capacities of people. Human resource development, therefore, may be a more realistic and reliable indicator of modernization or development than any other single indicator. (14)

To develop the innate capacities of the people, it was believed that public investments in formal education were essential.

Social scientists who studied the developing world during this period found moderate to strong correlations between a country's investment in schooling and its GNP per capita (Schultz 1961; Denison 1962, chap. 7; Harbison and Myers 1964). These findings were sometimes taken as support for human capital theory. At the same time, researchers recognized that some countries invested more in schooling than their economic level seemed to warrant and that other countries had comparatively dynamic economies in spite of low levels of investment in schooling (Harbison and Myers 1964). A good many researchers in the human capital school concluded that human resources development alone was not sufficient to produce economic growth. Harbison and Myers (1964), for example, wrote:

> Human resource development is only one of many factors which are associated with economic growth. The availability of petroleum and mineral resources, world markets for particular agricultural commodities, the population-to-land ratio, the stability of political institutions, social and cultural traditions, the existence of a will to modernize, and a host of other factors are also influential. (114)

Anderson and Bowman (1965) noted that pre–World War II income levels were a much better predictor of postwar income levels than were prewar schooling levels.

Later scholars raised new questions about human capital theory. Some felt that the less careful human capital theorists had assumed a causal relationship that the data simply did not support. Instead of investments in schooling creating a hardworking and skilled workforce to carry forward economic development goals, it might simply be the case that richer countries could afford to spend more on education (see, e.g., Collins 1979, chap. 2). Some writers even came to question the fundamental assumption of human capital theory that more educated workers are more productive workers (Berg 1970; Thurow 1973; Blaug 1987). They pointed out that people who were overeducated for their jobs might not be challenged enough to be very productive at all.

State-Led Development Theories

Today, social scientists have largely rejected the dependency and human capital theories in favor of a more complex view of the relationship between schooling and economic development. A well-educated labor force is often an important factor in development, and a poorly educated labor force can certainly be an impediment. However, other factors are at least as essential to sustained economic growth. These include effective economic policies and trade alliances, and the avoidance of war, political tyranny, overpopulation, and overborrowing. Economic development is like making a cake. Several ingredients are required—eggs, flour, sugar—and several others must be kept as far away as possible. Without one of the required ingredients, the cake will not bake properly, and the same is true if any one of the banned ingredients somehow gets into the mix. High levels of schooling are, therefore, best considered both a contributor to economic development and (more reliably) a consequence. Economically successful developing countries tend to invest heavily in human capital development through formal education. The opposite, however, is not as true: investment in human capital development does not in itself lead to high rates of economic growth. At the same time, it can contribute to economic growth, if mixed with the right development policies, by helping to create a disciplined and skilled labor force.

In the years following World War II, the most educated nations in Latin America were Argentina, Chile, and Uruguay, and none of those countries moved to the forefront of economic development in their region. Indeed, the social upheavals of industrialization and political conflict produced brutally repressive military dictatorships instead of the rapid growth reformers had anticipated. Their elegant constitutions were torn up, their congresses closed, their courts rendered a sham (Skidmore and Smith 1989:372).

We can better understand the relationship between economic and schooling development if we look in some detail at the world's greatest economic success story of the past quarter century: the eight high-performing Asian economies (HPAEs). In addition to Japan, these high-performing economies include the "four tigers"—Hong Kong, South Korea, Singapore, and Taiwan—along with Indonesia, Malaysia, and Thailand, which have joined the group within the past two decades. The four tigers are now poised to enter the elite club of fully industrialized, wealthy societies, and the other three developing countries are not far behind. Another Asian economy, "market-Leninist" China, has also shown remarkable economic gains. Figure 3.2 shows patterns of growth and income inequality in

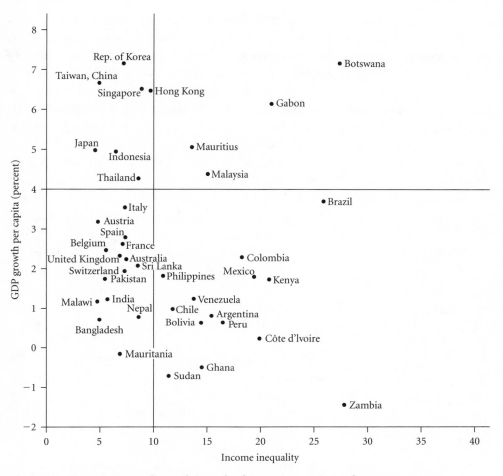

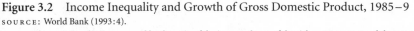

Figure 3.2   Income Inequality and Growth of Gross Domestic Product, 1985–9

SOURCE: World Bank (1993:4).

NOTE: Income inequality is measured by the ratio of the income shares of the richest 20 percent and the poorest 20 percent of the population.

several countries of the developing world since the 1960s. The figure shows that the highest-performing economies tend to be concentrated in East Asia and suggests, moreover, that growth in these economies has not been accompanied by the same high rates of income inequality found in the high-growth countries of Africa and Latin America. (It is important to note that data on levels of inequality are controversial; some analysts find the sources of this data to be unreliable. See, e.g., Moll 1992.) This concentration of East Asian economies at the top of the growth charts has encouraged social scientists to look for the sources of the East Asian miracle (see, e.g., Amsden 1989; World Bank 1993).

The high-performing Asian economies. By 1965, Hong Kong, Korea, and Singapore had achieved universal primary schooling, well ahead of other developing economies. Even Indonesia had a primary school enrollment rate of 70 percent. These high enrollment rates continued in later years through the secondary level and are now evident in higher education (World Bank 1993:43–6). In general, enrollment rates at different levels of schooling in the HPAEs have tended to be higher than predicted for their country's income level, meaning that they were investing more in schooling than countries at a similar level of GNP per capita. Between 1970 and 1989, for example, real expenditures per pupil at the primary level rose by 355 percent in Korea, compared with 64 percent in Mexico, 38 percent in Kenya, and just 13 percent in Pakistan (World Bank 1993:45). Remember, however, that per pupil expenditures mainly reflect economic growth, which allows more spending.

Schooling is far from a completely independent part of the "East Asian miracle." Educational institutions, like most other institutions in these societies, have benefited from lower birthrates than are found in the rest of the developing world. Lower birthrates mean that resources do not have to be stretched as far, class sizes are manageable, and everyone can be accommodated. They have also benefited from the absence of political conflict, famine, and disease factors that have limited progress in such nearby countries as Burma (now known as Myanmar), Laos, Cambodia, and Vietnam. They have clearly benefited from good family learning environments, which are built partly on the educational achievements of the previous generation and partly on the comparatively small number of children in each home. Instead of thinking of schooling as an important variable in the development formula, it would be better to think of it as part of a "virtuous circle" of influences.

Without doubt, the most important part of this virtuous circle is economic progress itself. As an economy grows, more resources become available for schooling children. The more people who are educated and the better the quality of the schooling they receive, the better the social environment they provide for the next generation. However, economic policies, not a commitment to human capital development, led the way in Asia. Indeed, it is entirely possible that the economic policies of the HPAEs could have been successful without a strong commitment to formal education.

Japan was the first Asian economy to reach full industrialization, and it provided a model for many of the later-developing HPAEs. Following World War II, Japan promoted the development of several weak industries by offering protective tariffs and formal incentives for introducing advanced technology. It also established so-called rationalization cartels to remove inefficient firms from export markets.

Government policies in the other HPAEs have not been based on a single model, but they have all actively supported export industries and imposed high tariffs on imports to protect domestic industry. In several countries, capital markets were not free. Governments repressed interest rates and directed credit to guide investments. The HPAEs have also developed an effective regional economic alliance for shared growth, with investment flowing first from Japan to the four tigers and more recently from these economies to Indonesia, Malaysia, and Thailand. The success of the East Asian economies is also built on comparatively low levels of social welfare spending, which reduces the threat of overborrowing to finance government debt. (See also World Bank 1993:79–103.)

Looking at the success of the HPAEs in relation to the rest of the developing world, it would appear that they have truly built the better mousetrap and that the mousetrap has been built by state-based development elites. Adrian Leftwich (1995) has listed four characteristics of the successful developmental state (many shared by fast-growing economies outside of Asia as well):

- A determined and cohesive developmental elite
- Relative autonomy of the development elite from intrusive political and military forces
- A competent, powerful, and insulated economic bureaucracy to carry out and monitor policies
- A weak set of social class actors, such as labor unions and local business interests

Export-oriented development (rather than the development of national industries to supply imported products) seems to be a centerpiece of most successful development states, as is the creation of strong trade and investment alliances with other regional powers. For example, Botswana, a comparatively successful African development state, benefited from trade with and investment by South Africa and Zimbabwe.

In thinking about the full implications of the high-performing East Asian economies, it is worth remembering that nearly all of these highly disciplined societies achieved economic success at the expense of political freedom and legal protections for citizens. All four of the little tigers were ruled by dictators, or near dictators, and the harshness of the regimes is legendary. In Singapore, even small infractions, such as spray painting private property, can bring a brutal caning at the hands of authorities, and political dissent is not tolerated. In South Korea, the civilian president, President Kim, used laws authorizing arbitrary arrest and detention, and those suppressing free association, expression, and assembly, to harass and control political opponents and labor activists. These same laws had been used to prop up decades of military rule. Schooling in the HPAEs reflects both the competitiveness of their economies and the authoritarianism of their political regimes. Little critical discussion gets in the way of drills on facts and principles, despite the avowed political liberalism of many schoolteachers.

Factors related to development success. We can now draw some conclusions about the role of schooling in economic development. Schooling can aid economic development, and economic development certainly tends to improve schooling, but the correlations hide as much as they reveal. Low-income countries in the developing world sometimes have high levels of literacy, high primary school enrollments, and good university systems. By the late 1970s, Kenya, the Philippines, Peru, and Chile, for example, all reported primary school enrollment rates well above 75 percent (Carceles 1979), but their per capita growth for the 1965–89 period lagged behind countries such as Indonesia and Brazil, which had yet to reach high levels of enrollment in the primary grades (World Bank 1993:31).

The problems of developing countries stem more often from political turmoil, overpopulation, disease, ineffective economic policies, and foreign debt than from schooling policies. The pitfalls into which developing countries can fall are many, and a strong commitment to schooling provides no magic ladder out. Only when a commitment to human capital development through schooling is combined with political stability, declining population growth, effective policies for the advancement of trade and industry, and macroeconomic stability to prevent overborrowing can a low-income developing society begin to experience strong rates of growth and development.

CONCLUSION

Most countries in the developing world have been independent for only 50 – 60 years. They inherited many features of schooling from the colonial powers. In their administrative and curricular structure, schools look very similar the world over. In addition, some particular practices of the colonial powers continued to stamp schooling in the newly independent states. Grade repeating, common in France, was, for example, also more common in the former French colonies.

The first generation of colonial leaders included many mass-mobilizing intellectuals and many status quo-oriented dynastic families and military rulers. The policies of these two groups tended to differ greatly. Mass-mobilizing intellectuals were schooling expansionists. They launched literacy campaigns, invested heavily in schooling, and were responsive to the schooling interests of the poor. Status quo-oriented leaders were more leery of schooling expenditures and repressed dissent that arose among students. Because of their relative indifference to the poor, their schooling policies tended to subsidize the well-to-do.

The second postcolonial generation has been marked by an increasing level of convergence in school policies, but increasing differences in economic conditions. The new standard model of schooling bears the imprint both of the decline of political passions in the Third World and the influence of donor agencies like the World Bank. The World Bank has successfully promulgated a model of schooling that encourages primary schooling and private spending, discourages vocational schooling, and evaluates schooling through a mix of efficiency and equity criteria. In spite of more standard policies, the poorest countries of the developing world have seen their school systems deteriorate as a result of economic stagnation, high indebtedness, and continued population growth. Most developing countries face problems of poverty, traditionalism, and physical insecurity. Where the problems of the developing world are greatest, so are the problems of schooling.

Three theories have sought to explain the role schooling plays in economic development. These are the dependency, human capital, and state-led development theories. The contemporary evidence tends to support the third of these theories, which focuses on the role the state plays in encouraging development through supporting export industries, regulating capital markets, and encouraging regional growth coalitions. Schooling in this theory is a factor of lesser importance in economic development than in the human capital theory, but it is a more important factor than the dependency theory allows. It is less important than state economic policies as an engine of growth, but it can play a role in economic development by helping to create a disciplined and skilled labor force.

In Chapters 2 and 3, I have discussed the structure of schooling in both the industrialized and the developing world. Drawing primarily on the work of macro-historical sociologists, I have shown why schooling systems have developed as they have and some consequences of different structures. We now turn, in Chapters 4 through 7, to a discussion of three major purposes of schooling in the contemporary world: the transmission of school knowledge, socialization, and social selection. These chapters rely primarily on work at the macro-historical and institutional levels of analysis. Chapter 4 begins this new discussion by looking at the defining purpose of schooling for most educators, the transmission of knowledge.

4 SCHOOLS AND CULTURAL TRANSMISSION

[handwritten notes:]
school knowledge
how curriculum chang.
global curriculum
multiculturalism
limited success in transmit
international test

Schooling has three major purposes in contemporary societies: *the transmission of school knowledge* (the topic of this chapter); *socialization*, the training of values, attitudes, and habits of conduct (the topic of Chapter 5); and *social selection*, the sorting of people for higher- and lower-level jobs in society (the topic of Chapters 6 and 7). These purposes underlie the familiar activities of schools. When students read silently at their desks or work on problems at the blackboard, they are studying the knowledge that one generation of educators considers important to transmit to the next generation of students. When students are told to sit still, concentrate, and do their own work, they are being socialized—in this case into habits of industriousness and independence. When they are directed on the basis of grades and test scores into more demanding or less demanding courses of study, they are being evaluated in ways connected to social selection.

By the transmission of school knowledge, I mean specifically the instruction of the uneducated members of a society by school authorities in the facts, theories, interpretations, and reasoning abilities that are considered to be consequential for the cognitive development of the individual and the transmission of culture in the larger society. In modern societies, the transmission of school knowledge occurs through a curriculum of subjects distributed over blocks of time in the school day. The *curriculum* can be defined as "a historically specific pattern of knowledge, which is selected, organized and distributed to learners through educational institutions" (Kliebard 1992:181). It is important to keep in mind that the knowledge transmitted through schooling is only a subset of all knowledge in the world.

As I will discuss it, the study of the transmission of school knowledge consists, first, of the subjects and course content that go into making up the curriculum, and second, of the extent to which this material is in fact successfully transmitted to the next generation. (The sociology of classroom interaction is discussed separately in Chapter 8, because teaching and learning are connected not only to the transmission of school knowledge but also to socialization and social selection.)

In my view, the study of cultural transmission should include investigation of what educational authorities want students to learn and how much of what is transmitted is actually learned by students. The chapter therefore takes up four topics: how the school curriculum developed historically; what the contemporary structure of curriculum looks like in different parts of the world; the social forces that have shaped curricula; and how well students in different countries actually learn course materials. The chapter begins by examining the relative importance of the transmission of school knowledge as compared to the other main purposes of schooling: socialization and social selection.

HOW IMPORTANT IS THE TRANSMISSION OF SCHOOL KNOWLEDGE?

It may seem obvious that the teaching of subject matter is the most important purpose of schooling. But is it really? Undoubtedly, some types of school knowledge—basic literacy and "numeracy," for example—are essential equipment for living. Everyone needs to be able to read the written word and to tally lists of numbers in order to survive independently in daily life. As one climbs the occupational ladder, higher levels of reading comprehension are usually required, and so, sometimes, are higher levels of quantitative understanding (Rosenbaum and Binder 1997).

Even so, some good arguments can be raised for the view that the transmission of school knowledge is for society a less important outcome of schooling than either socialization or social selection. Let's examine some of the more persuasive arguments.

- Both individuals and societies rely on a number of different knowledge systems for orienting conduct.

  In adult life, the knowledge taught in school does not necessarily count for more than other forms of knowledge, such as common sense, popular culture, merchandising, folklore, and religious belief. Nearly everyone recognizes that other knowledge systems compete with school knowledge for influence in everyday life. School knowledge might count more for those who run our institutions, but for the majority of people this is doubtful. Moreover, some of these other "knowledge systems," such as popular culture and religious traditions, have become more, not less important in shaping cognition.

- Beyond transmitting basic skills of literacy and computation, schools do not actually succeed very well in transmitting the lessons of the curriculum.

  Some students, of course, pull in school knowledge like magnets in a field of iron filings, but not the majority. Little that is taught in school sticks in most students' minds for long. A British book of humor, *1066 and All That*, contends that it is the first "truly memorable history of England," because unlike any other history book, it is the only one devoted to what adults actually remember from their school lessons, as opposed to what they are supposed to remember (Sellar and Yeatman 1931). In addition to "103 Good Things and Five Bad Kings," the book includes "Two Genuine Dates." Two of the four dates originally included "were eliminated at the last moment after research . . . revealed that they are not memorable." The book has the cheeky wit to say what most teachers could not dare to admit: school knowledge has a short half-life for most students, when it has a life at all.

- Much of what educators count as transmitting knowledge might be better interpreted as socialization messages or moments in the process of social selection.

  The treatment of value messages as cognitive content happens frequently. For example, some lessons in social studies are based on how other people see the world. The real lesson here is often that we shouldn't judge others too fast. The purpose of such lessons is more to create socially approved attitudes than to transmit a formal body of knowledge. But the problem of treating all school lessons as cultural transmission goes much deeper than this. When few students feel an intrinsic interest in the materials they study, and few use these materials when they are adults, knowledge might very well be regarded as more relevant to the process of social selection than it is to the process of cultural transmission. Learning is important here because it allows the schools to identify students who are academically able and who can, therefore, be encouraged to go on to higher levels of schooling. Sociologists have long argued that the adoption of high-stakes examinations carried a high price, because when they were introduced the selective function of schooling began to overwhelm and reorder the purely educational function (see, e.g., Sorokin [1927] 1959; Warner et al. 1944).

If we concentrate on the majority of students, rather than the academic elite, we might conclude that the transmission of school knowledge, beyond basic reading and calculating, is neither the most important nor the most successful activity of the school. This would not be a happy conclusion for many teachers, of course.

Even so, the curriculum and the transmission of school knowledge are important for sociologists to examine for several reasons.

- Mastering the school curriculum has practical importance as a means of gaining a livelihood for many people, and it also influences the way many people do their work.

  School knowledge is, in this sense, building material for much work, particularly in the upper reaches of the occupational structure. Of course, it is not the only influence on work activities. Even top professionals rely on practical knowledge gained at work as much as they rely on school knowledge, but school knowledge is a backdrop for gaining this practical knowledge and often it is also a direct reference point. Architects could not build without some knowledge of geometry and architectural design principles, even though building also requires selling clients on ideas and nurturing the loyalty of a work group.

- In every modern society, the subjects taught in school are, partly as a consequence of their importance in the upper reaches of society, surrounded with an aura of special significance.

  The prestige of the ideals represented by school knowledge is very often a factor in what people think they should be paying attention to. People may refer to school knowledge when they are trying to make a serious point or are communicating with high-status people. Recognition in the curriculum is a form of cultural status, and it exercises a kind of charismatic authority in society. For this reason, struggles for "symbolic centrality" can be fierce. People who advocate "intelligent design" against evolutionary theory, for example, do so partly because they want their intellectual views to be included in the symbolic center of society.

✗• The mental operations involved in learning curricula—reading, interpreting, calculating, making inferences, comparing, analyzing—are important features of adult life, whether or not adults remember much specific content from their school lessons.

From this perspective, the content of lessons is less important than the practice of engaging in mental activities connected to learning that content. To go a bit further, we might argue that without relatively difficult course content, it is unlikely that these mental capacities could be developed as well. Every report assignment requires students to learn skills of research and organization. Similarly, whenever a person draws an analogy or offers an alternative interpretation, those capacities of mind have been supported by earlier efforts to master course content in English or history classes. People could not make convincing arguments, in all likelihood, without prior training in examining a variety of perspectives and bringing evidence to bear on them. Efforts to solve problems in a step-by-step way may reflect processes learned in solving the problems posed in philosophy or math classes. Most people could not readily construct spreadsheets, for example, without considerable prior training in logical reasoning. Learning how to learn is another important part of the experience of schooling. A lawyer might not remember many of the cases discussed in her classes on torts, but she almost certainly remembers how to research cases and how to construct arguments on the basis of legal reasoning.

• Even those who do not carry the torch of secular learning into their adult lives do often find something of considerable value in their school lessons.

This value may come from a variety of sources—from a useful knowledge of correct grammar and pronunciation, or a way of dissecting arguments, or a flash of insight brought on by a particular work of art. A good many people gain the lifelong habit of reading through school; they become frequenters of libraries and subscribers to periodicals. It is also true that the high cultural aspirations underlying the teaching of the core subjects of curriculum can serve as an inspiration to teachers and their students. To be well educated is, ideally, to appropriate a cultural heritage—and, therefore, to be in a position to use and even advance some part of that heritage.

Are these contributions as important as the contributions that schools make to shaping students' attitudes, orientations, and conduct (socialization) or to selecting winners and losers in the "stratification sweepstakes" (social selection)? Possibly not, but they are important enough to warrant our full attention as part of our study of schools and societies.

CURRICULUM MAKING AND CURRICULAR CHANGE

Why do children study English, math, basic science, and social studies in elementary school, rather than, for example, business principles, computers, ethics and morality, and American ethnic cultures? Or, even further afield from current practices, why not ask students to study car maintenance, popular music, consumer awareness, and science fiction? Asking these kinds of questions leads us to the heart of the social organization of school knowledge.

One common way of looking at the school curriculum is to say that science and mathematics are taught because they explain why things happen in nature, and the humanities are taught because they represent the best that has been thought and said about human life. Ideas about increasing our understanding of our own and other cultures usually provide comparable justification for social studies. These ideas echo the famous lines of the nineteenth-century English educator and essayist Matthew Arnold ([1869] 1949), who argued that certain subjects and works must be taught because they represent "the best that has been thought or said" and therefore produce a fully humane reason, a mind that is not only logical and efficient but also fully open to experience and sophisticated in judgment.

However appealing these sentiments may sound (I confess they still sound appealing to me), they are not too helpful as a guide to how materials actually come to be represented in school curricula. They fail to provide an accurate historical grounding and suggest a greater stability than in fact exists. School curricula are not very stable over time. New subjects like social science gain ground over time, and old subjects like Greek and Latin decline in importance. Nor, except in scientific fields, are the major lessons taught very stable. Current judgments of intellectual value are not always very similar to past judgments, and outside of a handful of enduring authors, such as Homer and Shakespeare, the reputations of authors and works rise and fall continuously. Even the popularity of these authors is largely restricted to one cultural region, Europe and North America.

To understand the rise and fall of subjects and authors, it is necessary to move away from the philosophical humanism of Matthew Arnold to the less high-minded but more illuminating realms of social and cultural history. In fact, a few generalizations can be derived from the study of curricular history. This study suggests that a few factors have been most important in shaping the school curriculum:

- The purposes of different levels of schooling at the time they were first organized
- The interests and ideals of social actors (such as the upper classes and the state) insofar as they have been involved in curriculum making
- The formation of a ladder structure with each level defined relative to the others
- The shift from "moralistic" to "developmental" approaches as a basis for conceptualizing the relationship between children and society
- The changing composition and aspirations of student populations at different levels of schooling
- The maneuvering of rival bands of educators (and citizen support groups) for influence on the basis of their commitments to particular curricula

Each of these factors will enter into my discussion of the rise and fall of school subjects. By paying attention to these influences, sociologists can help to explain why boundaries exist between academic and nonacademic subjects, how these boundaries have been adjusted over time, why new subjects come into being, and why subjects gain and lose popularity over time.

Three Early Institutional Sources of Curriculum

Our contemporary schooling systems did not originate in any single curricular purpose. Instead, three distinct purposes played a role: rudimentary learning, liberal learning, and occupationally specialized learning. Each purpose was linked historically to a distinct level of schooling, and then migrated between levels as the current ladder structure of schooling, running from preschool to university, was constructed.

Primary schools, which have existed sporadically since ancient times, were developed to teach basic literacy and morality. Primary schools were often in the hands of private individuals or religious authorities. As Chapter 2 explained, our modern state-based mass systems of primary schooling had their origins in the nation-building efforts of eighteenth-century modernizers. Efforts to encourage loyalty to the king or emperor were important, but the original purposes also focused on the teaching of morality and basic skills of literacy.

Secondary schools have a connection to the ancient world of Greece and Rome. The "liberal arts" ideal played a decisive role. The term "liberal," in this context, means "freedom of the mind" and is opposed to the "servility" of following others blindly. The purpose of the ancient academies was to develop young men (they were all men) who were fit to govern by exposing them to the accumulated wisdom of great minds (and to challenge them constantly to defend their ideas), thereby preparing them for the active life of the citizen (Marrou [1948] 1982).

Universities developed primarily as institutions for professional skills training for men from the upper reaches of society. In the East, advanced training for occupational specialization existed since the time of the Han Dynasty (200 BCE). The ultimate aim of professional training was preparation for state service. In the West, universities were a product of the later Middle Ages. They grew up as bands of students surrounding renowned scholars and teachers (Rashdall [1895] 1936). Their underlying purpose was to provide training for a "learned profession"—that is, the clergy, medicine, law, or the teaching of these subjects. In this sense, the medieval universities were, at least in large measure, vocational in orientation. Yet, they were not narrowly vocational. Because they trained young men for "liberal" as well as "learned" professions, they were based on the premise that specialized occupational training should be founded upon and constantly supplemented by broad "liberal learning."

These three institutional sources of curriculum originally had little relation to one another. In the course of creating the integrated ladder structure of primary, secondary, and higher education that we have today, state elites and educational reformers mixed the originating purposes of the three levels in new ways. Perhaps most important, primary education absorbed some of the inspiration of the liberal arts ideal. The ideal of occupationally relevant education, associated with the medieval university, spread to secondary schooling, where it has coexisted, sometimes uneasily, with a continuing liberal arts emphasis. Universities have continued to offer a mix of liberal and occupational options, but occupational curricula retain the stronger influence. Since the rise of the German research universities in the nineteenth century, the pursuit of new knowledge through research has become an important third element in the curriculum of universities, together with occupationally specialized and liberal education.

Liberal learning. We can say that the ideal of liberal learning has had the most diffuse influence on public schooling in the West. The ideals of liberal learning have helped to differentiate public and nonprofit private schools from trade schools, because they assert that education is about more than becoming skilled at a trade or profession. The ideal can be described as aristocratic in origin, both because its ultimate purpose was to prepare students for governance and because, at the time this ideal originated, only aristocrats had the leisure to study.

In the West, the liberal arts tradition was born in a dispute between the two kinds of teachers, orators and philosophers, who prepared upper-class students for public life (Marrou [1948] 1982; Kimball 1986). For the orators, rhetoric and related disciplines were the culmination of education, because they prepared students for the active public life of the citizen. For the philosophers, scientific studies were most important because they provided training in the truths underlying the appearances of everyday life. Our contemporary humanities derive from the first tradition; our contemporary sciences derive from the second.

In the Hellenistic world created by the conquests of Alexander the Great, liberal education gained many of the connotations that it has today. The old dispute between orators and philosophers as to which form of knowledge was superior achieved a kind of curricular compromise in the Hellenistic world, with both branches included among the *septem artes liberalis* (seven liberal arts). The great contrast continued to be between "liberal" and "servile." Education for servility both in the Hellenistic and Roman worlds included all subjects intended to prepare students for a practical trade, rather than for political or cultural leadership.

The ideal of a liberal education, therefore, had from the beginning a status-defining character. But this status-defining character lost its association with the aristocracy, once it was adopted by modernizing states and their educational ministries. It is therefore wrong to reduce the social meaning of the liberal arts curriculum to its status-defining elements. Under the influence of the modernizing founders of mass secondary schooling, "liberal culture" provided an image, theoretically available to all, of what it means to have a fully formed consciousness. Indeed, it is one of the great triumphs of democratic societies to have aspired at times to make this "education for the freedom of the mind" available to everyone interested, rather than limiting its availability to the governing elite alone.

Modern curricular organization: Standard time blocks. The liberal arts have provided a content base and philosophical ideal that remains resonant to this day, but the temporal structure of curricular organization changed once the tutorial and academy forms declined. Before the era of mass schooling, master teachers worked with students in a much less formal and much more personal way. They read works with a single student or a few students, but not in a strictly ordered way and not always during strictly prescribed periods of time.

(This pattern persists in graduate schools and in the undergraduate colleges of Cambridge and Oxford in England.)

The contemporary arrangement of the school day into standardized blocks of time based on a sequence of subject matter is a product of the Protestant Reformation and, even more so, of the transition from elite to mass schooling under public control. The first appearance of the term "curriculum" occurs in Glasgow, Scotland, in 1633. Thus, the creation of deliberate order, each subject in its own time block, comes less from classical sources than from the ideas of the Protestant reformers. "Curriculum," writes David Hamilton, "was to Calvinist educational practice what discipline was to Calvinist social practice" (Hamilton and Associates 1980:14).

Public bureaucracy, with its need to coordinate large numbers of students and teachers, shows a strong affinity for more standardized forms of ordering and classifying knowledge (Goodson 1988; Bidwell and Dreeben 1992). Subject matter divisions, along with spatially separated classrooms and standard time units, are the kinds of highly organized, rule-bound practices that bureaucracies thrive on (Bidwell and Dreeben 1992:359). It is not surprising that the rise of urban mass schooling under public bureaucratic control led to far greater organization and monitoring of subject matter divisions.

The Conflict of Ideologies in the Modern Period

Many sociologists assume that the way in which a society selects and classifies knowledge "reflects both the distribution of power and the principles of social control" in the society (Bernstein 1971:47). This brings out an important point: the curriculum does not exist as an emanation from the brows of wise men; it has been created through the struggles of contending interests and ideologies. During the modern period, the main contenders have been educational researchers, wealthy idealists (and their educational allies), the business-oriented middle classes, government bureaucrats, and activists connected to social movements.

The cultural historian Raymond Williams (1961) suggested that curricular changes have reflected the relative power of these contending groups. Table 4.1 schematizes Williams's argument.[1] When considering arguments about the social bases of curriculum, it is important to avoid the pitfalls of overly schematic thinking: although specific groups can be identified with a particular vision of curricular priorities, not everyone in a group lines up in the same way—and when one vision becomes popular it attracts support from many different quarters.

In the era of mass public schooling, democratic reformers (led by patrician elites and liberal professionals) became interested in disseminating the advantages of liberal arts education more broadly in the population. Through the diffusion of liberal culture, reformers thought that democratic polities could retain the virtues of the ancient Greeks and Romans, while building popular support for elevating cultural standards. By contrast, the "occupational specialist" ideology carried by the business-oriented middle classes encouraged training for marketable occupational skills. Not surprisingly, when the commercial and industrial wing of the middle class has exercised the greatest power over curriculum, the study of

TABLE 4.1
A typology of educational ideals and policies

Social group	Ideology	Educational policies
Aristocracy/gentry	Liberal arts	Nonvocational courses in arts and sciences emphasizing cultivation, "character," and judgment
Merchants/upper professional classes	Occupational specialist	Higher vocational and professional courses, providing training for marketable skills
Democratic reformers (e.g., liberal professionals, some union leaders)	Liberal arts expansion	Expansion of "upper class" education, providing opportunities for the cultural development of all students
State planners	Utilitarian/technocratic	Lower vocational and semi-professional courses providing training for positions needed in the economy and state

SOURCE: Adapted from Williams (1961).

science and mathematics has usually been favored over humanities studies, because the former have practical applications to business and industry. Another influential group in the era of mass public schooling, government technocrats, have usually favored using curriculum as a mechanism of manpower planning, linking educational qualifications to labor market opportunities. Social movement activists have entered the picture episodically to demand better representation in the curriculum of the groups whose interests they represent.

The primary school curriculum has been shaped by the struggle between "traditionalists" who want to focus on mastery of a few core subjects, and "progressives" who want to encourage development of the "whole child." The first view has had more appeal to the conservative, business-oriented middle classes, while the latter has appealed more to intellectuals and liberal professionals. In the higher grades, the main contest has been between supporters of liberal arts/academic education and supporters of occupational/vocational education. These two groups have struggled against one another for institutional space in both secondary and higher education. The curriculum has changed to accommodate these two ideas about "the good society": a democratic ideology that has demanded equality and opportunity based on a common and "elevated" academic curriculum, and a utilitarian ideology that has emphasized individual ability and practical, job-relevant training. The mixing of the two ideals is evident especially in secondary education, where academic and vocational coursework developed at first as separate tracks, but now often exist as "core subjects" within broader courses of academic or vocational study.

In higher education, liberal arts education has become increasingly marginalized; it is now associated mainly with subordinate fractions of the middle class (e.g., artists, writers, social reformers, and teachers). Specialist education has, by contrast, triumphed among the dominant fractions of the middle class: business people, managers, and higher-status professionals such as engineers and lawyers (Bourdieu 1984). The role of technocratic planners in government has been to support the preferences of the business-oriented middle classes, and to broaden and rationalize the state's interest in manpower planning. They have introduced new occupational curricula into secondary and post-secondary education and linked support for educational programs to labor market projections.

Thus, the modern curriculum stands as a compromise between the major interests summarized in Table 4.1. Across the world the movement has been toward: (1) teaching basic skills in the lower grades to prepare students for academic studies, while adding other subjects that can contribute to the more complete development of the child; and (2) the retention of some liberal arts requirements in secondary school, together with the addition of vocational courses and tracks for all but an academically oriented minority. The United States, Japan, and a few other countries are exceptions, insofar as occupational specialization tends to begin later—and the liberal arts tradition remains strong both in secondary schools and during the first two years of university education. In most of the world, however, the market value of occupational education has become thoroughly ascendant both in secondary and higher education, and the status and personal development values of liberal education have been in retreat (Brint et al. 2005).

The Rise and Fall of School Subjects

The conflict of ideologies forms the background for the study of the modern curriculum, because it tells us where support has existed in society for the restructuring of secondary and higher education that has occurred in the modern period. Before we examine the contemporary structure of curriculum in countries around the world, it is important to see how much has changed over time in the subjects students are required to study—and to begin to think about more specific influences on the rise and fall of school subjects.

Consider the American secondary school curriculum. Like characters in a play, school subjects enter and depart the stage. Classical language and literature plays a leading role in the early acts, only to retire into the shadows in more recent acts. Physics, calculus, and foreign languages make a later entrance, are relatively silent at first, and then slowly swell into important supporting actors before falling back again into the shadows near the curtain's fall. "Life adjustment" subjects like money management and personal appearance come in as the stage is set for the twentieth century and are more or less dispatched during the Cold War period only to reenter in an altered form in the 1960s. If we take a long enough view, we can see a great pageant of comings and goings. What is true for subjects is true at an accelerated rate for authors, ideas, and theories.

How do sociologists explain these dramatic goings-on? The most important part of the explanation has to do with the reigning definition among educators about the purposes of a particular level of schooling. As understandings of these purposes change, so do the subjects in the curriculum. These understandings, in turn, often reflect the influence of new types of students entering the institution and the aspirations that these new students bring with them.

Primary school subjects. Primary schools at first focused on teaching basic literacy through reading and writing, and the reinforcement of moral precepts (Tyack and Hansot 1982). The integration of literacy training with moral instruction is clear in the readers and themes assigned by educators. As David Tyack and Elizabeth Hansot observe of nineteenth-century textbooks in the United States:

Above all, the textbook writers were careful not to confuse the pupils with wishy-washy morality. . . . The rules were always clear: *Never Drink, Never Smoke, Work Hard, Tell the Truth, Obey Authority, Trust Providence.* . . . [Student themes from the mid-nineteenth century] suggest how deeply the absolutist morality of the evangelical movement became interwoven with a work ethic and ideology favoring the development of capitalism. (Tyack and Hansot 1982:27–8)

From these rudimentary beginnings, many new subjects entered the primary school curriculum. These subjects include mathematics and science, arts and physical education, and social studies.

In some countries, including the United States, arithmetic already had strong advocates by the end of the eighteenth century. Because it was seen as having the power to "improve the logical and rational faculties of the mind," it was closely associated with ideas of civic virtue, and it was championed by such leading figures of the American republic as Thomas Jefferson and Noah Webster (Cohen 1982). France and Prussia also adopted arithmetic early. Here arithmetic was associated with ideals of rationality championed by the "enlightened despots" Napoleon and Frederick the Great. The addition of arithmetic to the primary school curriculum illustrates how children in the Age of Enlightenment were already coming to be seen as capable of enhanced mental development. However, it was not until the middle of the nineteenth century that most countries adopted mathematics as part of their primary school curriculum. The widespread adoption of mathematics was associated with the rise of industrialization (Kamens and Benavot 1992), and educators' sense that math could provide a practical benefit to children entering jobs in industrializing economies.

Science lagged behind arithmetic as a primary school subject, partly because it represented a threat to countries with national religions. The conflict between the Catholic Church and science created particular resistance in Catholic countries. However, by the middle of the nineteenth century, it too had entered the primary school curriculum in many Protestant countries, where it was seen as "adding to the capacities of individuals to be loyal and productive citizens" (Kamens and Benavot 1992:113).

Excellence in the arts and physical activities were among the classical ideals of education, and Swiss-German educators considered them important for all students from the beginning of mass primary education in Western Europe. But Anglo-American educators did not at first include them in primary school curricula, because they had a narrowly book- and morality-based view of essential educational subjects. However, beginning around the turn of the twentieth century, the image of children underwent a decisive change. No longer expected simply to conform, children were redefined under the influence of educational and cognitive psychologists as maturing organisms with developing capacities in many areas of mental, expressive, and physical life.

In the 1890s, G. Stanley Hall and others in the "child-study movement" led a campaign to rethink the curriculum "along the lines of a natural order of development of the child." The goal was to derive a curriculum "in harmony with the child's real interest, needs and learning patterns." Only then would the natural power within the child be "unharnessed," rather than constrained by strict discipline and dull recitals of facts typical of the teacher-centered school (Kliebard 1986:28). Under this new cultural understanding, public school-ing came to include aesthetic and physical education, as well as traditional subject matter. The new conception also led to much more attention to the socio-emotional development of children, and the use of trained professionals to counsel troubled children. The new "child development" philosophy gained a foothold in the schools for the first time in the 1920s, when many more students were beginning to enroll in secondary schools, and pri-mary schools were consequently shedding their identity as institutions providing only ru-dimentary and terminal instruction for the young.

One other change is noteworthy: history has ceded part of its share of the curriculum to social studies. This transition is far more recent, beginning in the 1960s and 1970s. Where history once focused on key personalities and conflicts in the rise of national power, social studies focuses on the groups and institutions that make up society—and sometimes also on comparisons with the styles of life and practices found in other countries. One contro-versial theory to explain this change is that the symbols of national power become less im-portant as the bureaucratic state ceases to depend on charismatic sources of authority. For the sociologist David Kamens, this transition represents the passing of the "heroic phase" of nationalism:

> The construction of national myths, symbols and monuments has given way to the prosaic
> work of institution-building. . . . As the sacredness of the "nation" declines, learning facts,
> names and dates becomes a less compelling task of schooling. [Moreover], other cultures
> and societies gain credibility as objects of analysis, from [which] useful lessons may be
> drawn. (Kamens 1992:77)

No doubt, this theory fails to account for wartime influences. War invariably increases the centrality of historical exposition related to the events and symbols of national power.

Secondary school subjects. Understandings of the purposes of secondary schooling have changed, in an almost mirror-like fashion, with the changing composition and aspirations of the students they have enrolled. With these changing understandings have come changes in curricular emphases. Martin Trow (1961) identified three major stages in the transfor-mation of secondary schooling in the United States: (1) secondary school as a preparatory institution for elites, (2) secondary school as a terminal institution for the majority, and (3) secondary school as a preparatory institution for the majority (who are going on to higher education). Each transformation, Trow argued, brought a new curricular emphasis in secondary schools.

When secondary schools played a preparatory role for only a small fraction of the age group, classical subjects predominated. Secondary education was education for member-ship in an elite status group with esoteric knowledge unrelated to occupational success. Those so trained could recognize one another as part of the educated elite. In the West, these classical subjects included Latin, Greek, philosophy, history, and geography, together with a smattering of mathematics and science; in the East, they included classical literary texts, calligraphy, and religious philosophy. Secondary schools became less singularly wedded to liberal arts as they became less elite. Although a residue of aristocratic humanism remained an important force in Europe, many of the subjects that were central to the classical curriculum (particularly Latin, Greek, and philosophy) declined greatly in centrality with the expansion of the number of students attending secondary schools.

As soon as large numbers of middle-class students were admitted to secondary schools, pressures built for a more "modern" curriculum. This modern curriculum included courses in rhetoric and English composition, French, German, Latin, astronomy, chemistry, physics, geometry, trigonometry, calculus, political economy, moral science, mechanical drawing, and bookkeeping (Labaree 1988, chap. 6). The transition from the "classical curriculum" based on Greek and Latin to a "modern, comprehensive curriculum" occurred much earlier in the United States than in Europe, more or less simultaneously with the introduction of the first public high schools in the 1820s and 1830s (ibid.). The comprehensive curriculum was closely associated with the democratic and utilitarian premises of American schooling, and it remained far more popular in the United States and in the Americas generally than in Europe or the rest of the developing world (Kamens, Meyer, and Benavot 1996:138).

Science began to be introduced in Europe in the mid-nineteenth century in lectures and demonstrations, but it did not become a formal part of the curriculum until the 1870s. The introduction of scientific education at higher levels of schooling was resisted by those with a strong status culture stake in the humanistic education of gentlemen. The classical curriculum held out longest in countries like England, in which higher education, as a preserve of the landed aristocracy and "learned professions" was highly independent from the modernizing interests of the state. It was not until the turn of the century that scientific specializations became available to secondary students in Britain, and then only in a limited way (Keeves 1986).

Throughout Europe, new curricular options in secondary schools, based on national languages and literatures or math and science, were introduced in the early twentieth century, but the classical curriculum retained its centrality until the great expansion of European secondary education in the 1950s and 1960s (Kamens et al. 1996:131). At that time, the two new curricula became increasingly popular: one for students concentrating in arts, humanities, and modern languages, the other for students concentrating in mathematics and science. The math and science curricula reflect not only their capacity to bring the natural world under human control, but, in particular, their perceived relevance to the workings of the industrial world. The secondary school curriculum remained academically oriented for the majority only so long as university enrollments were low and secondary schools enrolled relatively small numbers of students. Once secondary school replaced primary school as the terminal phase of schooling for most students, strong pressures developed to differentiate academic and vocational tracks. In the United States, the pressures to create vocational tracks began to build before the turn of the century,[2] but these pressures were largely resisted until the first decade of the twentieth century, when tens of thousands of new immigrants entered high schools. Demographic change pushed curricular change. By the 1920s, American high schools showed a "tremendous differentiation" of course offerings (Kliebard 1992), with educators everywhere arguing that easier, more practical work be offered to students not bound for college. In the 1920s, five out of six schools offered curricula in industrial arts and/or commercial subjects (Powell et al. 1985). So-called life ad-

4 students that were not college bound

justment curricula were also particularly popular during this period, with students study-ing such nonacademic subjects as how to manage money, personal hygiene, and dating be-havior (Cremin 1961, chap. 9). Explaining these changes, the educational historian David Cohen wrote:

> American educators quickly built a system around the assumption that most students didn't have what it took to be serious about the great issues of human life, and that even if they had the wit, they had neither the will nor the futures that would support heavy-duty study. (Powell, Farrar, and Cohen 1985:245)

In Europe, the change in the number and composition of students attending secondary schools led also to an elaboration of vocational options. The tradition of elite secondary schooling was modified to include practical training in one of two ways; in some countries, new vocational schools were established; in other countries, a lower tier of vocational stud-ies was added to existing academically oriented institutions. But the effect was essentially the same: schooling became less about preparing a cultivated elite for positions of power and more about preparing middle- and lower-income students for a wide array of jobs.

After World War II, secondary schools in the United States took on a new role as "mass transfer" institutions to colleges and universities. Vocational subjects once again dimin-ished in importance, because they served little purpose for the growing number of students who were now planning to attend college. Yet, because higher education remained relatively exclusive, more demanding academic subjects such as foreign languages, physics, and cal-culus also gained stronger support. In the United States, Cold War planners' needs for lan-guage specialists, area specialists, and physical scientists no doubt played an important role in the promotion of these subjects by the schools. The continued growth in higher educa-tion enrollments eventually led to declining enrollments of high school students in the most challenging academic subjects as well. Foreign languages, physics, trigonometry, and calcu-lus all enrolled a smaller proportion of secondary school students in the 1960s and 1970s than they had in the immediate postwar years (Goodlad 1984; Ravitch 1995). For the most part, only private schools and public schools in affluent suburbs continued to support them. With the shift from elite to mass higher education, colleges and universities became more an extension of secondary school than a distinctive prize for the academically tal-ented. Taking demanding coursework in secondary school was no longer necessary to suc-ceed in the growing number of nonselective higher education institutions.

In the early 1980s, social scientists and educational reformers began to note the impor-tance of rigorous curricula for persistence and success in college (see, e.g., Alexander et al., 1982). As a result, momentum grew to restore a more rigorous curriculum in the second-ary schools. The number of advancement placement tests given each year has doubled in the last decade and now stands at over 1 million (College Board 2005). Even so, fewer than one in five students completes an advanced science class, fewer than 15 percent of students take calculus, and fewer than 10 percent take four years of a foreign language (NCES 2004, Tables 21-1, 21-2, and 25-2). These percentages are rough indicators of the size of the stra-tum of students competing for admission to selective colleges and universities.

In Europe, class-divided secondary education persisted through the 1960s. In most countries, government planners have attempted to reduce class divisions and to increase higher education enrollments, but they have not done so by eliminating vocational programs from secondary schools. Instead, vocational qualifications proliferated (Stern, Bailey, and Merritt 1997), and policymakers have added new pathways from vocational programs to post-secondary institutions. This process has gone furthest in France, where a near-majority of university students now enter universities from the *lycées professionels*, which specialize exclusively in vocational and technical programs. But nearly every European country has found ways to improve access to higher education for secondary school graduates of vocational programs. Even in Germany, some graduates of the "dual system" are now admitted to universities and polytechnics.

Multiculturalism: A Case Study of Curricular Change

Course content—the specific authors, works, interpretations, and theories taught—naturally changes at a much faster rate than the broader subject matter requirements. Some have suggested that changes in course content reflect changing power relations in society (Bernal 1987). Such writers see a correspondence, for example, between periods of widespread social criticism and the popularity of the Romantic poets in English literature courses, and between feminism as a force in the political environment and gender as a popular topic in social studies courses. Of course, such correspondences do sometimes exist; curriculum can be a mirror to important movements in society and culture. However, movements of thought should not be reduced to a strictly social causation. New insights are often as important as new social conditions. Therefore, a complex attitude is required: we must be aware of the forces in the social environment that influence the reception of ideas, while also appreciating the particular insights of the ideas in play.

Studies of changes in course content are rare (see, e.g., Graff 1987). Given the limitations of existing evidence, I will not attempt to provide a comprehensive treatment of course-level changes in the curriculum. Instead, I will examine a single, dramatic case of course-level change: the rise of multiculturalism in the humanities and social studies curricula. In doing so, I hope to illustrate some of the ideas that sociologists use to understand curricular change at the course level.

The debate over multiculturalism. Henry Louis Gates, Jr., one of the protagonists in the debate over multicultural curricula, wrote:

> Few commentators could have predicted that one of the issues dominating academic and popular discourse in the final [decades] of the twentieth century—[at the same time as] the fall of apartheid in South Africa [and] communism in Russia . . . —would be the matter of cultural pluralism in our high school and college curricula and its relation to the "American" national identity. (Gates 1992:xi)

Indeed, this debate was conducted at a high emotional pitch. On one side of the controversy were defenders of traditional great works and traditional "Western values"; on the other, an alliance of minorities, women, literary theorists, and postmodern philosophers who wanted to revise the established canon of great works and, sometimes also, the scheme of identifications and values they saw as underlying it. One side argued for the permanent relevance of the classics of Western thought, the other at a minimum for the inclusion of new voices, particularly those of women and minorities.

The word "multiculturalism" barely existed in public discourse before 1980 (see Bernstein 1994:4), and the influence it has exercised in a period of less than three decades must be considered nothing short of phenomenal. As the conservative thinker Nathan Glazer (1997) remarked, with a tinge of resignation, near the end of the 25-year conflict over "multiculturalism": "We are all multiculturalists now."

The transformation of the curriculum is clearest in primary schools. Students now read African and Asian folktales, and they have their imaginative passports stamped with the impressions of countries throughout the world, rather than only those of Europe and America. The customs of many different lands are studied. Walls and hallways are decorated with pictures of famous women and famous men of non-European ancestries, as well as famous white men.

Many high schools have added minority and women writers to their English curricula, and some have introduced new "world literature" courses. High school textbooks have moved away from a concern with the doings of presidents and prime ministers and begun to play up the contributions of women and minorities. They have also frankly recognized the failings of American society in the integration of racial minorities (Fitzgerald 1979).

The scope of change is also impressive in higher education. A survey of some 200 institutions showed that one-third of colleges and universities had multicultural general education requirements, either as part of required core courses or as part of college distribution requirements (Levine and Cureton 1992). One-third of the schools also offered coursework specifically in ethnic and gender studies. More than half of colleges and universities reported efforts to introduce multicultural themes into departmental offerings. These efforts were largely in the nature of "add-ons" to existing curricula, rather than replacements for traditional courses (ibid.:29). At the same time, entirely new courses have been added, some of which attract a larger number of students than traditional courses. In recent years, the fastest-growing course offerings in university history departments have been Asia, Latin America, and Eastern Europe; Western European and English history courses have declined in number (Frank, Schofer, and Torres 1994).

Three Multiculturalisms

Despite the prevalence of multicultural course content, the debate over multiculturalism continues to be intermittently rancorous, largely because three very different visions all go under the same label.

The most moderate of these visions—which I will call "Multiculturalism 1" —is culturally expansionist. It is essentially another name for cultural pluralism, albeit a cultural pluralism with a stronger interest in the representation of women, minorities, and Third World cultures than earlier versions of cultural pluralism. This variant of multiculturalism advocates exposure to different cultures, but it does not necessarily advocate a devaluation of works traditionally considered to be classics of Western thought. This is the conception to which many well-established advocates of multiculturalism, such as Henry Louis Gates, Jr., self-consciously subscribe.

"Multiculturalism 2" adds a controversial dimension; it is culturally relativistic in addition to being culturally expansionist. Its advocates see all cultures as having a similar validity, and they therefore protest against an education based on the rank ordering of texts or cultures. For this second form of multiculturalism, the ideal curriculum would draw more or less equally from the works and histories of many different peoples.

The distinctive characteristic of "Multiculturalism 3" is ethnocentrism. It seeks to show the oppression of subject groups, and it is self-consciously critical of dominant groups, whose privileges are often interpreted as the result of the exploitation of subordinate populations. Most writers and educators associated with this form of multiculturalism are not really multiculturalists at all; they usually want to focus more or less exclusively on their own particular group and have very little interest in exploring the cultures of other groups. Afrocentrists, "critical race theorists," and some feminist scholars fit into this group (see, e.g., Asante 1987). The experience of minorities is seen as separate and antagonistic to the dominant order, not part of a common human experience.

The best solution might be to dispense with the term "multicultural" altogether and to substitute in its place three terms: cultural expansionism, cultural relativism, and ethnocentrism. These clearer terms would not solve another problem, however: the tendency of writers to collapse more moderate forms of multiculturalism into less moderate forms. Thus, the cultural relativist asks, "If we want to expand the representation of groups in the curriculum, why shouldn't we also treat each one as equal in importance?" And, the ethnocentrist asks, "If every group is essentially equal in importance, why not focus on the special contributions of the particular group with which I personally identify?"

Explaining the success of multiculturalism. Glazer (1997) argued that multiculturalism grew out of the failure of academic culture to integrate African Americans. Although it is clear that the alienation of minorities has fueled movements of collective cultural assertion, Glazer's is not a satisfying explanation. Multiculturalism is, after all, on the agenda throughout the world, not just in the United States.

Multiculturalism can also be interpreted as simply the successful stretching of the traditional cultural value of pluralism to include those who have, for no particularly good reason, been left out up to this point. It is true that ideals of cultural pluralism have been a part of the American creed since the eighteenth century (see, e.g., de Crevecoeur [1783] 1912), but opposition to cultural pluralism has usually been a more important influence in public schooling. The forces of "Protestant-entrepreneurial nation-building" have usually wanted to "Americanize" members of subordinate groups, not to recognize and appreciate their cultural differences. For this reason, it is too easy to say that multiculturalism triumphed because it resonated with American society's underlying support for pluralism.

For a more complete answer, it is necessary to look for the deeper social and economic currents that have been working under the surface controversies—and the mobilization of movements for change. Demographic factors are prominent among these deeper currents.

Both the university and the larger society have changed dramatically in their demographic composition since the 1950s. American society is still mostly white, but the white proportion dropped from 90 to 75 percent between the censuses of 1950 and 1990, and by 2000 white males made up only about a third of the population. Most immigrants no longer come from Europe, but from Asia and Latin America, and the fastest-growing groups are the three major racial and ethnic minorities (Riche 1991). Colleges and universities have also changed in ways that make both the student body and the professorate look more like that larger society. The new academic generation—those who have not yet reached the tenure stage—is more than 40 percent female and almost 17 percent minority (Finkelstein, Seal, and Schuster 1995).

Economic globalization was another important supporting current. Since the end of the Cold War, we have seen the full internationalization of capitalist exchange and the internationalization of the business elite. Japanese, European, and North American firms are tied through complex networks of joint ownership, joint capitalization, and franchising. Financial markets have become fully internationalized among the richer powers, with changes in one stock exchange affecting the other major exchanges. Travel and tourism continue to grow as a part of the global economy, and other forms of international exchange from scholarly conferences to food and musical influences also become commonplace. It is not surprising under these circumstances that multiculturalism has triumphed perhaps most quickly in elite institutions, including the once-Anglophile private boarding schools. These schools, like other elites spheres, have become internationalized over the past several decades. They admit increasing numbers of international students, and the parents of native-born students see, through their own experience, that their children will be living in a more globally integrated world.

Social movement mobilization is necessary to build latent forces into an active political force. As Gates (1992) observed: "Ours was the generation that took over buildings in the late 1960s and demanded black and women's studies programs and now, like the return of the repressed, has come back to challenge the traditional [curriculum]" (19). Indeed, much of the impetus behind multiculturalism can be found in the political protest and identity politics of the 1960s. "Consciousness-raising" through appeals to group pride (e.g., "black is beautiful" and "gay pride") became a central part of political mobilization during that period. Many of the battles between multiculturalists and their critics reminded outside observers of nothing so much as a superannuated version of Sixties generational conflict with older, but still angry, protesters confronting stooped, but intellectually unbending, defenders of the existing curricular canon of great works.

Legal requirements provided a final lever of change in some states and institutions. By the late 1980s, many U.S. states (beginning with California in 1987) added principles in their curriculum guidelines requiring "multicultural and gender-fair" perspectives (Rosenfelt 1994). Universities also changed their general education requirements to include representation of women and minorities in the curriculum. The institutionalization of multiculturalism in official policies lent legitimacy to efforts to take account of the contributions and experiences of minorities and women.

Given the demographic changes in all industrialized countries, it seems very likely that multicultural curricula will become more important in the future. But the extent of change could depend on how strong the countermobilization of educated whites and religious conservatives becomes. Highly educated parents indicate less interest than others in making multiculturalism a priority in schools: According to David Sikkink and Andrea Mibut (2000), "The status of the highly educated creates an interest in a rigorous academic regimen, which they see as in conflict with making diversity education a priority" (p. 41). It is possible that a coalition of the highly educated and religious conservatives could attempt to reassert the centrality of the Western cultural tradition, augmented perhaps by stronger appreciation for the significance of Christian texts in Western history. If so, schools in the future would see more clashes in the "culture wars" that have already divided religious and secular Americans for more than a generation (Hunter 1991). One point is clear: sociological study of the curriculum cannot ignore the influence of social movement activism, whether of the right or the left. A highly mobilized minority, especially if it has allies in political power, can often prevail over an unorganized majority.

GLOBAL STRUCTURES OF SCHOOL KNOWLEDGE

I have discussed the historical rise and fall of subjects. Now I will turn attention to the contemporary structure of curriculum, both in primary and secondary schools. Given the many changes in school subjects and curricular emphases over time, it is both notable and surprising that a high level of agreement exists throughout the world today about the major subjects that should be taught in primary schools and even about the amount of time that should be allotted to these subjects. Agreement is much less complete in secondary schooling, where divisions between academic and vocational orientations remains sharper, and governments have worked out a variety of accommodations between the two.

Global Curricula in Primary Schooling

The core subject areas in official primary school curricula throughout the world are national languages and literatures, math and science, social sciences, art and music, and physical education. Moreover, the amount of time allocated to these subjects is surprisingly similar throughout the world. Language instruction—reading, writing, and grammar—is the dominant curricular category in primary education; virtually everywhere in the world about one-third of class time is devoted to language instruction. Almost all of this instruction is in the national or official language. Mathematics and science have increased somewhat in importance over time, with about 20 percent of class time going to these subjects in the prewar period and closer to 25 percent now. In virtually all countries, math is given at least twice as much class time as science. Most of the remainder of class time is given over to arts and music, social science, and physical education. The time allocated to these subjects has been remarkably stable: approximately 25 percent of class time in the pre-World War II years and 25 percent of class time 60 years later (Benavot 2005; Cha 1992; Meyer, Kamens, and Benavot 1992).

Table 4.2 shows the amount of time governments have expected teachers to spend on primary school subjects in two time periods, the 1980s and the 2000s. Note that official government expectations do not necessarily correspond to how time is actually allocated in classrooms, where off-task activities, such as settling down, "fooling around," and teacher

TABLE 4.2

*Percentage of total instructional time allocated to subjects
in primary school curriculum, 1980s and 2000s*

	Grade 1	Grade 2	Grade 3	Grade 4	Grade 5	Grade 6
LANGUAGE						
1980s	38.4	37.6	34.5	32.6	31.4	30.7
2000s	38.6	37.8	34.7	31.4	27.8	26.2
MATHEMATICS						
1980s	19.4	19.4	18.7	17.8	17.3	16.7
2000s	19.9	20.1	19.4	18.7	18.0	17.5
SCIENCES						
1980s	4.3	4.6	6.4	7.3	7.9	8.8
2000s	3.6	3.7	5.3	6.1	7.2	8.7
COMPUTERS/TECHNOLOGY						
1980s	.3	.4	.4	.3	.4	.3
2000s	.9	.8	1.0	1.2	1.6	1.9
SOCIAL SCIENCES						
1980s	6.1	6.4	7.9	9.7	11.0	11.7
2000s	5.8	5.9	7.4	9.4	10.5	11.6
RELIGIOUS/MORAL EDUCATION						
1980s	5.7	5.8	5.5	5.4	5.2	4.9
2000s	4.8	4.6	4.5	4.3	4.1	3.9
AESTHETIC EDUCATION						
1980s	9.8	9.9	9.5	9.3	8.6	7.6
2000s	12.6	12.5	11.9	11.6	10.5	9.7
PHYSICAL EDUCATION						
1980s	7.1	7.1	7.1	6.6	6.1	5.7
2000s	6.8	6.7	6.6	6.5	6.1	5.8
SKILLS/COMPETENCIES						
1980s	5.6	5.6	6.4	7.0	7.7	8.7
2000s	3.3	3.3	3.8	3.7	4.7	4.6
ELECTIVES/OPTIONS						
1980s	3.4	3.3	3.5	3.1	3.5	3.9
2000s	5.0	5.1	4.7	5.1	5.4	5.3
NUMBER OF COUNTRIES						
1980s	83	84	83	83	81	77
2000s	124	124	125	125	127	125

SOURCE: Benavot (2005, Table A3, Table 5).

digressions sometimes crowd out instruction. But these data do provide a good sense of official priorities.

Although the similarities across the world are impressive, some atypical patterns do stand out. Teachers in Latin America and the Caribbean are expected to spend somewhat more time on foreign languages than are teachers in most other parts of the world. And teachers in both Latin American and Central Europe are expected to stress mathematics (Benavot 2005). Western European and North American countries have emphasized aesthetic and physical education more than countries in other regions, while Asian countries have given somewhat more institutionalized attention to moral education (Meyer, Kamens, and Benavot 1992:51).

Time spent in other subject matter spheres is not as consistent throughout the world. Religious education takes up one-sixth of class time in the Middle East and Islamic North Africa, but has no role in Eastern Europe and only a minor role elsewhere. Whether religion is taught in the schools seems to depend primarily on whether the country has an established national religion (ibid.:77).

In the past, global variation in primary school studies has been closely associated with economic development. Higher levels of development were associated with more time allocated for arts and mathematical education, and less time spent on practical education (ibid.:56). The causes of these associations are perhaps self-evident, given the preparatory role primary education plays in developed societies and the importance of mathematical reasoning in industrial and commercial life. However, practical education is now in slow decline throughout the world, while the amount of time governments expect teachers to devote to "modern" subjects, such as computers and the environment, is increasing. More countries are also allowing students to choose among elective subjects for a small part of the school week (Benavot 2005). In this data, we see both the progress of technology and the progress of efforts to control it. We also see a minor trend toward the individuation of culture.

Researchers led by John W. Meyer and Aaron Benavot have been largely responsible for collecting these data on trends in curriculum organization. According to their theory, the modern system of school knowledge is based on a vision of modernity, originating in the West, linking individual development and social progress. This vision of modernity has become institutionalized on a worldwide basis in large part because developing states have modeled their curricular structures on those of the core states in the world economy. In addition, the core states have taken an active role in helping to diffuse their ideals about the purposes of schooling and methods for realizing these purposes. To be accepted as a fully modern state, according to this theory, national leaders feel the need to adopt Western notions of how to link "rational persons" to "progressive nation-states" through the medium of mass schooling.[3]

Is the global system of school knowledge rooted in an abstract vision of modernity, as Meyer and Benavot argue? An alternative explanation might very well emphasize the practical politics involved in emulating the curriculum of core powers in the world economic system, or the cognitive advantages of Western-style curricular organization. But one point cannot be disputed: Meyer, Benavot, and their associates have done an enormous service by establishing just how similar curricular designs across the world are at the primary school level.

Global Variation in Secondary School Curricula

Comparative studies of secondary school curricula are more limited than those of primary school curricula, partly because much more variety exists at the secondary level. Changes in curricula are also frequent, as governments experiment with ways to motivate students to continue with their studies beyond the secondary level (cf. Kamens and Benavot 2006). Nevertheless, it is clear that essentially the same subject matter core exists at the secondary level of schooling as in primary school. Throughout the world, this core consists of language instruction, mathematics and science, and social studies. Moral and religious instruction, arts and music, and physical education are also prevalent, but of secondary importance. A great contrast exists between the European and American models, however. The European systems include many more occupational specialty programs. Until recently, the academic programs in Europe and East Asia were more demanding than those in the United States, but that is less true today, because governments in Europe and Asia have reduced secondary school requirements in order to encourage more students to continue their studies, while more U.S. students haven chosen rigorous courses of study to improve their chances for admission to selective colleges and universities.

In the developing world, secondary curricula show both the impact of Western influence and in many cases a special interest in science and mathematics curricula, which are privileged for their potential to contribute to industrialization. Specialized math and science programs have grown significantly in Asia and sub-Saharan Africa. These regions have been dominated by political elites committed to strategies of rapid industrialization (Kamens et al. 1996:134–5).

Academic streams. In the old core states of Europe, academic students are divided into separate curricular tracks, or specializations. These can be reduced to three major types: classical, "modern" humanities or social sciences, and math and science. Students enrolled in these curricular specializations take a different mix of coursework.

1. The classical curricula, which are now very much in decline, concentrate on classical languages (Greek and Latin), other languages, and a limited amount of science and math. Instead of social studies, they generally include history and geography. Philosophy is often required as well.

2. Modern humanities specializations focus on modern foreign languages and literatures. Languages and literature courses outnumber math and science courses at a ratio of approximately two to one. Classical languages and philosophy are generally minor or nonexistent parts of these curricula. As in primary schooling, social studies have grown in importance, compared to the older subjects of history and geography. In Sweden, social science has replaced humanities as the major "humanistic" specialization. Cultural studies are incorporated, but the emphasis is on such subjects as economics, policy studies, and sociology (Skolverket 2005).

3. Math and science specializations are a mirror image of the modern humanities curricula. About twice as much time is spent on math and science as compared to languages and literature. In addition, social science tends to be of minor consequence, with hours that would otherwise be allocated to social studies absorbed by additional courses in the math and science core. Math and science curricula are everywhere associated with economic progress. For this reason, math and science concentrations have become more prestigious than classical curricula even in many core European countries like France (Neave 1985), and they have been more prestigious in Japan from the advent of mass secondary schooling.

Secondary school curricula in Western Europe and East Asia were once renowned for their rigor. In recent years the number of compulsory hours and units has decreased signifi-

TABLE 4.3

*Compulsory courses in the first upper secondary year for university-bound students,
France and Japan, 1980 and 2000*

France 1980s	Japan 1980s
French (5 hours)	Japanese (5 credits)
History/geography (4 hours)	Social science (3.5 credits)
Modern language (3 hours)	
Physical science (3.5 hours)	Science (6 credits)
Biological science (2 hours)	
Mathematics (4 hours)	Mathematics (6 credits)
Physical education (2 hours)	Physical education (5 credits for boys, 3 credits for girls)

France 2000s	Japan 2000s
French (4.25 hours)	Japanese (4 credits)
History/geography (3.25 hours)	World history (4 credits)
Modern language (2.5 hours)	
Physical science (2.75 hours)	Science (2 credits)
Biological science (1.25 hours)	
Mathematics (3.5 hours)	Mathematics (3 credits)
Physical education (2 hours)	Physical education (3 credits)
Civic education (.25 hour)	
Second language (varying hours)	
1 elective course (varying hours)	1 or 2 additional course(s)[a] (varying credits)

SOURCES: Holmes and MacLean (1989:77, 209); Ministry of Education, Culture, Sports, Science, and Technology (MEXT 1998, Chart 3); Syndicat National des Enseignements de Second Degré (SNES 2004). Information on France provided by Christine Musselin. Information on Japan provided by Takehiko Kariya and Satorishi Ogawa.

[a] In Japan, additional required courses, to be taken at some point in upper secondary school, include arts, foreign language, home economics/home life, and information studies.

cantly, however, as governments sought to encourage entry into higher education. Table 4.3 summarizes the compulsory courses required in the first year of upper secondary school for university-bound students in two countries with national curricula, France and Japan, during the 1980s and the 2000s. In the 1980s, both countries had tougher required courses than the United States, and they also permitted a more limited range of electives for first year students. Electives were common in the final years of secondary school in France and Japan, but they had a very different meaning. They were used to prepare for secondary school leaving and university entrance examinations in the students' major field or fields of concentration. For example, a Japanese student expecting to specialize in science at the university would typically devote 80 percent of his or her electives to additional science courses (Holmes and McLean 1989:208). In recent years, the trend has been toward reduced course loads, both in France and Japan. Both governments have explicitly attempted to reduce what the Japanese call "curriculum overload"—the number of school subjects students are required to learn (Benavot 2005).

In the United States, separate curricular specializations do not exist, and a comprehensive curriculum dominates secondary schooling. English, math, science, and social studies each takes up one to two periods a day in both junior and senior high school. Math and science (if grouped together) become more prominent in the curriculum than language instruction as early as junior high school. Arts and physical education are somewhat more likely to be electives, but most students take them. Because the American government has taken a special interest in a rigorous ensemble of courses, rather than individual courses, it is difficult to know how many students take the most demanding courses. We do know that in the 1990s, less than a quarter of American students took physics in high school, and only about 10 percent studied calculus (Ravitch 1995). College-bound students were likely to have had at least two years of foreign language training, but only about 10 percent studied a foreign language for four years (NCES 1994).

In the view of critics, the elective system in American high schools has sometimes made secondary schooling look more like shopping malls than focused learning environments. Indeed, it is not uncommon to find a hundred or more courses listed on the books at the larger American high schools (Powell, Farrar, and Cohen 1985). American students can often choose electives from a large menu on the basis of casual interest as much as academic intentions. Lightweight courses, such as marriage and family and personal finance, continue to be popular with non-college-bound students. More college-bound students are, however, taking rigorous courses, a trend strongly supported by government policy analysts (Adelman 1999; Horn, Kojuku, and Carroll 2001). The number of advanced placement exams given each year has doubled to over 1 million in just a decade (College Board 2005).

Vocational streams. Academic preparatory curricula are, as a general rule, far more standardized than curricula leading out into the job market. Indeed, it is very difficult to generalize about secondary school vocational curricula across national boundaries, because of the tremendous diversity in these curricula and because of the frequent changes in occupational streams and options. European secondary schools offer as few as a handful of vocational programs, or as many as many dozens. In addition, as many as four levels of vocational qualification can be found in European schools: basic, intermediate, upper secondary (or "maturity"), and tertiary. Furthermore, some countries have introduced distinctions based on breadth or specificity of vocational qualifications. Thus, the English General National Vocational Qualifications (GNVQ) are broader than the workplace-based National Vocational Qualifications (NVQ).

The system of Scottish National Certificates (NC) represents an extreme in the custom-tailoring of vocational training. Through the 1980s and 1990s, National Certificates were available in 3,000 modules, each representing 40 hours of study. Students could use NCs to prove qualifications for particular occupational functions. In 1999, the NCs were replaced by an equally complex system, but one with a tendency to culminate in somewhat longer courses of study. Similarly, in France a wide array of vocational options is offered, accompanied by dozens of qualifying degrees. These include separate streams for commercial subjects (such as accounting and finance), human service subjects (such as social welfare work), and manual subjects grouped by processes (repair) or materials (metallurgy, electronics).

In other cases, governments have organized vocational education into a small number of national programs. The Swedish case provides one illustration. The 14 national vocational programs offered in upper secondary schools include: child care and recreation, business administration, construction, foods, electrical programs, energy, handicrafts, health care, hotel and restaurant management, industry, media, natural resources, technology, and vehicles. Like students in the academic programs, students in vocational programs are required to take courses in core subject areas (English, arts, physical education/health, math, general science, social studies, Swedish, and religion) (Skolverket 2005). The national programs are designed by the Swedish ministry of education, and the same course content is offered throughout the country. (The industry and technology programs focus on local occupational demand.) As in most other European countries, students in Sweden are able to transfer from vocational programs in secondary school to advanced occupational training programs in universities. In England, General National Vocational Qualifications are also awarded in 14 occupational fields, including several of the same fields covered in Sweden (but with more choices in arts and business specialty areas).

In the United States, the situation is more complex than in countries with national curricula, because variation exists from state to state and even from school to school. Most high schools now include vocational courses as options in a single comprehensive curriculum. The only way to determine which students are concentrating on occupational preparation is to look at transcripts. Those who take 20 percent or more of their classes in occupationally related coursework are often categorized as "vocational students." Vocational students usually sample a range of occupationally related coursework, rather than concentrating in any one area (as they would in Europe). They may also take quite a bit of nonacademic coursework that is not related to preparation for specific jobs (i.e., courses in typing, personal finance, or shop).

In schools serving working-class communities, a wide range of occupational courses (such as cosmetology, machine repair, and bookkeeping) may be offered, while hardly any vocational courses may be offered in schools serving upper-middle-class communities. Schools serving working-class communities may allocate more than two-fifths of their teachers' time to nonacademic courses, while schools serving affluent communities may allocate less than 15 percent of their teachers' time to them. This had led to concerns about the consequences of curricular "tracking" in poor communities, and occasionally to complaints about the few options for nonacademic students in affluent communities.

In recent years, many countries have experimented with new ways of integrating academic and vocational studies. In 1994, the Japanese introduced an "integrated" vocational-academic high school pathway that combines career development and university preparation. Enrollments in specialized colleges offering higher diplomas in industrial, commercial, and other vocational fields represent one-third of higher education enrollments in Japan. Further Education (FE) colleges in England offer a combination of academic and vocational training for students interested in obtaining vocational credentials following the end of compulsory schooling. In France, vocational education is threaded throughout the system, beginning in lower secondary schools. In Germany, the "dual system" has been continuously upgraded in intellectual content to the point that some now consider the apprenticeships comparable to the U.S. two-year college associates degree (Stern, Bailey, and Merritt 1997). Indeed, universities and polytechnic institutes in Germany have started to accept some "dual system" graduates. Even in the United States, long an advocate of academic secondary and higher education, integrated programs have shown some modest growth in secondary schools—and occupational programs now attract three out of five students in both two-year and four-year colleges and universities (Brint 2003; Brint et al. 2005).

SCHOOLING'S LIMITED SUCCESS IN CULTURAL TRANSMISSION

At one time, secondary schools were content to transmit knowledge in a few key subjects to children of the propertied and educated classes. Now they attempt to transmit relatively demanding knowledge content to all adolescents. By historical standards, the ambition of schools must be judged as impressive. But contemporary schools have had only limited success in transmitting the lessons of the curriculum to the majority of students. This limited success suggests that exposure to course materials may be more important for socialization, social selection, and practice in basic mental operations than it is for imparting specific cultural content.

Although most students fail to perform well on national educational assessments, this does not mean that they are necessarily lacking in motivation or intelligence. In fact, judging by IQ scores, today's young people are smarter than their parent's generation. James Flynn, a New Zealand researcher, discovered "massive gains" in IQ scores over time in 14 countries he studied (Flynn 1987). Flynn's findings should lead us to wonder whether kids are not smarter than they let on in tests—or perhaps whether our expectations for performance are unusually high by historical standards.[4]

The Nonintellectual Interests of (Most) Students

The acquisition of school knowledge is undoubtedly very important for the top 15–20 percent of students, who are competing for slots in selective colleges and universities. It is particularly important for the top 1 or 2 percent of students, who will become the scholars, intellectuals, and scientists of the future. These students develop a significant degree of mastery of course materials. Their successes are also important for society insofar as everyone profits from the knowledge and energy of this academically oriented stratum. Locating students with high-level intellectual potential is, of course, one of the main purposes of schooling, and schools succeed very well in these efforts.[5]

Schools are much less successful in transmitting knowledge to the majority of students, however. The facts are clear enough. Students do not remember much course content after the final test has been given (Collins 1979:17–9). What little they do remember continues to erode at a fast rate. When most students look back on their schooling, most people have vague memories of liking or not liking particular instructors, but they remember very little of the material covered in class and cannot clearly identify concrete knowledge they acquired.

Nor do the majority of students consider learning to be the most memorable feature of the schooling experience. Instead, they speak more often of the opportunity to socialize, to see and to be seen with their friends. Moreover, in the status system of adolescent society, academic success ranks low. Athletic and dating success are more highly esteemed, and in some national studies membership in the academic elite actually ranks lower than membership in a gang as a badge of status (Tye 1985). Even college students largely reject intellectual identities. Those who take a real interest in their coursework sometimes do not retain intellectual interests after they finish their schooling. Without support from a larger circle of friends and acquaintances, the intellectual interests developed in school tend to fade (Feldman and Newcomb 1969; Pascarella and Terenzini 1991, chap. 12). In many countries, including the United States, judgments of admirable qualities in others are much more likely to focus on economic success or moral character than on cultivation and intellect (Lamont 1992).

Declining Performance?

The apparently poor performance of American students on national educational assessments became a cause for widespread alarm in the 1980s. Diane Ravitch and Chester Finn's *What Do Our 17-Year-Olds Know?* (1987) was one of a number of studies and commission reports that called attention to the troubled state of learning among American high school students during the period. Ravitch and Finn reported average scores in the failing range on two national assessments: American high school students scored, as an average, only 54.5 percent correct in history, and only 52 percent correct in literature. Among the dispiriting findings for educators: only one-third of the students could identify the date of the Civil War within a 50-year time frame, and only about the same proportion could identify the theme of George Orwell's novel *1984*. Other reports of the era showed that 30 percent of high school seniors could not locate Great Britain on a map (Sowell 1992). Many studies showed evidence that student performance, particularly in secondary school, declined significantly between the mid-1960s and the late 1970s, a consequence in part of less demanding curricula.[6]

Assessments like these have been given on a national basis to fourth, eighth, and twelfth graders for some 30 years now through the National Assessment of Educational Progress (NAEP). The results of many of these assessments have improved in recent years, and it is particularly heartening that the gap between white and minority students is closing on most of the tests (Loveless 2003; Whitehurst 2005). Much of this improvement is due to the increasing proportion of students taking more rigorous curricula (Horn, Kojuku, and Carroll 2001). Yet, performance levels have remained low for the majority of students, if examined in light of the tests' standards of academic competence and proficiency. For example, in the 1990s approximately 40 percent of American students at all grade levels scored at a level "below basic competence" in mathematics, and only 20 percent in any grade level reached the "proficiency" level that the assessment's governing board considered within reach of *all* students (Ravitch 1995:79). These proportions have not changed significantly over the last decade (Whitehurst 2005).

A Manufactured Crisis?

Were American schools failing badly in the 1970s, or was evidence of failure exaggerated as part of a policy agenda determined for other reasons? This is a bitter debate—with contemporary relevance.

The debate originated in the heated atmosphere of the late 1970s, when policymakers believed that the poor performance of the American economy could be attributed, in part, to the defects in public schooling. Just as the Japanese economy appeared to be outperforming the American economy ("Japan is Number One" proclaimed one book of the time), so Japanese schools appeared to be outperforming American schools. In the formulation of the presidential commission report, *A Nation at Risk* (National Commission on Excellence in Education 1983), American society had declared "unilateral educational disarmament" by failing to insist on high standards from its public schools.

Were the "facts" behind the calls for reform true? Critics, led by the educational researchers David Berliner and Bruce Biddle, called them into question. In their book, *The Manufactured Crisis* (1995), Berliner and Biddle argued that very few national assessments showed a true decline in scores between the 1960s and the 1980s. The often-noted decline in scores on the SAT beginning in the late 1960s were real—but probably represented a difference of only about six to nine correct answers—on a test of 138 items. More important, the number of students taking the SAT increased during the period. "Sharply larger numbers of students from the lower-achievement ranks in high schools, from minority groups, and from poorer families began to take the SAT during those years. . . ." They argued that other tests, such as the National Assessment of Educational Progress (NAEP) showed essentially no change during the critical period, and some showed improvements for students from disadvantaged and minority backgrounds. "Surely this should have been a matter for rejoicing, not alarm," observed Berliner and Biddle (p. 20).

Berliner and Biddle were no less critical of international comparisons. Above all, they faulted these comparisons for failing to take into account differences in *opportunity-to-learn*. Not all eighth graders, for example, were exposed to algebra. It would be unfair to fault them for poor performance on items requiring knowledge of algebra. When American schoolchildren were compared to students in other countries who studied the same level of materials, they performed as well or better than these students. Berliner and Biddle also criticized the tendency of critics to focus on average scores and to ignore levels of dispersion around the mean. The real crisis in education, they argued, was the lack of attention to the educational needs of students from the poorest states and communities. True reform, they said, would aim to improve the educational opportunities available in these disadvantaged places.

Berliner and Biddle suspected that champions of educational vouchers played an important role in creating what they called "the manufactured crisis." If public schools were failing to educate students, advocates of vouchers could argue that students should be given an opportunity to choose private schools, using public funds to support these choices.

The Manufactured Crisis set off a firestorm of protest among the advocates of standards-based reform, and Berliner and Biddle were themselves criticized for slanting the evidence. Lawrence Stedman (1996) provided perhaps the best review of the evidence. Stedman concluded that overall well-controlled studies show high levels of stability in test scores between the 1950s and 1980s. However, more than one test showed declines in the 1970s. Only part of the decline in the SAT, which began in the 1960s, could be attributed to demographic change in the test-taking population. Perhaps half of the decline could be attributed instead to changes in schools or the value American society placed on learning. Stedman faulted Berliner and Biddle's data on "opportunity-to-learn," too. American students who took algebra in eighth grade did perform as well as Japanese and Taiwanese students, but it turns out that they were a far more selected group and studied much more algebra in eighth grade than did the Japanese and Korean students in the sample.

This controversy reminds us that political commitments can sometimes lead researchers (usually subconsciously) to collect and interpret data in ways that support their position. A complete picture of the evidence from the 1970s indicates that standards-based reformers had some valid reasons for concern, but that they also used data selectively, relied on flawed data, and exaggerated the dimensions of the "crisis." The same problems plague educational debate today.

Multiple-choice recall testing usually produces a bleak picture of how much students know. This "background knowledge" is not irrelevant to learning—most good students have lots of background knowledge that they can accurately recall. But it is by no means the only important end product we might want to measure. More authentic assessments provide evidence about whether students can interpret relatively sophisticated reading passages, solve challenging math problems, and produce cogent essays. We might also want to know if students have developed an enthusiasm for learning, or whether it has simply become an unrewarding "grind" for them. It may be true that the public schools were mislabeled as "failing" in the 1970s and 1980s, and that they are mislabeled as "failing" today. But they still have a long way to go if they hope to be truly successful in the ways that count for building engaged, reflective, deep-thinking adults.

International Comparisons

Do American students perform less well than students in other countries? Although differences exist among students from different countries, the evidence suggests that the "1066 and all that" effect is relevant throughout the world. It is hard work to master school knowledge, and the payoffs for this hard work are by no means self-evident to many students. School knowledge is not especially memorable to most students whether they are attending classes in Bangkok, Paris, Johannesburg, Cleveland, or Kyoto.

International educational assessments have been conducted since the mid-1960s in the core subjects of reading comprehension, mathematics, and science and also in a few other subjects. These international assessments provide evidence about how well U.S. students are performing in relation to students in other countries. Special precautions have to be taken when interpreting the findings of these studies, because a variety of technical problems limit the comparability of scores across nations (see, e.g., Husén 1979; Inkeles 1979; Noah 1987). For example, not all countries have sampled their schools adequately or looked at an exactly comparable set of students. If variables such as the poverty rates in different countries or actual exposure to tested materials are not included in the reporting of results, the gross results may be misleading to compare (Berliner and Biddle 1995:51–63). Perhaps most important, performance on standardized tests may not reflect the actual knowledge of students very well. Anthropologists, such as Jean Lave (1988), have shown that students are able to solve relatively complex problems when they are engaged in activities with their friends that are of immediate significance. The same students who give random, uninformed responses on tests may show a quick grasp of mathematics when they are cutting carpets for their families' businesses, or playing number games with their friends. Thus, the ability to express knowledge may be highly contextual.

We should be careful, then, not to make too much of these results. Nevertheless, if the findings are taken with the proper number of grains of salt, they can be used as indicators of how well schools are doing in transmitting school knowledge. They show that no country is consistently superior to all others across all subjects and age levels. Instead, the high and low performers in these assessments shift quite a bit from test to test, from grade level to grade level, and from year to year. Students in some East Asian countries (notably, Japan and Korea), some Western European countries (such as the Netherlands), and some Central European countries (such as Hungary and the Czech Republic) have performed well on most tests of mathematics and science. Students in some Western European countries (including England, the Netherlands, and Sweden) have achieved high scores in tests of reading literacy. Interestingly, students in countries with relatively high average scores often also show relatively little dispersion around the mean. This indicates that teachers in these countries are succeeding in pushing up performance among better students without leaving most other kids in the dust. We see this particularly in countries such as Japan and Korea, where math teaching is unusually effective.

Not surprisingly, the largest differences are between students from industrialized countries and students from developing countries. International assessments for grades 4, 6, and 8 show that students from high-income countries average in the 500 to 600 range on tests of mathematics, science, and reading, while students from low-income countries average 100 to 150 points lower (Ravitch 1995:83–9; NCES 1996). In some developing countries, like Burkina Faso, scores suggest essentially random responses to test questions. The international results also show a wider range of scores within developing countries, reflecting in part the very large differences in quality between urban and rural schools (Lockheed, Fonancier, and Bianchi 1989).

The mathematics and science tests perhaps bear the closest scrutiny. Mathematics and science are important subjects for technologically advanced societies. They are the best single indicators of students' ability to succeed well in higher education. In addition, the problems of translation that plague test constructors are minimized in tests of math, simply because the symbolic language of math is universal.

On the 1999 test of eighth grade mathematics, students from Singapore, Korea, Taiwan, Hong Kong, Japan, Belgium, the Netherlands, the Slovak Republic, Hungary, Canada, Slovenia, the Russian Federation, Australia, and Finland had significantly higher scores than students from the United States, and students from several of these same countries also showed higher mean scores in science than American eighth graders (Hiebert et al. 2003). However, American eighth graders had significantly higher mean scores than students in a majority of the countries participating in the assessments. On tests of mathematics and science, students from several East Asian societies (notably, Japan, Korea, Singapore, and Hong Kong) have usually outperformed American students by a considerable margin, and students from some Central European countries (notably, Hungary and the Czech Republic) have also generally scored higher than American students. Even in the highest-scoring countries, national averages typically fall below 67 percent correct on these tests. The amount of variation in scores within countries is always higher than the amount of variation in scores between countries. This shows that no country has a monopoly on high- or low-scoring students, and all countries must struggle to narrow test-performance gaps.

Variation between classes, races, and regions is higher in the United States than in most other countries, largely because inequality is higher in the United States than in most other countries. Even so, the findings of international assessments, far from demonstrating the dismal state of learning in the United States, actually support those who think that American students are not performing poorly compared to students in other countries. The average American eighth-grade student reads well by international standards, knows more about government and public affairs, and is above the international mean in math and science. Levels of proficiency are not as high as we might like—and particularly not for those at the bottom of the national distribution—but it is certainly time for our national educational scolds to stop berating American students for trailing far behind the international competition. They are much closer to leading than to trailing the pack.

Explaining Cross-National Differences in Test Scores

Country differences in average scores can be explained by a combination of factors internal and external to the schools. The important factors internal to the schools are the kinds of materials that are taught and the methods used to teach them. A well-focused curriculum, which requires exposure to higher-level knowledge and skills but does not attempt to cover too many topics, can lead to better average performance (NCES 1996:37–8). Teachers who have sufficient time to plan lessons; teachers who talk to other teachers about their lesson plans; and teachers who incorporate problems connected to students' everyday life experience are also more likely to have a positive effect on learning. (See also the discussion of teaching and learning in Chapter 8.) Individual classrooms and even whole societies can vary on these dimensions. The biggest differences between American students and students from higher-scoring countries is that American students are asked to cover too many topics and have fewer opportunities to learn more demanding curricular materials than their counterparts in East Asia and Central Europe. Teachers do not let lessons "sink in" through repetition and practice (Berliner and Biddle 1995:54–8; Hiebert et al. 2003).

The most important factors outside of the schools are parents' investment in their children's education, the availability of alternatives that draw children away from schooling, and the consequences for later life of school achievement. If parents invest time, effort, and money in their children's education, they will tend to encourage good performance. If regular times are set aside for homework and few alternatives exist either in informal socializing or work opportunities as a distraction from study, more students are likely to concentrate effectively on their schoolwork.

Finally, a strong link between school performance and later opportunities also focuses attention on school. When children do not feel that schooling is relevant to their futures, they will not take schooling as seriously. Again, both individual classrooms and societies can vary in these ways. Figure 4.1 provides a graphic representation of the forces I have described as relevant to different levels of performance on international mathematics and science assessments.

The example of Japan indicates that schools are most effective in transmitting school knowledge when students have the opportunity to learn demanding materials, have strong support for schoolwork from their parents and teachers, and have strong incentives to achieve.

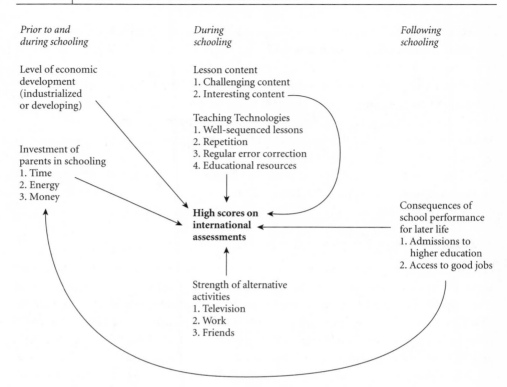

Figure 4.1   Model of National Achievement in Educational Assessments

Academic focus is partly a result of taking demanding courses. In the United States, educators define a "rigorous curriculum" as four years of English, three years of foreign languages, four years of math (including precalculus or higher), three years of science, three years of social studies, and at least one honors (or "advanced placement") class. About one in five high school graduates completes this rigorous curriculum. Researchers have shown that those who complete a rigorous curriculum attain significantly higher grades and have better persistence in college than students who have taken less demanding curricula (Adelman 1999; Horn, Kojuku, and Carroll 2001).

Academic focus is also an important influence on international test results in the developing world. Cuban children, for example, score significantly higher than children in other Latin American and South American countries on mathematics and reading assessments. These results persist even after controls for socioeconomic status are introduced. Martin Carnoy and Jeffrey Marshall attribute the success of Cuban schooling to the efforts of the government to provide the necessities of life to all families and to prevent children from being involved in activities that pull their focus away from school. The socialist government in Cuba, for all its faults in economic development and human rights, has created a greater equality and better social services than can be found elsewhere in Latin or South America. Cuban children consequently have few of the problems of hunger, homelessness, or poor health that are found in other developing countries. They have little or no access to such activities as drug use, gang involvement, or child prostitution. The government effectively restricts each of these activities. Neither classroom nor schoolyard fighting is tolerated, and this turns out to be a frequent and important disruption in some other Latin and South American countries (Carnoy and Marshall 2005).

National Test Performance and Economic Competitiveness

Newspaper editors and politicians like to use international comparisons to sound alarms about the threat that poor school performance poses for the future prosperity of the country. These kinds of warnings have in the past been effective for focusing attention on schools, but they are not based on sound arguments (see Collins 1979, chap. 1; Blaug 1987; Berliner and Biddle 1995). The truth is that international comparisons tell us next to nothing about the likely trajectory of national economies.

Consider just two counterfactuals: it is well known that the performance of American high school students took a nosedive in the late 1960s and throughout the 1970s (Ravitch 1995, chap. 3). Yet by the time these mediocre students began to take leading roles in the economic life of the country, the economy was humming along quite nicely. The United States rebounded from the economic slump of the 1970s in large part because a devalued dollar made U.S. industries more competitive in those industries in which it had lost market share (Berliner and Biddle 1995:92). The schools were responsible neither for the slump nor for the rebound. By contrast, the economic troubles of the 1970s occurred under the watch of the supposedly diligent students of the 1950s. In fact, it is unlikely that scores on standardized tests of school knowledge have any clear relationship to how well or poorly advanced capitalist economies perform. The evidence suggests that swings in economic performance have causes all their own.

Support is also missing for the related notions that more knowledgeable citizens will necessarily raise the level of public discourse, or that they can raise the tone of popular culture. If political discourse has deteriorated into dishonesty and manipulation—and who can say with certainty that it is worse now than in some earlier eras?—this has much more to do with the vastly increased scale of government and partisan organizations and the gulf that consequently separates average citizens from their leaders. Similarly, if public taste has fallen (and, again, who can confidently say that it has?) this must surely have more to do with the capacity of the media to stimulate the eardrums and galvanize the eyeballs.

In short, if the results of international comparisons cause people to feel dissatisfied with the state of knowledge transmission in the schools, they should justify improvement as desirable in its own right, rather than because it will magically boost competitiveness, strengthen democratic government, or improve public taste. It can be argued that better learning is desirable because learning alone has the capacity to improve students' faculties of logic and judgment and to deepen their experience of the world of thought. If a commitment to learning for the sake of understanding can eventually be shown to have positive spillovers in other arenas of economic and civic participation, so much the better.

Scores on international assessments are not completely unrelated to national economic circumstances, however. In all likelihood, they do tell us something about the level of mobilized human energy, or industriousness, in a society. It follows that international comparisons may be more important for developing countries than for industrialized societies. In the latter, work effort becomes part of the fabric of organizational life; it is regulated by what Max Weber called "the iron cage" of rules and incentives and, in some companies, also by technological surveillance. Better retention of school knowledge surely would not produce modernized economies overnight in the developing world. But together with political stability, wise use of resources, and relief from debt burdens, it might help to place the upcoming generation of students on a better footing to meet future development goals.

CONCLUSION

The transmission of knowledge is the most obvious purpose of schooling. To investigate the transmission of school knowledge, it is necessary to examine how subject matter materials become part of the curriculum and how successfully these materials are transmitted to students.

Contemporary structures of school knowledge originated in three separate interests: the state's interest in providing rudimentary literacy training, the aristocracy's interest in preparing its offspring to govern, and church and professional interests in reproducing occupational specialists. These were the important historical bases, respectively, of primary, secondary, and university education. Over time, primary schooling has broadened to encompass a wider range of mental, expressive, and physical capacities; secondary schools have become divided between academic tracks leading to the university and occupational tracks leading (in most cases) to the job market. Many polities have encouraged occupational qualifications to proliferate in both secondary and higher education, in order to encourage greater articulation between schooling and the labor market. Correspondingly, humanities and arts fields have become less important than science, technology, and business specializations.

In general, these changes reflect the growing importance of the utilitarian ideology of government planners at successively the higher levels of schooling. The changes are also closely connected to organizational developments (particularly the creation of articulated ladder structures linking primary, secondary, and tertiary schooling) and demographic influences (especially the increasing number of students moving from primary to secondary schooling and then on to higher education). Some "broadening" trends in the culture of the developed societies, such as the rise of "progressive" child development philosophies and increased sympathy for cultural pluralism, have also influenced curricular developments. Ideas about the well-rounded child have greatly influenced curriculum at the preschool and primary levels, and multicultural themes and sensibilities are making inroads throughout the world in the arts, humanities, and social studies fields.

Today, primary school curricula are very similar throughout the world. Most schooling concentrates on national language and literature and, to a lesser degree, math and science. The arts, physical education, and social science are also represented throughout the world, though they are not allocated as much time in the curriculum. Meyer and his associates (Meyer, Kamens, and Benavot 1992) have argued that this global curriculum structure reflects an originally Western, but now globally institutionalized, vision of modernity linking individual development to national purposes.

Secondary school curricula are far more varied. Except in a few East Asian and Anglo-American countries, the majority of secondary school students enroll in courses leading to vocational qualifications. Vocational students must take a number of traditional core subjects, however, during the course of their studies. European academic tracks feature earlier specialization between humanities, social sciences, and natural sciences as compared to American academic tracks. Until recently, vocational curricula channeled students directly into the labor market, while academic curricula channeled students into universities. The two tracks were sharply segregated and class-divided. In recent years, policymakers have created pathways from vocational programs into universities, and they have also experimented with new ways of integrating academic and vocational studies. The old distinctions between job training for the working classes and academic training for the middle classes no longer hold with the same force as before. However, elite tracks continue to exist in many countries, and these remain largely the preserve of affluent and highly educated families.

By historical standards, the capacity of contemporary schooling to transmit knowledge is impressive. In the early part of the twentieth century, fewer than 5 percent of Europeans even received an upper secondary education. Today, completion of upper secondary education has reached 80 to 90 percent in most countries of the developed world. Yet schools have not succeeded in bringing the majority of students to high levels of achievement. Only 15–20 percent of students in most industrialized countries show real proficiency in the mastery of school subjects. Students from industrialized societies tend to perform better than students from developing societies on these tests, but no countries consistently outperform all others. In general, American students score high on tests of reading comprehension, and East Asian and Central European students score high on tests in mathematics and science. In recent years, American students have begun to catch up in these subjects. Differences between countries largely reflect the greater opportunity students in East Asia and Central Europe have to learn more challenging and better-focused course material. Factors external to the schools also help to explain country differences in student performance. High levels of parental support for learning, the existence of regular times for study, and strong rewards in the job market for good school performance all contribute to better scores.

The results of national and international assessments have often been irresponsibly reported and used for political purposes. Contrary to many published reports, no convincing links have been established between a country's average score on international education assessments and its level of economic competitiveness, civic virtue, or public taste. Inaccurate and biased reports about student performance on international assessments have raised the level of public concern about schooling, but they have also misled many people about the true sources of economic and social problems.

SCHOOLS AND SOCIALIZATION

diff. types of socialization
socialization inside & outside
classroom.

The early nineteenth-century American school reformer Horace Mann observed that it is easier to create a republic than to create republicans (Mann, quoted in Cremin 1957:14). By this, Mann meant that the self-restraint and virtuous conduct that make representative government possible do not necessarily come naturally and must therefore be created by society's institutions, particularly by its schools. Mann's observation suggests the important role schools have long played in the socialization of children.

Sociologists use the term *socialization* to describe the efforts of the carriers of a society's dominant ways of life to shape the values and conduct of others who are less integrated into those ways of life. In schools, the teaching and administrative staff is the principal agent of socialization and students the socialized. (However, students can also try to socialize adults into the ways of student society—and some adults do end up adapting, at least in limited ways.)

The effort of school authorities to socialize students is undoubtedly one of the major activities of schooling, and it might be the schools' most important activity. Think how often students' attention and behavior is organized in school around the schools' ideas about acceptable conduct. Every time a teacher says, "I need your attention," she is implicitly socializing students to be responsive to authority. Every time she hands back a paper with a smile or a frown, she is socializing students to value work well done in the eyes of the school. The early sociologist Emile Durkheim ([1923] 1961) thought that the most important function of schooling in modern societies would be to develop habits of conduct. He argued that the schools should be organized to encourage students to build strong self-discipline, a capacity for attachment to groups, and sufficient autonomy for independence and creativity. Of these, Durkheim placed particular emphasis on self-discipline: "Indeed, what is most essential in character is the aptitude to exercise self-control, the faculty of restraint . . . that enables us to contain our passions and desires and to call them to order" (9). He thought the self-discipline required by study would be particularly important in democratic societies "because the conventional barriers which forcibly curbed desires and ambitions" in previous societies "have partly fallen away" (42).

Schools undoubtedly play a secondary role to families in socializing children. The more impersonal institutions of society cannot duplicate the powerful mix of emotional intimacy and consistent attentiveness typical of family life. Families create the capacity for trust and self-control out of which healthy egos develop. Even so, schools are organized to form personalities for a public world in which intimacy and attentiveness are not always in generous supply. Schools specialize in the creation of people who can adapt to impersonal work environments and who can pursue their interests with people who are neither kin nor close friends. Without lengthy exposure to the socializing environments of the school, most children would not be as well prepared as they are for adult life.

This chapter begins by describing the three types of socialization that take place in schools (behavioral, moral, and cultural) and then sketches the historical development of the schools' socializing role. The remainder of the chapter analyzes two distinct sites of socialization in contemporary schools: the classroom and the playground. By the playground, I mean all school spaces outside the classroom: the corridors, playgrounds, lunchrooms, and extracurricular activity rooms. Classrooms are the spaces in which lessons of industry and work-related achievement are principally taught. Playgrounds are the spaces in which friendships and coalitions are formed and broken, status hierarchies are expressed and challenged, and children learn to balance self-assertion and self-control in informal social life. If teachers are the primary agents of socialization in the classroom setting, the most popular boys and girls are the primary agents of socialization in these other school spaces.

THREE DIMENSIONS OF SOCIALIZATION

It is best to think of socialization as involving three dimensions: (1) efforts to shape behavior, (2) efforts to shape moral values, and (3) efforts to shape cultural styles. The differences in these dimensions become clearer when we consider how students who conform primarily on one of these dimensions are characterized. Students are described as "well disciplined" by authorities if they conform behaviorally, "good" if they are seen to conform morally, and "well adjusted" if they conform culturally.

1. *Behavioral conformity*. Training for behavioral conformity involves activities related to the body, its mechanical actions, and its instruments and adornments. In schools with strict disciplinary environments, students may, for example, be required to sit erect with their eyes on the teacher, to raise their hands before talking, to stay in their seats unless they are excused, to have their pencils sharpened at all times, and to have their textbooks with them in class. They may be subject to explicit dress and grooming codes. If students are punished for failing to comply with these requirements, the school is attempting to use its powers of control to socialize for behavioral conformity. Conduct is behavior regulated over a long period of time.

2. *Moral conformity*. Training for moral conformity involves activities related to the production of an internalized sense of "right action." Judgments of the goodness and badness of conduct are central in this domain, and they are typically based on the staff's advocacy of abstract virtues and values. Teachers may talk about the im-

portance of such virtues as honesty, tolerance, courage, hard work, or fairness. They may also assign reading materials that illustrate the consequences of not being guided by these moral virtues. At higher levels, more complex moral issues may be raised, involving the collision of two "goods" or finer judgments of others' actions. Clearly, training for behavioral and moral conformity overlap in practice. Most schools expect a movement from external discipline based on behavioral control to self-discipline in conformity with moral values. Nevertheless, it is possible to have a high level of behavioral conformity without much in the way of moral conformity, as the occasional cheating and sexual harassment scandals in military academies demonstrate.

3. *Cultural conformity*. Training for cultural conformity, or acculturation, is more a matter of learning approved styles and outlooks. In the better Parisian secondary schools, for example, students are expected to express themselves vividly, with memorable phrases and sharp wit (Bourdieu 1988). If a student makes a very witty remark in class, the teacher will smile in appreciation or attempt an equally witty riposte. By contrast, in secondary school in a Central European or Scandinavian republic, it may be more important for students to demonstrate conspicuous thoughtfulness: to probe beneath the surface appearances and to ask questions that get to the heart of a difficult problem. These styles and outlooks reflect the cultural logic of a particular group or time or place. It is, for example, reasonable to expect that centers of learning in cosmopolitan capitals like Paris will reflect the quick pace and brilliant surfaces of urban life, whereas those in relatively isolated regions show a gravity that frequently appears unduly stiff and reserved to urban sophisticates. Students of acculturation tend to be cultural relativists; they try to understand the social logic that produces distinctive cultural styles, but they do not usually think that cultural styles and outlooks have universal validity in every environment.

Even when schools emphasize all three types of conformity, they may be more successful in one area than others. For example, military cadets are required to conform to an enormous number of behavioral rules. If they don't salute in a crisp fashion, they can be sent back to barracks. If their boots don't show a "spit shine," they can be forced to clean out latrines. Because well-executed response to orders is vitally important (ultimately for survival and victory) in the military, behavioral conformity is a top priority. By contrast, faculty in art schools may expect students to take pride in thumbing their noses at behavioral and moral conventions, as the famous battle cry of bohemia, *"épater les bourgeois"* (literally, to shock or flabbergast the middle class) demands. But acculturation is unavoidable even in this nonconformist environment. To be accepted by other nonconventional people, would-be bohemians must conform to the expressive style and outlooks typical of their group. They may need to be able to talk knowledgeably about obscure poets or musicians and to shift smoothly between attitudes of enthusiasm for the offbeat and world weariness in the face of the familiar. A would-be bohemian who does not act in these ways is not well-suited for bohemian life.

Discussions of the role of schools in socialization are often muddled by the failure to keep these three dimensions distinct. Many contemporary conservative critics, for example, suggest that schools are failing in the area of socialization because they have stopped emphasizing moral virtues. In the introduction to his best-selling book, *The Book of Virtues* (1993), former U.S. Secretary of Education William Bennett wrote:

> Where do we go to find the material that will help our children in [the] task [of developing moral literacy]? The simple answer is we have a wealth of material to draw on—materials that virtually all schools and homes and churches once taught to students for the sake of shaping character. That many no longer do so is something this book hopes to change. (11)

Although Secretary Bennett raises an important issue in this passage, he is highlighting one dimension of socialization while playing down the other two.

Schools need to develop a certain minimum level of behavioral conformity, and they cannot help but acculturate students in some way. Nor have they abandoned the field of moral instruction as completely as Secretary Bennett and other critics contend.[1] However, as we will see, both the specific socialization messages and the techniques used to socialize schoolchildren have changed greatly over time.

SOCIALIZATION IN COMPARATIVE AND HISTORICAL PERSPECTIVE

School socialization environments can be described as fitting one of four major ideal types:

- The village/communal pattern is based on relatively lax behavioral control, relatively low levels of explicit moral training, and accommodation to the rhythms of village life.

- The industrializing pattern is based on very high levels of behavioral control, high levels of training for moral conformity, and acculturation primarily to the world of mechanical production.

- The bureau-corporate/mass consumption pattern is based on impersonal control through rules and routines, relatively lower levels of moral discussion and training, and many more choices in classroom and extracurricular life. Students are acculturated to a world of bureaucratic organization and mass consumption.

- The elite pattern has existed at the upper reaches of all societies, but the specific forms of elite socialization have varied greatly from society to society because of differences in the outlooks of the groups decisive in the formation of the schools, the geographic location of the schools, and other factors.

As societies change, so do the dominant patterns of socialization in schools. The first transformation is from the relatively free-flowing village/communal pattern to an industrial pattern characterized by very stringent demands for behavioral control and moral conformity. Some of the latter schools are evident in industrialized countries today. In these schools, students are closely monitored for behavioral conformity and are expected to follow a large number of detailed rules. The environment is more highly moralized, and work

TABLE 5.1
School socializing environments

Environment	DIMENSIONS OF SOCIALIZATION		
	Behavioral	Moral	Cultural
Village/communal	Relatively lax	Relatively weak emphasis	Accommodation to rhythms of village life
Industrializing	Strong explicit emphasis	Strong explicit emphasis	Preparation for world of industrial production and nation building
Bureau-corporate/ mass consumption	Embedded in rules and practices	Relatively weak emphasis and more pluralistic	Preparation for impersonal organizational life, cultural pluralism, and consumerism
Elite	Largely implicit (based on behavior modeling)	Relatively strong emphasis and highly ritualized	Preparation for world of power and status

U.S. A

assignments are typically based on rote memorization, filling in answers on rather undemanding worksheets (Bowles and Gintis 1976; Anyon 1980; Cookson and Persell 1985).

Today, the majority of schools in the wealthier societies have made a second transformation: from the industrial to the bureau-corporate/mass consumption pattern. Some of these changes are the result of conscious emulation of the leading organizations in society; some an unconscious reflection of changing expectations in the larger society.

Table 5.1 compares these four socialization environments.

It is important to avoid overly sweeping generalizations about how uniformly schools in any society fit this typology. First, cultural understandings of childhood often have an independent influence on how societies organize their school socialization practices. Some societies, such as contemporary Japan, draw a strict separation between the years of innocence and the years of responsibility. Early childhood is seen as a period of experimentation in which children require indulgence and unconditional support. They are not expected to conform to a highly disciplined style of life until later childhood (Stevenson and Stigler 1992). These views have been common historically in many European countries as well (Cubberly 1922). Second, the socializing environment in primary and secondary schools always differs somewhat. The personal authority of teachers over students is much more typical of primary schooling than of secondary schooling today. Choices are far greater in secondary schools. Therefore, the bureau-corporate/mass consumption pattern is more apparent at the secondary school level.

Within countries, the dominant socialization pattern does not necessarily sweep away the others. In some cases, a mix of elements may be present. Laurence Wylie (1974) describes a village school in the south of France in the 1950s that seems to mix elements of the village/communal and industrializing patterns. A favored child is allowed to wander unimpeded from classroom to classroom. Each teacher gives him a hug. The teachers do not have the same expectations for every child and are tolerant of those who are not succeeding. At the same time, the teachers maintain, and the parents insist on, a rather strict climate of authority in the classroom with severe punishments in the few cases of lying or stealing (Wylie 1974, chap. 4). The rule is: "Children must never dispute the word of the teacher."

One other qualification is necessary: the circumstances of the local economy or the social class composition of the school may influence socialization patterns. In the United

States, the bureau-corporate/mass consumption pattern now predominates in most middle- and upper-middle-class communities. But the other three socialization environments can also be found in some locations. The elite pattern continues, of course, in private day and boarding schools (and even in advanced placement tracks of some suburban public schools). The village/communal pattern can still be found in some of the poorest rural areas of the country; for example, among Mexican farm workers in the Central Valley of California or in the poorest sections of the Mississippi delta. The industrializing pattern can still be found in some urban working-class schools.

Parents tend to be strong proponents of class-conditioned socialization. Upper-middle-class parents expect more self-directed and creative schoolwork for their children, in large part because their own occupational careers require self-direction; working-class parents often demand tough discipline and strict compliance with the teacher's direction, in large part because they have found compliance at work to be a fundamental expectation of their employers (Kohn 1972; Bowles and Gintis 1976; Lareau 1987). Schools both reflect and reinforce these parental expectations.

The First Transformation: From Village to Factory

The least developed countries are those in which the routines of public life are also least entrenched, and where the intimate cultures of family and village still take precedence. The classroom environment in such countries tends to be relatively informal, and expectations for attendance, attentiveness, or performance cannot be easily enforced. Individual transgressions, such as poor academic performance and spotty attendance, are readily forgiven. Not too much is expected of teachers, either. A good example comes from Nancy Hornberger's (1987) fieldwork in rural Peru: "Over the seven day period, out of 50.5 hours spent at school by the children 30.5 hours were [spent out of the classroom] as follows: 16.5 hours in recreation periods, 4.5 hours in sports competitions, 3.5 hours waiting during adult meetings, 3.5 hours in which teachers were absent during school, and 2.5 hours in line-up activities" (211). She adds that a fifth of the classroom time consisted of housecleaning activities, such as sweeping up the classroom.

At somewhat higher levels of economic development, the classroom climate changes. Few countries have managed to achieve sustained economic growth without the "industrialization of schoolchildren." The informal ways of the village are replaced by values connected to readiness and exertion at industrial work. The value of strict obedience to authority is communicated to students through classroom discipline, and classroom life is consequently harsh. Many countries provide a warm and nurturing environment for early primary schooling, with rugs and overstuffed furniture easing the transition from home to school. Regimentation takes over in the later grades. In some countries, such as Germany in the later nineteenth century, the influence of factory-style discipline was heightened in the upper primary grades and secondary schools by a nationalist ideology that stressed preparation for war (Ringer 1979, chap. 2).

Not all countries leapt into the modern era on the heels of industrialized schools. In slow-industrializing countries, the era of mass schooling preceded industrialization. In these countries, socialization took a different path at first. In the early 1800s, the Swiss-

German reformer Johann Heinrich Pestalozzi argued that all children could develop their intellectual and moral capacities, if schools encouraged them to do so in a less regimented environment. He introduced methods of teaching in parts of modern Switzerland and Germany that aimed to inspire children's interest in learning, rather than to fill their heads with mechanical drill. This effort to adapt schooling to the natural interests and development of children dovetailed in these countries with the state's interest in separating formal schooling from religious control and connecting children to a new model of "modern" personality and national purpose.

The English, by contrast, developed mass schooling after rather than before industrialization. The industrialization of schooling also goes to the greatest lengths in England. At the same time that Pestalozzian ideas were adopted in the German-speaking world, the English were beginning experiments with the harsh "Lancasterian system." The system is named after Joseph Lancaster, who developed a plan in which one teacher, assisted by several of the brighter pupils, could teach from 200 to 1,000 students in one school. The pupils were sorted into rows, and each row was assigned to a monitor. The teacher first taught these monitors a lesson from a printed card, and each monitor took his row to a "station" at the wall of the room and proceeded to teach the other children what he had learned. The Lancasterian schools were organized in a largely mechanical fashion. *The Manuals of Instruction* gave complete directions for the organization and management of monitorial schools, the details of recitation work, use of apparatus, order, position of pupils at their work, and classification being minutely laid down (Cubberly 1922:341). The schools were very popular between 1810 and 1830 in England and other early industrializing countries, but fell out of fashion by 1840. The low expense of Lancasterian schools could not compensate for their inability to sustain the interest of hundreds of children at a time.

In many eastern cities in the United States, the first free schools were of this type, and indeed Lancaster spent most of the last 20 years of his life organizing schools in the United States (Cubberly 1922:360). In many locales, schooling in the United States remained highly repressive, even after the popularity of the monitorial system waned. No doubt Puritan asceticism, aligned with industrial work discipline, influenced the unusual severity of schooling in the United States. Children were relentlessly schooled to be obedient, regular, and precise in their habits. Classrooms were organized not so much to stimulate the intellect as to create well-disciplined workers. The phrase "toeing the line" still had a literal meaning. Joseph Rice (1893) visited hundreds of urban classrooms in the eastern United States to collect data for his book on the public high school at the turn of the century. In one school described by Rice, during recitation periods (periods in which students demonstrated that they had memorized a text), children were expected to stand on the line, perfectly motionless, their bodies erect, their knees and feet together, the tips of their shoes touching the edge of a board in the floor. The teachers, according to Rice, paid as much attention to the state of their toes and knees as to the words coming out of their mouths: "'How can you learn anything' asked one teacher, 'with your knees and toes out of order?'" (98).

Disciplinary practices varied, of course, but they were generally strict. At Philadelphia's Central High School, two evaluations were taken every hour—one for scholarship, the other for conduct. Demerits for disciplinary infractions (such as laziness or insubordination) were deducted from the student's grade point average at the end of term, influencing class rank and chances for promotion. In 1853, the principal of Philadelphia's Central High School described this system of discipline:

> The whole machinery of the school, like an extended piece of net-work, is thrown over and around [the student], and made to bear upon him, not with any great amount of force at any one time or place, but with a restraining influence just sufficient, and always and every where present. Some of the most hopeless cases of idleness and insubordination that I have ever known have been found to yield to this species of treatment. (quoted in Labaree 1988:18)

Teachers, too, were tightly controlled. In smaller communities, in particular, female teachers were told what they could wear, where they could travel, how late they could be out, and whose company they could keep. In many places, they were prevented from marrying or joining early feminist organizations. Men had more leeway in most communities. Nevertheless, rules such as the following from one southern California school were not uncommon: "Any teacher who smokes, uses liquor in any form, frequents pool or public halls, or gets shaved in a barber shop will give good reason to suspect his worth, intention, integrity, and honesty" (Oak Glen School 1873).

Nineteenth-century classrooms were also more highly moralized places than they are today. The schools taught a bundle of virtues that reflect three primary moral traditions: the *Judeo-Christian moral code* of honesty, decency, tolerance, love of goodness, and kindness; *the Protestant work ethic* of industry, enterprise, planning, and frugality; and *the republican-nationalist "civil religion"* of patriotism, bravery in battle, love of freedom, respect for the rule of law and the Constitution, and responsible participation in the institutions of political society.

The explicit moral teachings of the schools reflect the schools' historical interaction with three waves of "nation-building" ideas. The first and second of these waves occurred more or less simultaneously. From the eighteenth-century beginnings of mass schooling in Europe, children were taught to be good and patriotic subjects and also to follow the moral norms of the Judeo-Christian tradition (Bendix 1968). A third wave of ideas followed the advance of capitalist industrialization in the early nineteenth century. It encouraged thrift, sobriety, and hard work. The waves of social change brought on by the rise of the nation-state and industrialization left similar imprints in the socializing objectives and practices of schools throughout the world.

In the United States, most children in the mid- and late nineteenth century learned to read from the McGuffey Readers where "the rules were always clear: Never Drink, Never Smoke, Work Hard, Tell the Truth, Obey Authority, Trust Providence" (Tyack and Hansot 1982:27). Like a church with its Bible, the rural school with its McGuffey Readers was to be a small "incubator of virtue" (ibid.:4). Leading educational historians have argued that such rules were based on a tight interweaving of the "absolutist morality of the evangelical movement," the faith in "civic virtue" of eighteenth-century republicanism, and "entrepreneurial economic values." The common school supported capitalism by rationalizing wealth or poverty as the result of individual effort or indolence, and by making the political economy seem to be not a matter of choice but of providential design (ibid.:24). These schools were the natural seedbeds both for hard-driving entrepreneurs and their hardworking and abstemious laborers.

The same emphasis on behavioral conformity and stern morality found in nineteenth-century American schooling can be found today in industrializing parts of the developing world. Consider the following, rather extreme description of disciplinary practices in modernizing Lebanon: Those who received failing grades were asked to line up in the front of the room. The teacher took a long, thin wooden stick and slapped the first boy's open palms. Others were slapped across the face, on the hand, or across the body with the wooden stick. Once the punishment was meted out, the teacher began explaining the answers to the quiz in his seemingly relaxed, friendly manner (Howard 1970:129). Here, too, the interests of developing states in organizing self-discipline combine with religious injunctions to produce a climate of strict behavioral expectations and strong moralization.

"Well-adjusted" students in these authoritarian systems are, at least publicly, not very willing to criticize the harshness of their teachers. One boy explained why teachers hit: "He hits us because his conscience will hurt him when he doesn't help us to discover the good path. Truly, the teacher is a candle that melts and melts to light the road of virtue, love, and goodness. He is the messenger of civilization" (ibid.:130).

The Second Transformation: From Factory to Office and Shopping Mall

In later stages of capitalist development, the industrializing pattern gives way to what I have called the bureau-corporate/mass consumption pattern. This second transformation is at the heart of Americans' school experience today, particularly in secondary schools. A number of forces came together following World War I to produce the new pattern, which was less obtrusive in behavioral control (depending more on rules than personal admonitions), less highly moralized, and less single-minded in concerns with production. Instead of preparing students for factory work, schools began preparing them for work in bureaucracies and for a consumer-oriented life of choice and variety. These forces arrived somewhat later in Europe and the rest of the industrialized world than they did in the United States.

The Progressive Era's (1896–1918) emphasis on administrative solutions to social problems played the midwife in this transformation. The triumph of "scientific managers" moved the schools out of the hands of people who were obsessed with personally rooting out evil and put them into the hands of people who favored structural forms of control. With the right rules and organizational practices, educators like George Strayer and Ellwood Cubberly believed, it would be unnecessary to install a miniature tyranny in each classroom. Authoritarian methods were, in any event, coming under criticism by developmental psychologists, who saw them as creating a regime of fear in the classroom rather than an environment conducive to active exploration and learning.

At about the same time, schools came to be seen as institutions responsible more for the development of mental abilities than for the development of character. Secondary schools had always been more purely cognitive in orientation, but conflicts over what constitutes "good character" in a country newly self-conscious of its multiethnic population led both primary and secondary schools to tread more gingerly on moral topics than they once had.

If the movement toward a more student-oriented ethos began in social engineering and the desire to avoid controversy, it ended in full-fledged consumerism. First, schools were seen as a place to have fun as well as to work. Later, they were seen as places to choose among subject matter alternatives rather than to conform to standardized curricula.

Toward consumerism. As early as the 1920s in the United States, profiles in popular magazines of "heroes of production" (i.e., business, scientific, and political leaders) were giving way to profiles of "heroes of consumption" (sports and entertainment celebrities) (Lowenthal 1957, chap. 4). At the same time, football became popular and began attracting increasing numbers of students to college (Riesman and Denney 1951). Sports and later other extracurricular activities (band, glee club, drama, and others) became a focal point for high school students in the 1920s and 1930s. Arthur Powell and his colleagues (1985) quote one high school principal of the period observing the difference in interest generated by extracurricular activities and regular instruction: Extracurricular activity "pulsates with life and purpose," the principal noted, whereas the formal curriculum "owes its existence to a coercive regime, loosely connected and highly artificial" (257).

In the curriculum, social engineering justified as consumerism began in the early 1900s. Educators were determined to "meet the needs" of secondary school students who would not be attending college by providing more practical coursework. Under the influence of a "life adjustment" philosophy popularized after World War I, this emphasis on student interests gradually branched out to incorporate students in academic and general education tracks. Courses were provided to students to prepare them for balancing a checkbook, dating, driving, and raising children. After a swing back toward academic rigor in the Sputnik era, consumerism flowered again in the late 1960s and 1970s. The U.S. Department of Education counted thousands of course titles on high school campuses at the end of the 1970s, with the vast number in relatively undemanding "general education" programs, such as movie making, health education, and driver's education (Angus and Mirel 1995).

At the height of the era of student consumerism in the late 1970s, three social scientists, Arthur Powell, Eleanor Farrar, and David Cohen, studied a dozen American high schools and published their findings in *The Shopping Mall High School* (1985). How different their portrait is from the factory-like regimes described by Joseph Rice and others only a century earlier: "Most educators are proud of the mall-like features of high schools. 'The nice thing about [our] school,' a teacher explained, 'is that students can do their own thing. They can be involved in music, fine arts, athletics, sitting out on the south lawn and nobody puts them down for it.'" For Powell and his colleagues, the "shopping mall high school" was based on three distinctive features:

- *Variety.* The schools offered a wide variety of consumer opportunities, from curricular opportunities like fine arts to extracurricular opportunities like sports to noncurricular opportunities for socializing with friends.

- *Choice.* The schools placed choice in the hands of the consumer. The customer had real power not only to decide what to take and where to go but also how much effort to expend. Many schools, Powell and his associates found, allowed "negotiated treaties" between students and teachers rather than strict requirements handed down from above. If teachers agreed to keep requirements at an achievable minimum, students agreed to comply with the course requirements and to remain civilly attentive. The specific nature of the agreements were open to implicit or, in some cases, explicit bargaining.

• *Neutrality.* The schools were neutral about the choices students made. One choice was more or less as good as another (Powell et al. 1985:11).

Powell and his colleagues exaggerated the all-encompassing character of the movement toward consumerism, perhaps to bring out the changes in socialization practices as dramatically as possible. The term they coined, "shopping mall high schools," is, therefore, quite misleading: the socialization pattern found in today's schools includes socialization both for a world of consumer choice *and* bureaucratic regulation. Consider the ways organizational abilities are emphasized in the schools: students make appointments, manage time, fit things into their schedules, and are urged to plan and to keep themselves on track. Nor can it be convincingly argued that production pressures are ignored quite as much as the image of the shopping mall suggests. Teachers assign homework and expect it to be in on time. Bells ring and corridors clear. Tests, papers, and grades remain an obsession— even more so in recent decades given the schools' heavy emphasis on "accountability." Preparation for work life in a highly organized and competitive society thus remains at the center of the school's socialization mission, along with preparation for a life of variety and choice in the consumer marketplace.

Evidence from other industrial societies. The same transformation from the factory-like regimen of the nineteenth-century school to the bureau-corporate/mass consumption model of today can be seen throughout the industrialized world. However, in Europe this transformation began only well after World War II, when secondary schooling became for the first time a form of mass rather than class education, and it is only now beginning to develop in the industrialized societies of East Asia.

In the United States, the new environment was created by administrators looking for ways of appealing to the interests of new students while adjusting to the modern world of corporate organization. In Europe, students themselves demanded change, often against the resistance of academically oriented administrators. Student demands for more choice and variety in schooling became popular slogans during the student uprisings of the late 1960s. These demands built both on the large numbers of students moving on to higher grades and the greater affluence of the industrialized world in the second postwar generation. Student protest led to significant curricular change (Boudon 1979).

The changes could be seen even at Wylie's (1974) village school in southern France. When he revisited the village in the 1970s, Wylie was amazed that "the belief in hierarchy has given way to a concern for each individual's will, a mutual respect, a tolerance of differences that I would never have thought possible. In most families, there is acceptance [of the young people's new independence], though tinged perhaps with nostalgia . . ." (382–3).

In East Asia, the changes came even later, but they have now arrived in full force. Merry White (1993) described Japanese secondary school students as grumbling about the rules that regulate school life, concerned with the choices they are offered, and very interested in exploring cultural styles associated with "independence." Socializing and consumerism are as much at the center of Japanese adolescence as are the academic expectations of the schools. The schools have not compromised much to take these new realities into account, but they may very well be forced to do so in the future.

The new bureau-corporate/mass consumption socialization pattern may be an American original, but it has gained strength in all advanced societies, because it corresponds to the impersonal bureaucratic regulation, pressure for cultural pluralism, and mass consumption priorities of early twenty-first-century life.

Socialization in Elite Preparatory Schools

Elite schools provide training for students identified by school authorities as potential leaders of the future. At one time, wealthy parents, and particularly birth into a socially prominent family, would have been the major qualification for admissions. Since the 1960s, academic qualifications have become a more important factor. Academic promise has become increasingly important, because elite colleges and universities now seek to enroll classes with more uniformly excellent academic records. This has made the private schools a refuge for many academically gifted children, who might fail to thrive in public schools. Even so, because elite preparatory schools can cost as much as $30,000 per year and scholarships are rare, family economic standing remains a very important influence on who applies for admission to an elite preparatory school and, therefore, on who is admitted.

One of the great advantages of elite schooling lies in the area of training for the representation of power in face-to-face interaction. Through modeling the behavior of fellow students, children at private preparatory schools can acquire a refined sense of the accepted manner in which power is expressed in a democracy: good spirits and an easy manner with obvious social inferiors; an aloof attitude (which can be aggressively enforced, if necessary, through snubs and smirks) toward social inferiors who encroach too closely; and true frankness only with recognized social equals.

In addition to a rigorous academic curriculum, emphases on near-universal participation in sports and performing arts remain common at elite preparatory schools, because exceptionally competent and compelling public performance remains an important aspect of the expression and enactment of power and status in society. The powerful must be capable of performing with aplomb in public.

Otherwise, approved cultural styles in elite preparatory schools differ and reflect the idealized values and lifestyles of the primary stratum to which the school caters (or, in the case of very traditional schools, the stratum to which it catered at the time of its founding).

In the United States, private day and boarding schools were founded, for the most part, in the late nineteenth century for the children of the old, prominent families. They were founded as a way of maintaining social distance from *parvenus*, the large numbers of new rich who had risen during the Gilded Age. These schools, located in rural areas of New England, inculcated the values of American patricians: a very high level of self-control; taboos on discussions of wealth; a constant admonition to be involved in service activities for the public good; an efficient, businesslike approach to assignments; the expectation that knowledge is to be used rather than simply memorized; and a sense of earned entitlement to the privileges and power of high social status (Cookson and Persell 1985).

By contrast, British "public schools" (the equivalent of American private boarding schools) reflected the imprint of the colonial administration of the British Empire, with its emphasis on sports as a proving ground for the battlefield, chapel as an essential feature of a world-transforming Christian mission, and earnest effort in the classroom. In the most prestigious of the public schools, such as Eton, student styles also showed the imprint of the dandyism of the English aristocracy (McConnell 1985).

In Germany, the values of the *Bildungsburgertum*—the educated upper middle class—strongly shaped German elite secondary education following the university reforms of the early 1800s (Ringer 1969). This class sharply distinguished itself from the business-oriented upper middle class by emphasizing internal cultivation and external civility. It was highly intellectual and sought to distinguish the "higher court" of cultural values from the self-interested behavior of everyday commercial life (Ringer 1992). This outlook is typical of the cultivated professional classes in all early modernizing societies, but the sense of distinction between cultivation and commerce was carried furthest in Germany, largely because of the weakness of the German business classes in a country long dominated by the landed aristocracy, the civil service, and the military. Post-World War II changes have carried German elite secondary education in the direction of the rest of the industrialized world.

Acculturation in French elite secondary education, by contrast, was shaped by the powerful mix of Parisian wit and civil service precision, as these became embedded in the teaching traditions of the *grandes écoles* founded by Napoleon for the purpose of forming military, industrial, and administrative leaders for state service (Suleiman 1978). The *grandes écoles*, located in and around Paris, exercised a tremendous influence on the socializing patterns of the French academic secondary schools, not least of all because the leading stratum of French secondary school teachers were trained at one of them, the *Ecole Normale Supérieure*. Though carried on with public funds, the elite system has been maintained in France as a distinct track in upper secondary education (Bourdieu 1996), just as it has been maintained in the private boarding schools of the United States and England.

SOCIALIZATION MESSAGES IN THE CLASSROOM

Today's schools continue to buzz with socializing messages in the classroom and on the playground. But some of the most effective means of socialization are not part of the verbal buzz. Instead, they either frame the boundaries of acceptable behavior or are embedded in the very fabric of school routines. I will now look in greater detail at the practices of classroom socialization in contemporary schools and the extent to which these practices are successful in channeling behavior, belief, and students' orientations along school-approved lines.

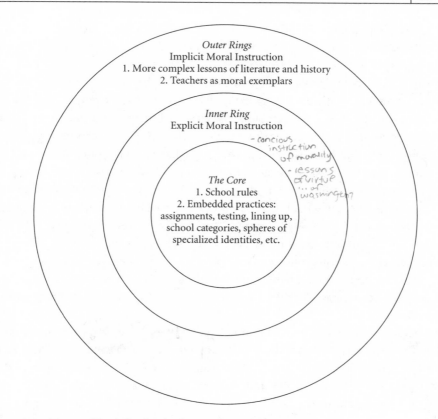

Outer Rings
Implicit Moral Instruction
1. More complex lessons of literature and history
2. Teachers as moral exemplars

Inner Ring
Explicit Moral Instruction

- concious
  instruction
  of morality
- lessons
  of virtue
  ...of
  washington

The Core
1. School rules
2. Embedded practices:
assignments, testing, lining up,
school categories, spheres of
specialized identities, etc.

Figure 5.1   Zones of Socialization in Contemporary Classrooms

It is helpful to think of classroom socialization as organized around a core of relatively effective rules and routines surrounded by rings of less insistent (and therefore less effective) moral instruction. The core consists of rules backed up by sanctions and routines of schooling that acculturate students to the worlds of impersonal organization and consumer choice. These embedded routines include such everyday features of schooling as lining up, working independently, choosing among options, and taking tests. Sociologists have sometimes used the term *hidden curriculum* to describe lessons of socialization that are embedded in the very fabric of schooling: in its official categories and constantly repeated routines. Surrounding this core are rings of moral instruction. One ring consists of explicit moral instruction—the overt teaching of moral virtues that is found mainly in the elementary grades. Another ring consists of implicit moral instruction. Some of this instruction occurs through exposure in later grades to the moral lessons of literature and history. Some occurs through observation of the exemplary actions of teachers and principals.

Figure 5.1 diagrams this conception of classroom socialization.

The Core: Impersonal Rules and Embedded Practices

Teachers and principals no longer force students to behave by whacking them across the bottoms or pulling the short hairs on their necks. Instead, students are socialized into an impersonal order in which rules and routine practices construct the boundaries of legitimate conduct; within those boundaries, students are relatively free to act as they wish. Because these rules and practices are built into the very fabric of schooling, they soon become taken for granted.

School rules. School rules define the serious infractions that require punishments: hurting other children, insulting teachers, being disruptive in class, cheating, and the like. School rules may also prescribe where students can be at different times during the day, and the conditions under which they may leave their classrooms. Rules represent the prerequisites of bureaucratic life: being where you are supposed to be, doing your job, interacting in a peaceful way with co-workers, and accepting the authority of bosses.

The number of socializing rules in schools varies by society and level of instruction. In the United States, primary schooling is very heavily encased by rules. Secondary schooling depends, to a greater degree, on the internalization of these earlier experiences with rules. This pattern is the norm in most of the developed world. In Japan, however, children remain strongly embedded in group-centered moral life through primary school and emerge into an impersonal, rule-bound setting only with the arrival of secondary schooling (White 1993). In the developing world, rules are frequently equally elaborate in primary and secondary schools.

The "hidden curriculum." In addition to explicit rules, sociologists have uncovered a number of embedded practices and school routines that play a role in socialization for the world of consumer choice and bureaucratic regulation. Sociologists often refer to these everyday practices of schools as the "hidden curriculum" of schooling, because the value lessons they impart are so embedded in the routines of schooling that they are all but invisible.

Many of the routine practices of schools are relevant to socializing students for life in bureaucratically organized settings. These encourage students to renounce their immediate impulses and gain patience; value individualism and individually earned achievements; deal effectively with authority and evaluation; and orient themselves to bureaucratic ways of seeing the self and others. These begin in primary school and continue to be embedded in schooling throughout secondary school.

Children are naturally egocentric and inclined to demand the regard of others and the freedom to pursue their own interests as they see fit. Schools as institutions are just as naturally opposed to allowing the natural egoism of children free expression. All of the "lining up" at school—for a turn at the water fountain, in anticipation of lunch or recess, for dismissal at the end of the day—requires students to learn patience. Because groups at school are relatively large, more patience and waiting for others is usually required than at home. Things happen at school not because students want them to happen but because it is time for them to occur. The denial of desire that schools require is "cumulatively important." The crowded condition of classrooms makes delayed gratification inevitable, as well as requiring students to deal with delays, denials, interruptions, and distractions (Jackson 1968).

School practices also socialize students into a life of evaluation based on individual performance. The three-step pattern of assignment, performance, and evaluation repeated over and over in schools reinforces the disposition to distinguish one's own efforts and feeds directly into the high premium placed on occupational success in modern societies. Evaluations at school are more formal, more performance-based, more public, and more consequential for adult status than those at home. Rewards are also generally for individual rather than group achievements. Because evaluation is so important in school, it teaches not only the norms of hard work and individual achievement but also various stratagems for managing evaluation while protecting the ego. As Philip Jackson (1968) pointed out, students learn how to enhance praise, how to publicize positive evaluations, and how to conceal negative ones (26). Those who are evaluated poorly may learn to disengage, to "play it cool," to not get involved, and to mask cheating.

School practices also socialize acceptance of authority. Every time a teacher invokes a rule, makes an assignment, or calls for an answer, her or his authority is reinforced. Obedience and even docility are part of the life of labor, and the transition from classroom to factory or office is made easily by "those who have developed 'good work habits' (which is to say responsiveness to authority) in their early years" at school (Jackson 1968). The spatial and temporal organization of schools itself expresses authority relations. Students are not allowed free access to certain spaces: the principals' offices, the teachers' lounges, or the counseling rooms. The staff even controls students' access to classrooms. Students are required to be out of hallways and off the grounds at certain times.

At least two other modes of orientation required by bureaucratic life are also taught in schools. One is the habit of considering oneself a member of some larger category of people. In schools, categories of people often matter more than individual personalities. Members of the "red group" may be first in line to use the computer during a particular week, and members of the "blue group" the next week. Third graders as a group may be given certain rights and responsibilities, such as the right to use certain equipment on the playground and the responsibility to clean up the playground on certain days. Through these repeated processes of grouping, schools give students experience in making social comparisons in categorical rather than particular terms. Pupils learn to distinguish between persons and the social positions they occupy. This orientation is important in bureaucratically organized societies, where people are constantly being asked to view themselves as members of particular categories such as those with a particular level of taxable income or having a similar job grade and to accept the duties and privileges consistent with those categories.[2]

Students also learn to express only specific, situation-relevant parts of their personalities. The whole person rarely matters in the school classroom. What counts is how good a math student the person is, or how good a social studies student. The whole personality is divided into parts, and students learn that only one or a few features of their whole personalities may be relevant at any given time. This type of understanding, too, is important in bureaucratically organized societies. It is not, for example, very important to a passenger whether a pilot is good company or likes sports as long as he or she can fly a plane properly.

The routine practices of offering variety and choice are the key to the consumer side of classroom socialization. Two colleagues and I found that variety was an important part of classroom life in eight primary schools we studied. Teachers interspersed periods of group work with lectures, problem discussion, and individual seat work. Students in some schools changed classrooms periodically during the week to be taught by subject matter specialists. They had options to explore different activity centers in the classroom. Even their textbooks

✳ TABLE 5.2
Structural differences between classrooms and families

Classrooms	Families
Yearly promotion	No yearly promotion
Relatively large group size	Relatively small group size
Heterogeneous composition	Homogeneous composition
Broken relationships	Unbroken relationships
High child to adult ratio	Low child to adult ratio
Narrow, homogeneous age grouping	Mixture of several ages
Narrow range of activities and events	Wide range of activities and events
Little privacy	Some privacy
Situation-relevant facets of personality	Complete personality relevant
Achievement-based	Affection-based

SOURCE: Adapted from Dreeben (1968).

emphasized variety. Literature texts sampled every genre, from poetry to journalism, usually in rather small bits (Brint, Contreras, and Matthews 2001).

The trend toward variety and choice in secondary schools may have been reaching its outer limit at the time Powell, Farrar, and Cohen published their study of shopping mall high schools (Ravitch 1995:48–58). Even so, the choices available to students at the larger secondary schools do continue to resemble the variety of choices they face on a Saturday shopping expedition: dozens of extracurricular activities, scores of electives, hundreds of social networks and possible identities, and only a relatively small number of common requirements.

Schools and families as socialization sites. Schools are well suited to prepare people for impersonal bureaucratic environments in ways that most families are not. In particular, school classrooms have two advantages over families for this purpose:

- Classrooms are the first performance-oriented bureaucracies in which children spend a good deal of time. Unlike families, classrooms are explicitly defined as performance-oriented places and organized by relatively distant agents of authority. Teachers are, in this respect, children's first "bosses" and schoolwork their first "job."

- Classrooms include many more children than families do, and the relationships that develop are broken at the end of the school year. Children do not have the same teacher every year or continue with exactly the same children. The large groups in classrooms and the annual discontinuity of classroom life limit the deep emotional attachments characteristic of families. The interest of teachers is, by necessity, limited to specific aspects of the child and is somewhat more distant emotionally. This impersonality becomes more evident as children progress from the early primary grades to the later primary grades, and it is more or less completely true by the time children reach secondary school.

Table 5.2 shows these differences between families and classrooms. Because parents are usually more concerned with the whole child and have a personal, direct authority in the household, "families lack the resources and competence to effect the psychological transition to adult life" in impersonally organized settings (Dreeben 1968:85).

Two Rings of Moral Instruction: Explicit and Implicit

It is often assumed that moral instruction has been completely drained out of public school-ing. No doubt, some school districts have become leery of stepping on toes by imposing one set of moral values, and others may feel that the traditional types of moral instruction are old-fashioned. Nevertheless, moral instruction has not disappeared from the public schools.

In a study of Southern California classrooms, two colleagues and I found that the values of hard work and persistence in the face of adversity were emphasized both in teacher-initiated interaction with students and in literature and social studies texts (Brint, Con-treras, and Matthews 2001). These are both "entrepreneurial" and effort-oriented virtues. We found less evidence for the centrality of such other traditional moral virtues as kindness, compassion, honesty, and fairness. Other researchers have found somewhat more support for these virtues. They find that many primary school teachers continue to use stories in-volving well-known heroes (such as George Washington and his apocryphal cherry tree) or familiar fables (such as the ant and the grasshopper) to inculcate moral virtues. Teachers (by overwhelming majorities) also say that schools should teach common core moral values, such as honesty, punctuality, responsibility, and industriousness (Farkas and Johnson 1996). And some social studies and reading textbooks continue to emphasize such traditional values as "honesty, courage, compassion, persistence, bravery" (Sharp and Wood 1992).

In our study of Southern California classrooms, my colleagues and I also found evidence for the importance of two relatively new school values. One is "self-esteem." Schools make many efforts to make children feel good about themselves through recognition in the class-room and school assemblies. One organizational reason for this is that, as higher levels of educational attainment have become the norm, school authorities have had a stronger in-centive to make every student feel a part of the school community. The other new value is "respect for diversity." This value was communicated through classroom activities, such as tracing ancestry on maps, and in the lessons of literature and social studies texts (Brint, Contreras, and Matthews 2001). Some 96 percent of teachers say they believe in "teaching respect for others regardless of their racial and ethnic background," and nearly every schoolroom now includes posters of famous women and minorities, along with the white men who once presided almost exclusively. Textbook studies confirm a dramatic increase in concerns with pluralism and the contributions of the many groups that make up American society (Fitzgerald 1979; Wong 1991; cf. Elson 1964).

Thus, recent empirical studies provide qualified support for the view that "the national [identifying symbolism] has been enlarged rather than abandoned" (Tyack 1999). Such a change would be consistent with Durkheim's ([1893] 1964) thesis that societies evolve from states of cohesion based on a common and obligatory moral order to states of cohesion based on pluralistic and balance-oriented moral orders, buttressed by the "cult of the indi-vidual," as their social structures grow more complex.

On the other hand, one of the remarkable features of contemporary schooling is how little of it is related to building the autonomy Durkheim prized as a foundation for inde-pendence of thought and creativity. A very large number of teachers' messages are directed toward gaining compliance; students are repeatedly told to follow directions and be quiet. But almost none are directed to encouraging independent thought, or supporting unconventional views. Also missing are explicit mentions of aesthetic or intellectual values (Brint, Contreras, and Matthews 2001). "Citizenship" is important in schools, but it has nothing to do with the right to speak one's mind or dissent. It has been translated into organizational terms to mean respecting others, following rules, and supporting the authority of the staff.

Cross-national variations in moral education. Some important cross-national variations exist in the organization and content of moral education. One of these differences is the extent to which schools create curricular boundaries around moral education. In most of the developed world, moral instruction is interlaced with the regular curriculum. In the United States, for example, discussions of Abe Lincoln's honesty take place in relation to lessons in American history. By contrast, many developing countries, as well as many developed Asian countries, devote explicit time every day to moral or religious education. Imagine an American student taking a test on morality in public school, which is commonplace in Singapore, Hong Kong, and elsewhere in East Asia. Separate periods for moral instruction presumably produce more commitment to moral norms, although they may create more transparent forms of hypocrisy as well.

Another important difference has to do with the location of control over moral instruction. In a few countries, the primary responsibility for enforcing behavioral and moral conformity is the student group, rather than the teacher. In Japanese nursery schools, for example, teachers do not pull children out of the group for misbehaving. Nor do they talk to children about behavior problems. Instead, they rely on other children in the class to censure those who are misbehaving. As Catherine Lewis (1995) notes: "[These] practices may promote strong internalization and ultimately high compliance while maintaining the role of the teacher as a benevolent, though perhaps not quite indulgent, figure" (84). In other words, group-based authority may increase the legitimacy of behavioral norms while allowing teachers and school administrators to be seen in a more sympathetic light than they might otherwise be.

A similar emphasis on peer authority can still be found in British "public schools" (which would be called "prep schools" in the United States). Sixth-form leaders (students of 16 to 17 years old) are selected to help the staff organize and discipline younger students. These "prefectures" both train selected students in habits of command and encourage student leaders to use their energies on behalf of the staff rather than on behalf of their potentially rebellious classmates. At Eton College, for example, the most famous of the British public schools, prefects are members of the Eton Society, also known as "Pop." The members of Pop wear fancy waistcoats, braided tailcoats, stick-up collars with white bow ties, check trousers, and a floral buttonhole. They enjoy tremendous prestige among the younger boys. In the past, members of the Eton Society could hand out whippings without the authorization of any housemaster, but corporal punishment by boys was banned in 1970. Today, members of the Eton Society must rely on words to keep their charges in line. Nevertheless, as one observer has noted, "Boy power is still strong and anyone coming [to Eton] from another school is struck by the weight and importance of boy opinion," represented at its pinnacle by the members of Pop (McConnell 1985:212). Just as in the case of

Japanese peer authority systems, the prefectorial system has long been credited as one of the hidden reasons for the cohesiveness of British elites.

The content of moral instruction also varies considerably around the world in response to particular political, religious, and pedagogical traditions. In the former Soviet Union, for example, respect for manual work, a centerpiece of communist ideology, filtered into moral instruction in numerous ways. Heroes of labor were celebrated, special times were set aside for manual labor, and the moral virtues of workers and peasants were celebrated (Bronfenbrenner 1970). In Japan, "principles of the Shinto and Confucian moral order, such as loyalty, filial piety, the discipline of group life, industry, cleanliness, physical strength and perseverance" are reinforced "by means of school rituals, courses of study and extracurricular activities" (Fujita 1986:330). In Israel, the rabbinical tradition of aggressively questioning what one reads, exploring paradoxes, and commenting on commentaries shows up in the qualities of mind that leading academic secondary schools try to cultivate. Singular individuals are also sometimes important. In areas of Europe (particularly Italy and Germany), for example, the progressive pedagogy of the Swiss school reformer Pestalozzi encouraged moral teaching based on a sense of the splendor and balance of nature.

Secondary schooling and moral complexity. As students move up the grades of public schooling, moral instruction either diminishes greatly or becomes increasingly implicit and complex. It diminishes most completely for students who enroll in general or vocational programs in secondary school. Industrial work values continue to be stressed (Oakes, Gamoran, and Page 1992), but otherwise moral instruction fades from the official curriculum. By contrast, moral instruction increases in complexity for students who enroll in the academic programs, particularly those who take a large number of courses in humanities. Exhortations to be honest, hard working, courageous, and kind are replaced by far more challenging lessons, just as in mathematics class simple addition is replaced by quadratic equations.

The moral instruction of the humanities works at a higher level than the illustrated lists of virtues that today's critics of schooling prefer. Not every student has the capacity to take moral lessons from literature and history, but these lessons are the stuff out of which the higher forms of moral judgment are created in the secular humanist tradition of public schooling. The widely assigned George Eliot novel *Middlemarch*, for example, expresses several of the more demanding perplexities of moral life: how, for example, a dedicated scholar, for all his knowledge and hard work, can suck the blood out of life, and how an otherwise admirable doctor can desire to please his beloved wife so much that he goes deeply into debt to support her expensive tastes. Through examples such as these, motivated students can learn that even widely proclaimed virtues will, at times, be pushed too far or fail to be sufficiently balanced by other virtues. Students may also learn that many situations in life involve not a choice between right and wrong, but between two rights. In *Huckleberry Finn*, for example, the meaning of civilization is debated from many sides. Is it obedience to the law and cultivated manners? Or is it the ability to empathize with the personality and situation of others, regardless of reigning conventions? A further question is raised: how do we judge a "civilization" that emphasizes the former and considers the latter to be relevant only for members of the subordinate status groups? Simple answers are not possible for some moral questions, but discussion can help to bring out what is at stake and the range of defensible positions.

Teachers as exemplars. Most schoolteachers are aware of their role in socializing the young and try to express values through their actions in the classroom. In the primary grades, for example, they usually express the values of kindness and empathy. They have, as Phillip Jackson observes, "a knack for discerning latent grace in the awkward gesture" and "applaud those who try no matter how slight their success" (Jackson, Boorstrom, and Hansen 1993:259).

Teachers have different strengths as exemplars, and what they have to teach is therefore more evident to some students than to others. One teacher may make precision and clarity important values in her classroom and express respect for these values through the carefulness of her handwriting, the persistence of her correction of imprecise language, her attention to detail in the working through of a proof. Another teacher may express the moral importance of truly engaged activity by throwing his whole body into a lecture, by beaming with pride when a student gives a good answer to a difficult question, or by cheerfully brushing off an annoying interruption. Another may express the moral importance of digging beneath the surface by patiently leading students ever deeper into a short story, by suggesting alternative interpretations, or by engaging in Socratic questioning of students' answers.

Dramatic gestures aid in the expression of teachers' values. An erect posture, neat handwriting, the lingering of a poised piece of chalk at eye level—all can express heightened respect for precision. Thoughtful stroking of the chin, dramatic exclamation at the discovery of a right answer, a long pause before sweeping away a shallow interpretation—all of these can convey a heightened respect for digging deeper.

How Successful Is Moral Instruction?

Sociologists have largely failed to study whether students actually internalize the schools' socialization messages. Many students of socialization apparently assume that the messages repeated most frequently are in fact absorbed (see, e.g., Dreeben 1968), especially if they affirm messages that are prominent also in families and popular culture. However, no one has really studied this very carefully. It is difficult even to know how this could be studied, since students do not live in a vacuum unexposed to influences outside of school. What we do have are ethnographic studies suggesting that students are only minimally attached to the behavioral norms of the school. In working-class schools, swearing at "mean" teachers when they are out of earshot is very common (Plank et al. 2001), and rebellious students, opposed to everything the school stands for, attract the admiration of many of their peers (Willis 1979; MacLeod 1987). Cheating, we know, is rampant in school; as many as four-fifths of students say that they have cheated.

Most students may pragmatically accept regulation by authorities, but they do not necessarily internalize the values of authority figures. Moral conformity, in particular, is not as easily gained as behavioral conformity. If the schools' values are supported by students' families and local communities, they are likely to be accepted. If they are not supported outside the school, they may be treated with a good deal of skepticism, or flatly rejected. The dominant moral culture of schools reflects the social conditions of people who have some authority in society (or identify strongly with those who do) and who are, in addition, not extremely cosmopolitan or worldly in outlook. It is, therefore, most congenial to those who are upwardly striving or located in the broad middle of the social structure. At a minimum, it always confronts opposition on at least two fronts: from the practical opportunism of the "have-not" classes and from the worldliness of upper-class sophisticates (see Bourdieu 1984; Collins 1988:208–25).

Even where the moral teachings of the schools are accepted in principle, they may not have a strong impact on behavior, because the temptations of selfishness, dishonesty, laziness, and cowardice are always great. Moreover, organizational biases sometimes undermine even simple moral lessons. Schools, for example, subscribe to the value of honesty, but often inadvertently reward cheats who are motivated by the equally high importance schools attach to achievement. Schools preach equality of opportunity, but are notorious for tamping down the ambitions of lower-status children. Most schools proclaim the importance of sturdy independence, but they do not approve of instances of student nonconformity if it threatens staff authority.

SOCIALIZATION MESSAGES OUTSIDE THE CLASSROOM

The school playground is an important part of childhood socialization, and it has been perhaps too little appreciated by sociologists. (By contrast, many children are obsessively interested in the "lessons" of the playground.) If classrooms are an introduction to bureaucratic life, the playground is an introduction to impression management and negotiating social networks. School experiences outside the classroom prepare children for adult life by teaching them about self-assertion and self-control among friends and colleagues. The values of the classroom and the playground often coexist peacefully, but in some secondary schools, adolescent values crowd out school values.

Like the classroom, the playground has important structural features that are different from those found in students' homes:

- On the playground, adult authority is present in the form of monitors, but this authority is in the background. Adult presence prevents anarchy, but adult distance allows a maximum opportunity for group-directed activity.

- Many children mix on the playground, and freely chosen interactions with a relatively large number of children are, therefore, theoretically possible.

- The members of school playgroups are usually similar in age, but are usually not close neighbors or family members.

Because they are spheres of monitored, but largely self-directed activity involving a variety of interaction possibilities among others who are neither very close nor very distant, playgrounds have advantages over close friends and family for the development of skills in informal social relations. Age similarity limits the social distance between children, but the aggregation of many acquaintances creates a wide opportunity for cementing, altering, and breaking relationships. The variety of possible contacts allows children to develop increasingly refined judgments about the possibilities and problems of social interaction.

The Playground and Informal Social Life

On the playground, children must learn to deal with bullies, "tagalongs," tattletales, false friends, snobs, and other familiar childhood types. Deciding how to react to these types of classmates can refine a child's social judgment. How should one deal with aggression from another child—by confronting the child, by raising a coalition against her, or by trying to avoid the harassment by diving under the bushes when she passes? Under what conditions should a higher authority be informed, and when is this action interpreted as failing to stand up for oneself? When does friendship fall over the line into dependency? How much should acquaintances be trusted with valuable information? When does such information cement a friendship and when does it increase one's vulnerability? How much effort should one make to win the friendship of an aloof but desirable child? When should one speak out and when should one wait to assess the situation further? How can one express pride in abilities and achievements without fostering resentment among others? Through confronting these and similar issues, children may become skillful navigators of relationships.

Without a great many experiences in dealing with these issues, children would be less well prepared for adult life. These lessons clearly apply in adult interactions with friends, potential mates, and acquaintances in the community. But they are no less applicable to social relations at work. Much occupational activity can be thought of as "political labor," in which people take and avoid taking stands and in which they maneuver to make useful alliances, to avoid encumbering connections, and to defuse potential conflicts (Collins 1979, chap. 2).

Some sociologists have long seen the experiences of the playground as an important socializing complement to the experiences of the classroom. Talcott Parsons (1959), for example, pointed out that not all high-status jobs in industrial societies require high levels of academic ability. Social skills are particularly important in many managerial and sales jobs and also in promotional and public service work. In Parsons's view, those who gain status on the playground but not as much in the classroom form the pool of future occupants of jobs that require high levels of social skill and emotional labor (e.g., salespeople, public relations people, entrepreneurs, actors and actresses). They are also the future central organizers of adult friendship networks. Those who gain status in the classroom but not as much on the playground form the pool of future occupants of jobs that require high levels of scholarly and analytical ability (e.g., scientists, engineers, professors, civil servants, technology managers). Those who gain status both in the classroom and on the playground are likely to be future achievers in the upper levels of occupational and public life (e.g., corporation executives and upper-level managers, college presidents and deans, doctors, lawyers, research entrepreneurs, politicians). Finally, unless they are late bloomers, those who lack status in both domains are unlikely to become socially dominant personalities.

Although the playground provides opportunities for experimenting with identity, it is far from a domain of true freedom and fluidity. Indeed, some inequalities are more apparent on the playground than in the classroom. While teachers usually try to mix boys and girls in classroom activities, for example, boys and girls usually separate from one another on the playground. In primary schooling, the dominance of boys is evident in their ability to control large, open play spaces, to label girls as ritually polluting (girls are primarily responsible for "cooties" on most playgrounds), and to invade spaces occupied by groups of girls. Thus, the playground can be a space in which some social relations—particularly gender and gender-related aggressiveness—are reproduced in a more faithful way than in the classroom (Thorne 1995). Status systems based on skills and attributes prized by the dominant children rule the social order of the playground. The social divisions of the playground—cool/uncool, jock/brain, tomboy/sissy—overlap with meaningful divisions in adult informal social life. Because these social divisions are strongly supported on the playground by the dominant children, they exalt some children more regularly and wound others more deeply than adult social divisions usually can. By the time young adults enter the labor force, they have usually developed emotional capacities that allow them to occupy positions close to the centers of work and/or community life, or a lack of confidence that leads them to retreat to the margins. Many of these cumulatively decisive emotional experiences occur on school playgrounds.

For all of its verbal violence, the playground is nevertheless an arena of experimentation and change. It is a place where children practice making and breaking friendships and where they try out new identities, which may prove rewarding. It is a place where children watch on the border of socially organized spaces and make forays across the borders at times, as when a popular boy decides to play with the girls for a day or girls join the boys' kickball game. It is a place where children learn to use verbal aggression to fight unwanted labels, as much as to enforce the existing status hierarchy.

Adolescent Society and the Schools

As children grow into teenagers, friends become an increasingly central part of the incentives to attend school. Because of the nonacademic interests of most adolescents, many adults fear that the influence of adolescent culture undermines adult authority and does not adequately prepare children for adult life.[3] This seems to be a perennial concern among adults, and there are enough examples of teenagers ruining their lives to keep up interest in the topic through the foreseeable future. But social science research makes clear that "adolescent society" is not as different from "adult society" as many parents fear. Even those teenagers who are deeply alienated may not stay that way; many alienated adolescents grow up into well-adjusted adults once they take on the responsibilities of jobs and families. In addition, adolescent friendship groups reinforce many of the same values as adults. For example, adolescents socialize emotional control by criticizing those who do not show it and calling them "crybabies." And, in most cases, if teenagers do not act with acceptable honesty or show up at appointed times, they will be loudly criticized until they conform or are forced to find new friends.

James Coleman and Adolescent Society

Before 1950, few young people had enough discretionary time and money to develop their own tastes, their own popular heroes, and their own sense of values. They were either children, under their parents' tutelage, or adults out on their own. The relatively autonomous stage of adolescence with its emotional passages, strong peer identifications, and ritualized rebellions against adult authority hardly existed. Some of the key forces bringing youth culture into existence were the freedom afforded by mass ownership of automobiles, the ability of teenagers to find part-time work while attending school, the relaxation of social mores to allow for earlier and less supervised dating, and the lengthening of the time children were expected to remain in school. In the 1950s, these forces came together to create for the first time a sense of adolescence as a separate stage of life. Young people developed their own popular heroes, such as Elvis Presley and James Dean, and they were serviced by multi-million-dollar popular culture and apparel industries. Similar forces were leading to the spread of a youth culture throughout the wealthier liberal democracies, with capitals of youth culture in London, Amsterdam, Berlin, and Paris.

About this time, educators began to worry about the harmful effects of adolescent culture on the academic commitment of the young. Many educators felt that the status hierarchy of young people reinforced values, such as sexual attractiveness and rebellion, which made the work of schooling more difficult. As in the Chuck Berry song, students couldn't wait for the last school bell to ring, so that their "real lives" could begin.

James Coleman (1961) was the first sociologist to examine the influence of American adolescent culture in an empirically rigorous way. Coleman's study of eleven Indiana high schools in the late 1950s confirmed the importance of alternative status systems running parallel to the official status system of the schools. In the American Midwest, Coleman found, it was not so much duck-tail haircuts and souped-up cars that posed the major threats to the academically oriented status order of the school. Instead, it was the more conventional alternative interests of teenagers: athletics and the opposite sex. Coleman asked high school students whom they admired most: outstanding students, outstanding athletes, or the students who were most popular with the opposite sex. Both athletic and popularity stars were far more likely to be admired than academic stars.

The "leading crowds" set the tone in the schools that Coleman studied, and they had the effect of accentuating values generally prevalent in their communities. In communities where academics had little status, the leading crowds were even less interested in academics.

Coleman expressed concerns about the influence of "adolescent society," but unlike the more rigid educational moralists of his time, he did not see adolescent society as a monolithic evil. Adolescents were not entirely cut off from adult society; their status systems recognized the values of adult society in many ways, not least in their tendency to ascribe highest status to the "all-around" boy and girl. Moreover, the effects of the adolescent society varied across the genders (girls were more responsive to adult authority than boys), from class to class, and from community to community.

How important is adolescent society? For the culture of adolescent alienation to penetrate deeply, the separation between the world of adults and the world of adolescents must be great and the amount of time adolescents spend exclusively with friends their own age must also be great. Both national and class differences are evident in the level of separation of the two worlds.

In Sweden, for example, greater balance has existed in the past among the reference groups influencing adolescent identities: the family, the school, the local community, and the friendship group. No single force has been as dominant as peer groups now are for many American adolescents. In Sweden, these four socializing forces each have had distinct times during the day and week in which they were considered legitimately central (Andersson 1969). In Japan, where schooling takes up such a large amount of time and consciousness, the role of the peer group is circumscribed throughout secondary school. In college, friendship groups play a much larger role, however. Some who have studied Japanese society argue that the primary function of college friendship groups is to prepare young adults for the intense work group culture of Japanese business and professional life (White 1993, chaps. 4 and 6).

In the United States and many other societies, however, adolescent society has for some time enjoyed great autonomy. The discretionary income that comes from part-time work, the freedom that comes from access to cars, and the distinctive sensibility that comes from the fashions disseminated by the popular culture industries all contribute to this autonomy. Moreover, adolescents spend most of their time out of school with one another. Thus, in the United States, the separation between the world of teenagers and the world of adults is great, and the time spent with peers is also great. If anything, the importance of adolescent peer groups has grown over time. In addition to cash, cars, and pop culture, another important element has been added: with more two-earner families, the amount of interaction between parents and children has declined. When they are not in school, most children now spend their time with friends or alone, "fooling around," surfing the Internet, or watching television (Boocock 1972:10; NCES 1996:66–7).

The sources of status in adolescent society remain decidedly nonacademic. The physical foundations of dominance—athletic ability and good looks—remain firmly in place. The social groups that form around athletic and attractive students continuously recharge the emotional energy of the leading cliques, and enforce boundaries between these cliques and other students. In a study of several thousand junior high school students, Tye (1985) found that "good-looking students" were identified as the most popular students in school by nearly two out of five students. Athletes followed them in popularity (23 percent). In this study, even "gang members" (15 percent) were considered more popular than "smart students" (14 percent). Academically oriented students were not at the bottom of high school status hierarchies—the large, neglected mass of "unpopular and unknown" kids were at the bottom. But they were miles from the top and subject to considerable verbal hostility, as the common put-down terms "nerd" and "geek" indicate (see also Clasen and Brown 1986).

Social class is a strong influence on the extent to which peer values become all-consuming in the life of adolescents. Even in the United States, the dominant pattern in the middle and upper-middle class (and also among upwardly mobile minorities) is *compartmentalization* of peer and adult influences. Peer values tend to dominate in areas related to informal social life and discretionary consumption: styles of language and emotional expression; dating practices; and preferences in movies, clothing styles, music, and the like.

Adult values tend to dominate in areas of long-range planning: the importance of keeping up good grades, going to college and preparing for high-paying and high-status jobs, and selecting acceptable people for dates (Boocock 1972:230–9).

Some more thoroughly alienated middle-class rebels exist, but in most suburban schools they have too few compatriots to form a self-sustaining critical mass (Willis 1979). In others, they band together as a small nihilist or bohemian minority.

Anti-school peer cultures. Although overstated, the concerns of adults about adolescent alienation are not entirely unfounded. Perhaps one-fifth to one-quarter of all adolescents is deeply alienated from adult middle-class society. And schools in the poorest communities must usually deal with much higher proportions of these alienated students.

Anti-school peer groups are increasingly common among adolescents who have little adult supervision and are not planning on attending college. The compartmentalization of peer group influence gives way to a more complete encapsulation of adolescent experience by the values of one's friends; in other words, adolescents become the central arbiter of all facets of behavior and orientation. This level of immersion in adolescent culture is strongly associated with the kinds of "problem behaviors" that are so disliked by adults: smoking, profanity, and vandalism among younger teens; drug and alcohol use, school dropout, and early pregnancies among older teens (Jessor and Jessor 1977). More or less complete anti-school peer group control is the dominant ambience in many nonimmigrant working- and lower-class schools, and also in cliques of "tough" and "unpopular" kids in middle-class communities. The same attitudes can be found in the peripheries of large European cities, where immigrant youth remain largely unassimilated into the dominant culture.

Sociologists have raised several objections to conventional ways of explaining the rise of counter-school cultures. Rather than drawing attention to deficiencies of character or family life, as many polemicists do, they have tended to look at disparities between the probable life trajectories of students and those assumed by the schools. Students who are most attracted to the counter-school culture are those who see no linkage between their current school activities and their anticipated adult status and activities (Stinchcombe 1964; Willis 1979; MacLeod 1987).

For boys and girls oriented to working-class jobs or a nonworking married future, the legitimacy of the "educational exchange" often fails completely. The educational exchange can be described as the exchange of respect and deference for valued knowledge: Students conform to gain knowledge that is valuable to them; teachers provide knowledge to gain conformity that is valuable to them. On the students' side, knowledge itself is of primarily instrumental value; it leads to qualifications, which in turn lead (so students hope) to higher status and income. When this chain of exchange breaks down, so do the foundations on which the socializing role of the school rests. When the breakdown is profound, the school is likely to confront an active counter-school culture.

The most provocative sociological portrait of a counter-school culture remains Paul Willis's (1979) study of "Hammertown boys" in the midlands of England. Willis makes the point that the most defiant boys he studied were the ones with the strongest sense of dignity and self-respect, not the most defeated. The kids who were upstanding and wouldn't take "bull" joined the counter-school culture—these Willis called the "lads"; those who were passive and compliant were part of the group the lads called "ear'oles" (for ear holes, that group's most prominent physical and moral characteristic, according to the lads). The lads were in some respects more realistic than the ear'oles. They refused to accept the official ideology of "equal opportunity" when the world, as they knew it, offered little real opportunity. Ironically, the lads with their boisterous high spirits, quick wit, and determination to have "laffs" at the expense of teachers and ear'oles alike paved their own paths into a life of insecure manual labor. They weren't tracked into lower-class jobs so much as they tracked themselves into those jobs. Their sense of moral superiority to students who passively conformed led them to embrace forms of labor that they considered a valid alternative to the tight controls of white-collar jobs. However, the form of work they chose as the better alternative would eventually tear at their high self-esteem.

England has had an aggressive and rather oppositional working-class adult culture, so it is not surprising that in America, where this sense of class opposition is largely missing, counter-school cultures reveal more drug- and alcohol-laced withdrawal than active rebellion. An American counter-school group studied by Jay MacLeod (1987) shared many of the values of Willis's lads, but had more trouble escaping the dominant culture's definition of success. Their outlooks were more pessimistic and resigned than those of Willis's lads. Unlike the lads, they saw no hope in working-class jobs for the expression of an independent spirit, and they expressed their alienation not by holding the authority structure up to ridicule but by consuming what MacLeod described as "huge quantities" of alcohol and drugs.

Can adolescent alienation be reduced? Some argue that the best approach to reducing adolescent alienation is to control the influence of counter-school cultures through tight security and strict enforcement of rules. These steps help schools in depressed neighborhoods to muddle through, but they are, by definition, unlikely to create any real sense of connection between alienated students and the school authorities that oversee them. At a time when many are aware of the problems of adolescent alienation, it is not surprising that calls for more job-relevant secondary schooling on the German model of apprenticeship training are also growing stronger. But unlike the German "dual system," vocational schooling in the United States, with its low status and uncertain connection to the job market, has not provided adolescents with a strong sense of purpose or motivation to succeed (see, e.g., Grubb and Lazerson 1975; Grasso and Shea 1979).

Some believe that the schools' current emphasis on accountability is leading to stronger commitment among "at risk" students, because they receive more regular feedback on the state of their academic skills (Carnoy, Loeb, and Smith 2003). The evidence is not yet in on this hopeful hypothesis, but some studies suggest that alienation and dropout have been largely unaffected by the accountability movement (Kaufman, Alt, and Chapman 2001). In some localities, a single-minded emphasis on accountability has further drained spontaneity out of the classroom and may in the end compound problems of alienation.

An alternative approach worth considering, according to MacLeod (1987), would be for schools and teachers to try to stimulate thinking while being more realistic about the life chances actually facing alienated young people who, quite realistically, do not believe that the middle-class success through academic achievement applies to them. Schools should provide more teachers who can relate to sthe students in nonstigmatizing ways and provide assignments that are materially relevant to these students' likely life trajectories. The one teacher who was able to reach MacLeod's alienated working-class kids dressed in a T-shirt and jeans and gave them assignments for papers on such topics as the origins of the Harley-Davidson motorcycle and the experience of life in prison.

Clearly, the mild hedonism of the adolescent society of the 1950s has given way to a more sullen and disenchanted mood in economically depressed communities today. The growing gap between rich and poor is an important backdrop against which this new mood has developed. And hopes about accountability notwithstanding, confident solutions to the problem of adolescent alienation are in short supply.

CONCLUSION

Schools may attempt to control behavior, moral values, and cultural orientations. These three dimensions of socialization overlap in practice but are analytically distinguishable. It is possible to define four historically important school socialization environments: (1) the village/communal pattern, (2) the industrial pattern, (3) the bureau-corporate/mass consumption pattern, and (4) the elite pattern. These patterns can be found at different stages of a country's economic development and, within countries, also in schools primarily serving different social class populations. Socialization practices in the industrial pattern are particularly harsh. They are based on personal control, rigidly organized work discipline, and a highly morally charged classroom setting. In the United States, the transformation of schools from the village/communal pattern to the industrial pattern occurred in the mid- and late nineteenth century, and the transformation of secondary schools from the industrial to the bureau-corporate/mass consumption pattern occurred in the 1920s and 1930s. Elsewhere, the second of these transformations occurred only well after World War II.

Classrooms and playgrounds provide distinct sites of socialization at school. The first is most relevant for socialization into institutional life, and the second is most relevant for socialization into informal social networks. School classrooms and playgrounds are organized in ways that allow them to acculturate students in ways that families cannot duplicate. In the classroom, the impersonality of adult authority and the annual breaking of relationships help to acculturate students to the demands of bureaucratic life. On the playground, the relative distance of adult authority and the presence of many nonintimate peers provide opportunities for children to learn to maneuver in informal social networks.

Classroom socialization practices in contemporary schools can be conceived of as involving a core of rules and routine practices and outer rings of moral instruction. The core of rules and practices create effective pressures for behavioral conformity and acculturation to bureaucratic and mass consumption ways of life. Embedded practices (such as lining up, working independently, making curricular choices, thinking of oneself as a member of a larger category, and being examined for special competencies) are often discussed by sociologists as elements of the "hidden curriculum" of schooling.

Although schools have been accused of renouncing moral instruction, primary school teachers continue to represent some ethical, entrepreneurial, and patriotic values in a positive way. Two new values have, in addition, become part of the moral curriculum: self-esteem and diversity. In secondary schools, students have the opportunity to learn more complex moral lessons by reading history and literature. Teachers also model much behavior that can properly be considered moral. Students resist the socializing messages of the schools if they are too discordant with the culture of their homes and neighborhoods. The organizational pressures of schooling, moreover, sometimes conflict with or even undermine their moral teachings.

The playground is the site of socialization for informal life in social networks. Here students learn skills in self-presentation, friendship making, conflict making, and conflict resolution. These skills help adults to maneuver in informal social networks. Although playgrounds offer many opportunities for developing these skills, they are also stratified in many of the same ways as adult society. Indeed, social divisions of gender and aggressiveness, at least, are stronger on the playground than in the classroom.

Peer influence increases as children grow into teenagers, but the degree of influence of adolescent society varies. In most middle- and upper-class communities, regardless of country, adolescent lives tend to be compartmentalized, with parents and other adults having the largest influence on long-term plans and peers having the largest influence on immediate life experiences and styles of expression. Anti-school peer cultures exist primarily among teenagers whose long-range life plans have least to do with schooling and who are therefore alienated from the basic educational exchange: opportunities to acquire valuable knowledge in return for behavioral compliance. It is likely that the number of alienated adolescents has grown over time as adolescent and adult societies have become more separate and as the income gap between rich and poor has widened.

SCHOOLS AND SOCIAL SELECTION: OPPORTUNITY

The goals of mass schooling at first had little to do with the awarding of credentials that would help people find work. Instead, schools were intended to teach basic literacy and calculating skills, shore up morality, and create loyal citizens. Before the early twentieth century, most men in the United States, for example, either inherited the family farm or trade, or they went off on their own to find the best work they could. Many were literate, but few had finished high school. Minorities were excluded from all but the most rudimentary education, and women, though more often educated beyond bare literacy, rarely worked for pay. Schools played a largely noneconomic role in other countries as well.

Now schools are central in the process of sorting and allocating people to jobs. This is true in every industrialized society. Not every child learns the course content or the socialization lessons of schooling, but every child is by definition subject to the schools' performance assessments. For this reason, social selection is, in my view, the most consequential activity of contemporary schooling. School performance from first grade through high school can lead one squirming six-year-old toward a life as a jet-hopping executive and another toward a life of shifting from one low-paid job to another.

The connection between schooling and social selection has become so important that I will devote two chapters to it. Schools are important both for providing opportunities for social mobility and for the reproduction of inequalities. Mobility and reproduction can be thought of as two distinct social processes. This chapter will concentrate on the themes of opportunity and mobility. The directing questions will be: Who gets ahead through schooling, and to what extent has the increased importance of schooling in the sorting process provided greater opportunities for people from less advantaged backgrounds to rise? Chapter 7 will concentrate on the theme of inequality. The key questions in that chapter will be: How do the circumstances of the lower social classes, members of racial and ethnic minority groups, and women contribute to the reproduction of inequalities through schooling, and to what extent do school structures, such as tracking, reinforce or exacerbate these inequalities?

The first part of this chapter describes the forces that have made schooling more important in the process of social selection. This section focuses on two key changes: (1) the expansion of schooling, which has encouraged a connection between educational credentials and mobility aspirations, and (2) the tighter connection between educational credentials and jobs. The second part of the chapter explores the characteristics of people who succeed in schooling and are thereby able to convert their educational credentials into good jobs. Many people believe that educational expansion has substantially improved the opportunities for children born into lower-status families, but the social science evidence suggests that this is not true. In fact, the correlation between fathers' social status and children's educational attainments has remained roughly constant over time—and the reproduction of family social status with the help of schooling has become, over the last quarter century, if anything, somewhat more common.

THE INCREASING SIGNIFICANCE OF SCHOOLING IN SOCIAL SELECTION

"To get ahead in life, you need an education." Most of us have heard this familiar refrain from our parents and friends. Income and labor market statistics bear out its truth. People holding master's degrees in today's U.S. labor market, for example, will earn on average about twice as much as high school graduates (the difference between $55,000 and $29,000 a year for full-time workers over age 25) and almost three times more than high school dropouts (on average $21,000 a year) (Day and Newburger 2002; U.S. Bureau of the Census 2003). Between 1980 and the early 1990s, income differences by educational level increased dramatically, the result of stagnation in wages at lower levels of education combined with growth in salaries at upper levels (see, e.g., Katz and Murphy 1992; Murnane, Willett, and Levy 1995).

The gap between people with higher and lower levels of education is larger in the United States than in any other industrialized society (OECD 2004:176). Where college graduates in the United States earn 86 percent more than high school graduates, the gap elsewhere is closer to 50 percent more—and in some highly egalitarian countries like Denmark it is as low as just 25 percent more (ibid.).

Opportunity Consciousness and Educational Expansion

To understand how schooling came to play such an important role in the process of social selection, we must first understand how the idea of upward mobility was reinvented in the early and mid-twentieth century as a promise of schooling rather than the expected outcome of hard work in a trade.

As you will recall from Chapter 2, the United States was a pioneer in the expansion of schooling, partly because schools became important in the "Americanization" of the millions of new immigrants who came into the country in the nineteenth century and partly because reformers believed that schooling could build skills and democracy at the same time. Even in the United States, however, expansion of secondary schooling was slow. As late as 1910, only 15 percent of American adolescents graduated from high school. But by 1940, high school graduation rates were already over 70 percent, and 15 percent of high school graduates were going on to higher education. These rates were three to five times higher than anywhere else in the industrialized world.

Schooling and opportunity in the United States. Before the Civil War, the United States was, economically, a nation of small-property owners—farmers and shopkeepers. Most knew how to read and write but had little in the way of formal education. Although opportunity was an important part of the national creed, in the early days of the American republic, opportunity meant the possibility for a person to grow to the full measure of his capacity, free of the limiting ties of feudal relations. This full measure of capacity had noneconomic as well as economic connotations. It referred to competence, character, and satisfying social ties, as well as to economic status (see Lasch 1995, chap. 3; Wuthnow 1996). The idea of opportunity as a chance to move into a higher status in the world only gradually entered American consciousness, and it did not become a very important view until after the Civil War (Lasch 1995:66–74).

Just before he became president, Abraham Lincoln ([1859] 1953) expressed a vision of the ideal of the "self-made man": "The prudent, penniless beginner in the world, labors for wages awhile, saves a surplus with which to buy tools or land for himself, then labors on this own account another while, and at length hires another new beginner to help him" (478–9). For Lincoln and many others of his time, business, not education, was the major road to opportunity for the self-made man. The self-made man grew his business or his farm by outthinking and outworking his competitors but not necessarily by getting more schooling than his competitors. (Many believed that luck played a role, too, as in the Horatio Alger stories that were so popular in the decades following the Civil War.)

The expansion of schooling was closely connected to an entirely new kind of "opportunity consciousness" than the one Lincoln expressed. With the rise of mammoth corporations and the closing of the frontier at the end of the nineteenth century, the fate of the self-made man became increasingly threatened. Self-employed farmers and shopkeepers were no longer the dominant economic group in the country. More and more people were becoming employees of large organizations. Clearly, if the American dream of individual advancement was to survive under these new conditions, other pathways to success would be required.

Schooling at first seemed an unlikely avenue. Businessmen regularly condemned college training, with its emphasis on fine thoughts and high-flown sentiments. They claimed that it made young people unfit for the "real world" (Wyllie 1954:101–5). Even so, some far-sighted philanthropists began to perceive the nation's school system as a replacement for the faltering promise of business entrepreneurship. Andrew Carnegie (1889), for example, believed that schools and colleges should be made into "ladders upon which the aspiring can rise" (663). In the late nineteenth century, the country's schooling system hardly fit anyone's idea of a well-built ladder. Professional schools did not require the completion of four years of college for admittance, and colleges did not require the completion of four years of high school. Over the next generation, however, the patchwork of American schooling was reorganized into the ladder structure that people like Andrew Carnegie advocated, thereby providing a mechanism to keep the American promise of opportunity at the very moment when fundamental changes in the economy were threatening to destroy it (Brint and Karabel 1989:3–6).

A suddenly awakened thirst for learning does not explain why young people began to graduate in large numbers from high school in the years between the two world wars, and why they began to attend college in large numbers after World War II. Instead, the most important factors were changes in the occupational structure and the increasing incentives for investment in education. Between 1900 and 1940, white-collar jobs almost doubled in the American labor force: from one out of six at the turn of the century to almost one out of three by 1940. Between 1940 and 1970, professional and managerial jobs also rose: from one out of seven to almost one out of four (U.S. Bureau of the Census 1975:139).

Shortly after World War II, American sociologists began noting that the channels of upward mobility through business ownership and shop floor advancement were drying up and that higher education was in the process of taking their place (Warner 1949). Some young people enjoyed schooling for its own sake, but many more then as now were primarily interested in using higher degrees as tickets to the better jobs in society, jobs that were becoming more plentiful during this period. And the government, convinced of the need for a more highly educated labor force, encouraged this view by supporting the building of secondary schools and colleges and by providing financial aid support, first in a limited way and then generously, for those who wanted to attend college but lacked the economic means to do so.

After World War II, the number of students attending college skyrocketed, helped at first by the federal government's loans and by scholarships for returning soldiers. In 1940, about 15 percent of 18- to 21-year-olds attended either a two-year or a four-year college. Just 30 years later, in 1970, the figure was well above 40 percent (U.S. Office of Education 1944:4; Peng 1977). Not everyone who enrolled in college after World War II graduated with a degree; in fact, only about half did. Even so, this kind of growth represents a tremendous increase in college enrollments, particularly given the nearly threefold increase in the numbers of 18- to 21-year-olds between 1940 and 1970 thanks to the postwar baby boom.

Of course, higher education did not simply replace entrepreneurship as an avenue to economic success. Indeed, the proportion of self-employed people has even grown a little in recent years. Some 7.5 percent of the American workforce is self-employed, most of them owners of small businesses with a helper or two (Hipple 2004). Self-made men and women can still be found, particularly in enclaves of the wealthy and in immigrant communities. Nevertheless, building one's own business is a risky and arduous task. Businesspeople must weather downturns in the business cycle, shifting patterns of consumer preferences, and changes affecting their business location. They may be aroused at night by phone calls reporting fires or theft. In view of the uncertainties of entrepreneurship, a large proportion of business people prefer that their children pursue the less risky path of professional training rather than following in their parents' footsteps as small enterprisers.

Schooling and opportunity worldwide. Demand for secondary and higher education grew much more slowly in the rest of the world than it did in the United States. Secondary schooling was, except in very unusual cases, off limits for the working classes throughout the nineteenth century and the early part of the twentieth century. European systems of secondary and higher education were set aside for those who could pay high fees and pass rigorous examinations. It is reasonable to call the European systems of secondary and higher education "status confirming" systems, because they helped to unite the upper classes as a common status group, culturally very distinct from the masses of people who had only rudimentary schooling (Collins 1977). Even in 1940, few European countries graduated more than 15 percent of young people from secondary school or sent more than 3 to 4 percent on to higher education (Craig 1981:185–6).

Loyal to their traditions, European educators fought the expansion of secondary and higher education as long as they could. Nor did politicians, themselves products of elite schooling, agitate very often for expanding secondary and higher education. But the same forces that led to change in the United States wore down the resistance of European educators and politicians a generation later. Once again, occupational change was an important factor. As corporations and state institutions grew, so did the need for white-collar workers. Perhaps even more important was the developing sense among politicians and ordinary citizens alike that schooling could be used as a "ladder of ascent" to a better economic future and to full participation in the modern world (Meyer, Ramirez, and Soysal 1992). After the end of World War II, and especially in the 1960s, much of the rest of the world adopted the American model linking schooling to opportunity.

Once governments decided on the necessity of mass schooling at the lower secondary level and, later, at the upper secondary level, the growth of enrollments in most countries showed an expansionary force that outstripped whatever might have been expected due to occupational change alone. No doubt parents' efforts to defend their families' social position are partially responsible for the vast growth of enrollments; at particular points, it becomes necessary to send children to higher levels of schooling, if only to protect them from social and economic disadvantage in the face of higher educational aspirations among other families in their communities. But a change in consciousness—the growing sense that schooling could provide opportunity—also helped to propel the educational revolution. This change in consciousness can be likened to what occurs in a large-scale social movement or religious "awakening." It was especially apparent in the Third World, where mass schooling was stimulated less by economic interests than by social and political ideals. Schooling had once been considered irrelevant to life (or even a resented feature of colonial subjugation), but it came to be viewed as "the way" to integrate people into "the grand project of nation-building" and individual development (Fuller and Rubinson 1992:12).

The Rise of the Credential Society

The desire for opportunity can be enough to increase the numbers of students attending higher levels of schooling, but it does not in itself improve the likelihood that such hopes will be realized. Only a tight link between educational qualifications and jobs can do that. The other facet of the schools' changing role in social selection, therefore, has to do with the rise of *credentialism*. By credentialism, I mean the monopolization of access to rewarding jobs and economic opportunities by the holders of educational degrees and certificates.[1]

All societies have mechanisms for allocating people to jobs. Indeed, a few have been even more inclined than the United States to use schools for this purpose. For instance, educational credentials played a more important role in social selection in the Soviet Union than they did in the United States, and they also became important for this purpose earlier in the Soviet Union than in the United States. Because entrepreneurship was not an alternative, socialism allowed ambition only one channel: through schooling. From the time of the great bureaucratization of Soviet society in the 1930s, the only means by which ambitious young people could succeed was through higher education credentials (augmented for the truly ambitious by Communist party membership). As one Soviet immigrant to the United States put it, "In the USSR, there is no capital except education. If a person does not want to become a collective farmer or just a charwoman, the only means [he or she has] to get something is through education" (quoted in Geiger 1968:156). The Japanese also placed an enormous weight on education to produce leaders for all sectors of society (Cummings 1985).

In most of the industrialized world, however, educational credentials played a smaller role for a longer period of time than in the United States. In-house promotion was the major avenue of advance for those who were ambitious. Middle managers and technicians were plucked off the shop floor, not off graduation procession lines. For example, in England, a very late developer of mass higher education, rates of upward mobility were not much different in the immediate postwar period than in the United States, but many more mobile people rose due to recognition for good performance on the job. They did not take higher-level jobs by virtue of their advanced educational credentials (Kerkhoff, Campbell, and Wingfield-Laird 1985).

Credentials and labor markets. Today, most societies have moved toward credential-based systems of social selection like the one that has become familiar to us in the United States. Higher educational credentials are now required for a wide range of professional occupations and for most other white-collar jobs in large organizations. These jobs represent a large proportion of the more prestigious and better paying jobs in today's society: ranging from accountants to zoologists. Even in the once less degree-obsessed sphere of business management, higher education requirements have become the norm for those interested in moving up the corporate ladder. Since the 1960s, a master's degree in business administration from a top-ranked business school has become an important ticket of admission to the executive suite (Useem and Karabel 1986).[2]

Thus, it is not surprising that with the advance of credentialism, higher education degrees have become important for some jobs that would in other days have been picked up through apprenticeships or on the job. For example, a health records technician degree from a community college may be required for those who want to help large hospitals and health maintenance organizations keep track of their patient, doctor, and insurance records. These jobs were once learned at work, but now they typically require two years of post-secondary study. Admittedly, medical records are more complicated than they once were, but it is debatable that they are complicated enough to require two years of formal study in an institution of higher education. Is a college degree necessary to manage a video store or fast-food franchise? Probably not if the intellectual demands of the job were all that counted, but most franchise managers do nevertheless have college degrees.

Educational credentials as screens and signals. Although it might seem like common sense that employers would want to employ highly educated people, credentialism has had its share of critics. Some early critics of credentialism argued that highly educated people would likely prove less productive in many jobs, because they would become bored if their jobs were not challenging enough (Berg 1970). Some irreverent social scientists took pleasure in showing that education could even produce a "trained incapacity" for some jobs—for example, that aloof and cerebral psychoanalysts might do less good for their patients than untrained people who simply showed empathy and acted as compassionate friends (Hogan 1979).

But most of the criticisms of credentialism were based on an economic logic. Indeed, the reasons why employers are willing to pay a premium for highly educated workers are not always obvious. After all, less educated people, if properly trained, might be able to do many jobs as well as people with degrees yet would not require the same high salaries. Why should employers pay more for those with a diploma? Educational credentials have also been criticized as signals more of background and breeding than of job ability. Those who subscribe to this view see educational credentials as essentially indicators of status group membership; people in positions of power see highly educated applicants as a kind of cultural kin, similar to themselves in language, dress, values, and demeanor. They are therefore inclined to hire and promote educated people on the grounds of cultural similarity rather than because jobs are complex and therefore require educated workers (Brown 1995; Collins 1979, chaps. 1–3). Critics of credentialism deny that most jobs are so complex that they require college graduates to fill them.

The critics of credentialism make at least one good point. Outside of a few highly technical occupations, the learning of academic content does not appear to be closely tied to the skills most jobs require. English majors may have characteristics that make them desirable employees, but those characteristics do not usually have much to do with their knowledge of Shakespeare or James Joyce. What's more, the information learned in school is not remembered long enough to do most students much good on the job. Most English majors cannot provide off-the-cuff quotes or interpretations of more than a passage or two from Shakespeare. Course knowledge in other fields has a similarly short half-life once final examinations have been turned in (Collins 1979: 17–9). Nor were grades in school more than modestly correlated, if at all, with success in work life (Capelli 1992; Dye and Reck 1989; Klitgaard 1985; cf. Bowen and Bok 1998, chap. 5). Social and political savvy—and old-fashioned good luck—were more important influences on careers.

But the critics erred in arguing that credentials are unrelated to job performance. The advance of credentialism has been propelled primarily by the applicant *screening* needs of large organizations and their willingness to accept credentials as plausible *signals* of economically valuable traits, including trainability (Bills 2003; Spence 1974). One of the most important characteristics that educational credentials signal is the ability of a job applicant to concentrate in a disciplined way on assigned problems—something that students obviously must do over and over if they are to succeed in school. Other organizationally desirable traits include reliability (showing up every day on time and in a work-ready state), the ability to handle nonroutine or self-directed work, and the ability to conform to the direction and desires of superiors. From the employers' point of view, it is a good bet that those who have survived all of the paper writing, problem sets, and examinations of a college education have developed these qualities to a greater degree than those who have not had such discipline-testing experiences (Squires 1979; Crain 1984).

The economist Lester Thurow (1973) argued that most employers were willing to pay a premium for people who could pick up new tasks quickly and that educational credentials were seen as a reliable signal of this capacity, which he called "trainability." Employers' judgments may privilege people from advantaged backgrounds, but the privileges are based not on economically valueless cultural similarities, indicating membership in a common status group, so much as on employers' interests in reliability, willingness to conform, and trainability. These noncognitive qualities have an economic value to employers, who can save on turnover and training costs by hiring people with more education.

In recent years, social scientists have begun to argue that educational credentials also signal that applicants have economically valuable cognitive capacities, such as the ability to conduct research, use information effectively, and reason well. As the number of college graduates has increased, employers have begun to look at grades and majors as selection factors, rather than concentrating primarily on degrees alone (Murnane, Willett, and Levy 1995). Even for entry-level blue-collar jobs, small employers will often go out of their way to develop close ties with teachers they trust to recommend only dependable and academically competent graduates for employment (Rosenbaum and Binder 1997). Cognitive skills seem to matter more at higher levels of business. Ishida, Spilerman, and Su (1997) showed that employers in one large U.S. and one large Japanese corporation used college quality as a signal of both cognitive and noncognitive skills. The results of this careful analysis are consistent with the hypothesis that cognitive skills are relevant to job performance at particular levels in the organizational hierarchy.

People who run large organizations have incentives to find efficient ways to process applicants and to fill positions. Educational credentials have proved to be the most cost-effective way to limit the pool of eligible applicants and to aid in the hiring of people with organizationally valuable qualities (DiPrete and Grusky 1990). Modern societies are consequently prone to credential inflation; once degrees become the norm for a given occupation, the pursuit of still higher-level degrees and specializations can easily become the most desirable option for those who want to differentiate themselves from the pack of "ordinary" degree holders. The aspiration for upward mobility can thus act to "ratchet up" credential requirements above what they might otherwise be. Colleges and universities have been only too happy to encourage this inflationary pressure.

The meaning and value of educational credentials remains controversial, however. This is largely because educational credentials play diverse roles in the labor market. Some credentials are what David Bills (2003) calls "information-rich" measures of competence (and, therefore, stand as meaningful indicators of "human capital"). These would include, for example, industry-certified training programs for entry-level computer systems jobs, and they would also include degrees from accredited engineering schools for higher level technical positions. Others are decent and low-cost, if imprecise, indicators of job-related skills, attitudes, and trainability. The community college degree in medical records technology would be a good example of a weak, but potentially valuable signal. Some other credentials may serve primarily as symbols of "background and breeding"—and have a status value quite distinct from their capacity to signal anything about job competence. Some nontechnical positions in the diplomatic corps are no doubt good examples of jobs in which background and breeding, burnished by private school education, can be decisive. So would some jobs involved in public relations and sales of expensive consumer goods. Still other credentials "may be trusted" and "yet provide misleading information about the productive capacity" of the people who hold them (ibid.:457), as is arguably the case in some psychotherapeutic and human services occupations. The early critics of credentialism argued that the latter two cases were typical, but this now seems doubtful.

The result of all these screening efforts of employers and signaling projects of job seekers has been the proliferation of specialized occupational jurisdictions off limits to anyone without the accepted educational credentials. Professional associations, governments, and educational institutions have each played a role in carving the job structure into this jigsaw puzzle of occupational jurisdictions controlled by the holders of specialized credentials. Each of these institutions has had a stake in the expansion of the "credential society": professional associations are evaluators in the accreditation process and, indirectly also, in their licensing examinations. They want to guarantee high-quality performance so as to maintain their respectability. Governments have a stake in the regulation both of occupations and colleges; and educational institutions provide the medium of exchange—degrees and certificates—that keeps the wheels of the system turning (Abbott 1988; Brint 1994, chap. 2).

Beneficiaries of the Credential Society

Educational credentials have come to play the stratifying role that family resources and family reputation once played. Statistical studies confirm that although family background was once the most important determinant of an individual's life chances, educational attainment is now more directly decisive (Jencks et al. 1979; Featherman and Hauser 1978; Hout 1988).

Not surprisingly, as schooling has become increasingly important as a determinant of life chances, people have raised questions about the fairness of the system. On the surface, an education-based system for sorting people into jobs can seem fairer than any previous system. It seems to provide greater opportunities for able and hardworking children from lower-status families to move up, while at the same time requiring children from higher-status families to at least prove themselves in school if they want to maintain their advantages. Among those who approve of the credential system, schools are likened to an elevator in which everyone gets on at the same floor but, depending on how well he or she does in school, gets off at a different floor corresponding to a particular level of occupational prestige and income.

Yet, almost from the beginning, some sociologists worried that exactly the opposite would occur: that advancement through schooling would be less fair to those closer to the bottom of the class structure than advancement through hard work or commercial enterprise had been. In 1949, the sociologist W. Lloyd Warner observed that the intense intellectual competition of the modern schooling system could easily deflate working-class aspirations more often than it nurtured and rewarded them. Warner (1949) observed that his own studies of social stratification offered something less than strong encouragement to those who would like to believe that education is providing an adequate substitute for entrepreneurship as a means of upward mobility (25, 29).

One important question, therefore, is how much schools are involved in altering inequalities from one generation to the next and how much they are involved in reinforcing the advantages and disadvantages that children from different backgrounds bring with them to school. Do schools really operate like elevators, giving everyone the same opportunity to get on at the ground floor and to go up as far as their ability and effort allow them? Or are they more like conveyor belts stacked one above the other, depositing people on floors not too dissimilar from the ones from which they began?

Two very different perspectives, corresponding to these two different images, have developed in response to questions about the distribution of opportunity in the credential society. The first can be described as a perspective based on the idea of *meritocracy,* and the second as one based on the idea of *social reproduction.*

Theories of meritocracy. The term "meritocracy" was coined by the British sociologist Michael Young in his satire *The Rise of the Meritocracy* (1958), a book about an acutely unhappy society of the future. In this society, people with high measured IQs rule with an increasing sense of entitlement while those with low measured IQs toil miserably without even the comforting sense of the unfairness of the world. In Young's satire, a populist revolt, led by women who had been left out of the meritocracy, eventually overthrows the system.

Although Young himself was highly critical of the pretensions and inequities engendered by meritocracy, the term has developed positive connotations today, and it has come to mean rule by the most intellectually able. Although effort is sometimes included as a criterion for membership in the meritocracy, other possible "merits" (e.g., of character) are usually left out of the discussion on principle. (It is difficult to identify "character" except when it is seriously challenged.)

The idea of meritocracy was in circulation before the term was coined. James Bryant Conant (1938, 1940), then president of Harvard University, wrote two important articles at the end of the Depression era laying out the rationale for a radical change in the organization of the social selection process. His ideas closely corresponded to the modern conception of meritocracy. Conant argued that democracy did not require a "uniform distribution of the world's goods" or a "radical equalization of wealth." What it required instead was a "continuous process by which power and privilege may be automatically redistributed at the end of each generation" (Conant 1940:598).

Conant and other mid-century meritocrats considered schools to be the primary mechanisms of this redistribution. They assumed that talent was not concentrated at the top of the social class structure but was instead rather widely distributed throughout the class structure. By giving every student from the most humble to the most privileged an equal educational opportunity at the beginning of life, society would be in a position to fairly select only those most qualified by brains and sweat to occupy the "command posts" at the top. Even better, this "aristocracy of talent" would be recreated fresh in every new generation.

The idea of meritocracy combined a principle of "aristocratic" leadership and a principle of democratic selection, or equality of opportunity. To the extent that the theory of meritocracy is true, we would expect the people at the top of the job structure to be those who are the most intellectually able and hardest working and that these people will come from a wide variety of social backgrounds. We should also find quite a bit of reshuffling of positions from one generation to the next.

Theories of social reproduction. Theorists of social reproduction have argued that Conant's "automatic redistribution" at the end of every generation does not occur. Instead, they have suggested, the "aristocracy of talent" is another name (and a highly misleading one) for what is in most cases inherited and socially transmitted status. Those already advantaged by the social order are precisely the ones who are most likely to be selected by it in the next generation under the guise of meritocracy. For these theorists, the supposed fairness of meritocracy does not exist because the schooling system frequently fails to see the potential of those who do not inherit the language, culture, and values of the upper classes. In the words of perhaps the best-known American theorists of reproduction, Samuel Bowles and Herbert Gintis (1976), "To reproduce the labor force, the schools are destined to legitimate inequality, limit personal development to forms compatible with submission to authority, and aid in the process whereby youth are resigned to their fate" (266).

Social reproduction theorists argue that the class structure limits society's ability to identify merit. They point to examples like the following: Imagine a girl born into a Spanish-speaking family in southern California. Let's assume that she has high cognitive potential. Nevertheless, linguistic differences may make a child shy in front of native speakers. She may have little in the way of consistent structure in her household, and this may make it difficult for her to adjust to the highly structured school environment. Because her parents have limited command of the English language and little formal education, they may not know how to stimulate her interests in school, or even think that this would be desirable. Lack of support for intellectual activity in the home may lead her to look for attention and praise in more consistently validated areas of life such as religion, socializing with friends, or feminine arts like crafts work and cooking. The children she plays with may care as little about school as her parents do, and they may even mock her if she expresses an interest in school. Her parents may feel uncomfortable talking to teachers and may therefore avoid school conferences or "working the system" on their daughter's behalf. This girl may be born with great potential but become less "meritorious" over time.

Social reproduction theory began in Europe as a critique of the social class biases in the schooling system (Bernstein 1961; Bourdieu and Passeron 1977). However, critically minded social scientists quickly began to argue that the educational deck can be equally or even more completely stacked against racial and ethnic minorities (Rist 1970; Ogbu 1978) and women (Byrne 1978; Hall 1983).

To the extent that the theory of social reproduction is correct, we would expect to see a high level of status transmission through the schooling system, rather than "automatic redistribution" of high-status jobs to the "best and the brightest" of every generation regardless of their social origins. Moreover, if social reproduction is a primary function of schooling, cognitive ability should count less than social background as a predictor of who gets ahead in both schooling and on the job.

SOCIAL BACKGROUND, ABILITY, AND OPPORTUNITY

When we examine the question of how much opportunity schools provide for students of lower socioeconomic backgrounds, it is important to separate the effects of occupational upgrading from the effects of educational attainment. In all industrialized societies, many lower-status jobs in farming and manufacturing have been gradually eliminated and higher-status jobs in the professional service sector and business management have increased.

Largely because of this change in the occupations that are available, more people have experienced upward occupational mobility than downward mobility in recent generations. Indeed, between 1900 and 1970, upward occupational mobility exceeded downward mobility by two or three to one in most industrialized societies (Erikson and Goldthorpe 1992, chap. 6).

People see that they have completed more education than their parents did. Many people also have the sense that their lives are improving in other ways compared with those of their parents. They have bigger houses and nicer cars; jobs in clean offices rather than grimy factories; more chances to travel and see the world. They are tempted to attribute these positive changes in their work lives and standards of living to the educational levels they have achieved.

But this attribution is not necessarily correct. Fifty years ago, the sociologists Seymour Martin Lipset and Hans Zetterberg (1956) pointed out that occupational upgrading was occurring in all industrialized societies, despite radically different historical experiences, widely varying forms of government, and sharply divergent schooling structures. Subsequent studies have affirmed that similar kinds of occupational changes do occur in all industrialized societies and that these changes occur whether a society has a restrictive or expansive system of secondary and higher education (Featherman, Jones, and Hauser 1975; Erikson and Goldthorpe 1992). For example, Switzerland, which until recently graduated less than 10 percent of each age cohort with university-level degrees, experienced occupational upgrading similar to that of the United States, which graduated 30 percent of each age cohort (OECD 1996).

Someone has to fill the new professional, technical, and managerial jobs even if educational systems do not expand at all. Indeed, in countries with few university-level graduates, less educated people are in fact recruited from the shop floor and the office pool to fill these higher-level jobs (Erikson and Goldthorpe 1992:303–4).

How Much Mobility?

Whether all industrial societies have similar rates of occupational mobility is a much-debated question in sociology. Seymour Martin Lipset and Hans Zetterberg (1956) provided one of the first answers to this question based on comparable cross-national data. Against the views of some celebrators of American exceptionalism, Lipset and Zetterberg argued that the level of mobility found in the United States was not substantially different from that found in a number of European nations. All modern societies seemed to show high rates of mobility, with more upward than downward mobility. Once industrializing societies reached a takeoff point, according to Lipset and Zetterberg, fairly common rates of mobility could be expected.

Later researchers discovered much more variation in the employment and occupational structures of industrial societies than Lipset and Zetterberg projected. Different occupational structures provide different distributions of occupations and therefore affect the rate of mobility. However, the intergenerational flows between occupational classes were similar (Grusky and Hauser 1984). When sociologists looked at flows from father's to son's occupations among just three major classes (professional / managerial, small business / routine white collar, and blue collar/farm workers), they found that between 40 and 60 percent of men have changed from their father's occupational class (Erikson and Goldthorpe 1992). Of these changes, upward movements exceed downward movements by between two and three to one and occasionally by more than three to one (ibid., chap. 6).

In the United States, 55 percent of men born between 1900 and 1970 moved within the three broad class categorizations and 45 percent were stable. Among men who were mobile, upward mobility exceeded downward mobility by almost three to one (40 percent upwardly mobile; 15 percent downwardly mobile). These rates, for the most part, fit comfortably within the range of other industrialized societies (Erikson and Goldthorpe 1992:330).

Today, the Lipset/Zetterberg thesis has been amended more than abandoned. Occupational structures are not as similar as Lipset and Zetterberg suggested, but flows among occupations appear to be similar across a wide variety of industrial societies (Featherman et al. 1975; Grusky and Hauser 1984; Erikson and Goldthorpe 1992). Like Lipset and Zetterberg, more recent researchers have found that the amount of upward mobility does not continuously increase with level of industrial development, nor is greater fluidity associated with the nature of a country's schooling or political system. In short, economic progress creates new occupational structures (especially more managers and professionals) and therefore more upward mobility from one generation to the next. If occupational change is the most important force behind intergenerational mobility, it is clearly wrong to attribute intergenerational mobility to the expansion of schooling. Instead, it would be more accurate to say that the expansion of schooling often accompanies economic progress and occupational change.

Such were the circumstances of the period between World War II and 1980. For the most recent generation, evidence is beginning to accumulate that rates of upward mobility have reached a plateau or are decreasing in advanced industrial societies like the United States (Bradbury and Katz 2004; see Scott and Leonhardt 2005:A18). One additional finding stands out: occupational mobility is greatest for countries where the level of economic inequality is lowest. Perhaps we should not be too surprised that the greater the equality of initial conditions between social classes, the greater the equality of opportunity for children born into the lower classes (Erikson and Goldthorpe 1992:388).

Once occupational upgrading is taken into account, researchers find quite a bit of individual-level mobility, based in part on superior school performance, combined with considerable continuity in the amount of class advantage. Recent studies suggest that men born in the top 10 percent of family income have had about a 40 percent chance of ending in the top 20 percent of income by mid-career, while those born in the bottom 10 percent of family income have about the same chance of ending in the bottom 20 percent of income (Bowles and Gintis 2005). This represents a significant degree of social reproduction but nothing like what we would expect in a system ruled by ascribed statuses. Indeed, statistics like these indicate that mobility, albeit mainly short range mobility, remains more common than status transmission. In a "hard" version of social reproduction, stickiness at the top and the bottom would be much greater than it is.

Neither theories of social reproduction nor theories of meritocracy adequately account for the patterns sociologists have found in mobility data. Instead, the findings suggest that we should see schooling as an important demonstration arena in which both brains and socially transmitted status characteristics attract positive notices and in which neither is entirely sufficient to ensure high levels of success. We may also be seeing a trend toward greater social class reproduction in societies like the United States that have allowed inequalities between social classes to grow.

How we weigh the evidence, however, depends on whether we take individual characteristics or group comparisons as our unit of analysis. The factors that bear on individual life opportunities do not necessarily tell us much about the circumstances faced by most people born into a given group. Therefore, it is important to look both at studies of individual achievement and those based on group differentials.

Who Gets Ahead? Individual-Level Studies

Most of the studies of the "who gets ahead?" question have examined the individual-level characteristics that make a difference in the kinds of jobs and incomes people eventually achieve. The classic studies in the status attainment tradition looked at adult attainment as a process in which circumstances at the beginning of the life course influenced outcomes later in the life course. In the earliest of these causal models, parental social status and individual cognitive abilities were seen as independently influencing educational attainment (Sewell and Shah 1967). Educational attainment, in turn, was seen as influencing adult occupational and income attainments (Blau and Duncan 1967). In social psychological versions of the status attainment processes, additional influences (such as parental and teacher expectations and peer influences) were also modeled (Sewell, Haller, and Portes 1969). These studies measured the net effects of attributes, such as social background or measured cognitive ability, by holding other variables in the model statistically constant. Thus, status attainment researchers who were interested in the independent effect of a father's occupation on adult attainments sought to compare people who were similar in every way except for their fathers' occupations—people who had the same measured cognitive abilities, the same levels of aspiration, and equivalent educational credentials. More complex models, developed in later years, included additional individual characteristics and experiences, such as racial-ethnic identity, course-taking patterns, and participation in extracurricular activities at school (see, e.g., Jencks et al. 1979).

Status attainment studies showed that most of the variation in American men's adult occupational and income status could not be predicted by characteristics like social background, cognitive ability, and educational credentials. Quite a bit of the unexplained variation in life fates had to do with the ups and downs of companies, industries, or regions (Haveman and Cohen 1994). Indeed, a good case can be made that although it is theoretically possible for school systems to select people on strictly meritocratic grounds, it is not possible for market economies to do so. Markets do not reward according to the same standards of merit as schools, but simply according to the economic value of goods and services offered (Goldthorpe 1996). Some of the variation in economic outcomes has to do with being in the right place at the right time, and other sources of good or bad fortune. People are subject to the vicissitudes of history, accident, employers' whims, and their own good and bad decisions. Many unmeasured individual differences are presumably involved, too, such as the ability to sense and act on market opportunities.

Both social background and measured cognitive ability show up as important explanatory factors for that part of the variation in people's adult attainments that can be explained statistically, primarily because they both influence the likelihood that a person will obtain more education. If a child has high test scores, she is more likely to end up with good educational credentials, even if she was not born into a high-status family. The opposite is also true: growing up in a high-status family means that a person is likely to end up with good educational credentials, even if she does not have particularly high test scores or top-flight grades.

Although background counts, cognitive ability has been the more direct influence on educational attainment. Grades and test scores have been the best single predictors of educational attainment (measured by number of years of schooling or highest degree level). Academic factors (defined as standardized tests scores, class rank, and academic course taking) have, for example, been by far the strongest predictors of college graduation rates (Alexander et al. 1982). Even so, background never disappears entirely as an influence on educational attainment. Even during the postwar period of expanding educational opportunity in the United States, family background helped to predict test scores, and it also had a modest direct effect on how much schooling a person was likely to receive regardless of test scores (Jencks et al. 1979; Featherman and Hauser 1978).

Here is an illustration of the role that cognitive ability and social background have played in the educational attainment process: At the height of the equal opportunity era in the United States (1946–1980), bright children whose fathers had blue-collar occupations were less likely than other children to obtain a college degree. According to the U.S. General Social Survey (GSS), children with the highest IQs (measured here as the top 14 percent on a word-recognition test) whose fathers were unskilled blue-collar workers and who reached college age in the 1950s and early 1960s had little more than a 50 percent chance of completing college (see Table 6.1).[3] Given the overall odds of the era (one in five), this is a very good probability of completing college, but it is not as high as the 80 percent likelihood of graduating enjoyed by people with the same high level of verbal intelligence and fathers who worked in professional or managerial occupations. And it is not even as good a chance as the 70 percent chance of completion enjoyed by all children, regardless of IQ level, who were lucky enough to be born into families in the top tenth of the occupational ranks (Hout, Raftery, and Bell 1993:46).

Yet, as Table 6.1 shows, the relationship between social background, verbal ability, and educational attainment has changed for more recent cohorts. Among men and women born between 1955 and 1971, background was substantially more important as an influence on obtaining a college degree, while verbal ability, as measured by the GSS word recognition test, was hardly important at all. The gap separating sons and daughters of professionals from sons and daughters of blue-collar workers nearly doubled between the earlier and later

TABLE 6.1

Chances of completing college by father's occupation and GSS word recognition score, U.S. men and women, born 1946–60 and 1955–71

	CHANCES OF COMPLETING COLLEGE (%)	
Father's occupation	Students with median scores (%)	Students with top 14 percent scores[a]
A. Respondents born 1946–60		
All occupations	20	70
Professional	38	81
Manager	26	82
Clerical/sales	18	65
Skilled blue-collar	15	60
Unskilled blue-collar	12	54
Father's occupation	Students with median scores (%)	Students with top 10.5 percent scores
B. Respondents born 1955–71		
All occupations	33	33
Professional	59	63
Manager	47	45
Clerical/sales	39	38
Blue-collar	19	18

SOURCE: General Social Survey (GSS). Cohort A (men and women born 1946–60) tabulated by Michael Hout. Cohort B (men and women born 1955–1971) tabulated by Kristopher Proctor.

[a] Verbal ability is based on a 10-item word-recognition test. Top 14 percent for cohort A = 9 correct. Top 10.5 percent for cohort B = 9 correct.

cohorts. But those scoring at the top of the word-recognition test were hardly more likely to finish college than those scoring at the median—and in some occupational strata were actually less likely to finish college than those scoring at the median.

This table is just one piece of evidence that the effects of family background may be increasing as an influence on adult attainments. Most studies suggest that growing income inequality lies behind this change. Berkeley economist David I. Levine notes that American children born into the elite have "a constellation of privileges that very few people in the world have ever experienced" (Levine, quoted in Scott and Leonhardt 2005:A17). At the same time, children born poor in the United States have disadvantages far in excess of those found in countries with stronger social safety nets and more equally funded educational systems. One recent study found that a child's family background was a better predictor of school performance in the United States than in several Western European countries (including traditionally class-conscious France) (see Scott and Leonhardt 2005). This is a finding certain to disturb Americans' confidence in their country's unique status as a "land of opportunity."

To be sure, class background and measured cognitive ability are not the only variables that count in the educational attainment equation. Other social and psychological characteristics also show an independent influence, after background and ability are statistically controlled. Factors bearing on educational attainment include all of the following: having an intact two-parent household, having families and friends who value education, taking academic courses (particularly academic courses in math and science), and having strong personal aspirations to succeed (Sewell, Haller, and Portes 1969; Sewell and Hauser 1975; Jencks et al. 1979; Jencks, Crouse, and Mueser 1983). Recently, several studies have found that taking rigorous academic courses in high school is a better predictor of college persistence than even standardized test scores or class rank (Adelman 1999; Horn, Kojuku, and Carroll 2001).

High-level education credentials, in turn, are the key to obtaining prestigious and well-paid jobs. The people who tend to move up are those who have the habits and skills that bring success in school: regularity, diligence, and reasoning ability. Not all credentials have the same weight in the market, of course. Business and technological disciplines are more highly valued, and the credentials of minorities and women are less highly valued than the credentials of white men (Treiman and Roos 1983; Goldin 1992).

The person with the best chance of later life success, then, is a white male born into an intact, two-parent, high-status family that values education; who has high tested intelligence and is surrounded by high-aspiring peers; and who takes lots of rigorous courses, especially in math and science, gets good grades in school, and maintains high achievement aspirations. Each of these characteristics makes at least a small independent contribution to explaining status attainment in later life. People who hold leadership positions in extracurricular organizations as adolescents also tend to have greater occupational success (Jencks et al. 1979, chap. 5; Willingham 1985; Howard 1986). People who do not have these characteristics certainly do get ahead at times, just not as frequently.[4]

This can make educational success seem like merely the product of putting the right set of variables together. In fact, the blunt language of sociological variables hides the truth that individual and group cultures create habits that can lead to success or failure. Sociological variables do not create the self-denying habits of study that encourage educational success. Only concrete people (helped by their friends and family) do that. Staying in school and achieving good grades is largely a product of the "academic ethos"—the self-discipline to study when others are out with friends, socializing and having fun (Rau and Durand 2000). Most people know someone like a former student of mine, Toby, who was born into a working-class (and non-English-speaking) family but spent hours and hours in the library in an effort to be the best-prepared student in class. They also usually know someone like another former student, let's call her Karen, who came from a wealthy and prominent family and had many rare life experiences (her family's name was attached to a performance hall on campus) but never felt the deep, inner need to work hard enough to stand out. To develop an academic ethos, students must have a sense that commitment will be rewarding. Many students, particularly minority students, hover on the edge of commitment, unsure that the benefits of commitment will outweigh the costs in lost friendships and the threats to self-concept represented by academic evaluators (Morgan 2005; Steele 1997).

Other factors that might plausibly seem important in later life success do not show up as statistically significant influences. These include good looks (as rated by peers) and good personality ratings from teachers and peers. Participation in extracurricular activities is not as important as taking a leadership position in extracurricular activities. In the past, sociologists were unable to show that attendance at "high-quality" secondary schools was an important independent influence on attainment (see, e.g., Sewell et al. 1969; Featherman and Hauser 1978; Jencks et al. 1979; Campbell 1983). But this may not be as true today. Recent data suggests that the college placement record of private, preparatory schools is impressive (Attewell 2001).

Status attainment studies went out of fashion in the 1980s, as stratification researchers began to focus on the challenges and barriers faced by specific groups (such as women and minorities) and on the economic structures that shape life chances. We must therefore be cautious about applying the findings of these studies to the contemporary period. Even so, these individual-level studies tell us many interesting things. The amount of mobility in the system was and no doubt remains high enough to make us wary of sweeping indictments of the "class system" or the "race system," as well as laments about the impossibility of breaching their barriers. In the industrialized world, many thousands of people do breach their barriers every year. The aspirations of one's families and friends and one's own drive to succeed make a difference even for people who are not born into very high-status families.

Perhaps most important, these studies tell us that people who finish higher-level degrees—whether due to family expectations, high intelligence, or just sheer persistence and ambition—have a "leg up" in the labor market, even if they are not otherwise advantaged. If a person had to choose just one characteristic on which to rank well above most of his or her peers—and was required to be average on all other characteristics—the best choice would be to have high-level educational credentials. Although it seems counterintuitive, studies suggest this would be a better choice than being born into a wealthy family (but being average in other ways), scoring very high on tests of intellectual ability, being exceptionally good looking, or having an unusually charming personality (Jencks et al. 1979).

Comparative Studies. For many years, the samples and measures used in status attainment studies in different countries were not comparable and therefore impossible to analyze in a rigorous way (Treiman and Ganzeboom 1990). Even today, consistently measured variables in comparative studies are limited to a small number of potential influences on attainment. Most comparative studies of status attainment look only at family origins, educational attainments, and adult status. Some studies have also looked at gender influences. The influence of cognitive abilities, aspirations, family size, race and ethnicity, and other factors that have proved to be important in the American case cannot be investigated, because good comparative data is still missing.

Nevertheless, some very general cross-national patterns are now evident. One is a pattern of underlying similarity in the process of status attainment. As in the United States, educational qualifications are now more important than social origins throughout the industrialized world in determining how likely people are to succeed. At the same time, social origins always help to determine how much education a person is likely to obtain. For the most part, the association between class origin and education falls into similar patterns across the industrialized nations. However, the formerly socialist countries of Hungary and Poland were apparently able to dampen the influence of social origins on middle-level educational attainments (and during some periods also on higher-level qualifications) by encouraging able working-class students (Ishida et al. 1995; Muller 1996). Conversely, France has stood out, until recently, for the persistent strength of the ties between higher-status families and the upper levels of the educational and occupational system (Garnier and Hout 1976; Muller 1996). It is not surprising that social reproduction theory originated in France. Until recently, mobility through schooling was distinctly limited in that country—as it was in England, another country in which social reproduction theory has been popular (Kerkhoff 1974; Garnier and Hout 1976).

Class inequalities are most severe, however, in the developing world. In countries such as India and Brazil, the class structure is less differentiated, higher levels of schooling are out of reach of the great majority, and stratification remains deeply rooted in family social standing (Kelley 1978; Treiman and Yip 1988). The elite send their children to private schools, and poorly financed government schools serve the poor.

Who Gets Ahead? Group-Level Studies

The findings for groups do not necessarily point in the same direction as the findings for individuals. One reason for this is that all the characteristics that make a difference for individuals are correlated. People born into high-status families are more likely to be pushed to achieve and to have friends that are similarly motivated. They are more likely to attend schools that place a strong emphasis on academics. And for reasons that partly reflect the economic and social advantages of a high-status birth, they are also more likely to do well on standardized tests of academic ability.[5]

Because all of the important factors in the "opportunity equation" are correlated, it is not possible to use individual-level studies to make final judgments about the opportunities of social classes or racial-ethnic minority groups. What is true for exceptional individuals may not be true for groups. If few people in a group have parents who are professionals or managers, the influence of prestigious parental occupations on educational attainments will be irrelevant to the fate of the vast majority of members of the group. An example of the level of correlation between several key individual-level characteristics is shown in Table 6.2 for a sample of American males in the 1960s, at a time of increasing educational opportunity. The data are from one of the world's best studied surveys, the first Occupational Change in a Generation Survey (OCG I), supplemented by IQ correlations from other surveys.[6]

There are many reasons to believe that group-level differentials may not have narrowed much in spite of the vast expansion of schooling. First, the upper classes care about passing on their advantages. Many upper-income parents will do what they can to give their children advantageous experiences, such as searching for the best schools in town, and perhaps providing extra educational resources in the form of tutoring, rare cultural experiences (such as travel to foreign countries), or opportunities for interaction with motivated peers. Cumulatively, the differences between families of upper and lower socioeconomic status (SES) may reach impressive proportions.

Schooling is capable of reducing achievement gaps between groups, even in the face of strong pressures encouraging the reproduction of class and racial-ethnic advantages (Alexander 1997). School systems can, however, also respond to increased demand for degrees in ways that do not reduce social class or racial-ethnic advantages. For example, educational expansion may be accompanied by a more differentiated structure of tracks and

TABLE 6.2

*Estimated true correlations, background, and status characteristics
of U.S. white non-farm males, aged 25–64, surveyed in 1962*

	1	2	3	4	5
Father's education					
Father's occupation	.640				
Education	.426	.485			
Early adult IQ	.358	.382	.680		
Occupation	.250	.440	.648	.502	
Income	.214	.287	.353	.349	.441

SOURCE: Jencks et al. (1972:322).

NOTE: Education is measured by highest grade attained; occupation is measured using the Duncan scale of occupational prestige; early adult IQ is based on the Armed Forces Qualifying Test (AFQT) given to men between the ages of 18 and 26; income is annual monetary income of respondent. AFQT scores were not available on the original survey. The correlations are based on the results of other surveys. Original data from Occupational Change in a Generation I (OCG I) have been corrected for measurement errors by Jencks and his associates (1972:330–6).

tiers, and lower-status children may be channeled (or channel themselves) into lower tracks and tiers, while upper-status children are channeled (or channel themselves) into the higher levels. When new class- or race-linked tiers arise, educational expansion may simply encourage a transfer of social differences in attainment to higher levels of the system. Thus, when lower-status children become better represented in high school, college may become the key to higher social status. When students from lower-status backgrounds begin to enter colleges, the meaningful lines of division in the system may shift again—to specific majors in college or to graduate school. Increased educational attainments may be completely compatible with stable (or even increasing) levels of social reproduction (Boudon 1974).

Findings of international comparisons. Most studies of group differences do find declining correlations between father's status and children's educational attainments over the course of the century. But this declining correlation does not necessarily mean that class inequality has been reduced at the highest levels of the system where credentials are most valuable. Instead, the lower correlation reflects two factors that tell us little about opportunity: (1) the higher average levels of schooling in the population; and (2) the decreasing variation in the amount of schooling children receive.

Robert Mare (1980) first proposed a method for distinguishing between quantitative results due to the expansion of schooling and those due to the selection and allocation of students. He did so by viewing the educational attainment process as a sequence of transitions (e.g., between elementary and lower secondary school and between lower secondary and upper secondary school). At each stage in the sequence, a student can either make a transition or discontinue. The odds of making any transition can then be computed by social background characteristics over a series of cohorts.

A recent study of 13 industrialized societies found that in 11 of the countries, class differences in transition rates to higher levels of schooling remained highly stable over time, in spite of a rapid rise in the average level of educational attainment in all 13 countries. The countries in the study were the United States, Japan, Israel, Canada, Great Britain, France, Germany, Italy, Sweden, the Netherlands, Hungary, Czechoslovakia (before its division), and Poland (Blossfeld and Shavit 1993). Only two countries, Sweden and the Netherlands, showed a clear pattern of decreasing class inequality over time at higher levels of schooling. In addition, the United States showed decreasing levels of inequality for some recent cohorts (Hout et al. 1993; see also Featherman and Hauser 1978:238–52). Thus, in the principal authors' words: "[while] the proportions of [students from] all social classes have increased [at higher educational levels], the relative advantage associated with privileged origins persists" (Blossfeld and Shavit 1993:22).[7] In most places, inequality between classes is effectively, though not maximally, maintained (Lucas 2001; cf. Hout 1993).

Although the odds of making higher-level transitions are greater for students from high-status families, they are not as high as social reproduction theory would predict. In the United States, for example, academically able men in the postwar college cohorts had a 20 percent greater chance of obtaining a college degree if their fathers came from the highest decile of occupational prestige than if they came from the middle of the occupational structure—the difference between a 70 percent and a 50 percent chance of obtaining a degree (Hout et al. 1993:47). We have to keep in mind that class advantages can be stable over time without being extremely large.

Ironically, the results of studies of educational transitions suggest that the societies ideologically most committed to eliminating class differences often failed most completely to eliminate them at the higher levels of schooling. For instance, leaders of the former Soviet Union periodically instituted periods of "class affirmative action," which substantially changed the composition of the educated classes, but only for brief periods. Findings from elsewhere in the former Soviet bloc suggest that policies designed to increase the opportunities of students from working-class families were usually undermined by political corruption before they could be fully institutionalized. The advantages afforded by university education were so great that anxious parents used the various means at their disposal from intimidation to bribery to win places for their children or for those of important clients. In Czechoslovakia and Hungary, corruption was commonplace, usually in the form of favors done for children of powerful officials, but sometimes also in the form of outright bribes, or "thank-you money" (Mateju 1993; Szelenyi and Aschaffenburg 1993). Corruption was so widespread, in the words of one critic, that far from suffering any disadvantage, "the elite and its successors were allowed to operate almost entirely free from meritocratic competition" (Mateju 1993:257).

Even in Japan, a country noted for its apparently meritocratic test-based system of educational selection, the patterns do not indicate lesser rates of social reproduction than elsewhere in the industrialized world. In fact, sons from professional and managerial class families in Japan have a very low probability of downward mobility. More advantaged parents typically buy additional private tutoring for their children in the attempt to ensure the kinds of educational successes that are necessary for white-collar employment (Ishida et al. 1995).

The Scandinavian difference. This leads to an interesting question: why did class inequalities decrease in Sweden and the Netherlands when they did not, for the most part, decrease elsewhere? In those countries, working-class students have more nearly caught up to middle-class students in their chances of achieving higher levels of schooling. These comparative findings show quite clearly that no universal law exists that "privileged classes always find ways to maintain their relative advantages" (Jonsson 1993:126).

A narrowing of class inequalities has occurred in Sweden and the Netherlands in spite of a relatively low rate of university graduation. Access to higher education has become more equal, but the effects of this change are limited for the period under consideration, because relatively few people graduated from universities. Instead, the key changes were at the level of secondary education, where social origins counted much less as a determinant of who completed. They also counted much less over time as a determinant of who was enrolled in academic as opposed to vocational programs.

In all likelihood, changes in the conditions and attitudes of Scandinavian workers themselves have been the most important cause for this change. Jonsson (1993) writes that the greater chances of working-class people over time are attributable primarily "to an equalization in living conditions due to decreasing income differences [and] welfare state redistribution. In addition, those characteristics of manual labor which limit workers' ability to give practical support and encouragement to their children [exhausting work, long hours, etc.] have become less common or severe" (126). Sweden and the Netherlands also have had unusually high commitments to equality of opportunity: they are both societies in which an egalitarian, social democratic influence in governmental policy (including educational policy) has been very important. These cases suggest that equality of opportunity may be greatest where equality of conditions is also greatest. (See also Erikson and Jonsson 1996.)

The Malaysian difference. Race can be as much an influence on mobility as social class— or even a stronger influence. Some racial and ethnic groups are more disadvantaged than working classes from the majority ethnic population. These include groups like the Maoris in New Zealand, the Koreans in Japan, and the Oriental Jews in Israel. In Europe, the peripheries of great cities are filled with immigrants from North Africa and the Middle East, who are very disadvantaged in competition with Europeans. The conditions encouraging greater ethnic equality in these circumstances are similar to those that have led to class equalization in Sweden and the Netherlands. Greater ethnic equality requires strong support in society for equalized conditions and governmental policies aimed at reducing inequalities in housing, schooling, and jobs. Affirmative action has in every case been an important influence on minority group prospects for mobility.

The most successful cases of reduction in inequalities between majority and minority groups are those in which minorities have already gained significant power in at least one institutional domain, such as government, the military, or religion. In Malaysia, a comprehensive government effort has reduced once-large inequalities between the Chinese, Indian, and Malay populations at the same time that educational attainments for all three populations had increased.

Ethnic Minorities and Equality of Opportunity

The few countries that have improved educational opportunities for ethnic minorities have generally made it a priority to do so. They have usually also built on relatively weak ethnic status boundaries, with some inconsistencies in power across sectors. Malaysia is a notable recent success story that illustrates these principles. The Chinese and Indian populations in Malaysia have traditionally controlled most of the wealth in the country, and the indigenous Malays have generally held political power. After years of tension and some racial rioting, the country's New Economic Policy (NEP) was introduced in 1971. The NEP mandated Malay representation in the economy through ethnic ownership quotas, hiring quotas, participation in the armed forces, and educational scholarships. The government also funded rural development, including irrigation and infrastructure projects. Between 1970 and 1990, the proportion of corporate assets owned by Malays rose from 2 percent to 20 percent, and the incidence of poverty declined by 35 percent (UNDP 1994).

Results over the last decade have continued to be impressive in some ways, but less impressive in other ways. Group income disparities have continued to fall, but income inequality within groups has risen since the late 1980s. Moreover, reports have increased of abuse of ethnic privileges by politically connected families. As the most recent *Human Development Report* put it, "National unity has proven elusive" in spite of the country's achievement of the socioeconomic targets in the NEP (UNDP 2004:70).

Where ethnic groups are completely shut out of the more prosperous spheres of the market economy and where sharp and consistent lines of ethnic and cultural stratification exist, even comprehensive government programs cannot usually improve the educational opportunities of minorities. Countries such as New Zealand and India, for example, have attempted at times to implement far-reaching plans to improve the condition of their primary disadvantaged minorities, but with little success. The difference seems to be in the relative status of the minorities in question. When minorities are very completely subordinated, reform polices will not be implemented with enthusiasm by the dominant group or embraced with enthusiasm by the disadvantaged group. The emotions of superiority and shame surrounding social boundaries in these systems can prove to be too much to overcome.

The Rise and Fall of Equalized Opportunity in the United States

Sweden, the Netherlands, and Malaysia are not the only societies that have experienced an equalization of opportunities for higher-level transitions as educational enrollments have expanded. During the period between 1945 and 1980, class and racial inequalities in higher education opportunities were also reduced in the United States (Karen 1991). The American path was based not on greatly improved conditions for the working classes but on a rapid expansion of higher education accompanied by very substantial state subsidies for lower-income and minority students. As Hout and Dohan (1996) put it,

> The Swedish path [to equality of educational opportunity] goes directly through existing class barriers, lowering them over the course of the century; the American path goes around them, expanding the system so much that class-based selection is irrelevant, because so few students are mustered out. (229)

Why did more women, minorities, and working-class kids go to college during this period? Both economic optimism and state support were at work. Real incomes were rising, and the long stretch of general prosperity supported an optimistic outlook among working people. They became more willing to invest in the possibility of an even better future for their children (particularly if they didn't have to invest too much). Moreover, thanks to the powerful postwar economy, professional and managerial jobs were growing at a much faster rate than other jobs. Young people and their parents were more willing to make the sacrifices required to attend college because they knew that good jobs would probably be waiting for them at the end of their studies.

Meanwhile, the government provided the means by which those who finished high school could go on to college without suffering crippling economic burdens. Public colleges and universities were well supported by state governments and required only nominal fees for attendance. The best public university system in the country, the University of California, for example, required students to pay fees of just $84 a year in the mid-1950s (less than $800 in 2005 dollars) (Liaison Committee of the Regents of the University of California and the California State Board of Education 1955:405), and these fees increased only moderately through the 1970s. For those who had trouble making the payments, generous financial aid packages were available. The GI Bill allowed World War II veterans to attend any college that would admit them. From the mid-1960s through the end of the 1970s, the federal government also provided subsidies for low- and middle-income students to attend college. Extremely high levels of institutional financial aid complemented these government subsidies. Financial grants-in-aid from all sources reached a peak of $20 billion in 1975–6 (Congressional Budget Office 1992:7).

These efforts had a measurable impact. Hout (1988) found that the effect of social origins on the subsequent career success of young men dropped by 50 percent between the early 1960s and the early 1980s. Hout attributed this change to the increased openness of higher education and the strong advantages of college degrees in the labor market. Although employers hiring at lower educational levels remained sensitive to applicants' social backgrounds, employers of college graduates adopted more "universalistic" selection practices. Thus, for the first time, college degrees eclipsed social background as a source of subsequent career advantages.

In the United States, the age of increasing educational opportunity ended around 1980 (Lucas 1996; Mortenson 2000). College enrollments continued to grow, but racial and especially class inequalities in college graduation began to increase. For African Americans who enrolled in college, graduation rates in the later 1980s fell to about half the rate for whites (GAO 1995:6). Similarly, after narrowing in the 1970s, the disparities between students from high- and low-income families widened (ibid.; Baker and Velez 1996). After 1980, virtually all the growth in the numbers of graduates came from the top quarter of the income structure. Graduation rates for students from the top quartile of family income approached 70 percent, but graduation rates from the second quartile of family income remained in the high 20 percent range (Mortenson 2005) (see Figure 6.1).

Public policy and social mobility. Since 1980, the United States has made fewer efforts to foster the socioeconomic mobility of children from lower classes and minority groups through education (Karen 2002; Lucas 1996). Most notably, the public resources available to support equality of opportunity at the college level have declined. At the leading private universities, tuitions are now substantially more than half the average family's total yearly income. Without scholarship aid, children whose families are not in the top few percent of

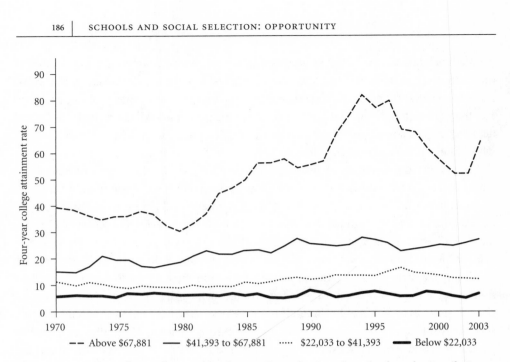

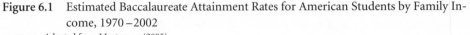

Figure 6.1 Estimated Baccalaureate Attainment Rates for American Students by Family Income, 1970–2002

SOURCE: Adapted from Mortenson (2005).

income cannot afford to attend these colleges, no matter how well qualified they may be. Even at public universities, fees have risen at nearly three times the rate of inflation since 1980, much faster than the incomes of all but the very rich. Students now very often wait to attend college until they are older or attend part-time while they are working 20 to 30 hours a week (Baker and Velez 1996). Many students from lower-income and less educated families are now limited to attending low-cost community colleges for at least two years, where they are surrounded by part-time and vocationally oriented students, and not as strongly encouraged by their peers to persist to the bachelor's degree.

Financial aid is also harder to come by. In the early 1980s loans replaced grants as the primary form of federally provided student financial aid (Congressional Budget Office 1992:7). Studies show that this shift has had little or no impact on high- and middle-income students but has appreciably affected low-income students. Many low-income students must now enroll in less expensive schools or drop out altogether (GAO 1995). These changes in financial aid had a particularly marked effect on black families, who have been reluctant to borrow to finance college (Hauser 1992).

The elite schools have begun to attract a more homogeneous applicant pool: highly qualified children of quite affluent parents. Qualified children from less well-to-do families became less likely to apply, stymied by tuition "sticker prices" that are now at $40,000 per year. In fall 2003, nearly 40 percent of incoming students at very selective private colleges and universities estimated their family's annual income at $150,000 or more (HERI 2003:78). This compares to 20 percent of freshmen in selective public universities who came from equally affluent families, and 16 percent of freshmen in all baccalaureate-granting institutions (ibid.). To put these numbers in perspective, just 5 percent of all

Americans reported annual family incomes at the level of $150,000 or more (U.S. Bureau of the Census 2003, Table 3).

Is IQ concentrated at the top? Some saw these growing class and racial inequalities as an ironic outcome of the triumph of meritocracy itself. This argument was popularized in Richard Herrnstein and Charles Murray's best-selling book, *The Bell Curve* (1994). By giving opportunity to less advantaged students from all social backgrounds, Murray and Herrnstein argued, the postwar meritocracy "creamed off" the most able children from lower-status families, leaving an increasingly large cognitive gap between the social classes in America.

This argument turned out not to hold up to serious scrutiny. People with very good test scores are simply not as concentrated at the top of the class structure as Murray and Herrnstein suggested. In the United States, sociologists found a narrowing, not a widening, of cognitive differences between social class and racial groups as one moved from older to younger cohorts (Weakliem, McQuillan, and Schauer 1995; Hauser et al. 1996). This increasing cognitive equality may be largely the result of a more similar cultural environment experienced by lower- and upper-income Americans thanks to television and the movies, or it may be due to the success of schools in raising intellectual standards (Alexander 1997). In either case, the reemergence of gross inequalities in educational outcomes cannot be attributed to the concentration of good brains at the top of the class structure.

Sociologists in the United States once scoffed at social reproduction theory, because it seemed ill suited to a society in which intergenerational mobility was the norm. Now the United States has a claim to being the clearest example of social reproduction theory at work. After a generation-long attack on the welfare state, the United States has become less a beacon of opportunity than a colossus of inequality. The policies of "free market" capitalism tend to increase, rather than narrow, the gaps between rich and poor. By contrast, "welfare state" capitalism as practiced in many Scandinavian countries has provided more equal education, economic supports for the poor and unemployed, and housing and other subsidies that level the playing field a little.

Would Americans trade the material wealth of a highly unequal, free-market capitalist society for the greater equality, but lower standards of living found in Scandinavian welfare states? Most affluent Americans would not; and lower-income Americans have not had much to say about this issue. Is the trade-off between wealth and equality inevitable? To some degree, perhaps it is. Yet, it is also true that in spite of facing the same challenges of global economic competition over the last quarter century, few governments in the developed world have abandoned the ideal of "equal opportunity for all" as completely as the government of the United States.

CONCLUSION

Social selection is the most important function that schools perform today. The importance of schooling in social selection is a recent phenomenon, however. It has depended on the rise of an opportunity consciousness, the attachment of this opportunity consciousness to schooling, and the tightening of the connection between schooling and jobs through credentialism. In this new system, educational attainment has become the single strongest correlate of getting ahead in adult life. All other factors being equal, it is more important to have high-level education credentials than to be born into a wealthy family, to have high measured intelligence, or to have good looks or a charming personality.

Two theories have developed to explain the connection between schooling and later life success. One theory argues that modern societies are meritocracies in which the brightest and hardest-working people tend to succeed, regardless of their backgrounds. The other argues that educational expansion makes little difference on the level of social reproduction in society. This level of social reproduction is thought to be both rather high and essentially stable, whether or not higher education is relatively restricted or relatively inclusive.

Both individual-level and group-level studies help to evaluate these theories. Individual-level studies are based on comparing the life trajectories of people with different sets of characteristics. These studies indicate that high cognitive test scores are the most important influence on educational attainment. Other factors also help people to complete higher-level degrees: support from family and friends, taking and doing well in demanding courses, and high personal aspirations.

Social background is an important influence, but it works primarily through these other variables. It is associated with high cognitive test scores for reasons that have partly to do with the ability of high-status parents to provide more stimulating cognitive environments. Higher-status parents also provide the motivation that leads children to do well in school, to surround themselves with supportive peers, to take harder courses, and to adopt high expectations for themselves.

Individual-level characteristics associated with higher attainments are correlated with one another. Group-level studies, therefore, provide a different perspective—one that emphasizes the distribution of opportunities between classes rather than individual variation within classes. Group-level studies suggest that class inequalities in attaining the most valuable levels of education do not typically decrease with the expansion of schooling. In most countries, correlations between social origins and high-level educational attainments have remained remarkably stable since the beginning of the twentieth century in spite of a rapid rise in the number of years most people stay in school. Sweden and the Netherlands are two exceptions to this rule, and they suggest that equality of opportunity may be greater in countries where equality of conditions is also greater.

The ideal of meritocracy requires, by definition, both rigorous selection procedures and energetic efforts to search as widely as possible for talent. The realization of this vision requires a set of societal supports, which include, at a minimum: (1) movements toward the equalization or at least the narrowing of the gaps between classes and strata in society, (2) high state subsidies for public higher education relative to the absolute costs of attendance, and (3) widespread availability of financial grants-in-aid for qualified lower-income students. The American experience since World War II demonstrates the importance of these societal supports. The era of equalized opportunities peaked between 1945 and 1980. Once these supports disappeared or declined in the 1980s, so did college graduation rates for lower-income and minority students.

7 | SCHOOLS AND SOCIAL SELECTION: INEQUALITY

The study of those who are not selected in the school sorting process is not as comforting to contemplate as the study of those who are able to use schooling to help them move up in the social hierarchy. Yet, for every few students who get through school successfully at every critical stage, many are left behind. In the United States today, for example, approximately one-fifth of high school students do not graduate with their classes, a figure that rises above 50 percent in the poorest minority communities. By the time the academic "race" finishes with the awarding of graduate and professional degrees 18 years or more after first grade, some 95 percent of each age cohort has fallen by the wayside.

As I showed in Chapter 6, neither the theory of meritocracy nor the theory of social reproduction adequately explains the distribution of opportunities linked to schooling. Too many factors other than academic merit figure into the status attainment process to sustain a theory of meritocracy, and too much mobility through schooling occurs to sustain social reproduction theory.

The theories provide no more certain understanding of inequality than they do of opportunity. This conclusion is perhaps a little surprising. Academic performance linked to meritocracy would seem to be the logical source of inequality in schooling. After all, the ranks of the academically successful seem to be erected on the backs of those the school system defines as not able or not willing to master the curriculum—those who read haltingly, calculate badly, and perhaps begin to consider most instruction "a joke." Certainly, differences in academic ability and motivation are intended to determine and to legitimate the unequal rewards of schooling.

But the theory of meritocracy is damaged by its assumption that school success represents an abstract quality of "merit" and school failure represents its opposite. It is true that children differ in their academic aptitudes, just as they differ in their aptitudes for soccer or art. But genetic advantages have to be activated and directed to make a difference. Nurture (the social environment) is, therefore, a co-determining factor from the beginning.[1] In a neglectful environment, even strong innate aptitude for cognitive activity can fail to be recognized and stimulated. In an attentive and stimulating environment, even modest aptitude may be maximized. The advantages of privileged parents help them to illuminate and direct sparks of acuity among their children. This is the major reason why good students are as common as crickets in some communities but rare specimens indeed in other communities. We often use the term "intelligent" to describe children who perform well on standardized tests. In doing so, we fail to appreciate the extent to which good test results are socially produced by families and communities.

Just as important, we also fail to recognize that tests measure only certain kinds of intelligences. Charles Darwin's son observed that Darwin used to say of himself that he "was not quick enough to hold an argument with anyone" (F. Darwin, quoted in Baker 1974:447). Darwin may have thought slowly, but he clearly thought well. Among other qualities, tests measure the ability to solve problems quickly, to check answers and not to guess, to eliminate obviously wrong answers, and the ability to stay calm under pressure. These qualities would be better described as "test-taking abilities" than as dimensions of intelligence. Intelligence might be thought of as the capacity to analyze and to make good decisions, both on paper-and-pencil tests and in life. A convincing underlying idea of intelligence includes a great many qualities that tests do not even attempt to measure—for example, the ability to change behavior to respond to challenging new situations, the ability to accurately judge the costs and benefits of different courses of action, the ability to "read" people and respond appropriately, the ability to express oneself forcefully and persuasively, and perhaps most important, the capacity to think deeply and creatively about problems and situations. These kinds of intelligences can be very relevant to life success, but they have little or no relation to doing well on tests.

Thus, although many people are conditioned to think of cognitive tests as measuring intelligence, this label is not completely appropriate. What tests do measure are kinds of intelligences and personal qualities that are particularly relevant to contemporary school systems, because schools, like tests, reward quickness, answer checking, calm nerves, and a good storehouse of cultural knowledge (Block and Dworkin 1976).

The problems with social reproduction theory are equally impressive. In its readiness to show that the educational deck is stacked against subordinate groups, social reproduction theorists often neglect important differences among these groups in the resources they hold and hostilities they face, important differences in the institutional structures they encounter from family expectations to labor market biases, and important differences in the adaptive strategies they develop for making the best of their circumstances.

Indeed, not all social inequalities are reproduced through schooling. It is true that low-income people and members of some minority groups face long odds in the school system, but what of another disadvantaged group, women? In many countries, their educational attainment has surpassed that of men in just a generation (Jacobs 1996). In the United States, they are more successful in enrolling and persisting in college, and they achieve better grades. Nor do subordinate groups face the same set of conditions in schooling systems. Schools may bear considerable responsibility for maintaining inequalities when they allow children to get past the first few grades without a solid basis in reading and writing (Farkas 1993) and when they employ tracking structures that contribute more to demoralization than to learning (Oakes 1985). But members of some subordinate groups enter schools that

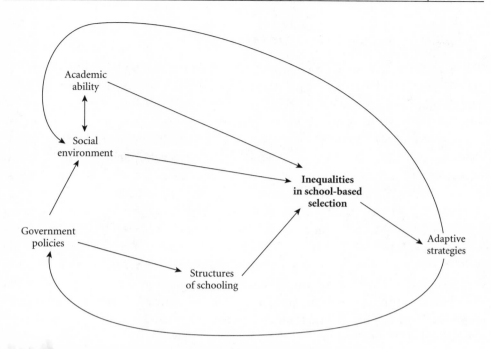

Figure 7.1   Factors Affecting the Development of Educational Inequalities

aim to equalize opportunities—schools, for example, in which tracking is de-emphasized and resources are directed toward those who need them. Overall, strong, well focused school systems are equalizing institutions more than they are institutions that increase inequalities. Learning gaps between groups, for example, tend to shrink during the school year and grow during the summer months (Downey, Von Hippel, and Broh 2004).

The view of schooling and inequality developed in this chapter is based on examining the interplay of group circumstances and institutional structures. The chapter concentrates on groups rather than on individuals, because larger structural patterns are most evident when groups are the unit of analysis. Group circumstances include the resources members of groups bring with them to school and the prevailing definitions of the group's place in society. Institutional structures include school tracking structures, labor market structures, and government policies (like compensatory programs for the disadvantaged) that are related to the reduction or persistence of inequalities. In addition, this view looks at human beings as actively developing strategies to improve their circumstances. Through their adaptive strategies, groups and their individual members can over time come to identify with the values of the schooling system, or to maintain their distance from schooling.

Figure 7.1 shows the factors that contribute most to explaining inequalities in school-based selection. Each of the factors ideally requires careful attention, but this chapter will not be able to address all five completely. In particular, I will have little more to say about academic aptitudes (which nearly all researchers now consider to be co-determined by heredity and environment), and I will only touch on the important subject of how government policies can affect educational inequalities.

THREE MAJOR BASES OF INEQUALITY

The first step is to think about what people from different backgrounds bring to the schools, and the best place to start is with groups on either side of the most important social divides. Three major bases of social inequality are class, race/ethnicity, and gender. Religion can be an important social divide as well, but it is often entangled with class and ethnicity, and for the purposes of this book it is most important as an institutional influence when it leads to the creation of schools run by religious authorities outside the public system. Age is also an important base of social differentiation, but it is less significant in schooling, because schooling is organized around the experience of homogeneous age cohorts.

Social class, race/ethnicity, and gender are not fateful to the same degree for educational attainment. The specific circumstances of subordinate groups bear on their success or failure in school. These group circumstances are based on the resources and experiences the group brings to schooling and how positively or negatively the group is viewed by the larger society. Public schooling is a system that requires and rewards academic commitments and academic performance. Thus, the group resources and experiences that are most directly important to success in school are cultural resources, attitudes about schooling, and motivational follow-through. Beneath these immediate influences usually lie deeper layers of economic and social support. Society's attitudes are also important, because they influence how subordinate groups are treated by dominant groups. High levels of social distance, which make it very difficult for members of a subordinate group to succeed, are at work in all societies with rigidly structured class, racial/ethnic, or gender divisions of labor. Social distance is communicated in many ways—from parents telling children that "he's not the kind of boy you want to be friendly with" or "girls don't do that" to teachers subconsciously lowering their expectations for members of racial and ethnic minorities. Frequently, members of the subordinate group experience feelings of inadequacy—or high levels of anger or resentment—as a response to the majority group's expressions of social distance and prejudice.

These two underlying factors—group resources and societal definitions of the group's place in society—will obviously vary from group to group and society to society. In fact, research shows that lower-class groups are nearly always highly disadvantaged in schooling; racial and ethnic minorities are sometimes even more disadvantaged than lower classes, but are also sometimes only minimally disadvantaged; and, at least in many affluent societies, gender differences may not be very disadvantaging at all in schooling, though labor market disadvantages persist. For these reasons, I will characterize class as a constant divide, race and ethnicity as a varying divide, and gender as a declining divide.

Social Class: The Constant Divide

Social class is based on the distribution of wealth, income, prestige, and power in society. These are the most valuable resources a society has to distribute, and they can be converted into additional advantages in position and opportunity. All societies distribute resources unequally, and so social class, our shorthand way of talking about people at a similar level in the distribution, is consequently the most durable and consistent social influence on educational inequality.

Sociologists often use indexes of socioeconomic status (SES) to measure social class. These indexes are based on weighted combinations of education, occupational prestige, and income. In many areas of life, wealth and income are the key resources of inequality. They allow people, for example, to buy houses in neighborhoods surrounded by other wealthy people and thereby to gain important contacts and the admiration of others who cannot afford to live in these neighborhoods. However, studies suggest that parental educations and, to a lesser extent, parental occupations are the features of SES that matter most for children's school performance and attainment. It is parents' own knowledge and past success in school—plus their ability and motivation to pass on knowledge and habits for success— that is most important. A parent without a secondary school degree or much interest in education might be able to buy an encyclopedia or a computer for her children, but this is no substitute for the daily usage of good grammar, advanced vocabulary, discussion of books, and help with computational skills that a more educated parent can provide.

Social class and educational advantages. Parental social status is strongly associated with how children think about and act in school. Students from more advantaged homes and neighborhoods are more likely to:

- enter school with knowledge and values that encourage school success,
- be surrounded by an atmosphere of parental support for and active involvement in schooling,
- have the economic resources to purchase instructional materials and educational services (e.g., computers, tutors, tuitions) that are not available to students whose parents have less money, and
- present themselves in ways that teachers associate with "good students" (e.g., standard, unaccented English; neat appearance; nice clothes; good manners).

This last point merits discussion. However hard they may try to remain fair-minded and clinical in their judgments, middle-class schoolteachers and counselors often feel subconsciously more comfortable with students who look and sound like themselves. They may feel indifferent, even averse, to students who do not. Many of these feelings are based on quite explicit status symbols: nice or worn clothes, good or poor grooming, deferential or boisterous manners.

Speech can be another factor. Teachers frequently make status associations on the basis of students' use of proper grammar and wide vocabularies. These linguistic abilities are typically the products of class environments more than innate intelligence. Training for public speech is itself class conditioned. The sociolinguist Basil Bernstein (1961, 1975) emphasized that middle-class and working-class speech patterns differ appreciably in the degree to which subject and object references are made explicit or left implicit. In public settings, middle-class speech tends to make all subjects and objects explicit. For example, a middle-class speaker would say: "The boy threw the ball through the window and the window broke" The working-class pattern leaves subjects and objects implicit. For example: "He threw it, and it broke." In Bernstein's terms, schools are built on the middle-class "elaborated speech code" rather than the working-class "restricted speech code." Teachers often judge users of the restricted code to be less intelligent than users of the elaborated code.

People from lower-status backgrounds sometimes tend to be less comfortable interacting with authorities, including teachers. A study by the sociologist Annette Lareau (1987) revealed the power of some of these "hidden advantages" of class. Lareau studied parents' involvement with their children's schooling in two communities. In the predominantly working-class community she studied, she found that parents weren't much involved with their children's educations not because they didn't care, but because they were ashamed of their own weak academic skills (such as a limited vocabulary or poor spelling). They were also likely to defer to teachers as "the experts." In the predominantly middle-class community she studied, on the other hand, the educational skills and occupational prestige of parents matched or surpassed those of their children's teachers. Middle-class parents were not afraid to intervene on their child's behalf for example, to bring up problems in the classroom or to request particular teachers for the following year. They also had the necessary economic resources to manage child care, transportation, and time off for meeting with teachers; to hire tutors; and to become intensely involved in their children's schooling. Different social classes, Lareau suggests, have the same affection and concern for their children, but different capacities for acting on these concerns.

Rungs in the ladder: Variation in class outlooks toward school. Class advantages and disadvantages set boundaries on ways of looking at the world and one's place within it. The French sociologist Pierre Bourdieu (1979) used the term "habitus" to refer to distinctive outlooks and forms of self-expression that arise out of recurring social circumstances. The insouciance and improvisational outlook of jazz musicians, as much as the hunched shoulders and dogged determination of scholars, can be seen as expressions of habitus insofar as both reflect the imprint of habitual practices in the conduct of a particular way of life. Bourdieu himself used the term most often to characterize recurring patterns of social class outlook and expression, which he saw as inculcated by families and reproduced over time under the influence of recurring social class conditions. Following Bourdieu, we can look at class habitus as an influence on the educational prospects of children.

Most of the very poor do not have the resources or the stability to treat schooling in a completely disciplined and attentive way. People who have grown up in relatively stable family circumstances fail to comprehend just how unstable life can be for Americans in the bottom fifth of family income. One of the most startling findings of a careful evaluation of one educational reform program in inner-city Milwaukee was that even the very highly motivated parents who enrolled their children in the program ended up moving at such a high rate (more than 50 percent changed schools from one school year to the next) that the impact of the program itself could not be truly evaluated (Witte, Bailey, and Thorn 1993). Bad nutrition, poor health, insecurity, and anxiety are common products of severely disorganized and stressful lives. So, too, following on their heels are irregular effort, confusion, alienation, and defensive boredom.

For the children of stably employed but low-paid workers, habitus encompasses a wider range of possibilities. The class habitus embraces both soldier-like conformity and hell-raising rejections of authority. There are those who choose a conformist path, but usually lack enough ease with intellectual materials to be considered promising scholars by their teachers; others who choose a path of rebellion, having "laffs" and engaging in small subversive acts at the schools' expense; and still others who withdraw behind a vaguely resentful wall of silence (Willis 1979; MacLeod 1987).

The creation of an identity as a "student" is no mean task even for very able working-class children if they have not been exposed to intellectual activity and high academic expectations in the home. Consider some of the hurdles that are involved in creating a "good student" identity: meeting difficult challenges successfully, accepting labels (ambitious, smart) that may seem ill fitting, overcoming doubts, and negotiating the skepticism or outright hostility of friends and family who may see success in school as an act of abandonment or rejection. The writers Richard Hoggart (1957) and Richard Rodriguez (1982) have provided rich portraits of working-class "scholarship boys" who soak up knowledge like a sponge, rack up awards for academic performance, but have no sense of intimate connection to the works they so compulsively absorb. Many are tempted to give up the chase, and some do give it up (Strauss 1959; London 1979).

Moving up the class structure, we see the habitus of the children of organization men and women. Students from these middle-class families exhibit more frequent and more accomplished conformity with institutional expectations, a matter-of-fact, businesslike approach to institutional life. Habits of regular behavior learned in the family allow for an easier negotiation of school demands, and higher parental expectations about schoolwork create an atmosphere of support for good performance in school. Children are able to balance their needs for a degree of spontaneity with the demands of formal organizations. Relatively few students at this social level may be truly intellectually oriented, but most will be able to perform up to an acceptable academic standard, because schools and teachers value regular effort and good organizational habits (including loyalty to the goals of the organization). In this stratum, students from families with high levels of "cultural capital" (academically valued knowledge resources) will be encouraged to engage with the intellectual side of schooling more than students from families with financial resources but less cultural capital (Bourdieu 1973).

At the top of the class structure, many children will have the resources and confidence to see themselves not just as vessels to be filled with knowledge but as active participants in the employment of culture, capable of using knowledge for their own purposes (Anyon 1980; Cookson and Persell 1985). They learn to advance their interests in an assertive way and to act on the school world as much as they are acted on by it. Here students may see themselves as colleagues of the teacher in the quest to understand and use knowledge. For its less academically inclined scions, upper-class habitus embraces a path of withdrawal from serious engagement with the school, and immersion instead in personal projects and the world of social contacts in preparation for making an impact on the world.

Of course, these are just sketches, and many shades of variation exist within social classes. But class defines the circumference of probabilities. It is very possible to be a working-class conformist, who dutifully follows the teacher's directions, or a working-class rebel, who flouts the middle-class pieties of schooling. But it is very nearly impossible to adopt the outlook of the organizational careerist or the aesthete, because these outlooks are not found frequently enough to serve as models within the milieu of most working-class students.

Preparing for Power

The "St. Grottlesex" private preparatory schools in New England are the most prestigious private secondary schools in the United States. They include such famous names as Andover, Exeter, St. Paul's, St. Mark's, Lawrenceville, Groton, and Choate. These schools are the core of the elite tradition in the United States. The families of as many as 40 percent of each school's students may be listed in *The Social Register*, the arbiter of elite social status in the United States. Other students come from newer generations of intellectually or economically prominent families. Other, slightly less well known private boarding schools can be found throughout the United States.

In their study of selective private boarding schools, Peter Cookson and Caroline Persell (1985) found that these schools are designed, above all, to socialize high-achieving students, many of whom come from upper-class backgrounds, for future positions of power. With their emphasis on character-building activities, challenging assignments, demands for creative engagement, and encouragement of self-reflection and intellectual debate, these schools provide a quality of educational experience that few public high schools can approach. Cookson and Persell refer to the schools as "status seminaries."

Students are required to read deeply and widely, to learn to interpret from a variety of angles, to see knowledge as something that they could use themselves for practical purposes. Students are encouraged to build facilities, write plays, and apply ideas to controversial public policy issues. Students are constantly set against star athletes, writers, and orators in competitions for extracurricular glory. Famous graduates, from presidents on down, come to visit, so that students can be close enough to touch power and personally observe the manners and attitudes of the powerful. And the schools provide resources for a wide range of educational experiences: from field trips to see the greatest works of the Italian Renaissance to internships with think tanks.

Even the landscape and architecture at these schools is designed to give students a sense of being in a special place:

> Andover students can read in the wood-paneled Oliver Wendell Holmes Library, look at works by American artists such as Eakins, Homer, and Whistler in the Addison Gallery or just relax in the Cochran Sanctuary, sixty-five acres of landscaped beauty which includes a brook, two ponds, and natural wild areas as well as manicured lawns and flower beds of rhododendron and laurel. (Cookson and Persell 1985:45)

The connection between beautiful surroundings, power, and high expectations is not lost on students. One headmaster reported the following statement from one of his charges: "This school requires quality in what I do, because I have leaded glass windows in my bedroom" (ibid.:48).

During the course of schooling, there are literally dozens of ways to disengage from the schools' demands for performance. The great majority of students do fall away from the demands of schools, either early or late in their careers. Social class influences the rate at which these disengaging behaviors are expressed. People with fewer resources for succeeding in school tend to express them early in their school careers. These patterns of disengagement include frequent daydreaming, frequent expressions of anxiety in performance situations, rejection of curricular materials outside a narrow sphere of interest, interpreting the classroom primarily as a stage for comic antics, and emphasizing social relationships as the only important feature of school life. Other patterns of disengagement are class conditioned in a more essential way. Self-protective, sometimes truculent defiance in the face of an unfamiliar academic culture is more common among the working classes and the poor, and feelings of intellectual superiority to the routines and rituals of school are more common in the upper classes.

Worldwide evidence of social class effects. Class advantages and disadvantages are very much the same the world over. Even socialist regimes did not succeed in integrating the poor equally into their schooling systems. The political scientist Walter Connor (1979) examined "obstacles to mobility" through education in the former Soviet Union, a state devoted in principle to promoting the interests of workers and peasants. He found that the children of the peasantry were disadvantaged in a number of ways:

- Peasant children lacked the heat in their bedrooms that would allow for uninterrupted study.

- Peasant children were less often disciplined for poor school performance than more privileged children were.

- Educated adult role models were absent.

- The interests of fellow students did not facilitate academic involvements.

- Peasant schools were poor in resources.

- Work competed for students' attention.

- Teachers were less able and experienced because of the low status of peasant schools.

- Stipends in higher education were inadequate, and students from families that could not supplement the stipends often had to take extra jobs. (Connor 1979:207–11)

In other words, class mattered, even in places where it was ideologically impermissible for class to matter.

The magnitude of the problems faced by the lower classes varies from one country to the next, but the types of problems are not fundamentally different. Differences in class circumstances nearly always lead to differences in school-related background knowledge, attitudes about schooling, and motivation in relation to schooling. As I showed in Chapter 6, Sweden, the Netherlands, and Malaysia are among a handful of cases in which class differences in educational attainment have narrowed over time. But in these cases greater equality of income and work conditions between the classes has been more influential than changes in school structures.

Communities and families as mediators of class. Clearly, not all people in the same social class face exactly the same circumstances of life. The rhythms and patterns of life vary greatly, for example, between urban and rural workers. Because their environment demands greater efficiency and organizational ability, urban working people in virtually every society acclimatize better to the schooling system than do peasants and farm workers. In addition, schooling is more relevant for urban occupations than for rural occupations and urban schools are often better supported and better organized than rural schools. For all these reasons, the lowest rates of school completion and the lowest test scores are invariably found in rural areas (UNDP 1994; Hannum 2003).

Community social context also matters. The working-class child attending school in a generally affluent community can receive the cultural benefits of the locale regardless of his or her family's economic situation (Fischer et al. 1996:83). These children are placed in an environment that expresses a higher value on good school performance than most predominantly working-class schools do. It is not surprising that graduation and college attendance rates are higher for working-class students who attend predominantly middle-class schools (McDill, Meyer, and Rigby 1967; Fischer et al. 1996). Conversely, children living in a neighborhood marked by concentrated poverty are more likely to associate with peers who are uninterested in school, and therefore to become themselves uninterested in school, both because of the models of status in the community and because of patterns of differential association (Wilson 1987, chap. 2).

Finally, family structures related to class, but not the product of class, can also make a difference. Children from broken homes often suffer greater disadvantages than other children, for both emotional and financial reasons. Thus, most studies find that living in a one-parent household (particularly a single-father household) has at least a small negative effect on children's grades, attendance, and behavioral adjustment to school (Biblarz and Raftery 1999; Entwisle, Alexander, and Olson 1997). In addition, larger numbers in a family often mean thinner emotional and social support rations. Thus, large households are less able to express as much attention and economic support per child (Downey 1995; Fischer et al. 1996:78). Many families in tight economic circumstances are tempted to choose the most promising child as the family "star" and to invest more heavily in this child's education (Conley 2004).

Race and Ethnicity: The Varying Divide

Racism can be defined as the unequal treatment of a subordinate group by a dominant group on the basis of skin color. Racism has been a feature of Western societies for more than 500 years, since the time of first contact between explorers from Spain and England and the technologically less advanced native peoples of the "new world." Racism was once built into law. Those days are now over, but *de facto* racism continues in many societies. In racist societies, contacts between majority and minority groups are rare, and relations between groups are marked by (often unspoken) prejudices and fears. The African American sociologist W.E.B. DuBois identified the problem of the "color line" as the major social problem of the twentieth century (Dubois [1903] 1995). It could be the major problem of the twenty-first century as well.

In the United States, race has been the most obvious social divide, and race relations the cause of the most troubling problems in American society. Native Americans were subjugated by whites and have lived largely outside of white society on reservations. In the South, blacks were denied formal education before the Civil War, and then allowed only in schools which were poorly funded and rigidly segregated (Walters, James, and McCammon 1997). The power of one group seems closely tied to the poverty and alienation of others. Racial disparities in education, occupation, and income continue to be profound. Even liberal school personnel have frequently encouraged dark-skinned people to set their sights low, on skilled blue-collar jobs, rather than on college.

Racial and ethnic hostilities are often in the news in other parts of the world as well—everywhere from Darfur to Paris. Once relatively homogeneous European societies now have large populations of workers from Asia, Africa, and the Arab world, and the tensions between native and immigrant populations have grown. Under the circumstances, it is not surprising that many people assume that race and ethnicity are the most important basis of social inequality.

But this is not entirely true. Racial and ethnic differences can, at times, be more consequential than class differences (as they have been between blacks and whites in the United States), but they can also be much less important. If skin color was the only thing that mattered, it would be hard to explain the great success of Cuban Americans and Korean Americans in the United States. The relationship between race and schooling depends on characteristics of minority groups themselves. The most important characteristics have to do with the cultural resources the group brings to school, its attitudes toward schooling, and how others treat members of the group. These characteristics, in turn, are typically related to the group's status at the time of immigration and to the size of its migration.

Social scientists have become increasingly skeptical of the concept of "race," because so much genetic variation exists within races and particularly because race is often used by bigoted people to make group differences seem more permanent and unalterable than they actually are. Sociologists are aware, too, that racial characterizations of groups vary over time and are therefore at least largely historical constructions. During the period of their peak immigration in the early twentieth century, the Irish, for example, were often considered "non-white" by "white" Americans (Jacobson 1998). The Nazis considered the Jews a separate "race," but now we think of Jews as members of a religious group formed of many ethnicities. For these reasons, many sociologists prefer to use the terms "majority group" and "minority group" to refer to people differentiated by both power and physical or ethnocultural characteristics. I will sometimes use these terms. However, because race is still firmly a part of everyday language and is also important for discussions of racism, I will also use the term "racial and ethnic minorities" at times.

Why do race and ethnicity matter so much in some cases and so little in others for a group's ability to take advantage of schooling opportunities? Stanley Lieberson (1961) argued that groups migrating voluntarily to a new land have strong incentives to assimilate to the culture of their new country. Although relations might very well be tense for awhile with the majority group, in the long run the new group could expect to be integrated into the host society. By contrast, he argued, groups conquered by a technologically superior power are less likely to be assimilated easily, both because the majority group is unlikely to fully accept those it has conquered and because the colonized rarely accept their conquerors. In our own country, those groups that have suffered most at the hands of European settlers—conquered groups (the Native Americans) and once-enslaved peoples (the African Americans)—have been less completely assimilated into American society, including the schooling system, than groups that have voluntarily migrated.

Lieberson's theory explains quite a bit of variation in racial and ethnic relations across societies. However, it probably fails to take sufficient account of the power of restricted economic opportunities, exclusionary laws, and cultural prejudices. These forces can make even voluntary immigrants into social outcasts, resulting in the kinds of deep antagonisms so often associated with conquest. Therefore, we should think as often of the social conditions groups currently face as of their original circumstances.

The special situation of "caste-like" minorities. Few people believe that Korean Americans or Cuban Americans are as disadvantaged in the United States as African Americans. The first two groups rank near the top of average incomes—higher than whites from English ancestry—the last near the low end. As compared to other minorities, those that are most disadvantaged are restricted by employers to the lowest-level jobs in society, live in highly segregated communities cut off from the rest of society, and are represented in the culture of the majority group in prejudicial ways, often some combination of the ugly adjectives of bigotry: as violent, unclean, greedy, promiscuous, unintelligent, or superstitious. In the West, these epithets have dogged the trail of minorities since the persecution of the Jews began during the European Middle Ages.

One problem for members of these "caste-like" (or "highly subordinated") minorities is that no way of acting helps to improve the judgment that members of the majority group make of them. If they are agreeable, they are scorned as servile. If they are assertive, they are criticized as overbearing. If they are good-natured, they are regarded as fools. If they are cautious, they are condemned as untrustworthy. With the group's increasing success in society, these responses change, although they often change in a very uneven and grudging way. Middle-class members of the group may be accepted, while lower-class members are as ill-treated as before.

Highly subordinated minorities develop responses to their situation that are characteristically different from those of less poorly treated minorities. They frequently reject the legitimacy of the institutions of the dominant groups and emphasize solidarity among themselves. Members of highly subordinated groups often develop a sense of themselves as victims and outcasts. Because they are denied status in the terms valued by the larger society, men from these groups, in particular, frequently develop an alternative status system based not on "respectability" but on "reputation" for eye-catching behavior. Margaret Gibson captures some of the dimensions of "reputation" in poor minority communities:

> You earn a reputation by how well you talk, by how tough you are, by your willingness to fight even if you lose, by how successful you are with women, by the dollars in your pocket and your willingness to spend them, and by your ability to lead others, no matter the direction. (Gibson 1991:180–1)

As a consequence, high levels of criminal activity and apathy are usually found among highly subordinated minorities, reinforcing the majority group's low opinion of them.

Highly subordinated minorities are found in many societies besides the United States. They include West Indians in Britain; Turks in Germany; Maoris in New Zealand; Burakumin, Okinawans, and Koreans in Japan; Gypsies in the Czech Republic; Arabs and Oriental Jews in Israel; and the Irish in Great Britain (Ogbu 1978; Fischer et al. 1996:192). Consider the following characterization:

> Members of [this] minority, many of whom were brought to the country as slave labor, are at the bottom of the social ladder. They do the dirty work, when they have work. The rest of the society considers them violent and stupid and discriminates against them. Over the years, tension between minority and majority has occasionally broken out in deadly riots. In the past, minority children were compelled to go to segregated schools and did poorly academically. Even now minority children drop out of school relatively early and often get into trouble with the law. Schools with many minority children are seen as problem-ridden, so majority parents sometimes move out of the school district or send their children to private schools. And, as might be expected, the minority children do worse on standardized tests than majority children do. (Fischer et al. 1996:172)

Who are they? They are Koreans in Japan, members of the same group that disproportionately number among the top achievers in the United States (Lee 1991).

No matter where or how racial stratification systems develop,[2] members of highly subordinated minorities invariably perform less successfully in school than do other minorities. Although the available data are not perfectly comparable, in every case reported these groups show a pattern of low commitment to schooling, low test scores, and low levels of educational attainment (Fischer et al. 1996:191–4). Frequently, these outcomes are taken by members of the majority group as evidence of the minority group's intellectual inferiority. However, the real causes are social: the restricted economic opportunities of these groups discourage a sense that schooling is a bridge to future possibilities. Residential segregation fosters isolation from more advantaged groups, and a differentiation of attitudes from the majority. And their stigmatized identities can create feelings of resentment and alienation from the authority structures of the larger society, including the schools.

Some voluntary immigrants, who express the expectation that the new host society will provide better economic opportunities, also develop a high level of separateness from the host society, because they experience discrimination when they arrive and because they emphasize religious or cultural practices that maintain the group's separate status. For this reason, the alienated culture of "caste-like" minorities can develop even when migration is entirely voluntary, as appears to be the case among many Muslims in contemporary Western European societies. While they give strong verbal endorsement of schooling as a way of getting ahead, Muslim youth often produce "very weak . . . attitudes, efforts, and persistence supporting the . . . pursuit of school success" (Merry 2005).

Gradual improvement in the circumstances of members of "caste-like" minority groups does occur in more open, pluralist societies, as the cases of African Americans in the United States and Oriental Jews in Israel demonstrate. But improvement often requires a very high level of commitment both by the government and by leaders in the minority communities. Only a few societies have succeeded in approximating multiethnic integration and equality.

Most of these societies are found in Latin America, where racial mixing (originally through force during the period of conquest), a history of class-based politics, and the humanistic philosophy of the Latin American Catholic Church have all played a role in reducing racial stratification (van den Berghe 1970: chaps. 2, 3, 6). However, even countries such as Brazil, with generally strong records of integration and intermarriage, have not achieved full social equality between racial groups.

Even in self-consciously pluralistic societies, immigrant groups usually experience ferocious prejudice and discrimination at first. The United States provides an example of long-term absorbing power combined with fierce short-term prejudice. The historical record shows that members of immigrant groups were regularly taunted by other children (and not infrequently by their teachers) for their foreign dress and manners and ridiculed for their unfamiliar accents. A memoir by the literary critic Alfred Kazin powerfully conveys the sense of strangeness that many immigrants felt and the anxiety induced in them by adult authorities (first represented by teachers and principals):

> It was never learning I associated with that school: only the necessity to succeed, to get ahead of the others in the daily struggle to make a good impression on our teachers, who grimly, wearily, and often with ill-concealed distaste watched against our relapsing into the natural savagery they expected of Brownsville boys. It was not just our quickness and memory that were always being tested. Above all it was our character. . . . The very sound of the word as our teachers coldly gave it out from the end of their teeth, with a solemn weight on each dark syllable, immediately struck my heart cold with fear they could not really believe that I had it. (Kazin 1951:17, 20)

Members of new immigrant groups usually appear not just lacking in "character," but also in intellectual ability, a conclusion that IQ tests were only too prone to validate. During World War I, for example, the average IQ score of U.S. enlisted men who were Polish immigrants or their children was 85 — a full standard deviation below the population average (Sowell 1981:9). These low test scores were more a function of unfamiliarity with the dominant language and culture than anything else. Men of Polish heritage now score above average on IQ tests. Nevertheless, in the first half of the twentieth century, many teachers and school administrators stereotyped Polish and other Eastern European immigrants as dim-witted and fit only for manual labor.

In later years, new immigrant groups, particularly those like Mexicans with limited English and darker skins, faced the same limitations in cultural resources, parents who could not help much with schoolwork because of overwork and limited English. And they faced the same pattern of educational discrimination: enrollment in less demanding schools, teachers who could not appreciate their circumstances or their latent abilities, and counselors who recommended that even the brightest students lower their sights to skilled blue-collar employments.

American society embraces the ideas of cultural pluralism and equality of opportunity. To some degree, schools act on these beliefs by developing programs to encourage talented children from disadvantaged backgrounds. In addition, living standards are higher than in most other parts of the world. Rates of incarceration are also very high by world standards.

These factors may help to explain why, in spite of high levels of residential segregation and limited labor market opportunities, blacks and Latinos in the United States do not express highly alienated attitudes toward schooling (Ainsworth-Darnell and Downey 1998). Schooling is seen as a way out of crime-infested high poverty areas. In this respect, the United States stands out from most countries; even though its treatment of minorities is far from perfect, it engenders relatively little of the alienation that is so frequently heard among minorities in other countries.

Explaining rates of "assimilation." One important reason that race and ethnicity are properly characterized as a "varying divide" is that some immigrant groups become assimilated into host societies and move up the socioeconomic ladder faster than others. The success of fast-rising minorities is often attributed to their superior drive or intelligence. However, the truth is that members of these so-called model minorities typically come to their new country with a host of advantages not enjoyed by other groups, and these advantages are more important than drive and intelligence (which are the products of success as much as the causes of success).

Highly mobile groups almost invariably bring urban skills with them to their new country. Although they were very poor, most immigrant Jews, for example, were urban merchants or artisans. In more recent years, Cuban, Korean, and Indian immigrants have come largely from merchant and professional backgrounds. These types of immigrants are well prepared for an urban, commercial society; they bring habits of conduct and experiences that help them succeed (Steinberg 1981). They are used to the fast-paced, calculating urban life and high levels of organization typical of cities. By contrast, less mobile groups have invariably come out of agrarian settings and traditional peasant cultures. This is true of Irish, Sicilian, Mexican, and African American immigrants. Cultures that celebrate study of the written word, sometimes for religious reasons, also help prepare children for success in schooling. By contrast, oral cultures, for all of their glorious banter and song, provide a much less advantageous preparation (Sowell 1981). Keeping just these two factors in mind, it comes as no surprise that the mercantile, Torah-studying Jews were one of the faster-climbing groups in the American educational system, or that the agrarian, storytelling Irish experienced a slow and difficult advance (Steinberg 1981; Sowell 1981).

The sheer number of immigrants is another factor that helps to explain the variable rates of assimilation and advance among ethnic groups. Sociologists have argued that "prejudice unfurls like a flag" with larger numbers of immigrants (Lieberson 1980). The phrase "Yellow Peril" was coined in response to the large surge of Chinese immigration in the late nineteenth century, not the small Japanese immigration during the 1890s and 1900s. Indeed, the groups that have had the most difficult time making their way in American society have been part of the largest immigrations. The nearly two million Irish who came to the United States between 1830 and 1860 were the largest immigrant group until the massive, four-million-person black migration from the South to the North in the 30 years between 1940 and 1970 (Sowell 1981:211). In the United States, the immediate effects of very large immigrations has been to reduce the level of prejudice against earlier-arriving groups, while intensifying opposition to the new group and placing it squarely at the bottom of the social ladder (Lieberson 1980).

Some groups encourage behavior patterns that lead to greater success in schooling. A typical pattern for children from Asian immigrant families is to study around the dinner table with older children helping younger children. These patterns of intense cooperative learning continue into college, where Asian children often form "study gangs," whose members organize their lives around common classes and shared academic goals (Miller 1995:276). Asian parents have more than high aspirations for their children; they enforce practices and standards that permit these aspirations to be realized. Children are rewarded for strong academic performance, and strictly controlled when their performance does not meet expectations. The Asian emphasis on "effort" as more important than "ability" no doubt reinforces the practices and standards that lead to school success.

Relatively large gaps remain in the school performance of the most disadvantaged racial-ethnic groups in American society and the more advantaged groups, but these gaps are slowly closing. Our best data come from the National Assessments of Educational Progress (NAEP) tests given annually in several subjects to national samples of 9-, 13-, and 17-year-olds. When the tests began in the early 1970s, African American and Hispanic students scored one standard deviation or more below European Americans at all three grade levels in both reading and math. This means that the average score of minorities was approximately at the level of the bottom third of whites. In recent years, the achievement gap has narrowed significantly; group differences will soon close to one-half standard deviation at the younger grades, and not much higher than that at the upper grades (Whitehurst 2005).

In the United States, bilingualism has been shown to be a factor conducive to the school success of Hispanic students. Students who speak both Spanish and English seem to have an easier time in school than students who speak Spanish only or English only. This is perplexing, since English is the official language. However, bilingual students have a wider range of potential contacts for information and help. They can receive help both from Spanish-dominant and English-dominant speakers (Rumberger and Larson 1998). Having to negotiate between two languages may also have some cognitive benefits. The same positive findings for bilingualism seem to apply for other ethnic groups as well, at least as long as both languages are strongly supported in the family (Portes and Hao 1998).

Schools have become far more attuned to ideas about ethnic pluralism than they once were, and they have introduced multicultural curricula in an effort to share the bounty of world culture and to make members of all groups feel welcome in school. These multicultural emphases in the curriculum seem, in fact, to help members of minority groups to feel less alienated in school, but they do not solve the fundamental problems of racial and ethnic stratification. They may even direct needed attention away from more important realities, such as investment in minority communities, development of economic skills and work-related habits, reduction of residential isolation, and confrontation of stigmatizing representations (and self-representations).

Gender: The Declining Divide

For most of human history, women have had much less power than men. Their status was tied to the reproductive cycle and enforced both by social expectations about women's roles and, not infrequently, by the physical strength of men (Blumberg 1984). Not until the 1820s and 1830s, with the upsurge of liberal and democratic ideals in Europe, were the first public calls for women's emancipation heard. Even though women made faster progress in the United States than elsewhere, through the 1950s they remained in a distinctly inferior position and were often frustrated by the narrow circumferences of their lives (see, e.g., Friedan 1963). Given the long history of women's subordination, it is amazing how much things have changed in a generation. Indeed, the changes have been so striking that we can fairly ask whether gender might become statistically irrelevant as a factor in social selection within the next half century.

From a global perspective, women are in a particularly complex situation today. In societies where women continue to be kept out of the public arena, they have essentially the same disadvantages as lower-class groups. They may lack the economic resources, the social ties, and the cultural experiences to compete with men. Some societies restrict women almost completely to the private sphere of family life. By contrast, middle- and upper-middle-class women in more gender-equal societies have the cultural background to navigate their way in society. They are increasingly developing the economic clout and supportive social ties that help as well. In their performance as students, women may even have some distinct advantages, owing in part to the concern with culture and social relationships that are part of traditional feminine roles. Yet a couple of distinct disadvantages of gender also continue to exist, even in contemporary industrial societies. Most important, women can be physically identified by appearance and are therefore relatively easy to discriminate against where discrimination is most advantageous to men.

Patriarchy and gender inequality. Differences in women's situations depend most on whether they live in patriarchal or less patriarchal societies. Patriarchies are societies in which men dominate more or less completely. Women are excluded from the public and business life of the society and are restricted to the family circle. Their main role is procreation and child rearing. In patriarchal societies, stereotypes about women's "incompetence" in male spheres abound, and men can get away with using physical force in their relations with women.

Although elements of patriarchy remain in every society, some societies have minimized these elements considerably over the past several generations. Factors that have led to the eclipse of patriarchy include having fewer children, typical of families following industrialization, and the technological advances that allow women to better control their fertility. They also include the rising expectations that come with women's participation in the paid labor force and with their increasing levels of formal education (Huber and Spitze 1983). A self-reinforcing cycle occurs: As women's child-rearing demands decline and their contribution to family income increases, their power in family decision making and the allocation of household tasks increases (Gerson 1985). Effective organization is another important reason for the changing circumstances of women. Encouraged by the broader social changes, women's organizations have lobbied effectively to change negative stereotypes, to improve women's opportunities in the workforce, and to expand legal protection against male violence (see, e.g., Stromquist 1993).

The world, consequently, is now divided between what we might reasonably call patriarchal and less patriarchal (though not quite "post-patriarchal") societies. The defining characteristics of patriarchy are still very much evident in the poorer countries of the Middle East, in nearly all East Asian societies, in South Asia, and in most of Africa. On the other hand, the United States, the other Anglo American democracies, large parts of Europe, and most Latin American societies can be considered less patriarchal. Gender discrimination has not entirely disappeared in these societies—far from it! But parity has been reached in some important spheres of social life, and the overall climate for women is no longer suffused with the assumptions of male power and control.

Patriarchal and less patriarchal societies show clear differences in how much educational opportunity women can expect. In the developing world, the largest disparities in the educational enrollments of men and women are found in African and Middle Eastern countries and the smallest disparities in Latin America (Stromquist 1989). Asian countries generally fall in between but still provide relatively few opportunities for women at higher educational levels. Women's college enrollments are, for example, half of men's in both China and India (United Nations International Conference on Population and Development 1995).

The poorer Islamic countries are the most notable examples of gender inequality. Girls represent just two-fifths of school enrollments, even at the primary school level (UNESCO 1994:6). These countries are often divided between the urban middle-class setting in which contact with the world is a given, and poorer urban and rural areas in which the religious culture of Islam remains the norm. By Islamic tradition, girls are sequestered at puberty, prohibited from contact with the opposite sex, and prepared for engagement and a "pure" marriage to a chosen man. To symbolize their conformity to these traditions, girls begin wearing veils to shield their faces from men. This induction to the traditions of "purdah" leads, predictably, to early withdrawal from school (Shah and Eastmond 1977). Beyond puberty, education is distinctly secondary to the social pressure on Muslim women to become wives and mothers.

We cannot say that Islam is invariably opposed to principles of gender equity in higher education or the labor market. For example, in oil-rich and Western-oriented Kuwait, more women than men are enrolled in higher education, and women are overrepresented even in science and engineering fields (United Nations International Conference on Population and Development 1995). In Indonesia, pre-Islamic cultural traditions have encouraged gender relations that are much more equitable and relaxed than in most of the Gulf States.

Societal correlates of gender inequality. The work of Roger Clark (1992) has shed considerable light on the forces that create and reinforce gender inequalities in the developing world. The study showed that countries with higher per capita incomes were more likely to have greater gender equality in schooling. As we have already seen, economic progress is strongly associated with conditions that make women's lives less restricted. On the other hand, Clark (1992) found that high levels of multinational investment were negatively associated with greater gender equality. (This may be because multinational investors feel more confident when men fill the high-status occupations and also discourage state labor regulation that would improve the conditions of women.) Countries with many ethnic groups generally had less gender equality, too, perhaps because it is politically difficult to extend educational opportunity when many ethnic groups are competing for preeminence. And, for the countries studied, Islam showed up as a negative influence on gender equality in the countries where it was the dominant religion.

In the industrialized world, a great deal more equality exists between men and women. In secondary school and higher education enrollments, women's enrollments are either equal to or higher than those of men. This carries over into higher education. Indeed, the number of women with university degrees is equal to or greater than the number of men with university degrees in 21 of 27 countries which are members of the OECD, an organization of wealthy democracies (OECD 2004). In most of these countries, women's educational parity is relatively recent. An exception is the United States, where women reached parity with men in secondary school and college attendance beginning in the late 1800s, partly because of the high female enrollment in teacher training colleges (Jacobs 1995). By contrast, Germany and the countries geographically and culturally close to Germany (Austria, Belgium, and Switzerland) remain notably unequal with respect to women's opportunities in higher education and, to a lesser degree, in secondary education. Gender inequality in education is the norm to an even greater degree in the richest countries of East Asia (Japan and Korea). But even in these countries, the tendency has been toward greater equality in educational access over time (Carceles 1979; Jacobs 1995).

Subtle forms of gender discrimination in school? Although women now experience few barriers to educational access and advance, the research is less clear about whether women continue to experience disadvantages in how they are treated in schools. The "microbehaviors" of teacher encouragement and control may still favor boys over girls—at least in some classrooms. In elementary school, boys show a more assertive style of commenting in class and also take up more physical space. Perhaps because of their very audibility and visibility, teachers can tend to give boys more "air time" and to allow them to interrupt more often than they do girls (Sadker and Sadker 1994). Boys also occasionally invade the space of girls on the playground with impunity and can effectively label girls in negative ways (Thorne 1995, chap. 6).

Early studies of the "climate" for women in college classrooms showed that instructors were more likely to maintain eye contact with men, to allow men to give longer answers in class, to allow men to complete answers without interruption, to nod and gesture in relation to men's remarks, and to amplify on men's comments. It was even common in some classrooms for instructors to attribute remarks made by a woman to a man (Hall 1983; Wilkinson and Marrett 1985). The situation today is clearly different. Reports of continuing discrimination against women, through exclusionary or demeaning micro-behaviors that lead women to feel uncomfortable in the classroom, are still heard at times, especially in science, math, and engineering. However, few such reports are heard in arts, humanities, and social science fields, where women are in the majority and frequently the most engaged and active students.

Even controlling for measured ability, gender remains a crucial element in choice of major (Davies and Guppy 1997). Some fields, such as art history and English, are dominated by women, but women continue to be less represented in math and science-related fields. In OECD countries as a whole, women make up only 30 percent of math and computer science enrollments, and less than that in some of the physical sciences (OECD 2004). Subtle forms of male resistance to women may be more evident in those fields, partly because the potential rewards for completion of degree programs are higher. Yet, in the United States, such remunerative fields as medicine, law, and business have all become "gender equal" over the past generation. Nevertheless, women still tend to fill more nurturing specialty areas such as pediatrics rather than surgery and family law rather than corporate law (Jacobs 1995; NCES 2005).

Whatever resistance remains has not stopped women from reaching parity with men and even surpassing them in school performance. More than 120 women are enrolled as undergraduates in the United States for every 100 men. Women also outnumber men in universities in the European Union, partly because they are far more likely to finish upper secondary schooling (Eurydice 2002). Women's grades are somewhat higher than men's in secondary school and college, and they are more likely to persist to complete degrees. Women outperform men on tests of verbal ability, and they are more likely to gain admission to academic honors societies. Indeed, many colleges and universities are experiencing a shortage of male applicants, and some scholars have even begun to talk about developing "affirmative action" programs for men. Much of the increased emphasis on sports in small colleges is directly related to the recruitment of male students. (Interestingly, men are found in disproportionate numbers at the very high end of cognitive test distributions, particularly in math and science, and also at the very bottom of the distributions.)

The reasons why women are better prepared to succeed in school are no doubt complex. First, middle-class women's traditional involvements in matters related to the arts and culture equips them well for success in academic fields where these interests are well supported (DiMaggio and Mohr 1985). Second, girls' emphases on cooperative play and interpersonal communication are well suited to classroom life, where a climate of order and civility rules. Competition, of course, is important in the classroom, but few boys experience academic competition in the same visceral way that they experience physical competition. It is possible that girls' skills in interpersonal communication help them to share valuable information about reading materials, assignments, and teacher expectations. Third, the capacity to concentrate and comply with authority over long periods of time may also be a factor. To the extent that women are expected to enforce propriety in families, they are well trained for the propriety climate of school, where students' willingness to comply with the teachers' authority over long periods of time is one key to success (Michelson 1989). Indeed, in some countries, the schools' emphases on high culture, cooperation, communication, and compliance are considered "effeminate" by boys from working- and lower-class backgrounds. This dismissive outlook greatly encourages the preeminence of women in the educational sphere (Gibson 1991).

Women and work. Women remain highly disadvantaged, however, in converting their educational achievements and credentials into high pay. At most educational levels in the United States, they earn on average about 70 percent of men's earnings; the same ratio holds for female and male Ph.D.s as for female and male dropouts. This is actually a little better than women's pay in other industrialized countries. In all OECD countries, women with secondary school credentials earn just 60 percent of male salaries, and women with university credentials only about 65 percent (OECD 2004). Field concentrations partly explain these differences at the higher educational levels, but they obviously can't help to explain the differences at lower levels. Instead, the inequities in earnings reflect the fact that occupations are more sex segregated than schools and that predominantly female occupations are poorly paid compared with predominantly male occupations (Reskin 1993). Some of the inequities also reflect the more interrupted work lives of women and their lesser chances of receiving specialized on-the-job training, which can perhaps be considered indirect consequences of male power. Most economists attribute the rest of the difference in the pay of men and women to the direct effects of discrimination (see, e.g., Osberg 1984, chap. 7; Goldin 1992).

The amount of job-related discrimination against women appears to be even higher in the developing world than it is in the industrialized world. Estimates from Latin America, for example, suggest that between 60 and 80 percent of the difference in women's and men's wages is due to discrimination rather than to "human capital" variables, such as formal qualifications, formal training, and work-related experience (Psacharopoulos and Tzannatos 1992). These figures are higher than comparable studies from the United States, which estimate that 50 to 60 percent of the wage gap is due to discrimination, rather than "human capital" variables related to training and experience (Mincer and Polachek 1974; Osberg 1984: 126–8). Throughout the world discrimination on the basis of gender remains a significant influence in the labor market.

Reasons exist to believe that gender will be a less significant influence in the labor market in the future. In the first place, more and more jobs in postindustrial societies involve communication and consultation in service industries, rather than heavy physical labor. Women are at least as well suited to these jobs as men. Moreover, as the pool of career-oriented women increases, men have more difficulty hiring and promoting men on grounds other than demonstrated competence. Women's organizations and women's support networks contribute to equalization of opportunity by continuing to challenge discrimination in an active way. As more women are promoted, men's sensibilities change, however slowly and unevenly. Education is not yet as useful a stepping stone to well-paying jobs for women as it is for men, but in the most advanced societies it might very well become as useful by the time the next generation of girls reaches working age.

SCHOOL ORGANIZATION AND TRACKING STRUCTURES

Social circumstances shape the resources and expectations that children bring with them to school. Society also looks at different groups through the lens of more or less disparaging stereotypes. Yet, if the circumstances of groups shape life chances, so too do the institutional structures of society. Therefore, an analysis of schooling and inequality cannot stop with an examination of students' social circumstances. The institutional structures of schooling—the way resources are distributed between and within schools; the way schools are tracked; and the tiers of the schooling system—also affect educational inequalities (Kerkhoff 1995).

School Financial Resources

Can school resources reinforce or even exacerbate inequalities? The answer is yes. In decentralized systems, school financing can be based, in large measure, on local property taxes. The higher the valuation of property, the more tax is collected for schools. School districts in suburban areas may spend two or three times as much per students as schools in central cities where property values are lower. Differences in spending at this level cannot help but maintain and reinforce social inequalities. Which student will want to go to school every morning: the student whose school is modern and up-to-date, with clean grounds and well-manicured lawns, or the students whose school is decrepit, with toilets that don't flush, grounds littered with cigarette butts, and walls covered with graffiti? Differences in spending lie behind differences in physical facilities. Often, they also lie behind differences in teacher quality, because good teachers are attracted to attractive schools with high-achieving students. In the United States, most states have now moved toward combined local and state financing of schools. This means that school funding has been substantially equalized across communities. Nevertheless, differences remain, partly due to the capacity of affluent communities to raise voluntary supplemental funds for their schools. Systems with central financing of schools—like those found in France, Sweden, and Japan—have the virtue of equalizing resources across communities.

But how important, really, are resources as an influence on learning? The conventional wisdom for many years was "not very important." This conventional wisdom reflected a key finding of the "Coleman Report" from the mid-1960s—that the social composition of schools mattered greatly for student performance, while school spending mattered very little once social composition was controlled (Coleman et al. 1966). When first publicized during the heyday of the Johnson Administration's "War on Poverty" this was a shocking finding; it threw cold water on the optimistic assumption that social problems could be solved if government had the will to spend the funds to solve them. The phrase "You can't solve problems simply by throwing money at them," became popular, particularly among conservatives, following the Coleman Report.

More recent investigations suggest that resources may be more important than we thought, although the issue remains controversial (Grubb, Goe, and Huerta 2004). Clearly, one implication of the Coleman Report remains true: resources alone won't be enough to improve schools (Hanushek 1996). Policy analysts can continue to point to any number of examples of well-funded schools in poor neighborhoods that have failed to turn around the educational trajectories of their students. In the 1990s, for example, under a court-ordered desegregation plan, Kansas City, Missouri, provided increased funding for a number of schools in poor neighborhoods. These schools were equipped with beautifully landscaped grounds, high-tech gyms, and state-of-the-art computer classrooms, but the impressive facilities alone could not overcome a climate of poor preparation and low expectations among students (Orfield 1994). Conversely, we can point to any number of modestly funded schools that have outstanding motivational climates and good learning results. In recent years, Catholic schools have often been cited as examples of schools with modest funding and good results (Bryk, Lee, and Holland 1993). Schools on military bases are another good example (Smrekar et al. 2001).

Even so, the conventional wisdom about school resources has been challenged around the edges in recent years. As researchers used more sophisticated methods to examine the distribution of resources within schools, they have discovered that schools distribute resources unequally between programs, thereby influencing how much learning occurs among different groups of students (Bryk and Raudenbush 1988). This is a salient issue for studies of inequality. If higher-status students, or the honors classes in which they tend to enroll, are disproportionately favored in allocations, patterns of inequality will be reinforced, rather than reduced. Research has also shown that additional resources can have a schoolwide influence, if they are allocated to practices and instructional conditions that enhance learning. Nearly everyone agrees that additional resources are well used when they create smaller classes or smaller instructional groups taught by very competent, motivated teachers who maintain order and consistency in instruction (Elliott 1998; Wenglinsky 1997). In all likelihood, these "good uses" of resources are more common in high-achieving than low-achieving schools and school districts.

In the developing world, the conventional wisdom suggested a reverse "Coleman effect"—that school resources were more important than socioeconomic composition in the production of learning (Heyneman and Loxley 1983). Many schools in developing countries lacked such basic materials as textbooks, maps, globes, blackboards, chalk, and school supplies. Little learning occurred under these circumstances, regardless of differences in the socioeconomic composition of the school. David Baker and his colleagues have recently argued that there is a "spreading Coleman effect" throughout the world (Baker et al. 2002). As mass education has become better institutionalized, they argue, basic materials for learning have become widespread in most developing countries. The schools' socioeconomic composition becomes more important under these circumstances, and remaining differences in resources less important. This issue is not settled. Baker's sample includes many countries that were not included in the original Heyneman and Loxley study, including quite a few that come from the more developed regions of the developing world. The Heyneman-Loxley effect remains in force in places like rural India, Myanmar, Cambodia, Sudan, Chad, Ethiopia, and Angola, where poverty and civil war have prevented the state from distributing basic educational materials to large sections of the population.

School Tracks and Tiers

In the sociology of schooling, the term "track" always refers to hierarchical structures that lead toward more or less advantaged destinations. Given the way the term "tracking" is used in the everyday language of educators, it makes sense to use the terms to mean hierarchical groupings and course structures *within* schools. These include, for example, ability grouping in elementary schools. The United States is not the only society in which ability grouping is common at the primary level. Students in Ireland and Hungary are also regularly divided by ability, or "readiness." Ability grouping is not very common in the more egalitarian societies of Scandinavia, or in East Asia (OECD 2004:410).

As I showed in Chapter 2, at the upper secondary level most national educational systems track students by curriculum and expected trajectory, either within "comprehensive" schools, or by splitting students into different institutions. The United States has less tracking at this level than most other societies. The most common form of secondary school "tracking" is based on students' choices between "honors," "general," and "basic" courses in each subject. Recently, the U.S. government has been promoting a new track structure, divided by the rigor of the package of courses taken. Those completing the "rigorous" curriculum take more math, science, English, foreign languages, and social sciences, and more demanding elective courses than other students (Horn, Kojuku, and Carroll 2001).

Hierarchically ranked educational pathways exist *between* schools, as well as *within* schools. If we take a broad view, these educational pathways might equally be thought of as "tracks," because they lead to more or less advantaged destinations. Indeed, attending a selective private high school, rather than a public high school, raises the chance that otherwise similar students will be accepted into prestigious private colleges (Attewell 2001). However, to avoid confusion, I will use the term "tiers" when I am talking about hierarchical levels that divide types of schools. Examples of tiers would include the distinct level occupied by private and public high schools and by two-year and four-year colleges. I will use the term "tracks" only when I am talking about hierarchical structures of courses and curricula *within* schools.

Justifications for tracking. Educators often feel that ability-based tracking is in the interests of students and teachers alike. They argue that it is only logical to group students with similar abilities and interests, because learning is enhanced when people are able to learn at a comfortable pace—when they are neither held up for "slower" children nor forced to keep pace with "faster" children. Educators (and parents) who approve of tracking also argue that different methods and curricula may be appropriate for students at different "ability levels." In theory, lower-track students are expected to gain confidence when they are not forced to compete with students who learn at a faster pace.

Most counselors want to do the best they can for students. Sometimes they will recommend that a student "try out" a less demanding curriculum and then later transfer to a more demanding curriculum. But not many students transfer back into more demanding classes. In places where opportunity consciousness is (or could be) strong, tracking can justly be described as a way of "cooling out" less advantaged and less successful students by encouraging them to lower their expectations to conform to the assessments educators have of them (Clark 1961). The dilemma for counselors is that low-achieving students placed in demanding classrooms can also fall behind and become alienated, if teachers are not attentive enough to their needs. In some classrooms, this can disturb the classroom focus for students who are more motivated to learn.

Tracking has strong arguments on its side, but strong arguments also exist against it. The question for sociologists is: What does the research evidence indicate about the consequences of tracking? Are lower-status children channeled into lower tracks? Does tracking make a difference for students' trajectories over and above what we would expect on the basis of background and measured academic ability alone?

The channeling of lower-status children. The research indicates quite clearly that lower-status children are more likely to end up in lower tracks. As I showed in Chapter 6, children from higher-status families usually bring more school-related knowledge and higher aspirations with them to school. And most tracking structures, even if they do not rely exclusively on ability and performance measures, do depend considerably on such measures to help determine track assignments, or to provide guidance for parents.

Because children from lower-status backgrounds are more likely to have lower grades and test scores, they are also more likely to be assigned to less demanding courses or lower tracks (Oakes, Gamoran, and Page 1992). Estimates from the early 1980s in the United States suggest that low-SES students were approximately twice as likely as high-SES students to participate in vocational programs in high school (NCES 1985:58). They were also highly underrepresented in math and science courses, and black and Hispanic students were severely underrepresented (ibid.:32). These track choices and track assignments, in turn, were strongly correlated with subsequent school trajectories. Students in college preparatory tracks were three to four times more likely to enroll in four-year colleges compared with students in general and vocational tracks (Peng 1977; NCES 1985). By contrast, students who take a large number of vocational courses in high school were more likely to drop out (Mann 1986).

Partly because of tracking practices, lower-class and minority students receive less instructional time, less demanding and lower-quality educational materials, and less imaginative teaching than other students (Oakes 1994). They are frequently held to much lower standards than other students (Dreeben and Gamoran 1986). It would be wrong to blame teachers for this state of affairs. Without doubt, teaching is a tough job in classrooms marked by student apathy and low achievement (Good and Brophy 1987:365). Nevertheless, when little is expected of students, those who are disadvantaged by virtue of their social circumstances can be expected to fall still further behind.

Even where track choices are left entirely up to parents and students themselves, children from lower-status backgrounds may "track themselves" in ways that influence their long-term life chances. In many cases, decisions are made on the basis of "practicality consciousness," a way of thinking strongly conditioned by class circumstances. Children from lower-status groups may feel the need to obtain job-related training, because they do not see any real likelihood of attending college. People who cannot afford four years of college will often try to save money, for example, by starting at an inexpensive two-year college. But starting at a community college remains a less promising avenue for eventually obtaining a bachelor's degree than starting at a four-year college.

In other cases, the power of social expectations can be decisive in enrollment decisions. Although Japanese women perform as well as men in most educational fields, male power is still a strong enough factor in Japan to shape expectations about appropriate courses of study. For this reason, women predominate in Japanese two-year colleges, whereas men are more numerous in four-year colleges and universities (OECD 2004).

The Net Effects of Tracks and Tiers

The research also suggests that tracks and tiers do sometimes have at least modest negative effects on students' learning opportunities and later life chances net of other influences on attainment. This is a strong statement, because it takes considerable statistical power for any variable to show effects once student background and ability measures are taken into account.

The evidence suggests (but does not conclusively demonstrate) that tracks and tiers add net explanatory value to other attainment variables when: (1) average *motivational intensity* differs greatly between the tracks or tiers, or when (2) *tight institutional linkages* are maintained to the more desirable locations at the next level of schooling or the labor market. Ability-based tracking, for example, can lead to large differences in motivational intensity, and elite private secondary schools can be very tightly linked to selective colleges. We can expect net track and tier effects under these conditions. In addition, tracks and tiers may widen inequalities between students if (3) they have *highly crystallized prestige* in the eyes of key gatekeepers. Prestige has confirming effects, independent of the characteristics of the individuals involved. Ivy League institutions provide prestige to those admitted, even if they are in the bottom quarter of their class. The principle here is the same for individuals. Thus, winners of prestigious fellowships, such as the Rhodes Scholarship, are identified by gatekeepers in society as having exceptional talent, and they may be rewarded with many more opportunities than runners-up for these prizes whose qualifications were very nearly identical (Ilchman, Ilchman, and Tolar 2004).

Ability grouping. At the elementary level, ability grouping in key curricular areas, such as reading and math, may raise mean achievement levels a little over what mixed-ability grouping would accomplish (Oakes et al. 1992:590–1). Many young students learn more effectively when they are grouped with peers who are at roughly the same level of readiness. At the same time, it is very important to eliminate stigma associated with grouping by ability or "readiness level," because children are highly sensitive to stigmatizing identities and can begin to treat one another differently because of them.

The story for secondary school tracking is more complex, and studies have not yielded consistent results. The best contemporary evidence suggests that advanced courses produce better performance among upper-track students than mixed-ability classrooms, but basic courses produce significantly lower performance among lower-track students than mixed-ability classrooms. These results are not surprising: higher-track students are given interesting assignments, have more challenging expectations, are surrounded by well-motivated peers, and may be assigned more dynamic and effective teachers as well (Gamoran and Mare 1989; Oakes et al. 1992). Lower-track students, by contrast, are given dull work and surrounded by unmotivated peers. Higher-track students do not appear to benefit as much from tracking as lower-track students suffer. The weaker competition and easier material do not improve the self-esteem of lower-track students. Instead, they lead to less interest in school. Dropout rates among lower-track students are approximately 10 percent higher than would be expected for otherwise similar students in untracked schools (Gamoran and Mare 1989).

The sociologist Jeannie Oakes has provided dozens of student self-reports that tell us much about the experiences of tracked students and the outcomes of concentrating high and low achievers in separate classrooms in secondary school. When asked what they have learned in a class, high-track students respond by saying things like: "I've learned to analyze stories that I have read. I can come with an open mind and see each character's point of view." Or: "[I've] learned about different theories of psychology and about Freud, Fromm, Sullivan and other psychologists." Low-track students respond by saying things like: "Nothing" or "[How to] waste time" (quoted in Oakes 1985:67, 69, 70, 71). Do these differences simply reflect the "native ability" and motivation of students? Most social scientists have concluded that the concentration of students with peers in classrooms marked by very different motivational climates and very different expectation levels have an independent, net effect on students' schooling experience.

Both motivational concentration and institutional linkages help to explain these patterns. Engaged students are further reinforced by being surrounded by like-minded classmates, whereas the effects are opposite for disengaged students. Moreover, basic course levels and vocational tracks in high school are often stigmatized and have few strong connections to desirable jobs. The incentives to finish a vocational program, under the circumstances, are relatively weak. If we are interested in learning and opportunities, the old saying "It's better to be a big fish in a small pond than a small fish in a big pond" leaves a lot to be desired. Although the challenges to the ego are greater in the more competitive big pond, in terms of learning and life opportunities it is usually better to be swimming in a big pond, whether big fish or small.

Some of the disadvantages of tracking can be mitigated if track placements are less rigid and permanent, and if students have choice about the courses they take. When schools allow more mobility in their tracking systems, inequalities between students are reduced (Sorenson 1970; Gamoran 1992). Tracking may also not be necessary to achieve the efficiencies that its advocates value. Even in primary school, where tracking does often show positive effects for both "fast" and "slow" groups, it is not the only way to achieve efficient learning. Studies of cooperative learning programs, where faster learners help to teach slower learners, suggest that these kinds of programs, if they are carefully designed, can benefit both groups. They can give faster learners a chance to learn the arts of explanation, and they can give slower learners exposure to more able and motivated children (Cohen 1984; Slavin 1994; Slavin and Oickle 1981).

Although tracking can reinforce and even add to inequalities among students, this does not mean that schools should adopt comprehensive "de-tracking" as the preferred approach. Placements in basic courses, if they allow for mobility and are seen as temporary, can be much preferable to placing a student into a high-achieving class for which he is completely unprepared (McPartland and Schneider 1996). The issue of tracking is vexing precisely because there are no easy solutions to teaching students who come to schools with widely differing levels of preparation and interest. Major problems arise, however, when some students are slotted into lower-level courses for their entire school careers, surrounded by the same peers, and therefore come to be seen by other students as part of the underachieving, "burn-out" group. In these cases, the conditions for a self-fulfilling prophecy are created, in large part, by the school itself. Fortunately, the once-common rigid form of tracking is now rare (Lucas 1999).

Tiers that matter. I have distinguished tracks (hierarchical structures *within* schools) from tiers (hierarchical structures *between* schools). The same qualities of tracks that I have emphasized so far—motivational climates, institutional linkages, and prestige stereotypes—also help to explain why some tiers matter over and above what we would expect on the basis of student characteristics alone.[3]

The separation of academic and vocational schools is an important form of tiering. When these tiers separate children at an early age, they are disadvantageous for children from the lower classes. These early branching systems create different motivational climates, different institutional linkages, and have highly crystallized prestige identities. The inequalities that result from these structures are consequently demonstrably large. For many years, working-class students have been less strongly represented in pre-university programs in Germany than in any other country (Husén 1971). This is not surprising. At age 10, many children have not had a complete chance to prove themselves before they are channeled away from preparation for academic secondary schools and professional employment opportunities.[4] Most studies have shown that the abolition of early branching systems significantly improves the performance and the educational chances of children from lower-status backgrounds (Husén 1965; McPherson and Willms 1987).

Torsten Husén and Swedish Educational Reform

In the years immediately following World War II, no country in Europe moved more decisively away from the traditional European pattern of early tracking than Sweden. A large share of the credit for the reform of Swedish schools in the 1950s and early 1960s goes to social scientists and especially to their leader, Torsten Husén.

The tools of social science came to Sweden first in education departments, rather than in psychology, sociology, or the other social science disciplines. Thus, the institutional infrastructure for a large-scale research effort on education existed before policymakers developed a strong interest in reorganizing Swedish schools. At the same time, research and policymaking were assumed to go hand in hand in Sweden, perhaps because many Swedish academic social scientists had become leaders of the long-time governing party in Sweden, the Social Democrats.

The reform movement was fueled by two key studies. Using military service records, Husén discovered a large reservoir of highly able working-class men whose circumstances had not encouraged them to continue schooling. A colleague of Husén's, Kjell Harnqvist, followed a sample of all fourth-grade students for 10 years, estimating "talent loss" on the basis of the large number of able lower-class students who did not enter the academic ladder (Husén 1965).

Reformers, however, faced a powerful opponent. Most Swedish professors and academic secondary school (gymnasium) teachers resisted reform ideas. The majority of educators expected the movement toward comprehensive schools to harm everyone involved. Comprehensive schools would, they felt, place excessive academic demands on less able students, and more able students would be held back by mixed-ability classrooms.

Nevertheless, in 1950, the Swedish parliament passed an educational act providing for a nine-year test of comprehensive schools. Swedish social scientists, under Husén's leadership, studied the consequences. The most interesting and important of these studies capitalized on a naturally occurring experimental situation. The City Council of Stockholm decided to implement pilot comprehensive schools in the southern part of the city while retaining the dual system for a short time in the northern part of the city. The two parts of the city had socioeconomically similar populations, so any differences in student outcomes could not be attributed to class differences. Holding the students' social backgrounds and initial ability levels statistically constant, Nils-Eric Svensson found that the comprehensive system performed better overall. The brighter students suffered no negative consequences, and the lower-ability students performed better throughout their school years than their peers in the tracked system (Husén 1965).

Husén and his colleagues had ingeniously questioned the assumptions underlying the selective system, and their results were finally accepted "without reservation." The Education Act passed by the Swedish parliament in 1962 mandated comprehensive schools for all students between the ages of 7 and 16.

A form of tiering familiar to Americans is the differentiation of public and selective private secondary schools. Selective private secondary schools have a modest independent effect on enrollment in selective colleges, even controlling for student background and ability (Attewell 2001). The motivational climate in these secondary schools is highly focused on achievement and encourages an active relationship to knowledge. Network links between these schools and selective private colleges and universities are also actively maintained. Counselors stay in close touch with admissions officials at selective colleges and universities, and they may even socialize with them. They counsel students on how to prepare winning applications, and they follow up themselves by urging admissions staffs to give their top students careful consideration (Cookson and Persell 1985). Students at competitive public high schools suffer, by contrast, from the tendency of these high schools to focus their college admissions energies on one or two top students (Attewell 2001). Studies of the most selective private colleges show that graduates have significantly increased chances of entering top-rated graduate and professional programs and attaining high incomes, even after background and test scores are controlled (Bowen and Bok 1998; Kingston and Smart 1990).

We can also see the importance of motivational press, institutional linkages, and prestige stereotyping by looking at cases in which one or more of these influences are missing. Studies have shown that otherwise similar students are more likely to complete their degrees if they start at four-year colleges rather than community colleges (Dougherty 1994; Dougherty and Kienzl 2006; Monk-Turner 1990). Community colleges have traditionally combined low-effort motivational climates and relatively weak linkages to jobs. Most of the students have done relatively poorly in high school, so they do not reinforce a strong academic learning climate among their peers. Because most students attend part-time and none live on campus, the schools also tend to lack cohesive campus cultures. Students therefore often feel little attachment to the goals of the college. Although community college officials emphasize the strong links between community college vocational programs and good jobs, the linkages are usually not as strong as officials suggest. The colleges have too few resources to cultivate relationships with employers, though individual teachers may do so. Overall, for-profit colleges often spend much more time cultivating ties to employers, and they do so more effectively than community colleges (Ruch 2001).[5]

At the same time, vocational programs that are strongly linked to good jobs can help students in later life. Arum and Shavit (1995) showed that students in vocational programs that offered skills strongly demanded by employers stayed in school longer and earned higher pay than students in generic vocational tracks. This is consistent with findings for the German "dual system" of vocational training, which is well supported by employers and linked to good jobs (Maurice, Sellier, and Silvestre 1986).

ADAPTIVE STRATEGIES OF GROUPS

People do not simply accept in a passive way the circumstances they encounter. Faced with a range of opportunities and constraints, they develop strategies, either consciously or sub-consciously, in an effort to make the best of their circumstances (Bourdieu 1979). At any given time, the choices people make about where to invest their time and energy reflect the relative advantages they have and the options available to them. In relation to schooling, these strategies can be seen as investments and disinvestments in amounts and types of schooling, in the labor market, and in particular occupational "beachheads" already occupied by members of the group. Time and time again, we can see individuals and groups making the most of the resources they have—investing in credentials where they have cultural advantages, and using social ties to build employment networks in work where they lack the cultural advantages or the money to continue in education.

As I showed in Chapter 6, one condition that affects investment decisions is the availability of alternative resources for making a living. It is not surprising that investments in schooling are lower than would otherwise be expected among the children of owners of small businesses and farms (Ishida, Muller, and Ridge 1995). These people do not usually have the same incentive as children whose parents are wage and salary workers to use schooling as a means of gaining economic security. (As the offspring of people who are used to "running things," it is possible that they may also tend to find the bureaucratic authority structure of schooling less congenial.)

The choices people make partly reflect the existing state of the credentials and labor markets. Indeed, in contemporary capitalist democracies, market forces are perhaps the most pervasive influence on individual and group strategies. Improving labor markets increase the supply of credential seekers, and declining labor markets decrease the supply of credential seekers.[6] We tend to think of this market orientation as a modern phenomenon, but historical research suggests that it has been influential since the seventeenth and eighteenth centuries, at least among groups able to afford secondary and higher education. As the historian John Craig (1981) observed, European societies experienced a growing demand for clergy and teachers thanks to the Reformation and Counter-Reformation, and the growth of centralized power increased demand for civil servants. This led to an early surge in higher education enrollments. The later stagnation of higher education reflected the greater returns to entrepreneurial activity.

Group strategies sometimes aim to maintain the market value of those degrees to which the group has better-than-average access. David Labaree (1988) described an interesting example of this process in his study of one of the first high schools in the United States, Central High School in Philadelphia. Central High was for many years the only high school in the city. It was highly selective; students had to pass very rigorous exams to be admitted. Even once admitted, students had no guarantee of finishing. Only about a quarter did finish. But those who finished the degree generally found very good employment in the

Philadelphia business community. Many went on to become civic and business leaders in the city.

The high market value of the degree helped create strong and ultimately successful pressures for more high schools and more high school degrees. This plenitude reduced the value of the high school degree, however. In an attempt to create a new kind of credential-based market monopoly, the high school curriculum was eventually divided into college preparatory and vocational tracks. Much educational history can be written as a conflict between strategies for limiting access to valuable credentials, popular agitation for access to these credentials, fears of declining market value in the face of increased access, and new strategies of monopolization at a higher level in the system developed by those whose position has thereby been threatened. This dynamic expresses a common conflict between market monopolies and democratic politics, and is one important source of credential inflation (Collins 1979; Labaree 1988).

At any given time, schooling may appear to be a relatively more advantageous setting for some groups than work, or work may appear to be more advantageous than schooling. In the United States, for example, African Americans and women have tended to invest heavily in education as a means of improving their access to desirable jobs. In a race- and gender-sensitive age, they faced a more favorable climate in schooling and in the sectors of the labor market demanding educational credentials (e.g., the professions and the civil service) than they did in the more entrepreneurial sectors of the economy. Given a choice, white males of average ability have been more likely to invest in work than schooling, because their relative advantages were typically greater in work environments and their opportunity costs were lower.

Latinos, by contrast, have adopted a more mixed strategy. Those from the least educated families, seeing limitations to their advancement through schooling due to linguistic and cultural disadvantages, have developed strong niches in skilled trades and entrepreneurship (Bailey and Waldinger 1991). Given these strategic investments, it is not surprising that Hispanics have the highest secondary school dropout rates of any group in American society. Nearly half of Hispanic students who were born outside the United States drop out of high school (Kaufman, Alt, and Chapman 2001). By contrast, native-English-speaking Hispanics have invested as heavily in higher education as other minority groups (Alexander, Pallas, and Holupka 1987).

Strategies sometimes reflect the more specific mix of resources that students bring to schooling. At higher levels in the educational system, students from well-educated families who are not top achievers themselves more often move into humanistic fields, such as literature and art history, where their early family-based cultural advantages can pay off in the prestige market, if not so much on the earnings scale (Bourdieu 1984). By contrast, very high achievers from less educated families tend to move into high-paying technical fields, both because they lack the family-related cultural knowledge to succeed in many humanistic disciplines and because they are usually less attuned to prestige competition than to economic security (Davies and Guppy 1997).

At the broadest societal level, mobility strategies depend on how closely linked schooling is with employment. In countries such as England and the United States, which have relatively weak links between schooling and work, a wider range of mobility strategies comes into play. Family resources may be concentrated on education or, alternatively, on securing jobs in skilled trades or entrepreneurial business. By contrast, in countries such as Hungary, Japan, and Germany where stronger education-to-employment links exist, a narrower range of mobility strategies is sensible. The best strategy (and the one most frequently followed) is for families to invest heavily in education and job-related training before employment (Erikson and Goldthorpe 1992:304–5).

CONCLUSION

Neither theories of meritocracy nor theories of social reproduction are entirely adequate for explaining patterns of inequality in school performance and educational attainment. Theories of meritocracy embrace an unwarranted tautological definition of merit (i.e., those who succeed are meritorious), and social reproduction theory is too sweeping and blunt-edged to be fully satisfying. By focusing on the connections between group circumstances, institutional channels, and the adaptive strategies groups develop over time, we can develop a better explanation. Group circumstances include both school-relevant resources, such as cultural knowledge and motivational commitments, and the stereotypical definitions of groups in the larger society. Institutional channels include school tracking structures, labor market circumstances, and government policies.

Social class, race and ethnicity, and gender are major bases of inequality in societies. These social divisions are not, however, equally fateful determinants of school success and failure. Social class is strongly related to school performance and attainment nearly everywhere, because it is consistently associated with the distribution of cultural resources and motivational attitudes. Race and ethnicity is a varying influence. In some cases, it is even more important than class; in others, it is of marginal importance. Highly subordinated minorities are restricted in employment, segregated in housing, and stigmatized in the dominant culture. These groups invariably perform poorly in school. Racial and ethnic groups that, by contrast, assimilate rapidly are usually those that come to a host society voluntarily and with urban, commercial skills. Often, they also have religious traditions that place strong emphasis on the written word. Gender is a declining factor in educational inequality. Girls are often well socialized for the cultural emphases and orderliness of schooling. In addition, the power of patriarchal social structures has declined in the industrialized world as women have gained control over fertility, won legal rights, and begun to participate more regularly in paid employment. Women still face considerable discrimination in the workplace, however.

Schools can accentuate preexisting inequalities. Although school resources are not an exceptionally important influence on educational attainment, resources can accentuate inequalities within schools if they are devoted primarily to already advantaged students. Track and tier systems are developed to improve school efficiency by grouping students with similar abilities or interests. School tracking and tier structures can, however, sometimes reinforce and accentuate social inequalities. This is especially true for tracking structures that are highly concentrated in terms of motivational climate, are strongly connected to either high- or low-status trajectories, and have strongly crystallized prestige in society. Early branching systems and rigid academic and vocational tracks in secondary schools are among the most likely to reinforce and accentuate social inequalities.

It is wrong to think of groups as passively conforming to their social fates. Instead, they develop strategies to improve their circumstances by weighing the relative advantages of investing in schooling or work, and in different kinds of schooling and work. These investment and disinvestment strategies cumulate into the distinctive paths by which groups make their way in the structure of social stratification.

8 | TEACHING AND LEARNING IN COMPARATIVE PERSPECTIVE

Extraordinary teachers come in a great many types and temperaments. Some, like Mr. Bixby, Mark Twain's guide to the mysteries of the Mississippi River, are irascible and demanding, content only with seemingly impossible feats. Others, like the nun who helped Richard Rodriguez overcome his childhood fear of reading, are patient and quietly persistent:

> At the end of each school day, for nearly six months, I would meet with her in the tiny room that served as the school's library. . . . The old nun would read from her favorite books, usually biographies of early American presidents. Playfully she ran through complex sentences, calling the words alive with her voice, making it seem that the author somehow was speaking directly to me. I sat there and sensed for the very first time some possibility of fellowship between a reader and a writer. (Rodriguez 1982:60)

Still others are charming and enthusiastic. Louisa May Alcott describes Jo's mentor in *Little Women*, the German philosopher Friedrich Bhaer, as "turning only his sunny side to the world."

For all their differences, writers' descriptions of extraordinary teachers usually feature a highly personal relationship between teacher and student. The lessons come in private tutorials on a river, in a music practice room, or in the professor's office or lab. And they come at a time when the student is eager to learn. Frequently, the student's old ways have proved insufficient for mastering a new situation, and the student is therefore particularly open to changes. The full force of the teacher's personality and understanding are focused on a mind willing to be transformed.[1]

Literary portraits of the more impersonal setting of schooling often convey exactly the opposite impression. Teachers are usually depicted as dull, mind-numbing pedants or vengeful persecutors surrounded by anxious and fearful captives. Consider, for example, George Orwell's memories of his boarding school life at St. Cyprian's School in England around the time of World War I:

> The [headmistress] was a stocky, square-built woman with hard red cheeks, a flat top to her head, prominent brows and deep-set, suspicious eyes. Although a great deal of the time she

was full of false heartiness, jollying one along with mannish slang (*"Buck* up, old chap!" and so forth), and even using one's Christian name, her eyes never lost their accusing look. It was difficult to look her in the face without feeling guilty, even at moments when one was not guilty of anything in particular. Your home might be far from perfect, but at least it was a place ruled by love rather than by fear. At eight years old you were suddenly taken out of this warm nest and flung into a world of force and fraud and secrecy, like a gold-fish into a tank full of pike. Against no matter what degree of bullying you had no redress. (Orwell ([1952] 1968:331, 349)

Of course, some great teachers are also found in larger group settings. We have only to think of such virtuosos of the classroom as Jaime Escalante, who exhorted, joked, and goaded his class of mostly working-class Latino students to top marks on the Educational Testing Service's advanced placement calculus test. Some books, such as *Goodbye, Mr. Chips* and *To Sir with Love*, have explored the transformations extracted from jaded and cynical students by great classroom teachers.

But in the United States we do not normally expect schools to be places where the joys and deep pleasures of learning prevail. Perhaps the most comprehensive study of schooling over the last 25 years depicts a "general picture of considerable passivity among students and emotional flatness in classrooms" (Goodlad 1984:113). Why is that? What prevents so many classrooms from fulfilling the empowering promise of education? And why do some classrooms overcome the odds to hum along with energy and purpose?

This chapter takes a close-up view of the interaction between teachers and learners. Even so, larger structural influences must be addressed, because they bear on the character and quality of classroom interaction. This chapter will therefore start from outside the school before moving into the classroom. It begins by examining the identities and interests teachers and students bring with them to the classroom. It then examines features of school and classroom structure that affect teaching and learning, but are determined by higher-level authorities or are inherent in the work of teaching. These include the bureaucratic setting of teaching, the number of students in the classroom, the way that the school day is divided, and the inherent uncertainties of success in instruction. Only after the stage is fully set does the chapter take up the lines and gestures of the actors themselves and show how they can lead either to enthusiasm and learning or boredom and frustration.

FOR WHOM THE SCHOOL BELLS TOLL

To understand life in classrooms, we must first look beyond the classroom doors. Both teachers and students bring with them certain experiences that are relevant to what happens in the classroom after the school bell rings. The key is to think about what kinds of experiences foster high energy and expectations and what kinds of experiences diminish interest and energy or draw it away from the classroom.

Who Are the Teachers?

Before teachers ever set foot in a classroom, they are first recruited and trained. Partly because of the people who are recruited and the rigor of their training, teachers step into the classroom with a certain status in society. These circumstances have an influence on how teachers teach and the kinds of expectations they hold for students.

Comparative studies show that American teachers once ranked near the bottom of the scale of teacher preparation and status in the industrialized world. Teaching now recruits higher-quality college students than before, but the preparation of teachers remains inadequate in some states. In the absence of further reforms of teacher training, we should not expect great improvements in the way that schools work.

Personalities and preferences. Teachers who were themselves good students and who were trained in rigorous academic programs are usually enthusiastic about academics and will set somewhat higher standards for their students than will teachers who were not themselves good students. In the United States, schoolteachers are recruited mainly from the middle two quarters of high school students and from the bottom half of college graduates. The college entrance test scores of education students have been consistently lower on average than those of students in other disciplines (Stevenson and Stigler 1992; Berliner and Biddle 1995:103–5). These scores have been going up in recent years, but they remain below the national average.

Prospective teachers also have distinctive preferences that influence their choice of career. People who go into teaching do not indicate as much interest in "making money" as those who go into high-paying fields or as much interest in "working with ideas" as those who go into science, medicine, or academe. Instead, their most common characteristic is that they enjoy "working with people." More than 80 percent of teachers say their major satisfaction comes in "making a difference in the life of a child" (Lortie 1975; Kottkamp, Provenzo, and Cohn 1986). Nor do secondary school teachers think of themselves primarily as subject matter specialists. No more than a third of American teachers say they are subject matter oriented. These subject matter specialists gravitate, if they can, toward private schools and wealthier suburban school districts. Most teachers say they are primarily interested in the rewards that come from seeing children develop and mature (Kottkamp, Provenzo, and Cohn 1986).

The dominant "people orientations" of American teachers have some decided benefits for students. American teachers may be more approachable and sympathetic toward children than their counterparts in much of Europe and East Asia. As the sociologist Philip Jackson and his colleagues observe:

> American teachers tend to look for strengths rather than weaknesses. They take what students say in class—their contributions to a discussion, for example—and turn these remarks around until they make better sense, asking questions about them or rephrasing them in a way that makes them more substantial than they were when first stated. They applaud those who try, no matter how slight their success. They have a knack for discerning latent grace within the awkward gesture. (Jackson, Boorstrom, and Hansen 1993:259)

At the same time, American teachers who are far removed from the spirit of academic learning often do not have expectations for students that are as high as those of their European and Asian counterparts. Think of how different doctors, the archetypal clinicians, are from American teachers in this regard. For most doctors, all that ultimately matters is that their patients improve. They diagnose what ails the patient and then prescribe remedies in light of the diagnosis. Few teachers regard their students in such a clinical spirit. For many, pleasures come not just from seeing intellectual growth but also and often primarily from nods and smiles and similar signs of affirmation. Rewards may also come from seeing children improve in their social skills, becoming "better adjusted" to their peers. These approval-based satisfactions are not inappropriate, but they are very different from the more exclusive interest in improvement that would be typical of a clinical occupation, or the interest in purely academic mastery that is characteristic of teachers in some other industrial democracies, such as South Korea and Japan.

Recent accountability legislation has encouraged higher standards in teacher training and teacher certification. At the same time, by introducing punitive measures for schools that do not meet performance standards, it has also opened the way to the "deprofessionalization" of teaching. Scripted learning formats, prepared by textbook publishers, have become increasingly popular among educators who are eager to find a quick fix for problems in meeting performance goals (California Educator 2002). These scripted learning formats undermine the initiative and autonomy of teachers by organizing teachers' work for them. If scripted learning becomes more popular in the future, it will make teaching a technician's job, rather than a professional job. Professional jobs encourage a broad skill set and independent judgment; technicians' jobs do not.

Recruitment and training. Teacher training in the United States was once notorious for its lack of rigor as compared to training in other industrialized countries. On this subject, the frustrations of critics sometimes reached the boiling point. According to one, "The worst of the (education) schools are certification mills where the minimally qualified instruct the barely literate in a parody of learning" (Kramer 1991:220).

This observation is no longer as true as it once was, and is becoming less true by the year. Most prospective teachers now take 20 to 30 percent of their courses in education and the rest in other subject matter fields (Berliner and Biddle 1995:107). Education courses vary considerably in quality, but education schools have improved their standards by offering more rigorous courses and by introducing minimal grade requirements and proficiency examinations (ibid.:107–8). Even so, it remains true that prospective secondary school teachers who are education majors take fewer classes in their subject matter specialty than other majors would.

Thanks to the work of educational researchers such as Linda Darling-Hammond (2000), we have a good idea about what kinds of qualifications help to improve teacher performance in classrooms. Measures of general intelligence do not correlate strongly with teaching effectiveness. Strong preparation for subject matter teaching is more important in ratings of teacher effectiveness, and knowledge about teaching and learning are even more important than subject matter knowledge. "Those who enter with little professional preparation tend to have greater difficulties in the classroom, are less highly rated by principals, supervisors, and colleagues, and tend to leave teaching at high rates" (Darling-Hammond 2000:47).

Undoubtedly, it would be helpful to certify these competencies through competitive examinations, as well as classroom observation. But many prospective teachers in the United States still do not sit for competitive examinations to receive their teaching degrees. To receive their certification, all they must do is pass their coursework and participate in a minimal amount of classroom observation and practice teaching. In an effort to improve standards, many American states now require teachers to pass proficiency examinations, but these tests do not require competence above what would be typical of an attentive high school sophomore. In the California test, for example, math questions are limited to basic computation and elementary algebra and geometry (Green 1988).

In no place do primary school teachers think of themselves as subject matter specialists. However, in many places they are recruited from among the better secondary school students, and they also usually express an interest in the intellectual development of their students more than in their social and emotional development. In Japan, for example, prospective teachers do not stay as long in school as American teachers do, but they are more highly selected. Only the top fifth of candidates for teaching jobs pass rigorous screening examinations and are able to obtain the jobs they seek (Stevenson and Stigler 1992). Japanese teachers also spend much longer observing experienced teachers before they are given their own classrooms. In Japan, 20 hours of in-service training is required during the first year after certification. In Germany, requirements are stiffer still. Primary school teachers and teachers in nonacademic secondary schools are now almost all university graduates. Specific requirements for certification vary somewhat from state to state, but all states require prospective teachers to study two academic subjects in addition to education. They then take a first state examination in their academic subjects and in education. During the practical phase of their training, following graduation, prospective teachers practice as student teachers for two years and prepare for a second state exam, which they must pass to be certified (Bailey 1995).

Even greater differences in training separate secondary school teachers in Europe and Asia from American junior high and high school teachers. In France, Germany, and Sweden, prospective secondary school teachers take their training at universities and major in academic subjects rather than in education. They generally have to pass rigorous national examinations as well. In Germany, less than half pass these examinations. The second state exam consists of a thesis on an educational topic, two observed and graded lessons, and an oral examination (Stallmann 1990). By this point, teacher training has lasted for seven or eight years. Even so, teachers must continue for three years or more on probation before they receive tenure (i.e., secure employment over the lifetime). During this time, school supervisors and administrators periodically evaluate teachers (Bailey 1995).

Social standing and salary. Partly because of how they are recruited and trained, teachers have a markedly higher social status in parts of Western Europe and Japan than they do in the United States. This status, in turn, helps to bring very able people into the profession. In the United States, teaching is a respectable occupation, but it does not carry the same prestige as most professional occupations. Some of the low social status of children (who are both loved and disdained for their lack of adult responsibility) rubs off on those who teach them. In other industrialized countries, secondary school teachers and college professors are considered to be involved in fundamentally similar work, which they pursue in a fundamentally similar spirit, as intellectuals. Public opinion polls in Germany, for example, place teachers in the top 11 occupations that deserve respect (Bailey 1995:39). High status is communicated in the terms used to refer to teachers. The Japanese term for teacher, *sensei*, implies great respect and applies equally to teachers at all levels, including university professors. In France, where secondary schools are tightly linked to the universities, secondary school teachers are referred to as *professeurs*.

This high status is associated with concrete forms of recognition as well. In recent years, teachers' pay has been highest in Japan, Korea, Germany, and Switzerland (OECD 2004: 380). In Japan, teachers by law must be paid 10 percent more than other civil servants of the same seniority levels (White 1993:90). In Germany and Switzerland, teachers are paid on the scale of high-ranking civil servants, and their pay includes supplements for spouses, children, and housing. The average secondary school teacher at mid-career earns about 85 percent the salary of the average engineer (Bellinger 2004; NCES 2001b). By contrast, in Japan the average secondary school teacher earns about two-thirds the salary of the average engineer, and in the United States, she earns less than half the salary of the average engineer (Costlow 2001; NCES 2001b). Teachers' pay in the United States varies considerably from community to community. Among primary and junior high school teachers with 15 years' experience, salaries average about $40,000 a year—relatively high by world standards, but close to the lowest salary for professional occupations in the United States. Wealthy communities do sometimes pay teachers much more than the norm, though cost-of-living is also higher in these communities. Salaries per instructional hour are significantly higher in many European and East Asian countries, largely because American teachers spend longer hours in the classroom and less time preparing outside class (OECD 2004:378). Figure 8.1 illustrates teachers' salaries in different countries.

Teachers in the developing world. Poorly prepared and poorly qualified teachers are a far more important problem in the developing world than they are in the industrialized world. Indeed, because more qualified teachers cannot be found, many primary school teachers have incomplete secondary educations. As the educational researcher Marlaine Lockheed (1993) noted, "Where teacher education requirements are low, many primary school teachers have a weak background in the subjects they are teaching" (29). In Nepal, nearly a third of primary school teachers have not even set foot in a secondary school. In several African countries, as of the early 1990s, a majority of primary school teachers were not graduates of secondary schools (Lockheed 1993). Those who have little formal education are frequently unfit to teach.

Teachers in poor, developing countries have other hurdles to overcome. Most seriously, they cannot always show up for work. They may have to travel long distances to work or to be paid, and these travels contribute to absences. Supervision of family festivals and religious celebrations sometimes keep teachers out of class. Months at a time can be lost to teacher strikes, which are relatively common. Some countries allow for maternity leaves but do not make provisions for substitute teachers. Thus, the rhythms of natural and communal life, along with the inefficiencies of poorly working bureaucracies, make education in the Third World a more irregular phenomenon than it is in the United States. Here the occasional snow day is something that children look forward to for months, and substitute teachers, however embattled they may find themselves in the classroom, do show up in a predictable way when the regular teacher is ill.

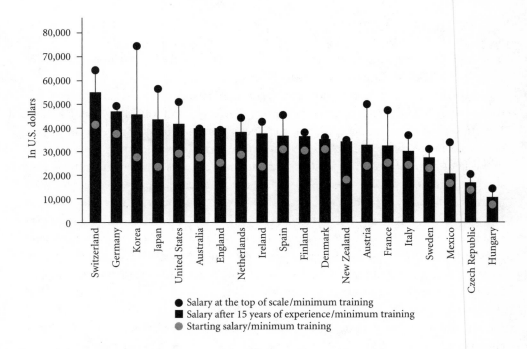

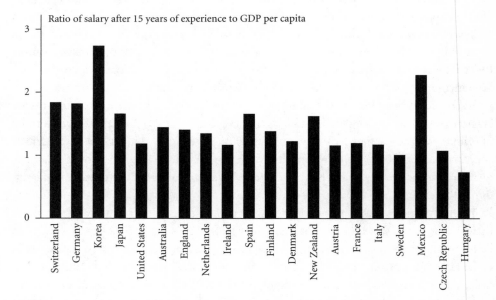

Figure 8.1   Teachers' Salaries in Lower Secondary Education, Selected Countries, 2002

SOURCE: Adapted from OECD (2004:380).

NOTES: Equivalent U.S. dollars converted using proportional purchasing power (PPP). Countries are ranked in descending order of teachers' salaries in lower secondary education after 15 years of experience and minimum training.

Who Are the Students?

Just as teachers come to class with experiences that influence their attitudes and behavior in class, so do students. Chapters 6 and 7 discussed the influence of social class, race and ethnicity, and family motivational climates on students' outlooks toward schooling. These factors are without doubt the most important determinants of how well equipped and well disposed students are to achieve in school. But several other factors also bear on the level of *interest* students bring to learning. These factors include the importance of schooling for job prospects, the outside-of-school activities in which they are engaged, and community pressures for achievement, as well as differences in learning styles.

Engagement and disengagement. Throughout the world, students share in the same universe of possible feelings about school. Some enter school full of excitement and confidence, with a reasonably clear sense of what is expected and parental support for their efforts. Others enter school with great trepidation, confused about what is expected of them, and unclear that they will be able to succeed. Still others seem to be at odds with school from the beginning, either because they are resentful of adult authority or because they would simply prefer to be otherwise occupied.

Societies vary in the proportion of "engaged" to "disengaged" students. Students in the United States say they are relatively satisfied with their schools and teachers but often report that they are bored or uninterested in what is going on in class. One study, using an innovative methodology involving self-reports of engagement and disengagement at random times during the school day found that students reported being engaged in their lessons only slightly over half of the time. Interests outside the classroom proved to be a challenging rival to teachers, occupying students 36 percent of the time (Yair 2000). Students in Asia, by contrast, report much stronger positive feelings about school and seldom report feelings of boredom or restlessness (Stevenson and Stigler 1992:61–7).

In cross-national comparisons, levels of student engagement appear to depend primarily on three influences: the extent to which school performance is relevant to success in adult life, the number and demands of outside-of-school involvements, and the level of pressure exerted by parents and communities for engagement with school.

In places where school performance is not particularly relevant to adult jobs, student engagement with schooling is low. With opportunities for higher levels of schooling limited, many also do not see the relevance of secondary schooling to their later life chances. As school-based opportunities for mobility increase, so does the importance of schooling in the life of the young. A longitudinal study comparing three villages in Papua New Guinea, for example, found that only in the community with an increasing number of middle-class jobs linked to schooling did children perceive schooling as a particularly valuable activity. In the villages relying on traditional economic activities related to fishing, school dropout rates were high and young people indicated little interest in schooling (Pomponio and Lancy 1986).

American students have been prime examples of the problems that exist when democratic openness is not accompanied by strong community pressure to maintain high academic standards. Except for a minority of academically motivated students (perhaps 15–20 percent of the age group), "getting by" without working hard has been the long-accepted norm among American secondary school students (Powell, Farrar, and Cohen 1985; Steinberg 1996). Another very common pattern is to pay attention and study hard only in the courses that are of special interest. Although acute levels of disengagement are more common in lower-class and among students from ethnic minority groups, they are a prominent feature of middle-class schools as well. Many American students admit to coasting during school hours. Between 33 and 40 percent of American students reported that they are neither trying very hard nor paying attention in class (Steinberg 1996:67). A statistic like this might mean that "coasting" attitudes are "socially expected" more than that they are an accurate reflection of students' true levels of engagement, but social expectations are themselves revealing because they show what passes as acceptable and appropriate in student culture.

As students have become aware of the increasing income and status gap between college graduates and those without higher degrees, schooling has become more interesting to American students (Public Agenda 1997). Even so, students still must balance the demands of schooling against the attractions of other activities. In time allocation, school work ranks below part-time work and social life for most teenagers. Although estimates of adolescent paid work hours vary, the best recent estimates suggest that more than half of American high school students work part-time (Rothstein 1999). Working students average 15–20 hours per week at after-school jobs—not for the most part because their families depend on the money, but because students themselves want to have spending money. Teenagers spend perhaps another 20 to 25 hours a week on average socializing with friends. They spend an average of about 15 hours a week on extracurricular activities, such as sports or music. And another 15 hours a week are given over to watching television (Steinberg 1996:164). Although paid works helps to familiarize students with the labor market and the expectations of employers, one important impact of this busy lifestyle can be insufficient sleep. Working long hours after school is associated with later bedtimes, shorter total sleep time, and reports of fatigue and sleepiness at school (Mitra et al. 2002). Those working more than 20 hours per week are, in addition, at risk for dropping out of school and other problems. In most of Europe and East Asia only fewer than one in five adolescents works 15–20 hours per week (Rothstein 1999). In Sweden and Switzerland, two countries with high educational achievement, only 10 percent of teenagers work such long hours.

Student engagement with school is also higher in East Asia, because families and communities maintain strong pressures on children to succeed in school. Where parents and the community insist that school is the main priority, student engagement usually remains high. Where the family and the community do not insist on schooling as a priority, secondary schools become "warehouses" for many bored and disengaged students. Simply offering the promise of opportunities through schooling is not enough to keep student motivation high. It is easy enough for students to see this as an empty promise, or (where access is open) merely their birthright. Social pressure supporting the priority of schooling is necessary to maintain real engagement.

Learning styles. American educators have pioneered studies of student learning styles. The term "learning styles" is contested, however; some conceptions focus on cognitive functioning; others on cultural differences among students. Studies of learning styles provide a persuasive picture of conflict between children who bring a range of cognitive approaches, sensory strengths, and cultural predispositions to classrooms, confronted by classrooms that are organized in a more single-minded, single-sense, single-culture way.

The term "cognitive styles" refers to how children absorb and process information. Cognitive psychologists are certain that children acquire different styles and strategies of learning, but they do not agree on how best to think about these differences (see, e.g., Presseisen et al. 1990). Some students are predisposed to learn through reflective observations and others through active engagement with materials. Overall, students report more engagement when working in lab groups, when preparing individual or group presentations, and during class discussions. Each of these is a more active form of learning. Students report lower engagement when listening to lectures or watching videos (Yair 2000). More active learners may feel bored in class unless they are engaged in handling materials, asking questions, or making comments. More reflective children sometimes feel uncomfortable and anxious in such a challenging environment and learn better by reading alone or listening to teachers lecture (Boocock 1972:129–33). Experienced teachers mix their methods of instruction to accommodate both more active and more reflective learners.

Children also vary in their capacity to extract information from different media; visual and aural media can help children who are not able to learn well from print alone. The appeal of television and film has certainly influenced the use of visual and sound media in classrooms. However, the movement toward multimedia classrooms reflects advances in learning theory as much as changes in the popular culture. (Book lovers can take solace, however, from the likelihood that print will remain as the primary classroom learning medium. The written word lends itself, much more than images or sounds, to abstraction, review of ideas, and internal dialogue.)

Some differences that cognitive theorists root in brain functioning, cultural theorists root in the life circumstances of majority and minority groups. Some learning theorists have argued that both social class and ethnicity create cultural differences in learning styles. One theory contrasts "analytical" and "relational" learning styles, the first associated with higher-income, ethnic majority homes and the second with lower-income, ethnic minority homes (Cohen 1969; Hale-Benson 1982). These terms are used to describe two ways of thinking in and about the world:

- The *analytical style* emphasizes the ability to remove objects from their context and to group them together on the basis of some common property. For example, a tree, a cucumber, and a flower might all be grouped together as "vegetation." Students comfortable with the analytical style can look at a sentence, identify the noun from the context of a sentence, and generalize about the properties of nouns, where they come in sentences, what relationship they have with other sentence elements, and so on. The analytical style is comfortable with abstraction.

- The *relational style* is "self-centered" in its orientation to reality and tends to lump objects together as all appropriate to a particular context, rather than splitting them apart analytically and free of context. For example, a comb, lipstick, pocketbook, and door might be grouped together under the conceptual umbrella of "getting ready to go out" (Boocock 1972:109). In this way of thinking, each object has meaning in connection with the other objects in the relevant context. Students whose thought processes are based on the relational style would tend to think of nouns, verbs, adjectives, and other grammatical elements, not as conceptually distinct, but as having a meaning in the context of the sentence as a whole. The relational style is less comfortable with abstraction.

For cultural learning theorists, cognitive styles are rooted in home and community practices. Parents who are used to distancing themselves from their immediate surroundings and who use grouping and abstracting concepts to experience the world encourage the development of the analytical style in their children. These parents are prevalent in middle-class communities. By contrast, parents who are simultaneously more communal and more egocentric in their relation to the world encourage the development of the relational style in their children. These parents are more likely to experience the world through particular things, people, and events, rather than abstractions. Detachment from context is a less frequent cultural experience. These parents are more often found in lower-income and minority communities.

A similar hypothesis underlies the sociolinguistic work of Basil Bernstein (1975), who argued that middle-class parents and communities teach children to express themselves in ways that are more often context free. Indeed, some cultural theorists prefer the terms "high context" and "low context" learners.

Schools do undoubtedly favor the analytical style. After all, meaningful abstraction is at the center of the western intellectual experience of the world. The analytical style is now the dominant cognitive style around the world. The schools' preference for the analytical style can therefore be justified on both pragmatic and egalitarian grounds.[2] As the political scientist Andrew Hacker has written:

> The abilities and outlooks associated with the analytical style can no longer be adequately thought of as "white" or "Western" or "European," but are in fact part of a dominant global culture, which stresses not only literacy and numerical skills, but also administrative efficiency and economic competitiveness. (Hacker 1990:24)

Schools can, however, do more to encourage students who bring a more relational style of thinking to school. Research by Robert Slavin (1980) and others has shown that lower-class and minority children learn better in cooperative learning environments, where members of a group all work together on a lesson. They may also appreciate more continuous feedback. One reason that cooperative learning works well with lower-class and minority children is that it makes these children feel less lonely in the classroom. Another may be that it is compatible with the comfortable, communal style of participation found, at least in the best of times, in their families and neighborhoods.

STRUCTURED INTERACTION AND CLASSROOM LIFE

Teachers and students come to classrooms with socially conditioned experiences and ways of seeing the world, and they meet in a space that is itself socially structured. Features of this space also affect what goes on in the classroom. In this section, I will focus on three important aspects of the socially structured space of the classroom: (1) its bureaucratic setting, (2) its "ecological" features (such as the number of students in class and the methods of grouping students), and (3) its instructional culture. These are the stages and frames within which classroom interaction occurs.

Craft Production Ideals, Bureaucratic Realities

In a famous essay on organizations and social structure, the sociologist Arthur Stinchcombe (1959) made a distinction that helps to explain why most literary memoirs of outstanding teaching are set outside of formal classrooms. The distinction is between two types of production systems:

- *Craft production* involves the use of a variety of nonstandardized materials, many nonroutine processes, and the creation of individualized products. Fashion design, custom-made furniture, and specialized computer software programs would be examples of craft production industries. Craft industries usually have few levels of management, and managers are generally considered to be less important in the operation than the craftspeople or professionals who conceive and execute the work.

- *Bureaucratic production* involves a standard set of raw materials, routine processes, and standardized products. Paper mills, smelting plants, and automobile assembly plants are examples of industries organized along the lines of bureaucratic production. Because production processes are routinely repeated, coordination and control are typically more relevant concerns than creative work with the materials themselves. Managerial hierarchies are steep, and managers are more important in the operation than the people who make the products.

Schooling should ideally be organized as a craft production industry. Students are the "raw materials" in this process, and they are obviously highly varied when they come to the classroom. They come into schools with many different personalities, interests, capacities, and motivations. The processes that teachers need to use to reach and transform these students are varied as well. Some students require constant prodding, even expressions of exasperation to get them involved. Others might require imaginative, hands-on play. Still others might need large amounts of emotional support coupled with high expectations. Even the final products will not be precisely the same; they should be "custom built." Certainly, graduates should meet minimum standards of knowledge, maturity, and self-confidence, but individual talents and interests ought to be given a wide opportunity for development as well.

Although schooling ideally fits the craft production model, it is organized along the lines of bureaucratic production. Students are grouped together in batches and treated as more or less standard vessels into which knowledge can be poured. Teachers have too little time to get to know each student personally, and they must think in terms of methods that work better on average in large groups. The teacher's authority is central in such a setting rather than the learners' progress. The classroom is organized by a large number of rules. These may be necessary to keep order in a grouped setting, but they discourage the disorderly discussions out of which important insights and debates can grow.

The deep personal connections that are a vital part of memorable educational experiences do not usually have the time or space to blossom in bureaucratic settings. The care and creativity we associate with craft production is, consequently, frequently overshadowed by the efficient processing structure we associate with bureaucratic production. Few students receive as much personal attention as would be desirable. This tendency becomes more and more pronounced as students move from primary grades, where they spend all day with the same teacher, to higher grades, where they pass from one teacher to the next as they follow their class schedules.

Because teachers in public schools work with large groups of students all at once, they tend to rely on a standard set of teaching techniques, primarily seat work and lectures interspersed with questions. Under these circumstances, they cannot know whether every student who is physically present is also mentally engaged. Their success as teachers is measured primarily by whether they cover the curricular material, whether their students move along without causing too many problems, and perhaps also by their subjective sense of how well their students are doing. Standards-based testing, which promises "accountability" for short-term retention, is a popular bureaucratic mechanism of evaluation appropriate for the bureaucratic setting of school.

The imprint of bureaucratic efficiency is found also in higher education. This no longer shocks us, but it did shock some of the thinkers who were alive at the time that universities began to resemble businesses. Thorstein Veblen's turn-of-the-twentieth-century satire on the "industrialization" of American higher education focused on the consequences of "academic accountancy" for the spirit of scholarship:

> Because of the difficulty of controlling a large volume of perfunctory labor, such as is involved in undergraduate instruction, the instruction offered must be reduced to standard units of time, grade and volume. Each unit of work required . . . in this mechanically drawn scheme of tasks must be the equivalent of all the other units. . . . These . . . units of academic bullion are increased in number and decreased in weight and volume; until the parcelment and mechanical balance of units reaches a [diminishing] point [which would be surprising] to any outsider who might naively consider the requirements of scholarship to be an imperative factor in academic administration." (Veblen [1918] 1957:75–6)

Veblen's satire retains its sting because we can see that mass education is a far cry from the intimacy and personal relation between master and apprentice required for the craft production of scholars. The system of "academic accountancy" allows universities and other schools to process large batches of students, but it is not well designed to invigorate and challenge the mind through long-term personal interaction with serious thinkers. In our bureaucratic, batch production systems, students learn to "jump through hoops," but they rarely catch the spirit of learning.

To organize schooling as a craft production industry would require one-on-one tutorials and small-group sessions rather than dozens or hundreds of students following a single teacher's lectures and questions. No society has the resources to spend even a fraction of the money required for such a form of learning. Instead, schools have tried to make bureaucratic education more enjoyable through improved lecture presentations, elective courses, and extracurricular activities. (The only places where tutorials remain the center of education are the two ancient and highly selective English universities, Oxford and Cambridge.) This is one reason why the tutoring industry is booming in places like Korea, Japan, and the United States, as parents attempt to supplement low-cost bureaucratic education with brief periods of high-quality craft attention.

How Much Has Teaching Changed?

Have you ever wondered whether teachers in your parents', grandparents', and great-grandparents' generations taught in the same way as teachers today? Many people assume that teachers were stricter in the past, more likely to "stick to the book" and, perhaps, less forgiving of errors. Yet no one has really known whether these impressions are true. No one, that is, until Larry Cuban decided to find out.

In his book *How Teachers Taught* (1993), Cuban, a former high school social studies teacher and school administrator, looked at a tremendous amount of data to decide how much had changed over the course of a century. He examined photographs of teachers and students in class. He looked at textbooks and books used by teachers as resources. He gathered student recollections of their classroom experiences. He collected teacher reports of how they taught. He combed through reports from journalists, administrators, parents, and others who visited classrooms. He looked over student writings in school newspapers and yearbooks. He collected research studies of teaching practices. And, finally, he read descriptions of classroom architecture. From these sources, he gathered detailed descriptions of over 1,200 classrooms for the years 1890 to 1990. These descriptions were embedded in a larger set of data that indirectly revealed teaching practices in almost 7,000 other classrooms.

Cuban divided teacher-centered classrooms from student-centered classrooms and he also allowed for mixed forms. In the teacher-centered classroom, activity follows a strict routine of lecturing, board work, and seat work. Students are not free to move around the classroom, and they sit in rows with attention focused on the teacher. Cuban found that highly teacher-centered instruction is most common today, especially at the secondary school level, and it was also most common 100 years ago. However, some hybrids dating from periods of reform have slowly changed the character of American classroom life at the primary school level. Today's primary schools have more activity centers, more field trips, and more student movement around the classroom. Some student-centered reforms have not been adopted, however. Few elementary school classrooms, for example, allow for joint teacher-student discussions about what to study.

In Cuban's view, the need felt by teachers to maintain their authority in the classroom explains why some student-centered reforms have fallen by the wayside. Teachers have become less strict and less formal, but they continue to feel the need for control over the essential aspects of classroom organization. Therefore, they implicitly differentiate between an inner core of instructional authority and an outer periphery of social relations. The core includes the lesson content, lesson techniques, and tasks to be done. The periphery includes the arrangement of classroom space, the amount of student movement, the amount of grouping, and the amount of classroom noise tolerated. Teachers have felt the need to defend their authority over the core features of classroom life, but not as much over peripheral features. As Cuban (1993) observed, "Substantial numbers of teachers, concerned with maintaining order and limiting classroom noise, yet attracted to the new ideas about children and their development, struck compromises between what were viewed as essential teacher prerogatives and the new beliefs [about student-centered learning]" (p. 269).

The ambiguous and uncertain work of teaching. The sociologist Dan Lortie (1975) provided a now-classic portrait of schoolteachers that increases our appreciation of the difficulties of the teachers' task in a bureaucratic, mass production setting. As compared with other professions, Lortie argued, school teaching is distinguished by four characteristics: (1) work with large, heterogeneous groups of students; (2) work that requires high levels of group concentration but is marked by many interruptions; (3) work that has multiple goals rather than a single, overriding goal; and (4) work that is performed in an environment generally lacking in collegial support. The first three of these distinguishing characteristics make the work of teaching objectively difficult. The fourth leads to a sense of isolation that reinforces the uncertainties of teaching and has some unique consequences of its own.

1. *Large groups, mixed abilities.* Teachers typically work with groups of 30 or more students. These students have a mix of abilities, motives, and interests. Even when they are predisposed to learn, they may learn in very different ways. Obviously, under these circumstances, a teacher cannot know with any certainly that he or she is getting through to every student. Even if the teacher is getting through, the payoff for the student may not come immediately. A great teacher may, so to speak, turn over the soil without harvesting the crop; lessons may need to "sink in." Moreover, even very good teachers inevitably fail with many of their students. And, to make matters worse, even when teachers seem to be succeeding, they may not be succeeding very well. Those children who seem to be doing well may simply be gifted students who would do well no matter who they had as a teacher.

   This situation, Lortie argued, creates a pervasive sense of uncertainty among teachers. Some two-thirds of the teachers Lortie interviewed said they encountered problems in assessing their work, and most of those felt the problems were serious. As one told Lortie, "I feel very inadequate and hopeless at times." Another said, "It's only every once in awhile when you do see progress. . . . You can go on for an eternity with nothing" (Lortie 1975:143–4).

2. *Permeable boundaries.* The objective difficulties of single-handedly teaching large, mixed-ability groups are compounded by the many interruptions during the average school day. For learning to occur in a bureaucratic setting, students must concentrate together on the lessons. However, teachers often find it difficult to control the boundaries around their classrooms. Public address announcements may break in at any time. Distractions, from clanging ambulances to bellowing marching bands, may be within earshot of the classroom. Parents may arrive to chauffeur a

child to an appointment, disrupting the flow of activity. The children themselves may be difficult to control or quiet down. These interruptions make it difficult to preserve the high levels of concentration that allow students to learn and practice most efficiently.

3. *Multiple goals.* The mixed goals of schooling in the United States create conflicts in the minds of many teachers about what they should expect from their students. Academic goals are by no means the only goals that schools care about. Schools also want their students to be socially well adjusted, to become good citizens, and to be able to develop their specific talents (e.g., in music or art). Increasingly, schools are also asked to provide nutritional, emotional, and moral support to children whose families are unable to do so. Although academic goals are usually most important, they may not be the most important goal for every student. Many teachers are unclear about what priority they should give different kinds of child development goals. Teachers wonder if they are doing their job acceptably if, for example, their students seem to be self-assured and self-controlled but aren't making great progress academically. Conversely, those who feel that their students are making progress academically may feel insecure if they don't detect evidence of social and emotional progress as well.

4. *Isolation from colleagues.* Unlike therapists, social workers, doctors, and other professionals in human services work, teachers are essentially on their own. Therapists-in-training talk to their supervisors about every patient encounter, but teachers only rarely interact with their principals or with other teachers on matters of practice. Principals rarely visit classrooms or review class notes. Nor do most teachers have a strong collegial culture with respect to the sharing of craft skills. Team teaching is rare, and, perhaps because of the uncertainties of the craft, conversations in the teacher's lounge only occasionally take up issues of practice. The norm is to learn to teach "through trial and error in the classroom" (Lortie 1975:79). Many teachers jealously guard the perimeters of their classroom, for fear of interference with the one area of professional life they feel they can control: how they teach subject matter materials.

The isolation of teachers is reinforced by the lack of staging in the teaching career. Although teacher pay goes up with seniority, few schools have rank systems, with statuses such as "apprentice teacher" and "master teacher." Ranks in professions, like all prestige hierarchies, can be useful for a number of reasons. First, they potentially provide senior guidance for younger recruits. A teacher hierarchy may also stimulate ambitions for career advancement, leading practitioners to give more thought to their craft. In the current unranked structure, many talented teachers simply leave teaching for what they hope will be more lucrative pastures.

Behavioral consequences. According to Lortie (1975), these four occupational characteristics encourage a common set of attitudes among teachers:

- *Defensiveness:* a desire to protect the sanctity of the classroom from any outside interruptions or any deviations from schedule

- *Conservatism:* a tendency to rely on trial and error rather than any more reliable guide to effective practice
- *Pragmatism*: an unwillingness to experiment and a hostility to the kind of idealism that asks teachers to do more than "get through the day" without major catastrophes
- *Elitism*: a tendency to favor the few students who provide rewards to teachers through good performance or expressions of approval, rather than looking for across-the-board improvements in an impartial and clinical spirit

It is easy to see how these attitudes might develop out of the structural circumstances of teaching. People who feel insecure tend to be defensive about what they can control and unwilling to try new ways that could lead, at least in the short run, to further insecurity. They may also be more likely to overvalue signs of acceptance, such as nods, smiles, and words of appreciation. These tendencies are reinforced by the recruitment of so many who are "people oriented," looking for emotional rather than clinical satisfactions from teaching. (Certainly, where success is often tenuous and failure common, teachers cannot be blamed for looking for satisfaction from a few high-performing students, the unconscious elitism that Lortie notes as characteristic of teachers.) Finally, people who lack the social support of collegial culture or supervision from more experienced and knowledgeable colleagues are unlikely to change their "tried and true" methods.

Recent studies of teaching reveal a somewhat more mixed picture than Lortie found. The uncertainty of teaching remains as strong as ever and has, if anything, become more severe as more students come to school poorly prepared for learning and teachers are expected to show yearly annual improvement in students' test scores. The sense of isolation that Lortie emphasized remains strong (Hargreaves 1993). Political pressures to legislate what goes on in the classroom and cultural clashes between teachers of different backgrounds and philosophies have reinforced some teachers' already strong desires to build impregnable walls around their classrooms.

The isolation of teachers may be slowly changing in the direction of climates that encourage more sharing of craft knowledge. In many countries, teachers share experiences, lesson plans, and other craft knowledge on a regular basis. Some observers argue that the collegial culture of Japanese and Korean teachers helps to explain the good performance of Japanese and Korean students on international assessments (Hiebert et al. 2003). Teacher collegiality also has strong advocates in the United States, and it is possible that more schools are encouraging teachers to develop collegial cultures. Some research suggests that the new accountability legislation has encouraged more frequent discussions of teaching craft in schools threatened by negative performance assessments (Siskin 2003). At its best, teacher collegiality can create "a shared vision" of what counts for high-quality teaching and learning refined over time through ongoing collaborative activity and reflective dialogue among teachers (Louis and Marks 1998). But collegiality is not easy to sustain in the face of the daily demands of teaching (Pomson 2005). Some writers argue that teachers choose isolation because it allows them to conserve scarce time and energy to meet immediate instructional demands (Flinders 1988:25) and shields them from the "digressions and diversions involved in working with colleagues" (Hargreaves 1993:58).

Teachers' desires to seal off their classrooms are apparently strong enough that experiments in staging the teaching career have not succeeded. New teachers often appreciate "master teachers" for the advice and reassurance they can provide. But they are treated more as potential intruders than as pedagogical leaders by more experienced teachers (Griffin 1985; Tauer 1996). Until teachers' work is better paid and gains higher status in society, it is unlikely that efforts to professionalize practice through clinical discussions will go far (Ingersoll 2005).

The "Ecology" and Instructional Culture of Classrooms

In environmental science, ecology is the study of the relationship between organisms and their environments. Ecological studies can include analysis of the size and type of terrain, the climate, the number of species and their population size, the patterns of their interaction, and the forces that change the balance of relationships. If we stretch the metaphor a little, classrooms can be thought of as having an ecological order, too.

Dimensions of classroom ecology provide a frame for interaction. Classrooms may be relatively rich in instructional resources (such as maps, textbooks, and posters) or relatively poor. They may include relatively many or relatively few students. They may or may not have the help of teachers' aides. Instructional periods may be long or short, punctuated by rest periods or not. The school day and the school year may be long or short. Children may be grouped by ability or work in mixed-ability groups, with student leaders assigned to each group. Students' work may be organized in whole-class instruction most of the time, individual work, or small-group work.

Organizational researchers have shown that dimensions of classroom "ecology" can affect the amount of learning that occurs (Barr and Dreeben 1983). Classrooms with more resources have the capacity to provide enriched learning experiences. Classrooms with fewer children and those with more aides often produce more learning (Finn et al. 2001). Classrooms that devote more time to learning than to socializing activities can achieve better learning results (McPartland and Schneider 1996). Grouping patterns can also speed up the classroom, or slow it down (Barr and Dreeben 1983). The most important of these influences are the number of children (better few than many) and adults in the classroom (better many than few) and the amount of time spent "on task" rather than on socializing and transitions. Otherwise, ecological variables do not consistently affect learning. They always provide a frame for interaction, but the frame is too loose to be consistently associated with learning outcomes. For example, we know that learning resources are not always used well; disruptive fights can occur even during well-spaced recesses; and potential student leaders may find themselves placed in classroom groups they cannot effectively lead.

Instructional culture can be defined as the accumulated understandings about teaching and learning that are dominant in a society. Comparative studies bring home the extent to which instructional cultures vary. Some instructional cultures, such as the British, are highly verbal. Others, such as the Chinese, are document-based (Cummings 2003). In some instructional cultures, students are expected to be ashamed of their errors as a sign of incompetence. In others, errors are honored as the only path to learning. In some instructional cultures, teachers tend to use many problems from everyday life. In others, problems are presented abstractly and are not directly connected to problems of everyday life.

The work of educational researchers Harold Stevenson and James Stigler (1992) provides a stimulating window into the cultural dimensions of classroom organization in Japan and China, as compared to the United States. Based on intensive study of classrooms in six cities (two cities in each country), Stevenson and Stigler observed a number of variations in the three countries that show how student expectations and consciousness can be shaped by differences in the instructional culture of the classroom.

In Japan and China, differences in ability were downplayed and differences in effort placed in the foreground. Errors were not considered to reflect lack of ability, but rather lack of attention to the source of the error. Stevenson and Stigler (1992) describe one scene from a Japanese classroom that would likely never occur in a public school classroom in the United States. A young Japanese student was having trouble drawing a three-dimensional cube. The teacher called the boy to the board and asked him to draw the cube. The boy failed repeatedly, but the teacher kept the boy at the board, providing help and asking the class whether the boy was improving. The boy showed no signs of embarrassment. Errors were not a cause for embarrassment in this classroom or a threat to self-esteem. They were treated as an index of what still needed to be learned and as a necessary means to improvement. The boy remained at the board for nearly the full hour until he finally produced a passable three-dimensional cube. This type of intensive focus on a particular problem or topic was also more characteristic of Asian classrooms than the race to cover many problems or topics, typical of U.S. teaching culture. Many more problems were introduced in Asian classrooms with familiar, hands-on examples. Students in one classroom, for example, learned about measuring volume by first comparing the amount of liquid contained in bottles of various shapes and sizes.

Time use was also markedly different in the Asian and American classrooms. Teachers were in the classroom fewer hours in China and Japan, but they were expected to work on lesson preparation after hours. They had much more organized and informal discussion with fellow teachers, which reduced the isolation characteristic of American classrooms. As Stevenson and Stigler (1992) point out, if teachers are overworked in the classroom, they cannot be expected to prepare interesting lessons after hours. The organization of class time also differed. Students were taught to quickly perform classroom routines, such as sharpening pencils, so that teachers had more time to spend on lessons. Most important, Japanese and Chinese classrooms included many more recess breaks, once after every lesson and at least five a day. This schedule helped to refresh the children and made it easier for them to concentrate on the next lesson.

Almost as striking were the differences Stevenson and Stigler found in grouping patterns. Instead of dividing students by ability level, as is common in American classrooms, Japanese and Chinese teachers faced mixed-ability groups. In the Japanese *han* (or small group), faster learners were expected to help those who were having trouble, in effect becoming assistant teachers. Asian teachers spent more time in whole-class instruction than in individual or small-group instruction. Stevenson and Stigler speculated that children felt more involved in class activity if they were learning with their fellow classmates rather than alone at their seats completing workbook assignments. American students, they observed, seemed lonelier than Asian students more on their own and less supported by others. In another notable difference, Asian primary school students also helped with classroom discipline, acting as delegates of the teacher in quieting disruptive children.

Although American parents lament the size of their children's classes, class size did not explain the differences Stevenson and Stigler (1992) found in the effectiveness of teaching practices. Japanese and Chinese classrooms actually included more students than American classrooms, averaging between 38 and 50 students. Nor did Asian schools have more teachers. By reducing the time spent on routines and by relying more on whole-class instruction, Asian teachers could effectively teach groups as large as 45 to 50. The fewer number of hours Asian teachers spent in the classroom allowed them to remain relatively fresh for the high-energy performances of instruction.[3]

CONSTRUCTING CLASSROOM INTERACTION

Teachers and students enter an environment that has been created for them by previous generations and existing rules. They have little control over what curriculum they will study, the number of students assigned to the classroom, or how many recesses they will be allowed during the day. Once they enter the classroom, however, they also begin to construct a world through their own actions and interactions. This last section of the chapter explores the process by which classroom reality is constructed through the interaction of teachers and students.

The Bottom Line for Teachers: Classroom Order

The first focus of the teacher's interaction with students is toward the creation of a sufficient degree of order for learning to occur. If students are whispering to each other, throwing objects at one other, running around the room, or openly ridiculing fellow students, the classroom will be too chaotic for learning to occur. Not surprisingly, research shows a strong positive association between good order in the classroom, teacher confidence, and higher levels of learning (Arum et al. 2003; Coleman, Hoffer, and Kilgore 1982; Newman, Rutter, and Smith 1989). Moreover, principals who do not back up teachers' efforts to maintain order are cited as a more important source of low teacher morale than job demands or hard-to-reach children (Moeller 1964; Liu and Meyer 2005).

Willard Waller (1932), the first important American sociologist of schooling, observed that a natural conflict exists between the teacher's need for order in the classroom and the spontaneous interests of children. He noted that teachers must simultaneously create a rapport with students and exercise enough authority to maintain classroom order. Waller observed that teachers of his day often worked to create this "mixed rapport" (i.e., rapport mixed with respect or fear) by evoking role types with high cultural prestige (such as "the officer and gentleman," "the patriarch," "the kindly adult," even "the love object"). Some of these cultural reference points of Waller's era are dated. However, teachers continue to face the problem of how to create a rapport mixed with respect for classroom order. Somehow teachers must walk the line between too much firmness, which makes some children afraid to try, and too much friendliness, which makes some children feel that "anything goes." Most teachers today depend on a clearly communicated and graduated set of responses to misbehavior in the classroom.

More than order is necessary, however. A minimal consensus on the value of learning is also necessary for classrooms to work well. This consensus is not as easy to establish as order. For many students, real agreement about the value of learning would require something like a "conversion experience"—a change of loyalties from peer group and pop culture to books and ideas. Teachers, however, have three resources for gaining minimal consensus on the value of learning. The first resource—and historically the most important—has been students' acceptance of the authority of the teacher. The second is the school's implicit offer of a valuable exchange—the exchange of marketable knowledge and credentials in return for cooperation and respect (Willis 1979). This has become a much more common form of control over time. The importance of the exchange mentality can be seen in the pervasive use of rewards such as pizza parties, candy, and early release for compliance in the classroom (Brint, Contreras, and Matthews 2001). Finally, some students—but not many—are attracted by the substantive interest of the materials and activities of the classroom.

Understanding and Misunderstanding in the Classroom

In Chapter 1, I observed that teachers and their students communicate through symbolic expressions, interpretations of those expressions, and responses in light of those interpretations. This complex interaction process occurs simultaneously on both sides of a communicating pair. One reason that clarity in teaching is of such central importance is that children are not experienced in filling in background information or unstated steps in an argument. Without great clarity and quite a bit of repetition, shadows are likely to fall between the expressions of teachers and the interpretations of those expressions by students.

Some children will find all lessons difficult to understand. Teachers therefore walk a fine line between repeating enough so that all students understand, and repeating so much that the better students become bored. Because many children are only occasionally engaged with the classroom, a fair amount of the teacher's time is spent monitoring students' attention levels. How often have teachers asked a student what she or he thinks, and the answer is: "Huh? Oh, I must not have been paying attention." Teachers must also gauge levels of understanding. Teachers repeat the question: "Do you understand?" frequently, because answers to this question are necessary for teachers to feel that they can go on. One reason why more exciting discussions do not occur in most classrooms is that basic understanding is hard enough to achieve. Unfortunately, even in advanced courses, the amount of material covered rarely permits much in the way of free-form discussion. Comprehension is the *sine qua non* of schooling systems, not the exploration of ideas.

Even so, ample room exists for incomprehension. Words are misheard or misread, and ideas that seem straightforward to teachers are anything but straightforward to students. Students' malapropisms prove this, if any proof is necessary. According to one student essay, "In the state of nature, Man is nasty, British, and short." And another: "The government of England is a limited mockery." Fledgling essayists write about such topics as "intravenous fertilization" and "cereal killers." Subject matter may be a translucent plate for teachers, but it can be a thick fog for students.

Of more direct interest to sociologists, misunderstandings can also arise from the clash of cultures in the classroom. For example, Asian and Native American children are taught that it is rude or impertinent to look adults in the eye. White teachers may interpret this aversion as a lack of confidence or forthrightness. Similarly, many working-class children do not learn something that is a norm of middle-class society: if you don't understand something, you generally don't admit it and rather assume that it will eventually become clear. Middle-class teachers may experience the "obvious" questions of working-class students as indications of "dullness," when other students may be equally perplexed, but too savvy to admit it.

Status cues are among the most prevalent unconscious influences on teacher interpretations of their students' behaviors. A well-known study by the sociologist Ray Rist (1970) showed how important these status cues can be. Rist found that teachers in kindergarten classes he studied in Washington, D.C., unconsciously connected indicators of social status with indicators of academic aptitude. Children who wore clean clothes, whose hair was nicely combed, who addressed the teacher respectfully, and who spoke standard English were placed in the top reading group and received the most attention from the teacher. Children who were unkempt, unclean, ill mannered, or poor English speakers were relegated to the back of the class. By substituting status cues for more direct evidence of academic potential, teachers inadvertently undermined their expressed commitments to equality of opportunity. Other studies have confirmed the emphasis of the Rist study on the powerful, but largely unconscious, influence of status cues (see, e.g., Bernstein 1975, chap. 6; Erickson 1975).

Who Are the Effective Teachers?

The Rist (1970) study is a useful cautionary tale, but it would be wrong to assume that only people who are very much like one another in social background are capable of communicating effectively. Teachers need not come from the same background as their students or adhere to one set of "ideal teaching behaviors" to be effective in the classroom.[4] By the time most students reach second or third grade, they are relatively skilled in symbolic interaction. They are able to read, adapt to, and learn from different types of personalities. They learn to interpret a teacher's gestures in the context of his or her particular manner of communicating. Most teachers are practiced in drawing out different kinds of students. Moreover, norms of fairness place boundaries around teachers' social prejudices. Even studies that find social bias in evaluation usually find that "objective" criteria of student performance, as measured by grades and work effort in class, have a stronger influence on teachers' and counselors' assessments of students (Erickson 1975; DiMaggio and Mohr 1985).

"Traditional" versus "progressive" pedagogy. Some teachers are demonstrably more effective than others in reaching their students. Students in their classes learn more and are more engaged while in class. What are the qualities and practices of effective teachers? In the

United States, advocates of two very different answers to this question have pursued a debate for over a century.

Those who support *traditional pedagogical theory* believe that effective teaching consists of clarity in explanation, step-by-step mastery of subject matter, repetition, and continuous feedback on performance, culminating in letter grades "with real meaning." In the late nineteenth and early twentieth centuries, advocates of what came to be known as *progressive pedagogical theory* challenged traditional educators (Dewey [1916] 1966; Cremin 1961). Progressive pedagogy took a child-centered view of learning, arguing that stimulating a child's natural curiosity is the key to effective learning. Educational progressives argued that teachers should provide curricula of interest to children, rather than curricula that educators alone find enlightening or uplifting. They also felt that teachers should vary their methods, using field trips, hands-on projects, and student-centered discussions to complement lecturing, board work, and seat work. In general, the progressives believed in de-emphasizing evaluation and emphasizing getting to know children's strengths and weaknesses and, above all, allowing them to learn through doing.

Both schools of thought have something important to offer, and both, left to their own devices, can also go badly astray. Studies of teacher effectiveness in the United States have converged on the conclusion that both *task leadership* and *socio-emotional leadership* are essential. In this way studies of pedagogy replicate the conclusions of leadership studies in other institutional settings (Perrow 1986, chap. 2). Task leadership, a strong point of traditionalists, involves such matters as efficiently organizing activities and schedules, providing clear instructions, monitoring performance, and providing feedback. Socio-emotional leadership, a strong point of progressives, involves such matters as developing rapport in the group, creating a considerate and positive environment, contributing to the social pleasures of a work group's life, listening to concerns of members of the work group, and discussing thoroughly any issues that come up in accomplishing the work.

Table 8.1 summarizes the following discussion of effective teaching techniques from both perspectives.

One of the most consistent findings in the literature is that the sheer amount of time on task is related to the amount of learning (Edmonds 1979; Dreeben and Gamoran 1986). Thus, the more time spent on curricular materials and the less time spent warming up, following classroom routines, housekeeping, and sharing nonschool experiences, the better for the learning climate. As seemingly trivial a matter as increasing the number of school days from 175 to 185 has been associated with increased achievement (Goodlad 1984:96), as have summer learning programs (Heyns 1978). Many students lose a lot of what they have learned during the summer months, when schoolwork is the last thing many children want to think about (Downey, von Hippel, and Broh 2004). Also supporting the traditionalists' view, researchers have found that effective teachers have high standards that they expect students to reach. To be precise: expectations should be high but not out of reach, and they should be very clearly communicated and consistently maintained.

One especially interesting study by Robert Dreeben and Adam Gamoran (1986) brings home the importance of high expectations. Dreeben and Gamoran examined 13 first-grade classrooms in three Chicago area school districts. When they compared children who had

TABLE 8.1
Characteristics associated with effective teachers

From traditional pedagogy	From progressive pedagogy
Concentration on task-oriented activities	Varied daily routine
Emphasis on reading and writing	Use of many different types of learning materials
Clearly communicated expectations	Student participation
High (but not out of reach) expectations	Hands-on activities
Quick correction of errors	Less lecturing; more labs, projects, and discussions
Diagnostic quizzes	Positive emotional tone, rather than flat tone
Clarity and repetition in lectures	Responsiveness to individual student's experiences and needs
Frequent assessments and feedback	Ample (but not overly-generous) praise for students' achieve-
Strong (but not exclusive) emphasis on	ments and contributions
meaningful grades	

had similar levels of reading readiness at the beginning of the year, they found that scores on reading tests administered at the end of the year varied primarily by the sheer amount of time spent on reading and by the number of words covered over the school year. Neither students' race nor their family's socioeconomic status showed a significant influence on reading achievement once "time on task" and total word coverage were taken into account. However, both race and socioeconomic status were correlated with the amount and difficulty of instruction offered by the schools. Dreeben and Gamoran conclude that poor children are often short-changed because their teachers fail to give them assignments challenging enough to stimulate their potential intellectual growth.

Continuous and serious monitoring of performance is another emphasis of traditional pedagogy that appears to be essentially on target. Prompt correction of errors is necessary so that students know what they need to work on. Frequent diagnostic quizzes can be a major help for this purpose. Indeed, good evidence exists that the learning climate of virtually every classroom would be improved if teachers gave short, three- or four-question diagnostic quizzes at the end of every class meeting to see whether students were paying attention and whether they learned the most important points of the day's lesson.

Although these elements of traditional pedagogy are well supported in the educational research, an overly rigid conception of the traditional approach can be counterproductive. Students need to feel that teachers are interested in them and have their interests in variety, experimentation, and exploration in mind. Traditionalists can obtain outstanding performance from the most motivated students (and those with strong needs to please authority figures), but they can also turn off less motivated and more rebellious students by failing to spark an imaginative connection with the materials studied.

For reasons like these, the research suggests that effective teachers also draw on practices associated with the progressive tradition. They draw, in particular, on students' experience and natural interests in the world. For example, children can learn about quantities by repetitive practice of sums or, more effectively, by working in an imaginary store and making change for their "customers." Effective teachers also make their classrooms inviting places by hanging attractive posters on the walls and decorating in other ways. They vary the daily routine, using different kinds of learning materials from instructional videos to small-group discussions to field trips. Most of all, they encourage students' active participation by frequently breaking lectures for discussions. Discussions, if they are well led, can make students feel like an important part of the class. They seize on student participation by accepting and clarifying student answers and by using their ideas where possible. They provide praise for good performance, although they do not praise so effusively that praise itself becomes devalued. Finally, effective teachers convey a sense of deep interest and enthusiasm in their own work as teachers. They vary voice pitch and gestures to maintain a vibrant emotional tone, just as anyone who was truly interested in a subject would.

It is not easy to be a good teacher; and being a great teacher is a magnificent achievement. The great teachers must combine the skills of an intellectual, an actor, a digital media designer, a coach, a diplomat, and a psychologist. (See, e.g., Boocock 1972:129–49; Goodlad 1984, chap. 4.)[5]

Some students are well prepared to focus on curricular materials for long concentrated stretches. But for younger children and children who are less able to concentrate over long periods, classroom organization must sustain shorter bursts of interest. Some teachers have the gift for organizing activities that build student commitment to the classroom and ultimately to its academic mission. As Michael Huberman (1993) writes: teachers can try to build interest by "acting out legends, singing in class, conducting an apparently aimless physics experiment suggested by pupils, reading parts of a play. . . . [Many teachers] suspect, perhaps with good reason, that [their students'] reactions of amused curiosity or real engagement will pay off further down the line" (43). Student engagement seems to be highest when students are working on labs, individual or group projects, or participating in discussions (Yair 2000). Engagement is not the same thing as learning, of course, but for most students it is a precondition for learning.

Effective teaching practices are less common in secondary schools than in primary schools because of differences in school and classroom organization. Primary school teachers have the same children all day. They are able to get to know their 30 children better than a secondary school teacher can possibly get to know the 150–200 students he or she sees during the school day. Primary school teachers may, therefore, feel the need to make the children's "home base" an attractive place to be. They also have more flexibility in managing time; they are not chained to the 50-minute subject period, as secondary school teachers are.

These factors increase the incentive of secondary school teachers to communicate their curricular materials as efficiently as possible. Teacher-centered lecturing, combined perhaps with a small amount of discussion, is widely believed to be the most efficient method for communicating the relatively complex ideas of secondary school courses (see, e.g., Cuban 1993, chap. 8). Secondary school teachers could probably do better if they were to implement some of the findings from the research literature, but many are understandably more concerned about "getting through the day" in a challenging environment than they are in using research to rethink tried-and-true practices.

The increasing importance of content standards and testing for accountability has encouraged a search for efficiency in primary school classrooms as well. Many teachers complain about the large number of content standards they are expected to teach every month. They feel the need to find effective ways to communicate large amounts of information in a short time. Progressive educators made a good case that techniques of "drilling" students on knowledge content were "killing" for the spirit of learning, but the constant pressure of performance standards means the days of "drill and kill" are definitely back. Short-term gains in retention may be found using these methods, but perhaps at the expense of long-term interest in a deeper engagement with anything school has to offer.

Teacher expectations and student performance. Before the accountability era, perhaps the greatest teaching deficiency in the United States was that teachers did not expect enough of their students. Indeed, teachers often reacted to signs of student disengagement by trying to make school less taxing and more enjoyable. Because they feared losing students, they substituted light material they felt would stimulate their students to try harder and to be more interested in school (Sizer 1984, chap. 5; Powell et al. 1985; Steinberg 1996:75–6). Even today, as compared to teachers in other industrial countries, American eighth-grade mathematics teachers, for example, tend to introduce problems of relatively low complexity (Hiebert et al. 2003). Unfortunately, instead of trying harder when offered light material, most students respond by further disengaging from their studies (Yair 2000). They assume they can pick things up when they need to for the test (Sedlak et al. 1986; Metz 1993).

High expectations, we know, play a role in learning, but how important are they? Can high expectations lead struggling students to achieve great things? A famous study by Robert Rosenthal and Lenore Jacobsen, *Pygmalion in the Classroom* (1968), is often cited in support of the contention that teacher expectations are the single most important key to student performance. In the original study, the researchers chose 20 percent of students at random from each of six classes in a San Francisco school. They gave a test to all students participating in the study, a test they misrepresented as predicting "intellectual blooming." Rosenthal and Jacobsen then told the teachers of the six classes that the test indicated which students were destined to show large intellectual gains during the academic year (the experimental subjects, of course). Pre- and post-tests showed that among first and second graders the experimental subjects did in fact show higher than average gains from the beginning to the end of the year. The obvious interpretation is that teachers had high expectations for the predicted "bloomers" and that these expectations made a difference in how the children performed. By "facial expression, posture, and perhaps by her touch, the teacher may have communicated to the children of the experimental group that she expected improved intellectual performance" (Rosenthal and Jacobsen 1968:180).

A closer look at Rosenthal and Jacobsen's study, however, encourages doubt about just how powerful teacher expectations really are. Changes in line with the "self-fulfilling prophecy" did not occur in the higher grades, and in a few cases the change scores of the experimental subjects were actually lower than those of the group of students who were not predicted to "bloom" during the year. Subsequent replications of Rosenthal and Jacobsen's study have tended to confirm a more qualified view of the power of teacher expectations. It may be that by grade three most children have acquired an academic self-conception that is difficult to revise much in the course of a year. Some may not be capable of doing more challenging work. Many more may not think themselves capable of doing it. Still others may not see enough relevance of schooling to their life goals to exchange respectful attention and hard work required by schooling for the advantages of better understanding and higher grades. Teachers' expectations are important, but they are not all-powerful.

Cultural Matches in Classroom Interaction

Teaching methods that mix traditional and progressive elements generally work well in the United States, but they would not necessarily work well elsewhere. A "kind and caring" American-style teacher might simply confuse Asian students, just as a glib and cultivated European teacher might seem insufferable to American students. Indeed, different societies provide rather different conceptions of what ideal teaching looks like. These divergent ideals suggest that effective teaching practices are not universal. To be effective, teaching practices must align with the pedagogical ideals of the culture in which they are located and thereby fit the expectations of students who have become attuned to that culture. Where these alignments do not occur, students are likely to be confused or hostile, and teachers less effective than they would otherwise be.

The ideal teacher in China and Japan. In Asia, the ideal teacher is a skilled performer. As with the actor or musician, the substance of the curriculum becomes the script or the score; the goal is to perform the role or piece as effectively and skillfully as possible (Stevenson and Stigler 1992:166–7). The teacher's job is to lead students through coherent and engaging lesson plans that bring them eventually to new knowledge. Thus, Asian teachers are expected to be lively and responsive to students, and they do not feel much pressure to be sensitive and nurturing. Indeed, Asian teachers are perceived as strict. They give out fewer high marks than American teachers, and they are more likely to scold students (Ban and Cummings 1999). Stevenson and Stigler (1992) found that the teachers they surveyed in Beijing, China, chose clarity and enthusiasm as the most important attributes of good teachers, whereas teachers in Chicago chose sensitivity and patience far more often (166–7). Thus, the cultural ideals of teaching in Asia can be described as skillful performance, clarity, and coherence in lesson planning. As I noted earlier, Asian teachers also show a marked appreciation for the role of effort in the process of acquiring new knowledge, and the importance of errors to the process of learning. Errors are no shame in China and Japan. They are impediments that can be overcome on the path to knowledge, not indicators of limited "aptitude."

Teaching styles, of course, vary among the East Asian societies. In Japanese mathematics classes, teachers make an average of eight shifts between whole-class and individual work during each class period. They focus on a few problems during each period, and explain those problems thoroughly. Japanese teachers try to make connections between new material and previously studied material. They also repeat and summarize frequently, so that most, if not all, students are able to understand new material. Teaching in Hong Kong, by contrast, tends to emphasize "practice, practice, practice." Students go over procedures until they know them by heart. Both countries show high levels of success in mathematics instruction, but this is not because teachers have the same style. More likely, it is because the expectations of students and teachers are well aligned and because teachers in both countries are not afraid to ask their students to work on complex problems (Hiebert et al. 2003).

The ideal teacher in English and French elite education. At the upper reaches of English and French secondary and higher education, teachers embody an entirely different cultural style. The most admired teachers often have "a certain gracious demeanor and a talent for witty and pleasant conversation" (Rothblatt 1968:190). In this respect, the ideal teacher is the person of broad knowledge who is nevertheless at ease with the repartee of polite society. The "humourless college authoritarians" have always been found in these settings, as well, but the most admired teachers worked hard to present the appearance of effortlessness. They displayed their learning through intriguing lecture themes and provocative questioning, and they encouraged bantering exchanges between themselves and their students. The English literary critic Cyril Connolly provides a reminiscence of one such teacher at Eton College, the leading British preparatory school:

> Wells taught the classical specialists; he was a fine cricketer and a judge of claret, a man of taste with a humour of understatement in the Cambridge style. [He] was theatrical, he liked knotty points and great issues, puns and dramatic gestures. He was . . . fond of paradoxes and we learnt to turn out a bright essay on such a subject as "Nothing succeeds like failure" or "Nothing fails like success." (Connolly [1938] 1973:220)

Corresponding to the values of their teachers, elite English and French students are expected to show signs of brilliance, not mere correctness or competence. In France, the cult of brilliance reaches its apex in the *grandes écoles* and in the schools preparing students for admission to these highly selective institutions. The sociologist Pierre Bourdieu (1988) conducted a study of some 150 student records from one such preparatory school for girls. Bourdieu analyzed the remarks made by instructors supporting grades on each of five or six exercises submitted by the girls. He found that the descriptive adjectives "careful," "conscientious," and "thorough" were located closer to the pole indicating poor performance (the latter marks supported by such adjectives as "simplistic," "vulgar," and "insipid") than to the pole indicating excellent performance (supported by such adjectives as "masterful," "cultivated," and "ingenious"). Nor were the adjectives "sensible" or "right" terms of praise in this hierarchy of professorial judgments (Bourdieu 1988:195–208). They, too, were slightly closer to the pole indicating poor performance.

The persistence of the cultural ideal of aristocratic brilliance is a tribute to the staying power of "court society," where serious matters of state mixed with the lightness and wit of high society. As the aristocracy receded in importance in the age of commerce, new classes adapted the old cultural ideals to their particular situations. The gentry (men and women of property and established name in the English countryside), urban professionals, and intellectuals, each in their own way, took up the old aristocratic cultural ideals as a means to express a lifestyle and values markedly different from those of the more consistently sober-minded and profit-conscious business classes. Wit and erudition have often been appropriated as weapons in the struggle for status by culturally privileged segments of the dominant class.

Today, the cult of aristocratic brilliance remains important only in those institutions and disciplines least marked by the democratic and bureaucratic revolutions of the era of mass education—in self-consciously elite preparatory schools in continental Europe and in the humanities departments of highly selective undergraduate colleges in the United States. Democracy and science favor the sober and dedicated specialist over the brilliant and cultivated generalist. Even so, it is still too early to write an epitaph for the man of letters as a cultural ideal. So long as there is something to be gained in status from the expression of conspicuous learning united to wit, the cultural ideal that originated in court society will undoubtedly continue to live on as a weapon in the status struggles of the educated middle class.

Homo Academicus

Throughout his career, the French sociologist Pierre Bourdieu was sensitive to the relationship between language and social power. From his earliest studies of the French educational system (Bourdieu and Passeron 1977), he has emphasized the connection between professorial evaluations and students' social class backgrounds. Few students, Bourdieu argued, have the kind of experiences that allow them to present themselves as highly cultivated. Few travel widely, listen to sophisticated discussions at the dinner table, or are encouraged to read serious literature. Professorial judgments, therefore, are in large part social class judgments.

Professorial affinities for cultivation and sophisticated wit are, according to Bourdieu, a form of "symbolic violence" directed against the lower classes. Categorizations of one student as "brilliant" and another as "dull" are, he argued, reinforcements of the social hierarchy in linguistic terms. The terms are meant to seem to be unbiased assessments of underlying aptitudes, but what they really assess is the cultural capital of the home environment. In one of his studies, *Homo Academicus*, Bourdieu continued his critique of symbolic violence by correlating descriptive remarks on student exercises with the social class background of students. Although the correlations were not perfect, Bourdieu did find a relatively strong pattern. Those exercises characterized in the most positive terms tended to be written by children of professors, doctors, diplomats, and executives. Those characterized in the most negative terms tended to be written by children of tradesmen, clerks, and craftsmen (Bourdieu 1988:195–208).

Bourdieu's work can be interpreted as having greater relevance to French and other Western European societies than to societies like the United States, in which familiarity with art, literature, and history is not a decisive marker of status (see, e.g., Lamont 1992). Nevertheless, Bourdieu should be credited with pioneering efforts to unmask the hidden social codes of academic evaluative language and the role these codes play in the intergenerational reproduction of the "culturally dominant" segment in society.

Third World teaching styles. Cultural models in the Third World provide a contrast both to the skilled performers of Asia and the clever gentlemen-scholars who help to prepare elites in Britain and France. Teaching styles in most developing countries are teacher-centered to an extreme. Students are expected to copy what is on the board and to memorize textbooks; they are not expected to engage with their textbooks or lessons in any more probing way. The authoritarian methods typical of many Third World classrooms are evident in a study reported by Pfau (1980), which compared classroom behaviors in several fifth-grade classes in the United States and Nepal. In Nepal, some 80 percent of class time was spent on lectures. In the United States, lecturing accounted for just 40 percent of class time. Pfau counted three times as much student speaking and teacher questioning of students in the United States as in Nepal. Group projects, student demonstrations, library research, and field trips were almost unknown in Nepal. In the United States, they accounted for small but measurable increments of activity, approximately one-fifth of class time overall. The findings are similar for other developing countries (see Lockheed, Fonancier, and Bianchi 1989; Lockheed 1993:31).

In the United States, teacher-centered classrooms typically include a strong emphasis on testing. In the developing world, however, teacher-centered methods often go hand in hand with a decided lack of interest in evaluation. In the Philippines, less than one-third of fifth-grade science teachers, and those mainly in the cities, reported using tests frequently (Lockheed et al. 1989). In Nigeria, only 10 percent of primary school teachers said they relied on testing (Ali and Akubue 1988), and in Botswana, students were observed taking tests only 1 percent of the time (Fuller and Snyder 1989).

The sources of autocratic teaching in the Third World are similar to those that made autocratic teaching methods common in eighteenth- and nineteenth-century America. Teachers are poorly prepared and teach under difficult circumstances. Children do not reliably show up for class and are often not prepared even when they do attend. Resources are often extremely limited. Only the unusual teacher is willing to take risks by loosening the reins of authority in such circumstances. The pressures that teachers feel to focus attention on themselves are reinforced by traditional models of authority, which emphasize the decisive role of the leader and the unquestioning deference of followers.

We need, then, to take a complex view of cross-cultural differences. Specific kinds of societies give rise to specific teaching ideals, and these ideals shape the expectations of teachers and students alike. At the same time, some basic principles of effective teaching are apparently universal. In developing countries, for example, research shows that significant gains in student performance are associated with many of the same factors that also make a difference in the United States. These include better qualified and more knowledgeable teachers, larger amounts of time spent in class on academic studies rather than on ancillary activities, more opportunities for students to participate actively in class through questioning and discussion, and continuous evaluation of student progress through the use of tests and other feedback (Fuller and Clarke 1994).

CONCLUSION

Study of teaching and learning requires looking at the characteristics that teachers and students bring with them to the classroom, the social structure of classrooms, and the process of interaction itself.

Teachers and students meet in the classroom, but their capacities and interests are largely formed outside the classroom. Teachers are most likely to have high academic standards when they have done well themselves in school, have had a rigorous subject matter training, and are highly respected and well remunerated by society. Students are most likely to be engaged with classroom activity when their parents and their communities provide high levels of support for learning, when they have enough time to study, and when they see the relevance of schooling to their adult life plans. Some learning theorists suggest that students differ also in the learning styles they bring to school and that schools need to provide opportunities keyed to these differences.

Most portraits of great teachers describe one-to-one relationships, because teaching ideally occurs between an individual teacher who knows how to bring out the best in a student, and an individual student who is motivated to learn from that teacher. These portraits suggest that schooling ought ideally to be organized as a craft production industry. Of course, for reasons of cost it is actually organized as a bureaucratic production industry. Teachers in bureaucratic settings face a number of problems. They are subject to a great many rules and can be interrupted from teaching by a number of intruding events. They work with large numbers of diverse and unequally motivated students. They therefore cannot be certain of succeeding with many of their students. In addition, academic achievement is only one goal of schooling; thus, teachers must decide priorities in a climate of competing expectations. Under these uncertain circumstances, many teachers try to wall off their classrooms, thereby depriving themselves of collegial support. These occupational circumstances can create attitudes of defensiveness, conservatism, pragmatism, and unconscious elitism among teachers.

Teaching and learning are further conditioned by classroom organization. These organizational features include the number of students and aides in the classroom, how they are grouped for instruction, and how time is divided during the day. Smaller numbers of students and larger numbers of aides often help with instruction, as do frequent recess periods during the day. Instructional culture can also be considered part of the classroom structure and is another important element that can affect learning. Instructional culture refers to the assumptions about teaching and learning that prevail among educators. The instructional culture in East Asia emphasizes in-depth coverage of a smaller number of topics than American teachers cover. It also encourages a more favorable attitude toward errors and a sense that effort, rather than ability, is the most important factor in learning. Other societies have developed different cultural understandings of teaching and learning.

Once teachers and students gather in classrooms, they also construct a world through their actions and interactions. Classroom order is a prerequisite to all other effective communication. Even in orderly classrooms, communication can break down due to misinterpretations of teacher or student behavior or because of poor instructional techniques. In the United States, a long-running debate has divided advocates of traditional and progressive techniques. The research evidence supports some aspects of traditional pedagogy (such as clarity and repetition, high expectations, quick feedback, and rigorous evaluation) and some aspects of progressive pedagogy (such as hands-on learning, use of frequent discussion, and use of varied media to convey lessons). The ingredients for effective teaching are not, however, universal. Comparative studies indicate that a wide variety of pedagogical styles can be effective, so long as the pedagogical styles of teachers are aligned to the expectations of students.

9 SCHOOL REFORM AND THE POSSIBILITIES OF SCHOOLING

Sociology can tell us a great many things about how schools operate as social institutions in different societies, but can it also help us to make improvements in schools? To some extent, the kinds of changes people want to see in schools reflect their values, and sociology cannot tell people what to value. But sociology can clarify the range of values that inspire reform movements, and it can show what kinds of reform policies have been most likely to succeed.

The term "reform" has a complex history. For most of the twentieth century, it was used to refer to changes in schooling that reformers expected would lead to more attention to the interests of students, or more fairness and equity for disadvantaged groups—in other words, for changes that we might today call "progressive reform." However, over the last generation the term "reform" has been enthusiastically embraced by conservatives, who have seen it as a way to provide a positive image for policies that are intended to make the schools more demanding and more market efficient, but not necessarily more student-centered or more equitable. (This adoption of the "reform" label mirrors what has happened to other concepts, such as "empowerment," "compassion," and the "public interest." All have been adopted by conservative politicians as a way to suggest positive connotations for policies that reflect values that are far from the liberal roots of the term "reform.")

School reform in most societies has been a largely top-down affair. Political leaders have developed plans for reorganizing schools and then mobilized support for those plans. Top-down mobilization is also common in the United States, but school reform has often been accompanied by much higher levels of popular involvement in the United States. Even today, at a time when the public has grown indifferent to many government activities, which are perceived as distant from everyday life concerns, public schools remain an object of intense public interest in the United States (Rose and Gallup 2004). Because Americans expect much of their schools, and invest so much of their hopes as a society in schools, they are keenly disappointed when the schools seem not to be measuring up. It is not surprising that periods of dissatisfaction with the schools have been as common or nearly as common in the United States as periods of satisfaction.

I will depart a little from the comparative focus of *Schools and Societies* in this concluding chapter. I will focus on school reform primarily in the American context. No other country has placed as much faith in its public school system to lead it toward the economic progress and social justice it seeks. The American case is also unique in the range of policies that have been promoted under the rubric of "reform."

This chapter discusses the range of reforms that have been proposed for American schools and why some reforms have been successful in changing the organization and effectiveness of schooling, and others have failed. It discusses why efforts to raise standards became so important in recent years and the various programs that were introduced for improving educational standards. It focuses considerable attention on efforts to improve schools in the inner cities, because urban schools face the most difficult circumstances and reformers have focused much of their attention on them. The chapter concludes by using the research on reform to discuss the ingredients that go into producing high-quality schools.

A TYPOLOGY OF SCHOOL REFORMS: THE FOUR E'S

Four primary values have informed American school reform movements: desires to improve efficiency, to raise standards of excellence, to enhance children's full range of powers, and to increase equity. It is, therefore, only a small stretch to say that the "three R's" of school curriculum (reading, 'riting, and 'rithmetic) are matched by the "four E's" of school reform: efficiency, excellence, enhancement, and equity.

The first reform impulse, and the one with the most enduring appeal to school administrators, is connected to improving the *efficiency* of schooling. These reforms reflect bureaucratic organizational principles and (often) preference for market principles of efficient allocation of students to tiers and tracks within tiers. They involve the introduction of new forms of categorizing and organizing personnel, curriculum, and school practices. They sometimes also involve the introduction of entirely new types of schools and curricula (such as secondary school commercial and vocational tracks).

The second and third reform impulses have their strongest roots in the teaching staff, but administrators often find them appealing as well. These are reforms connected to *excellence* (or improved academic standards) and those connected to *enhancement* of children's full range of intellectual and emotional powers. Reform movements aimed at improving academic standards may encourage stiffer requirements, more time in the school day, new evaluation procedures, more demanding educational materials, and the like. Reform efforts aimed at enhancing children's development may include such "add-ons" as music and art programs, physical education, extracurricular activities, and multipurpose or special purpose rooms. They may also involve more child-centered activities, such as field trips, hands-on science projects, class or schoolwide arts projects, and more colorful and interesting classroom decor.

Finally, movements aimed at improving *equity* are the project of democratic reformers, who wish to use the schools to make society more just. These reforms involve educational programs intended to provide additional or compensatory education for members of dis-

TABLE 9.1
Types of school reforms: The four E's

1. Efficiency reforms
   a. New types of schools (e.g., junior high schools, community colleges)
   b. New tracks within existing schools (e.g., vocational and commercial tracks in high schools)
   c. New standardized categories (e.g., course credit units, standard divisions in the school day, standardized educational requirements for teachers)
   d. New forms of district-level organization (standard-sized schools and classrooms, articulation arrangements between levels, etc.)
2. Excellence reforms
   a. Demanding new curricular subjects (e.g., computers)
   b. New instructional methods (e.g., "new math")
   c. Upgraded teacher training standards
   d. Upgraded graduation standards
   e. New and more challenging forms of evaluation (e.g., state or national proficiency tests)
   f. Tougher grading standards and/or higher expectations in classes and schools
   g. Longer school days or school years
3. Enhancement reforms
   a. New types of schools (e.g., kindergartens, alternative schools)
   b. Facility/activity "add-ons" (e.g., multipurpose rooms, extracurricular activities, computer labs)
   c. New child development–related curricular subjects (e.g., art, physical education)
   d. New "student-centered" instructional methods (e.g., "learning by doing," field trips, "open classrooms")
   e. New forms of "whole child" evaluation (e.g., portfolios)
   f. New classroom amenities (e.g., posters, artwork, movable desks, activity centers)
4. Equity reforms
   a. New compensatory programs (e.g., Head Start, Title I, aid for students with disabilities)
   b. New social integration programs (e.g., busing for purposes of integration, bilingual education)
   c. New prevention programs for "at-risk" children (e.g., drug education, parent education, AIDS education)

advantaged groups (such as Head Start, which was aimed at the urban poor), integrating socially subordinate groups into better schools (such as desegregation plans), or preventing self-destructive or otherwise dangerous behaviors on the part of socially alienated at-risk groups.

Table 9.1 lists some of the school reforms that fall into each category.

Cyclical Theories of Reform

A common image of school reform is that it occurs in cycles, marked by alternating periods of "liberal" and "conservative" reform. In these *cyclical theories*, liberal reforms are defined as those that make the schools more responsive to previously excluded groups, such as children from minority groups, or that take a more child-centered and creative approach to learning. Conservative reforms, by contrast, are defined as those that go "back to basics" and insist that students work harder to meet rigorous academic standards.

In such theories, the 1840s and 1850s (the expansionist phase of the common school movement), the 1920s and 1930s (the age of John Dewey's progressive education), and the 1960s and early 1970s (the period of the Great Society and the "War on Poverty") are seen as periods of liberal reform. The 1890s (the era of administrative reform and "the one best system"), the 1950s (the era of the Sputnik scare and "meritocracy"), and the 1980s and 1990s (the era of public alarm about economic competitiveness and "accountability" reforms) are seen as periods of conservative change. In some cyclical theories, periods of liberal and conservative reform are thought to be systematically linked: The more relaxed and inclusive standards brought on by liberal reforms feed into dissatisfaction among conservatives, leading to a new period of conservative reform. But the rigidity of conservative approaches eventually fuels demands for more inclusive and child-centered schooling, leading to a new period of liberal reform, until the cycle begins anew (cf. Tyack and Cuban 1995:40–54).

Although cyclical theories contain kernels of truth, they present too many problems to be accepted as convincing descriptions of the main historical eras of school reform activity in the United States. Some reform efforts do not easily fit the liberal/conservative typology, because they do not have a clearly identifiable political character. (What is the political character of the once-innovative idea of separating junior from senior high schools, for example?) Others do not fit, because they do not fall neatly into the popular designations of liberal and conservative periods. The 1980s, for example, were marked by movements both toward multicultural curricula, a liberal equity reform, and toward greater academic rigor, a conservative reform. Indeed, the terms "liberal" and "conservative" do not reliably identify the constituencies for school reforms in every case. Today, some political conservatives accept programs to diversity the curriculum, and many liberals support efforts to raise academic standards and increase accountability.

Perhaps most important, as the historians David Tyack and Larry Cuban (1995) have emphasized, cyclical theories tend to overemphasize policy statements and underemphasize what is actually going on in classrooms. Schools do change—by adding new forms of organization, new technologies, and new kinds of students—but "institutional developments in education may have an internal dynamic of their own only loosely connected with the periods of widespread and intense attention to schooling that we call periods of educational reform" (Tyack and Cuban 1995:47).

Correlates of Successful Reforms

Some reforms fade quickly after a year or two of experimentation. Who now remembers the vogue for "whole language" approaches to reading, or for "fuzzy math"? These were popular curricular movements only a decade ago. Indeed, many reforms heralded in their day have failed to make a lasting impact. Some educational prognosticators, for example, thought educational television would eventually make teachers obsolete, except as masters of ceremonies for transmissions from the tube.

The historical record suggests a great deal more immediate and enduring acceptance of reforms that do not radically alter the prevailing organization of schools, with principals at the center of administration and teachers at the center of a clear structure of classroom instruction and curriculum. These nonthreatening reforms contribute to increasing the engagement and success of staff and/or students. Some recent curricular innovations, such as "whole language" approaches to reading and "fuzzy math" proved to be confusing for some students and teachers alike. By contrast, reforms that make school more interesting for students, such as extracurricular activities and field trips, have been popular and therefore proven easy to assimilate. Reforms that compromise, or seem to compromise, the ability of teachers to discharge their duties and retain their authority in the classroom are ignored, treated with foot-dragging reluctance, or adapted only at the margins. This explains why some instructional technologies, such as radio and television, promoted by many as revolutionary forces, did not make important inroads into the classroom. They shifted too much authority away from teachers, and were therefore used sparingly. They also failed to grab students' attention as much as more active forms of learning.

Some reforms try to create greater equality in social relations through schooling. Examples include school desegregation and bilingual education. These social reforms are connected to the fourth "E" of school reform: equity. Too often, we discount the improvements that are possible due to equity-based reforms. Head Start programs for preschool children, services for disabled students, and even bilingual programs have proven effective and continued to be popular, or were at least popular for many years after they were initiated. However, social reforms that are threatening to important constituencies or cost too much for the perceived good they deliver will always come under criticism. Even relatively effective and low-cost reforms may become unpopular when the balance of political power changes, as happened recently in the case of bilingual programs. Successful equity reforms mobilize important constituencies that refuse to let the reforms die. Typically, they are also mandated into law in a way that allows compliance to be easily monitored. These factors help to explain, for example, the success of bilingual education programs, which were maintained in many states for decades, in spite of the constant criticism they received from "English first" conservatives on pedagogical and political grounds (see Porter 1990).

David Tyack and Larry Cuban (1995:57–8) summarize the conditions under which school reforms are more likely to be adopted. Reforms are more likely to be adopted and to last when they

- create more efficient organization for administrators;
- permit teachers to use more involving instruction (provided that the reforms do not threaten to displace teachers or create burdensome time demands);
- give students more incentives to attend school;
- do not threaten important political constituencies; and
- are backed up by the mandate of law, particularly if compliance can be readily monitored.

CONTEMPORARY SCHOOL REFORM

The school reform efforts of today fit into this larger context. Although cyclical theories of reform are not completely convincing, it is true that at various times in the nation's history public attention has focused more on one of the "four E's" than the others. Reformers at the end of the nineteenth century, impressed by the new world of business organization, wanted to make the schools into paragons of efficiency along corporate lines. In the 1910s and 1920s, progressive educators wanted to make schoolwork more creative and to encourage the expressive faculties of children as a way to engage their minds. This is the period in which movable furniture, eye-catching posters, hands-on experiments, and field trips were introduced into the schools. During the "War on Poverty" in the 1960s, equity issues were squarely at the center of reform efforts. To increase the opportunities of the disadvantaged, reformers developed a large number of programs from preschool Head Start programs to Pell grants for low-income college students.

Before Accountability: A Crisis of Declining Standards?

Since the 1980s, "excellence" has been the watchword of school reform. Educational standards became the dominant issue among school reformers for some good and some not very good reasons. The recent era of reform began in the late 1970s, when educators and the public became troubled by the perceived decline in American secondary schools. Some educators saw declining quality as an unintended consequence of the previous era's emphasis on equity (see, e.g., Ravitch 1983). Others pointed a finger at lowered expectations and watered-down curricula designed more for short-term relevance than for long-term educational value (see, e.g., Hirsch 1987, chap. 1).

Many indicators from the period do suggest growing problems in American schools. High levels of choice among electives tended to reinforce the generally anti-intellectual flavor of secondary school in the United States. The "general track" (which in some places included such courses as driver's education, typing, training for adulthood, and home economics) enrolled more than 40 percent of all students in the late 1970s, up from 12 percent in the previous decade (Adelman 1983). By the late 1970s, only the top 5 to 10 percent of students took languages for four years or advanced math or physics. Many schools, perhaps as many as two-thirds, dropped calculus and physics altogether (Holmes and MacLean 1989:34). Average SAT scores fell, verbal scores by more than 40 points. Reports of school violence were also increasing during the period. Each month, some 7 percent of high school students were assaulted by fellow students and as many as 10 percent were robbed (Toby 1980).

The alienated atmosphere in many high schools created foreboding and fear. Billy club- and bullhorn-wielding principals like Joe Clark in Elizabeth City, New Jersey, briefly became popular heroes for their no-nonsense approach to school violence. State legislatures hurried to pass minimal-competency exams for students and teachers. Portraits of "good schools" and high-achieving classes in troubled neighborhoods became a popular staple of educational sociology (see, e.g., Comer 1980; Lightfoot 1983; Ravitch 1985).

Researchers also propounded lists of the core elements of "effective schools" (Edmonds 1979; Rutter et al. 1979). Most of these lists played into the worries of the age about declining discipline and lowered expectations. According to the educational reformer Ron Edmonds (1979), even schools in the poorest communities could be effective provided that

- the academic mission of the school was pursued diligently by hard-driving principals,
- a disciplined and orderly atmosphere was carefully guarded and enforced by principals and teachers,
- teachers were well trained and academically oriented,
- students spent their time in class on task,
- students had regular and demanding homework assignments, and
- students received regular individualized attention.

A widely publicized study of private and public high schools by James Coleman and colleagues (Coleman, Hoffer, and Kilgore 1982) bolstered Edmonds's conclusions. This study found that order and discipline were higher in private schools and that expectations were also higher. The findings held for Catholic schools, even those enrolling students from low-income backgrounds. These academic climate characteristics, lacking in the public schools, had a salutary influence on learning. In the study, this influence was apparent even after student background characteristics and academic abilities were statistically controlled.

A number of important commission reports from the 1980s urged concerted national action to meet the crisis in American secondary schools. The most famous of the reports, written by a presidential commission, was entitled *A Nation at Risk*. Like the other reports, *A Nation at Risk* recited dismal statistics suggesting educational decline and widespread dissatisfaction with public schooling, and it linked the fate of the American economy in a competitive world to the fate of America's schools. "History is not kind to idlers," the report warned. "We are now faced by determined, well-educated and strongly motivated competitors. There is a redistribution of trained capability throughout the globe. We have committed acts of unthinking, unilateral educational disarmament" (National Commission on Excellence in Education 1983:5–6). Social reform movements need to mobilize resources and emotional support, if they are to succeed. The *accountability movement* of the 1980s certainly mobilized a tremendous amount of emotional support. As many as 20 prestigious commissions weighed in with complaints about the state of American schools, and the press was filled with reports of danger and suggestions for reform.

As I showed in chapter 4, the accountability movement exaggerated the crisis. American schools during this period were not guilty of "unilateral educational disarmament." In fact, some indicators suggest that the schools were performing better than they ever had before (Bracey 1991; Carson, Huelskamp, and Woodall 1992; Berliner and Biddle 1995). The declines in SAT scores partly reflected the increasing numbers of students who were taking the test during the period. Because of the way test scores are calculated, small decreases in the number of correct answers show up as large declines in average scores. At the top end of the scale, one error can drop scores by 50 points (Berliner and Biddle 1995:16). While providing more opportunities for minorities and women than in the past, the United States continued to produce more scientists and engineers than other industrial countries (Berliner and Biddle 1995:95–100).

Nevertheless, the crisis rhetoric and worrisome statistics of the commission reports precipitated a great outpouring of reform legislation and programmatic activity to improve schooling. A majority of states increased high school graduation and teacher training requirements. Many also raised teacher salaries (Johnson 1985). School leaders tried to implement Edmonds's (1979) and others' principles for creating "effective schools." These efforts produced a good record of improvement. School achievement among American secondary school students increased in the 1980s and 1990s, and American students began to look very good on most international assessments of educational achievement. Racial gaps in achievement remained sizable, but were reduced in half or nearly in half. Some analysts credit state-level reforms of graduation requirements and teacher training as the most important causes of these improvements (Ravitch 1995:70–85; Darling-Hammond 2004).

The "No Child Left Behind" Act

By 1994, the federal government was building on state efforts to mandate accountability assessments in the public schools by requiring such assessments as a precondition for receipt of federal funds. The movement toward greater accountability for student performance culminated in the enactment of the "No Child Left Behind" (NCLB) Act of 2001 by a large, bipartisan majority. This Act has been the subject of intense controversy. Many educators laud it as the most important effort in the history of the United States to ensure that every child is making adequate progress in learning important subject matter materials. Indeed, the Act was passed as a deliberate effort to demolish the "soft bigotry of low expectations," especially for poor and minority students. Others accuse the Act of ensuring a massive failure of the public schools, thereby leading the way to increased demands for turning public education over to the private sector. Rarely has a piece of educational legislation aroused such strong and contradictory emotions.

The major provisions of the Act required that schools report "adequate yearly progress" (AYP) toward meeting the goal of 100 percent "proficiency" in reading, mathematics, and science by the year 2014. Although definitions of AYP and proficiency were left up to the states, the Act required that any state receiving federal funds for education must agree to test all children in grades 3 through 8 every year. The tests must be based on "challenging" standards. Schools were required to demonstrate AYP overall and separately for all major ethnic and socioeconomic groups, for special education students, and for English Language Learners.

The Act included very stiff enforcement standards. Schools were required to test 95 percent of their students, and even one student below this cut-off could lead to the school being designated as failing to make adequate progress. States were required to publish report cards of their progress each year. If schools as a whole failed to meet their AYP goals two years in a row, they came in for increased attention and could receive funds to encourage improvement. Students in these "program improvement" schools were guaranteed the right to transfer to any other district school that was meetings its progress goals. Schools that failed to meet AYP goals for three years in a row were subject to more severe sanctions, including the firing of "low-performing" teachers, the replacement of the administrative staff, and even the abolition of whole schools and school districts.

An important part of the philosophy of NCLB is that students learn best when they are taught by well-qualified teachers. For this reason, the Act required that all current teachers in schools receiving NCLB funds must be "highly qualified" by 2006. Newly hired teachers must also be "highly qualified." By "highly qualified," the Act meant that teachers must hold at least a bachelor's degree, have full state certification, and not have had any certification requirements waived on an emergency or temporary basis.

The Act's advocates have argued that only very high expectations and powerful sanctions can get the schools moving along the right lines. They point to evidence that schools in Texas, which were subject to NCLB-type accountability standards, made better progress after high-stakes testing than before (Carnoy, Loeb, and Smith 2003; cf. Haney 2000). They have also documented many cases of teachers starting to talk to each other more about effective teaching tactics, and of principals providing emotional and material support for meeting AYP goals (Siskin 2003). Studies like these suggest that the law can have a positive impact.

Critics argue that any benefits of NCLB are likely to be short term. They believe that NCLB sets unrealistic long-range targets, which are enforced by overly punitive sanctions. The educational psychologist Robert Linn has noted that at current rates of progress, American schools will meet "proficiency" targets (as measured by the National Assessment of Educational Progress, or NAEP) for fourth-grade math in 57 years, for eighth-grade math in 61 years, and for twelfth-grade math in 166 years. To meet the targets by 2014, as the law requires, schools would need to increase their current improvement rates in grades 4 and 8 by a factor of four and their twelfth-grade improvement rates by a factor of 12. This would be equivalent to the big automobile manufacturers being required to produce engines averaging 288 miles per gallon by 2014 (Linn, cited in Bracey 2003). Because "proficiency" in NCLB has a fixed and absolute meaning, even schools that are showing progress—but not enough progress to meet "proficiency" levels—may be labeled "failures" rather than being rewarded for improvement.

Moreover, because children in "failing" schools are encouraged to leave for better-performing schools, critics argue the Act could, in principle, lead to AYP failure across the board, as high-performing schools begin to accept larger numbers of students who have not performed well in the past. Because NCLB has not been funded at the level originally authorized by Congress, the funds that might help schools to improve are in relatively short supply. It is no wonder that some critics refer to the law as the "Let No School Succeed" Act and wonder whether the Act was intended to ensure the failure of the public system, thereby paving the way for vouchers and other forms of school privatization (Bracey 2003).

Although most parents have not left "failing" schools, parents have reacted with confusion to the proliferation of test results bearing on the performance of their children's schools. Most states have set the AYP bar low; a few have set it high. For this reason, some good schools in the most demanding states have been unable to meet AYP goals and are now labeled "low-performing." By contrast, in states with lower standards, schools with modest records have been hailed as successful. The federal government has used "proficiency" levels in the NAEP as a check on state assessments. "Proficiency" standards in the national test are higher than those used in most state tests. Differences between the states and federal standards have sewn confusion in the minds of many parents. Many schools that are ranked as "excellent" by their states are considered "low-performing" by the federal government. Parents at these schools wonder who to believe and may be discouraged by the effect of negative labeling on school morale—and, perhaps, even on property values. Because 95 percent of all subgroups in a school are required to participate in testing, a few untimely absences can lead to the labeling of otherwise excellent schools as "low-performing" (Dillon 2004). Americans, in general, have reacted in ambivalent ways to NCLB. They rate the quality of schooling nationally higher than before it, but they express many doubts about the long-term effects of NCLB. They continue to express concerns that the public schools are inadequately financed (Rose and Gallup 2004).

Some of the weaknesses of NCLB could be corrected by greater standardization of proficiency measures across the states, by the allocation of more funds for school improvement efforts, and by review and revision of the technical deficiencies in the Act's assessment and enforcement protocols. Even with these corrections, however, it will be difficult for the public schools to weather what appears to be, in effect, a determined effort to challenge the morale of school administrators and teachers by requiring them to succeed to a degree that no schools in the modern era of mass schooling have ever succeeded. The Act contains no recognition that the social and economic conditions of communities bear on the capacity of students to reach national proficiency levels within the 2014 time frame. In this respect, the outlook of NCLB is utopian; it is unrelated to the world that we actually inhabit.

If NCLB continues with few modifications, the public schools are likely to be transformed in ways that many Americans will not welcome. Over time, a *high-stakes testing regime*, as represented by NCLB, will almost certainly lead to the diminishment and regimentation of schooling. As in the fast-food business, low-cost, standardized products will likely be served to consumers by low-skill, standardized workers. Already, textbook publishers are beginning to organize teaching in highly standardized ways—telling teachers exactly what and how to teach to meet state learning standards. Many schools in California and other states have adopted "scripted learning" programs in which teachers are told exactly what to teach word-for-word (California Educator 2002). In "low-performing" schools, subjects not tested in state assessments are starting to be crowded out of the curriculum by tested subjects.

Progressive educators spent years working on methods to encourage well-rounded children, whose aesthetic and social capacities are developed as fully as their self-discipline. These years of effort are in the process of being reversed. Teachers who try to engage students through creative, hands-on projects may come to think of these projects as not worth the time and effort. Historically, teachers have been interested in maintaining autonomy over instructional practices (Ingersoll 2003). Teachers who want to invest creativity in instructional design may increasingly leave the field to those who are comfortable equating the objectives of tests with the objectives of schools. The same fate may befall teachers who are interested in the social development and psychological maturation of children. One wonders whether the industrialized classrooms borne of NCLB will generate sufficient warmth and enthusiasm over the long term to serve as effective learning environments.

Programs to Improve Urban Schools

Educational improvement has remained elusive in the poor and racially isolated communities of urban America, where public schools face the toughest problems financially and socially. The tax base in the cities lags well behind that in suburban communities, and children come disproportionately from the lowest rungs of the socioeconomic ladder. Many of the urban poor grow up in unstable families, surrounded by the wreckage of drug and alcohol abuse, and in a culture of alienation from majority institutions and values.

In this unpromising terrain, the reform spirit of the 1980s made heroes of educators who claimed to know how to turn around failing school systems. These reformers thought they could turn the schools around through new kinds of instructional work in the classroom, through new kinds of relationships in the community, or through new organizational designs. The efforts of these reformers led to less well-known legislation that encouraged efforts to rethink schooling for the poor in comprehensive ways. These efforts remind us that "accountability" through high-stakes testing is only one path to the national goal of improved schooling for all.

Standards-based solutions. One set of solutions, following Edmonds's (1979) effective schools argument, emphasized greater intensity in academic work and higher standards. Among the best known of these standards-based solutions were programs designed by three university professors, Robert Slavin ("Success for All"), Henry Levin ("Accelerated Schools"), and Theodore Sizer ("Coalition of Essential Schools").

"Success for All" began in Slavin's home community of Baltimore in the early 1980s and spread to many other cities. It provided intensive instruction in reading for inner-city children in kindergarten through grade 3. Tutors were the most important feature of the program. They received special training and worked individually with children who were failing to keep up with their classmates in reading. Children were organized for the program by reading level rather than by age. Staff worked with parents to help them work with their children out of class. The children's progress was monitored on a regular eight-week cycle with feedback to parents (Slavin et al. 1990).

Levin's "Accelerated Schools" were based on the idea that all children should be treated as "gifted students" and given enriched educational materials rather than the "watered-down" curricula that had become commonplace. Special efforts were made to design curricular material that would be interesting to students but also challenging. The program emphasized thematic units that integrated a variety of subjects into the study of a single topic (Levin 1990).

Sizer formed a consortium of schools largely serving the urban poor. Participating schools committed themselves to maintaining "essential" intellectual goals for all students in a supportive environment emphasizing active learning. The schools otherwise showed little uniformity in approach, but did meet together periodically to discuss common issues and progress (Sizer 1986).

Community involvement programs. Another set of solutions attempted to increase the community's involvement in the schools. Many of these efforts focused on parental involvement; others on business-education partnerships.

James Comer, a professor in the Yale School of Medicine, was perhaps the best-known advocate of community-based solutions. Comer's program, which began in New Haven schools in the mid-1970s and soon spread to other states, was based on the premise that parents are potentially schools' most important resource. Comer's program organized administrators, teachers, counselors, and parents into three interacting "teams": the school planning and management team, the student and staff support team, and the parent team. To facilitate parental involvement, Comer's management and governance teams designed and carried out a social activities calendar for the school year, with parents playing a primary role in implementing the activities. In addition, parents were encouraged to volunteer in the schools as teacher aides, librarians, study hall monitors, and the like. The Comer program also included a social skills curriculum to teach students how to make good decisions in their interactions with others and "mental health teams" to deal quickly and comprehensively with specific behavioral problems in the schools (Comer 1980). The guiding principles of Comer's program are that a positive attitude about the school, community-building, and collaboration can lead to student achievement gains.

Community outreach also occurred through efforts to involve the business world in the schools. By the mid-1980s, nearly every large city and nearly every large corporation had some type of "business-education partnership." The New York businessman Eugene Lang stimulated these efforts when he offered to pay for college for every sixth-grade student at his Harlem alma mater who stayed in school and kept up good grades. (Ninety percent of the children took him up on the offer.) Following Lang's lead, hundreds of corporations (and many wealthy individuals) "adopted" schools in the 1980s. They sent equipment, money, and mentors to local schools to help with instruction and inspiration. Other programs, like the Boston Compact, were implemented by consortia of area businesses and district school superintendents. Participating businesses guaranteed part-time and summer employment to students who stayed in school and kept up their grades (Deng 1991).

Organizational restructuring. A third set of solutions sought changes in the organizational structures of schools to overcome bureaucratic rigidities and political intrusions. Of these structural solutions, "school choice" programs gained the most attention. John Chubb of the Brookings Institution and Terry Moe of Stanford University became well known for advocating "choice" programs that encouraged schools to compete for student consumers. Chubb and Moe (1989) foresaw a time when many specialized schools would spring up to attract children with special interests. Parents would be free to choose among a variety of schools in the public and private sector. A variety of *"choice" programs* sprang up at this time, each one based on a strong faith in the "magic of the market." These included some within-school district plans involving only public schools, some inter-district plans involving public schools (including, in Minnesota, a very large-scale statewide plan), and some usually small-scale and experimental public-private programs. In the public-private plans, parents were typically given a *voucher* to pay for their children's schooling if they chose a private school, or the schools themselves were reimbursed by the public school district.

Magnet schools were another popular structural solution. These schools allowed children with special interests in a particular subject (such as computers or the performing arts) to attend schools designed around those interests. Although magnets were originally associated with "gifted and talented" programs, these quickly became a small minority of the magnet offerings. The vast majority of the programs (almost 90 percent) were based on a particular subject matter emphasis or instructional approach or some combination of specialized curriculum and method (Blank, Levine, and Steel 1996). Some magnet programs specialized in particular instructional approaches, such as open classrooms, the Montessori method, or basic skills. Most were implemented as part of desegregation plans, in the hope that special schools would retain some nonminority families in urban school districts, while providing minority children with more appealing school options. By 1991, some 230 school districts, enrolling a quarter of all the country's schoolchildren, offered magnet school programs. The number of curricular emphases grew proportionately, to include everything from aerospace technology and biotechnology to "travel and tourism," ROTC, cosmetology, and animal care (ibid.).

Charter schools also date from this period and are a variant on the theme of "school choice." Charter school legislation, beginning in the early 1990s, provided disaffected parents a way out of the public school system by allowing them to form their own publicly supported, but privately organized alternative schools. Charter schools are granted considerable autonomy from existing school regulations in return for promises of accountability for academic results. Charter schools are allowed to vary from other public schools in philosophy, curriculum, pedagogical approaches, attention to special populations, and size. (Most are small, averaging only about 250 students.) The "charter" establishing these schools is a performance contract detailing the school's mission, program, goals, students served, methods of assessment, and ways to measure success. Most charters must be renewed after 3–5 years based on an acceptable record of management and performance. Several types of parent groups were involved in the founding of charter schools: some were minority parents hoping to escape failing urban schools; some were white parents with similar motivations; and still others involved parents seeking alternative pedagogical approaches or more personalized attention to the special needs and interests of their children. By 2004, some 3,000 charter schools had been founded in 37 states, with some states, such as Arizona, Florida, and Texas, strongly encouraging their development (Renzulli and Roscigno 2005).

School-based management, another structural reform, advocated the reorganization of authority relations rather than enrollment patterns. Its champions argued that "empowering" principals and teachers by moving decision-making authority from the superintendents' office to the schools themselves would be enough to make a substantial difference in how well the schools operated (Clune and White 1988; Malen, Ogawa, and Kranz 1990).

Comprehensive School Reform Evaluations

In policy discussion and newspaper headlines, the national NCLB program has eclipsed these efforts to improve urban schools, but the programs have not disappeared. Indeed, government efforts to evaluate and "scale up" comprehensive school reform (CSR) received a boost during the Clinton Administration, when the federal government passed Comprehensive School Reform Development legislation and set criteria through which schools could qualify for federal funds to aid comprehensive reform. This legislation was later absorbed into NCLB. Comprehensive school reform is one of the most interesting experiments in American educational history, because literally dozens of designs have qualified for CSR support. These designs are now in operation at thousands of schools enrolling millions of students. Because designers are required to show that their programs improve academic achievement, CSR legislation has also encouraged more and better evaluation than previous eras of education reform.

Government funds supporting implementation of comprehensive reforms have been targeted largely for the schools most in need of help: high-poverty schools with low student test scores. CSR designs are eligible for government support if they can show that they are based on effective practices and include provisions for parental involvement, professional training for school staff, annual evaluation plans, and meet other mandated criteria (see

Borman et al. 2003:127). Some of the urban school reform plans discussed earlier, such as business-education partnerships, do not meet the criteria for CSR support, but they continue in a piecemeal fashion. Others, such as charter schools, have achieved their own authorizing legislation and have grown rapidly (Renzulli and Roscigno 2005).

Some CSR programs have now received dozens of evaluations in multiple sites, and over many years. It is possible to sift and weigh these evaluations and to make judgments on average effects based on analysis of evaluations that meet scientific criteria (Borman et al 2003).[1] More sophisticated evaluation strategies are also underway, which compare more than one of the reform programs using the same methodology (Rowan et al. 2004). Because of these efforts, we are in a position to begin to assess which reforms work in high-poverty areas—and which ones are as yet unproven. We can also use social theory to understand the patterns shown in the evaluations.

Successes and Disappointments in Urban School Reform

Dozens of comprehensive school reform programs have been developed and evaluated. These programs range from the exotic and adventurous to the scripted and tame. Among the more adventurous are academic-athletic programs involving periods in the classroom and periods in nature, and programs that focus on "different ways of knowing" using arts-infused curricula and teaching based on theories of multiple intelligences. Sociologists have known for some time that bursts of energy often follow the initial introduction of a change, any change. This phenomenon even has a name: *the "Hawthorne effect,"* after the General Electric factory in Hawthorne, California, where it was first observed. But the improvements that result from initial interventions may fade as the novelty of the intervention wears off.

Few of the comprehensive school reform programs have as yet been evaluated frequently enough or well-enough to satisfy hard-nosed researchers that they have consistent, positive effects on learning. For example, neither Henry Levin's "Accelerated Schools" nor Theodore Sizer's "Coalition of Effective Schools" has been evaluated thoroughly enough by independent researchers to provide strong evidence of effectiveness (Borman et al. 2003). Others, such as "site-based management," show an inconsistent pattern, depending on the quality of site plans and personnel involved.

The assessments thus far point to two conclusions: well-designed, very traditional instructional programs seem to be producing the best results, and programs providing very strong incentives for achievement to all students can also produce good results. These findings underscore the military-like training aspects of mass schooling, and the importance of incentives in a competitive, capitalist society. Community-based programs also show some promise, but the inclusive and collaborative features of these programs work best when they are linked to a very strong academic ethos promulgated by principals and teachers. Finally, "choice" programs, based on market models of human motivation, have shown mixed results. Their popularity is also limited. Statewide voucher programs have been strongly opposed by teachers' unions, and they have thus far failed to gain necessary majorities when they have appeared on statewide ballots. Local experiments (and experiences in other countries) suggest that, as in many markets, low-income parents lack information, time, or other resources (such as transportation) to take advantage of opportunities to change schools. The competence and commitment of personnel involved in charter schools varies, and the mixed findings of charter school evaluations seem to have more to do with practical difficulties of the supply side (applying to all business "start-ups") than with the more dramatic flaws in the logic of the demand side of the market model, as revealed in studies of vouchers.

Effective comprehensive school reform programs. Robert Slavin's tutor-based and reading-intensive "Success for All" program is one of the clearest examples of a successful comprehensive school reform program (Slavin et al. 1990). Slavin's program has been rigorously and repeatedly evaluated. The results show significantly enhanced language and reading skills in preschool and primary grades, reduced special education referrals, and reduced numbers of grade repeaters. These results are consistent with the work of researchers who argue that weak preparation in reading is the single most important cause of instances of poor school performance among inner-city children (Slavin, Karweit, and Madden 1989; Farkas 1993). Once remediation is necessary beyond grade 3, it is often too late.

"Success for All" can be an expensive program (nearly $300,000 for one-year implementation schoolwide), because it requires that additional teaching staff be brought into the classroom. However, schools have been able to use compensatory education ("Title I") funds from the federal government to implement the program (Slavin et al. 1994), as is true for other CSR designs.

> ## "Success for All"
>
> Is it possible to give all children a strong foundation in reading, even those who are at risk of early failure? Robert Slavin has shown that it can be done. Slavin and his associates (Slavin et al. 1990) believe that students must be prevented from needing remedial attention beyond grade 3.
>
> Here's how the program works: tutors work directly with students who are having trouble keeping up with their reading groups. First graders have the highest priority. They take students out of their homerooms during periods other than reading and math. In general, they stress the same skills as the student is currently learning in reading, but they also attempt to identify learning deficits and to use different strategies to teach the same skills. Tutors and teachers meet regularly to coordinate their approaches to particular students. Once students begin to read primers, the program uses cooperative learning activities built around story structure, prediction of story lines, summarization, vocabulary building, decoding practice, writing, and direct instruction in reading comprehension skills. Student progress is assessed every eight weeks. Family support teams work to encourage parental involvement and to help students who are not receiving adequate sleep or nutrition, who need eyeglasses, who are not attending school regularly, and who are exhibiting serious behavior problems.
>
> We can be reasonably confident that "Success for All" works because Slavin's group has been careful to evaluate the program rigorously, usually using more than one measure of reading competence. Where possible, "Success for All" schools are matched with a control school similar in poverty level, historical achievement level, ethnicity of the student body, and other factors. The results of evaluations of the first 15 "Success for All" schools in seven states showed that the program improves student performance in reading and that it usually

continued to be successful.

has the largest effects with the bottom 25 percent of the class. In these evaluations, significant effects were not found on every measure at every grade level, but the program showed effects in a great majority of schools and grade levels on measures of reading competence. In many cases, "Success for All" students read several months or even a grade level ahead of the students with whom they were matched. Indeed, the only school that failed to show positive effects of "Success for All" was a school in rural Caldwell, Idaho. This had less to do with a weakness in the "Success for All" program than with the unusual strength of the control school with which it was matched.

Subsequent evaluations have continued to produce positive results for reading comprehension and vocabulary (Borman et al. 2003). The program's greatest importance, according to Slavin, has been to demonstrate that substantially greater success for disadvantaged students can be routinely ensured in schools that are neither exceptional nor extraordinary—schools that were not producing great success before the program was introduced (Slavin et al. 1994:647).

In addition to "Success for All," at least one other popular CSR design has shown consistently positive results and has been evaluated frequently enough by independent researchers using replicable designs to merit the designation "very likely" to be effective (Borman et al. 2003). Siegfried Engelmann of the University of Oregon developed this program, "Direct Instruction." It is quite similar to "Success for All" in many of its main features: it is very structured and based on continuous assessment of progress. The program is based on highly scripted lesson strategies and extensive writing assignments. Lessons are interactive, and presented to small groups of students.

If well-focused instructional help in the classroom is one promising factor, strong incentives for achievement can be another. When Eugene Lang offered to partially finance the college tuition of every member of a Harlem sixth-grade class who made it to college, he found himself paying for more than 90 percent of the students in a school where a 75 percent dropout rate had been typical! (Lang also helped with counseling and motivational support for the families of his "adopted" students.) This is, needless to say, a very expensive offer. Where incentives are not as strong as those promised and delivered by Lang, success is usually also not as strong.

Local business communities can sometimes get together to stimulate better performance at a less daunting price tag than Lang's college sponsorship program required. But these partnerships take tremendous work to produce strong results. The Philadelphia High School Academies, for example, showed a good record by using the promise of full-time employment in supporting businesses as an incentive to improve attendance and school performance. The Boston business community promised to hire thousands of high school students in summer jobs and to give preference to graduates of the city schools for permanent entry-level employment, if the Boston school system improved the attendance and achievement of high school graduates and reduced the dropout rate. The business community delivered on its promises, employing thousands of local high school students. However, attendance and achievement in the schools increased only modestly (and no more statistically than the improving national trends would have predicted), and the program later faltered on disagreements about whether the business community and the schools were living up to their ends of the bargain.[2]

Thus, although the evidence is not entirely conclusive, two factors appear to be frequently associated with successful urban school reform programs:

- Enrichment of classroom life through well-focused and continuous instructional aid, using field-tested curricula and continuous evaluation of progress

- Encouragement of student achievements through practical incentives for achievement in the form of jobs or help with college tuition

The promise of community-based reform programs. Some community participation-based programs have shown good results over the short term, but they have not yet dispelled suspicions that they depend on the charisma of a singular leader to be effective, and are difficult to institutionalize on a long-term basis in poor, unstable communities. Both the sense of promise and the nagging doubts go back to the 1960s. At that time, principal Samuel Shepard of St. Louis, Missouri, was the only urban school reformer who proved that he could bring children up to national grade-level performance. Shepard went house to house and had parents sign contracts to monitor their children's schoolwork and to set aside a clean, well-lit place for their children to do homework. He also brought parents into the school to participate and help out. However, when Shepard retired, the program faltered.

The Comer program (also known as the "School Development Program") is based on similar principles of community involvement, plus the formation of parent-teacher teams to build community engagement and to treat behavioral issues on campus. Evaluations showed evidence from the beginning of success in the schools in which Comer himself was directly involved (Comer 1980). Fortunately, evidence is beginning to accumulate that the Comer program can be successfully institutionalized, even in settings where Comer himself is not continuously involved. The research, while encouraging, is not yet completely conclusive; too few good studies have been conducted by researchers independent of Comer and his associates. Comer has observed that the program's success depends less on "mechanisms" than on the energy and commitment of participants.

Community-based reforms work best when they work not only on building parental involvement but simultaneously on creating a strong academic ethos on campus. We know that parental involvement alone is no panacea. Indeed, the research suggests net negative consequences when parents are heavily involved in school governance (no doubt because of the contentiousness and favoritism that can develop in such situations) (Borman et al. 2003). However, when increased parental involvement is connected to a strong academic ethos, good things can happen, even in high-poverty schools. The educational researchers Anthony Bryk, Valerie Lee, and Peter Holland (1993) showed that Catholic schools achieve better results among the urban poor than public schools, even after the social and academic characteristics of students are statistically controlled. The better performance of Catholic schools, the researchers concluded, is the result of their ability to keep children focused on academic pursuits, their ability to create a communal environment, and their continuously disseminated inspirational values. Catholic schools have a more focused academic orientation than public schools and do not allow for as much individual choice in course-taking patterns. Teachers are not notably stronger classroom instructors than their public school counterparts (Bryk and his colleagues suggest that they may in fact be less good overall), but they make extra efforts to be engaged with their students and to involve parents. Absences for commitments outside of school, such as athletics or other performances, are frowned upon. In return, teachers and principals expect reciprocation on the part of students and parents. Many decisions are made after wide consultation and discussion rather than handed down from on high. An "inspirational ideology" uniting concern for every individual and for the school as a whole is at the center of this "communal model" of urban school reform.

> Fundamental to Catholic schools are beliefs about the dignity of each person and a shared responsibility for advancing a just and caring society. When such understandings meld to a coherent organizational structure with adequate resources, desirable academic and social consequences can result. (Bryk, Lee, and Holland 1993:312)

Whether the Catholic school model can be exported into the public school system is certainly debatable. Catholic schools charge tuition, and parents willing to invest in their children's schooling are likely more committed to education than other parents. Religious homogeneity is another factor that can encourage above average commitment and sacrifice. However, the Catholic school model deserves further study, because Catholic schools have shown that their model can work even when the school draws the great majority of its children from poor and immigrant communities.

Promises and problems of "school choice" programs. Voucher programs, magnet schools, and charter schools all involve efforts to create more "choice" for families who would otherwise be assigned to their neighborhood school. They build on public skepticism about the effectiveness of public bureaucracies that are protected from market competition. This same skepticism has encouraged tens of thousands of parents to leave the public system altogether, either for private schools (Davies and Hammack 2005) or for home schooling (Stevens 2001). Public systems have consequently experimented with several approaches to building in more opportunities for parental choice.

The form of choice differs significantly between voucher, magnet school, and charter school programs. Vouchers make parents into consumers; they put educational resources in the hands of parents to use as they wish. Magnet schools give options to parents who feel that their children would profit from a particular curricular emphasis or teaching philosophy. Charter schools allow groups of parents to organize their own schools, provided that they meet government-mandated requirements for planning and evaluation. School choice programs have proven to be popular with conservative policymakers and with parents who are dissatisfied with their public schools (Elmore and Fuller 1996), but the results of experiments with school choice are mixed.

Without a doubt, some schools that grew up as "alternative schools" in early choice experiments, schools such as Principal Deborah Meier's Central Park East schools in East Harlem, are beacons of light. The programs at Meier's four Central Park East schools were tailored to attract students' interests and housed in small communities of 250 students. The schools achieved strikingly strong results: 90 percent of Central Park East students went on to college from a school district in which dropout rates of more than 50 percent were common (Meier 1995, chap. 2).

However, most voucher programs have proven to help mainly the best informed and most highly motivated families. The evidence points to a "creaming off" phenomenon, in which bad schools do not improve to keep up, as the market model predicts they should, but rather stagnate or sink further as the more motivated families leave (Moore and Davenport 1990; Wells 1991). These kinds of effects have been shown in several U.S. school districts (see, e.g., Lee, Croninger, and Smith 1996; Martinez, Godin, and Kenerer 1996; Wells 1996; Witte 1996) and also in the most comprehensive study of choice in Europe, a study of the Scottish experience (Willms and Echols 1993). As I indicated in Chapter 3, evidence from Latin America and Sweden also suggests that the most advantaged parents gain the most from vouchers, while the poor gain little—and are likely to remain in poor-performing neighborhood schools (Carnoy 1998).

Voucher programs depend on an assumption that parents will invest time and energy into learning about schools and will choose to transport their children to better schools. But costs of transportation and information are high, and poor parents typically do not have the wherewithal to bear them. The policy analysts Richard Elmore and Bruce Fuller (1996) have concluded that in the absence of serious progress in improving classroom instruction in schools serving the urban poor, "it is unlikely that choice will do anything other than simply move high achievers around from one school to another, mistaking the effect of concentrating strong and motivated students for the effect of the choice system" (Elmore and Fuller 1996:200).

Magnet school programs often show the same undesirable consequences for district inequalities as other choice programs. Magnets attract better educated and more highly motivated families and therefore can lead to the concentration of less highly educated and less motivated families at the bottom schools (Archbald 2004; Blank 1989). However, some "controlled choice" magnet plans create choices for parents without exacerbating racial and social class segregation. They convert all schools to magnets, provide centrally supported information and transportation to all parents, and work within the context of fixed goals of racial and socioeconomic diversity (Archbald 2004). Definitive studies have not been conducted on the effects of magnet schools on student achievement. Logically, the roughly half of magnet schools now geared to specialized subject matter (such as performing arts or animal care) seem unlikely to raise performance in subjects outside the school's major area of emphasis. On the other hand, those geared to distinctive instructional approaches may have positive effects on achievement by attracting students with similar learning styles. It will be interesting to see if they do.

Charter schools are a form of choice that allows parents a major role in creating the climate and pedagogy of new schools supported by state funds. The positive impacts on learning expected of charter schools have not thus far been proven, and the best evidence available suggests that the results of charter school experiments have in fact often been disappointing. National studies, with controls for student background characteristics, have shown that charter school students have performed somewhat worse than regular public school students on tests of math and reading (Schemo 2004; NAEP 2005; Carnoy et al. 2005; cf. Hoxby 2004a, 2004b). Charter school advocates have tried to explain the performance gap by arguing that charter schools serve more disadvantaged populations, but this argument is not true. In fact, charter schools tend to serve a slightly more advantaged population than regular schools (Carnoy et al. 2005, chap. 4). Running a school is hard work, and idealism can fuel it only for so long. Some charter schools have failed to provide a stable management environment. The enthusiasm of volunteers and management board members can erode once the hard realities of running a school are faced on a daily basis over a long period of time.

The findings on choice programs and magnet schools encourage ambivalent feelings. Surely, we should not sacrifice motivated families to failing school systems. But at the same time we might legitimately worry about the further isolation of schools at the bottom if they are deprived of precisely the kinds of parents who are likely leaders in creating a positive learning climate and support for the teaching and administrative staff. Still more troubling is the finding that even the highly motivated families who take advantage of school choice opportunities do not always gain very much from their participation. Studies of the Milwaukee public-private choice experiments suggest that turnover in school populations is so great in poor urban areas that the continuity needed to sustain a learning community may be difficult to achieve. The performance of choice students has varied from year to year, but they do not appear to show better achievement overall than similar low-income students who have remained in their neighborhood schools (Witte 1996:130). Schools in communities like inner-city Milwaukee need a strong academic ethos, orderly environments, consistently high levels of parental participation in the life of the school, and academically focused principals more than they need "school choice" or other purely organizational "fixes."

THE POSSIBILITIES OF SCHOOLING

Schools of the future may very well be different in some important respects from those we see today. For one thing, computers, with their interactive and multisensory potential, will become more central in the classroom. Although they are now still mainly used for drill work (Pelgrum and Plomp 1993), they may in the near future help to open up the world for children in ways that textbooks alone cannot do (see, e.g., Papert 1993). Many more one-on-one tutorials will be possible using computer-aided instruction with feedback. In addition, we may see more specialized secondary schools focusing on particular subject clusters or pedagogical methods, in the future. Multicultural and global curricula, already a force, seem likely to become increasingly important as well.

Computers in the Classroom

Computers will almost certainly play an even more important role than they now do in classrooms of the future. This is a little surprising, considering that technology has often been a bust in the classroom. Radio, television, and film have all failed to make large inroads in classroom life (Tyack and Cuban 1995). The difference between these earlier technologies and computers is that computers are interactive and offer a wide range of choice in learning experiences for teachers and students alike.

Computers began to enter classrooms some 25 years ago. Their entry into school life has not been without problems. Some schools remain "unwired," and the existence of computer resources has become one of the major stratifying resources in school systems, as the term "the digital divide" suggests. Just as computer use for analytical purposes has become more and more a marker of high-level jobs, so computer resources have become a marker of better schools. Many teachers continue to use computers for unimaginative drill work, whereas others substitute net searches for learning experiences. In the latter cases, "data smog" or information overload can be a problem.

Where they are used effectively, computers can be a tremendous learning resource. From the beginning, some teachers were able to take advantage of the interactive quality and versatility of computers. For example, one school in rural Louisiana used computers to develop a folklife archive about their community. The students interviewed friends and relatives for reminiscences, folktales, recipes, crafts, and celebrations. They transformed these interviews into files that combined text, graphics, animation, and sound, creating interactive documents with multiple layers of information. The archives fed into classroom activities. Native Americans came into class to help students build authentic Choctaw huts, famous cooks came in to instruct on local recipes, scuba divers came to talk about sea life in the Gulf. Photographs taken at these events were integrated with text in the archives (Gooden 1996, chap. 2).

At a school in south Philadelphia, science instructors used computers to aid in the building of a greenhouse and the study of plant life. Computers were used to record growth data, conduct plant growth simulations, and write reports on topics from photosynthesis to acid rain. Students got hands-on experience with plant life in the greenhouse and intellectual reflection on natural processes through the computing facilities. Students and teachers also began to use electronic bulletin boards and networks to do research and to establish links with other schools. They shared statistics on water and air quality and other data (Gooden 1996, chap. 3).

In addition to the information resources of the Internet, some teachers now have access to enormously sophisticated educational software. Children can simulate the growth and management of towns and cities, follow intergalactic space travelers to solve problems that help them save the universe, look at and listen to different countries of the world while learning history. Thanks to these creative programs, children who attend today's best schools will be learning how to do research and how to think in an integrated way at an earlier age than any previous generation.

But these innovations alone cannot create the well-ordered, academically enriched learning communities most people want their schools to be. These are not the "magic bullets" that some of their advocates imagine. Other panaceas have been proposed in the past, and most have fallen short of the expectations of their promoters. There is a "sticky quality" to what can be done in bureaucratic, group-learning systems, especially those like public schools, which attempt to transform students with such a wide range of capacities and interests. Most reform, therefore, requires slow, persistent, patient work.

In this book, I have intended to explain mass schooling as a social institution: where it came from, why different patterns of organization and practice exist, and what consequences these different patterns have for societies and their individual members. In these last few pages of the book, I would like to look at schooling in a more prescriptive way, that is, in terms of the ideals that schools can represent and how they might represent those ideals more effectively than they currently do.

Which Educational Values Should We Promote?

The first question for those who presume to prescribe is: What constitutes health? The first conclusion is that all the major values associated with school reform movements represent desirable goods:

- Efficiency is associated with the economical use and conservation of scarce resources.
- Excellence is associated with high cultural attainment.
- Enhancement is associated with the fostering possibilities for more complete development.
- Equity is associated with prevailing standards of social justice, opportunity, and fairness.

And yet we often lack a metric for deciding whether one good is more important than another. To promote efficiency, we might give children with different aptitudes different kinds of schooling. But this efficiency would be purchased at the expense of equity among groups. Which value should take priority? In many instances, logical solutions cannot be defined; the values are incommensurable. Tradeoffs may be possible, but how these trade-offs are made will depend on how the two goods are weighted and also the thresholds below which a minimal value on the good seems unacceptable.

Much depends, therefore, on how we weight various goods and what thresholds we consider acceptable. Having looked at schooling systems for many years, I believe that the best protection for a progressive, democratic society and the best hope for individuals occur when the state provides essentially the same education for all through secondary school and when educators do not trim their commitment to high standards of academic and personal excellence.

The political theorist Benjamin Barber titled his book about schooling *An Aristocracy of Everyone* (1992), and this title captures the spirit with which I look at the possibilities of schooling. As Barber observes, the great dream of the Enlightenment was that ordinary people could gain the cultural knowledge and refined understandings that were once reserved for inherited wealth. Most liberals of the seventeenth and eighteenth centuries believed that a market society required the widespread diffusion of knowledge and good standards of social behavior. Certainly, this was the view of John Locke, the most important advocate of a social order based on the maximization of individual freedoms (Gray 1989). Democratic and republican forms of government required self-limiting virtues and just discriminations, and these could be produced only through schooling that aimed to produce excellence in all citizens.

In contemporary work on schooling, however, the idea of excellence has become tied more or more exclusively to a narrow, test-based version of academic merit. But tests alone do not measure merit. Beautifully written and vigorously argued essays, well-crafted research projects, provocative questions—these too are marks of inquiring and able minds. Worse yet, the reasons political leaders put forward to justify pursuing academic excellence are exclusively tied to prospects for economic advancement, either at the individual or societal level. The economic rewards of academic excellence are important, but they are not the only important rewards: people who think well will also have the opportunity to experience a richer appreciation of the world they inhabit and a greater self-awareness. Schools can also foster excellence in character, in the conduct of social relations, and in community life. Well-rounded, deep thinking people are more likely to take an active role as informed citizens.

Today, a narrowly economic outlook threatens to override the ideals of high-quality education for all that animated the American common school movement and its Enlightenment precursors. Although we retain faith in the power of the schools to provide training and good work habits that help in the labor market, we have already, to some degree, lost our faith in the power of the schools to lift our minds and spirits and to build the foundations of a democratic community. Educators themselves are partly to blame for these diminished aspirations. When educational leaders accepted differentiated secondary school curricula in the early twentieth century in the name of "social efficiency" and "student interest," they helped to reduce the democratic faith in the possibilities of schooling. Too many classrooms today remain dull places, where teachers march through textbook chapters in an effort to keep up with the "standards express" and children's minds frantically race to shovel in the facts but remain largely disengaged from the subject matter. These tedious marches through forests of facts and interpretations are punctuated by the few truly arousing events during the school week or month—campus controversies or sporting triumphs. These moments are close in spirit to other mass entertainment spectacles in our society. The works of political theorists like Benjamin Barber, of empirical social scientists like Anthony Bryk, and of school reformers like Deborah Meier remind us that we do not have to settle for a diminished version of what schools can be educationally.

Which School Qualities Should We Prefer?

Thanks to these and other writers, we have good evidence about the school characteristics that can enhance the possibilities for children: the possibilities that they will become self-disciplined and considerate in their conduct and accomplished in their thought processes. Like Ron Edmonds's (1979) principles of effective schools, this list emphasizes the importance of good order and high standards, but it also includes some other qualities. Good schools, regardless of location, have the following qualities:

- They have adequate resources.
- They are of a relatively small size.
- They express high academic expectations and are organized in ways that reflect those expectations.
- They are staffed by well-trained and highly motivated teachers.
- They include strong elements of communal organization.

w/ business / family
- sense of community

• schools in poor neighbourhood are more equitably.
• Catholic schools perform better than secular school, very strong inspirational tendency due to religion.

- They mobilize the voluntary involvement of students, parents, and others in the learning and social activities of the school.

The first point is the most basic, and it is often taken for granted: good schools require adequate resources. An appropriate physical plant is critical for high-quality learning. Well-maintained schools signal to children and their families that education is important and may help to inspire children to make the commitment to learning. By contrast, dilapidated and overcrowded buildings signal that education is not a high priority. Maintaining an appropriate physical plant, especially in older cities, can be an expensive proposition. The need for adequate resources seems like a truism (and may even seem like an invitation to waste, as it has been at times in New York and other cities), but it means that taxpayers will need to continue their historically strong commitment to schooling. The market is an alternative to public support, but it is not as equitable an alternative.

Second, good schools are relatively small. As the school reformer Deborah Meier (1995) wrote, "Large schools neither nourish the spirit nor educate the mind. What big schools do is remind most of us that we don't count for a lot" (p. 107). Being known (and therefore at least potentially appreciated) is among the strongest benefits of small schools. As Meier notes, students in large high schools often find that no teacher knows them well enough to write a college reference letter that sounds authentic. But at her small secondary school in East Harlem, "the shyest and least engaged student would not have suffered the fate that the average big school student takes for granted" (ibid.:112). The empirical evidence indicates that small schools pull more students into active participation in the life of the school community and thereby create a stronger sense of satisfaction and engagement (Lindsay 1982).

Small schools also foster the natural interpenetration of adult and student cultures, rather than a strict separation between the two. Interacting on a regular basis with adults outside the classroom is important for the kinds of conversions that schools hope to make:

> In part, after all, we teachers are trying to convert our children to a set of adult intellectual standards and appreciations—our love affair with literature and history, science and math, logic and reason, accuracy and precision. . . . This in turn requires joint membership in an attractive community representing such values as well as a myriad of interactions across generations. . . . [Small schools] offer a chance, not a guarantee, that children will glimpse possibilities that make them want to be grown-ups.[3] (Meier 1995:113)

Evidence is accumulating that small classes also produce better results, though starting early in small classes and continuing for at least years may be necessary to assure long-term carry-over effects of small classes (Cotton 2001; Finn et al. 2004). It is possible, but not yet proven, that small classes are particularly beneficial to minority students (Finn et al. 2004; Nye, Hedges, and Konstantopolous 2000).

Schools in poor neighborhoods are now playing roles that are more than simply educational. They provide parental counseling, baby-sitting services, an oasis out of harm's way, in some places a one-stop social services agency (Graham 1993). The difficult circumstances of these communities have led some reformers to believe that schools need, above all, to offer encouragement and support rather than challenging academic standards. This is a prescription for decline. Schools have the opportunity to help children to develop their minds and their spirits, to transmit socially useful skills and personally useful habits of behavior. But schools can do this only if they create commitments to the learning community rather than only to the "support system" of the school.

Good schools keep their priorities straight by expressing high expectations and a real passion about learning. Good academic standards in turn cannot be built on weak foundations. Children cannot learn unless their basic language skills are adequate. When school districts have extra resources, the research suggests these should go into providing classroom aides in the early primary grades to make sure that all children are at or above grade level in reading. Effective schools are, moreover, intellectually challenging places. Teachers are well trained both in their subject matters and in the art and science of good teaching (Darling-Hammond 2000; Wayne and Youngs 2003). The academic focus of the school is communicated through the structure of expectations and the consistency with which these expectations are communicated. Teachers spend their time in class on task and assign regular homework. Basic rules of conduct are consistently enforced.

These good standards do not mean that teachers spend less time thinking about how to make their lessons engaging. Good teaching is a creative joining of opposites: passion and rationality, imagination and instrumentality, objectivity and compassion. Children learn by separating things into analytical bits and joining things together into integrative wholes, by thinking and speaking, by memorization and play. Teaching is an art of activating interest and preserving important tensions, as much as it is a science of conveying information and understandings. Because good teaching is difficult work, good schools provide ways for teachers to talk to one another about their craft, but they allow effective independent-minded teachers to go their own way.

Some of the most important qualities of good schools cannot be mandated; they have to grow. Communal organization is one of the most important of these. Communal organization means high levels of interaction guided by common values and many opportunities to share in governance. Communal organization cannot be achieved without either highly involved families (the typical case in affluent suburbs) or leadership that builds consensus and trust and actively reaches out to families (the more common case in poor urban settings).

In many schools, communal organization also requires consistent representation of an inspirational ideology that gives meaning to the life of the school community. Anthony Bryk and his colleagues (Bryk, Lee, and Holland 1993) have provided a vivid depiction of how important such an inspirational ideology is in the life of urban Catholic schools. Other integrative ideologies can more appropriately reflect the values of other communities, but all integrative ideologies find a way to celebrate the importance of each individual life and to link these individual lives to a meaningful, larger purpose.

Good schools find ways, finally, to mobilize commitments. For this purpose, perhaps the most important quality of all is simply the well-focused effort of those who care about learning to act on their commitments. Not long ago, the educational historian Patricia Graham wrote a book about school reform titled *S.O.S.* (1992). The familiar abbreviation stood for a less familiar idea: sustain our schools. In Graham's view, communities, families, government, higher education, and business do not need to *save* the public schools so much as to *sustain* them: "Most of all, the schools need people who will be knowledgeable about their fields, skilled in their pedagogy, passionate in their concern for their students, and committed to educating all our children well" (Graham 1992:170).

Teachers and principals search for the right metaphors to convey these understandings. One teacher likens the process of sustaining learning to planting seeds. "Some [seeds] fall on inhospitable ground and don't grow, some of them aren't going to be watered or taken care of, but some of them grow and produce other seeds and pretty soon you have a forest." Another suggests that the reason for her school's success is that the principal is "out there in his hip boots helping with the cement work" (Gooden 1996:74, 79).

In life, there are virtuous as well as vicious cycles. Wise and persistent involvement in the life of schools by parents, volunteers, and other community members can stimulate virtuous cycles. Even a little effort can be reciprocated, and even a little reciprocated effort is an important base on which to build.

CONCLUSION

Unlike other chapters of *Schools and Societies*, this chapter has focused on one society, the United States. Expectations about the contribution of schooling to society have been higher in the United States than elsewhere, and a wide variety of plans for improvement have fallen under the label "school reform." The meanings of reform cluster around four goals, which I have labeled the "4 E's" of education reform: efforts to improve efficiency, to create higher levels of teaching and learning excellence, to enhance the facilities and activities that contribute to student learning, and to create more equity in educational opportunities.

Some historians have argued for a cyclical view of educational reform, with periods dominated by conservative efficiency and excellence concerns alternating with periods dominated by more liberal enhancement and equity reforms. It is possible to show the broad outlines of more conservative periods in the 1890s, the 1950s, and the 1980s, and more liberal periods in the 1920s and the 1960s. However, this cyclical framework is not adequate for capturing the complex dynamics of educational reform. Some reforms, such as the introduction of junior high schools, do not easily fit into either a conservative or liberal category, and most periods show a complex mix of conservative and liberal reform initiatives.

Evidence on the implementation of reforms indicates that reforms are most likely to be successfully implemented when they do not significantly challenge teachers' authority in the classroom, make school more interesting for students, have measurable results, are relatively low cost, and create a mobilized constituency that will defend the reform. Many widely heralded reforms, such as the introduction of media-based schooling, have failed to take hold because they challenged teachers' authority and could not engage students as much as their proponents expected.

The current era of reform, dating to the early 1980s, has been dominated by excellence concerns, and particularly the introduction of accountability measures in the schools. These accountability efforts have led to increased high-stakes testing as a way to measure student learning outcomes. The No Child Left Behind Act, passed by Congress in 2001, mandates that all schools must make adequate yearly progress in state-developed tests of student proficiency. Although research evidence suggests that accountability measures can improve student learning, NCLB has produced considerable confusion by allowing each of the states to determine its own standards of student proficiency independently of all other states. Not surprisingly, many states have produced easy tests that allow their schools to avoid the punitive consequences imposed by the federal government on schools that fail to show adequate yearly progress. The consequences of NCLB could extend also to the narrowing of curricula and the deprofessionalization of teaching.

Although overshadowed by the No Child Left Behind Act, another federal program, Comprehensive School Reform, may have a longer-lasting influence on school improvement efforts. Comprehensive School Reform allows for federal funds to be allocated to schools, mainly in high poverty areas, that make a commitment to implementing and evaluating programs of comprehensive change. Thus far, two programs that change instruction by providing more structure, more regular feedback, and additional staff in the classroom have shown consistently positive outcomes. Programs that provide incentives for students in the form of jobs or college opportunities can also work, but these are usually rather expensive programs to implement, because businesses (or businesspeople) must commit jobs or tuition funds as incentives. Findings on community involvement programs and school "choice" programs have been more mixed. They rarely succeed unless attention is given to the development of a strong academic ethos in target schools.

The research evidence suggests that a recipe for the creation of good schools does exist. Good schools have adequate resources; are of a relatively small size; consistently express high academic expectations and are organized in ways that reflect those expectations; are staffed by well-trained and highly motivated teachers; include strong elements of communal organization; and mobilize the voluntary involvement of students, parents, and others in the learning and social activities of the school. The creation of good schools requires inspiring leadership and widespread staff dedication, but so too does every other successful organizational effort.

The current dominant philosophy of schooling in the United States (and much of the rest of the world) defines the highest goals of education as making a contribution to economically valuable work skills and work discipline. This philosophy submits that the only acceptable way to measure educational success is through standardized test results. These legitimate, but narrow ends and means can diminish the potential of schooling to make contributions to society through the cultivation of well-rounded, aware, autonomous, and engaged young people. No one should wish to jettison the gains attributable to the accountability movement, but we have reached a point of imbalance in our vision of schooling, one that can be corrected only by a broader vision.

REFERENCE MATTER

NOTES

CHAPTER 1

1. Among the last generation of critics of schooling, see, for example, Goodman (1960), Neill (1960), Holt (1964), and Kozol (1968). This is a criticism that resonates with the larger social critique of European Romanticism and originates particularly in the writings of the French political philosopher Jean-Jacques Rousseau ([1762] 1911).

2. In the discussion that follows, students who have studied sociology before will see the influence of some important sociologists of the past. The discussion of the macro-historical level of analysis is inspired by the work of the great German sociologist Max Weber ([1921] 1978). The discussion of the institutional level has its roots in the work of two mid-century American sociologists, Robert K. Merton ([1949] 1968, chaps. 2, 10–11) and Philip Selznick (1949, 1957) and one contemporary sociologist, John Meyer (Meyer and Rowan 1978). The discussion of the micro-interaction level is influenced by the socially structured interactionism of Willard Waller (1932) and Erving Goffman (1959, 1974), the symbolic interactionism of Herbert Blumer (1969), and the dramatism of literary theorist and social critic Kenneth Burke (1969).

CHAPTER 2

1. The poorer countries of Europe resemble other European systems in structure but not in the outcomes they produce. Portugal, Ireland, Greece, Poland, and at least the southern region of Italy and nonmetropolitan Spain have lagged in school development throughout the modern period despite strong rhetorical commitments to mass schooling. Modernizing leaders in these states were not able to decisively gain the upper hand over the landed nobility, the traditional church, and communal resistance (Soysal and Strong 1989). Compulsory schooling laws were passed, but enrollments remained low. Even today, educational attainments remain somewhat lower in these countries than elsewhere in Europe (OECD 1996:33). Compulsory schooling tends to end earlier than elsewhere in Europe, at ages 14 and 15. Dropout rates before the completion of secondary schooling are high (ibid.:124), and government expenditures on schooling comparatively low (ibid.:

65). The problems of Italian schooling were for many years compounded by a higher education system poorly adjusted to labor market conditions (Barbagli 1982).

2. The right of school districts in the same state to spend different amounts on children was affirmed by American courts beginning with *Serrano v. Priest* (1971). The settlement of *Williams v. the State of California* (2000) obligates the state to pursue limited remedies to redress substandard school resources and facilities. See Grubb, Goe, and Huerta (2004).

3. At the elementary school level, industrial societies also differ in one other important way: by how much of education is under public as opposed to private control. In the Netherlands, for instance, private schooling has developed in defense of linguistic and religious differences. In countries such as Spain and France, where the Roman Catholic Church once controlled education, Catholic private education very frequently remains a popular alternative to public schooling. In Japan, private schools mainly provide opportunities for students who are struggling in the public sector. Only in England and parts of the United States are parts of the private sector primarily associated with the desire of professional and managerial elites to avoid the public sector. The private sector rarely counts for more than 10 percent of total primary or secondary enrollments. (See Table 1.2 in Chapter 1.)

4. Other efforts to construct typologies of educational systems include, notably, Allmendinger (1989), Cummings (2003), Hopper (1968), Kerkhoff (1974), and Kerr (1979).

5. The number of universities in the two countries is more similar than these figures suggest. Of the 325 institutions of higher education in Germany, 112 are universities. Of the approximately 2,400 four-year colleges and universities in the United States, just 156 are research universities. The great majority of U.S. colleges are small comprehensive colleges, liberal arts colleges, or specialized institutions, such as theological seminaries or art institutes.

6. As compared to Sweden and France, some countries (such as Denmark) have somewhat smaller vocational enrollments in upper secondary school. Others (such as Belgium and Switzerland) have higher vocational enrollments. The latter lean in the direction of German-style limits on academic schooling, and they frequently provide a considerable amount of apprenticeship training, again following the German model. The contrast between Social Democratic egalitarianism and German-style "hierarchization" and skill building helps to explain these divergent tendencies.

7. It would be wrong to overstate the differences between Japanese students and American students. According to reports beginning a decade ago, Japanese secondary school students now spend more time watching television than studying, and they also spend significant time, just like American students, shopping and "hanging out" with friends at the mall (White 1993). They are far from "round the clock grinds." Moreover, Japanese universities are renowned for their lax standards; they are often described as approximating a four-year vacation between the rigors of secondary schooling and the rigors of the business world (Rohlen 1983). The oft-noted propensity of Japanese teenagers to commit suicide due to the pressures of testing also appears to be badly outdated (Zeng and LeTendre 1998).

CHAPTER 3

1. The World Bank is not omnipotent. Even in countries with significant debt obligations, alternative educational policies may retain popularity for historical or partisan political reasons. For example, the ideas of the radical educational reformer Paolo Freire have remained popular in his home country of Brazil, even at the highest levels of the educational ministry. Freire's influence led, first, to a massive literacy program in the 1960s (interestingly, under a military government), and, later, to many efforts to increase teachers' professional autonomy and community involvement, and to keep populist political ideas alive in the schools, including ideas about the "oppressive structure" of global capitalism (Bartlett 2003; Teodoro 2003).

CHAPTER 4

1. Herbert Kliebard (1986, 1992), the American historian of curriculum, emphasized essentially the same social interests as Raymond Williams, but used different terms to characterize them. I have adopted Williams's terminology.

2. In 1893, a famous statement by the National Education Association's "Committee of Ten" called for a common secondary school curriculum for all students regardless of their origins or likely destinations. This resistance melted away by 1910, as secondary school attendance continued to double each decade and new, less literate populations of students began to enter secondary schools. In 1906, the Douglas Commission helped to legitimate public vocational education by arguing that children who leave school at the completion of seventh grade would find further training of a practical character attractive if it prepared them for industries (73). In 1918, a statement of Cardinal Principles by the National Education Association called for increased choice in curricular offerings so that each individual could find his [proper] place.

3. The Stanford team collected this information by examining a wide range of official policy statements, collected by United Nations agencies among others, and also more specific historical studies. The data have to be approached with some caution. Not all continents are proportionately represented in each time period. Several countries in which mass education is poorly institutionalized are missing altogether. Most important, official proclamations about what is supposed to happen in school and actual practices in school may differ substantially in many countries (Meyer, Kamens, and Benavot 1992, chap. 3). This slippage no doubt reduces the accuracy of the findings. It is well known, as we saw in Chapter 3, that rural schools in poor countries do not strictly follow government-sanctioned plans. Lessons may make up but a small part of the school day, in the midst of taking care of the classroom and the school grounds, playing, and getting settled for work (Hornberger 1987). On the ground studies of anthropologists generally reveal gaps between official rhetoric and actual practice (see, e.g., the field reports in Anderson-Levitt 2003). Official policies affect the actual practices of schooling, only where a relatively high level of consensus or tight administrative controls exist (Stevenson and Baker 1991).

4. Clearly, something has changed in the culture to produce the higher IQ scores found by Flynn. But what is it? Some have argued that visual and computer gaming cul-

ture, with its ultra-fast pace and nonlinear narrative structure, has encouraged more complex cognitive development (Johnson 2005). Others argue that higher-quality schooling has also contributed to the "Flynn effect" (Blair et al. 2005).

Yet, something is odd about this. In their everyday experience, teachers encounter many students who do not read much, do not engage deeply with print materials, and do not think abstractly with ease. It may be that the qualities of mind encouraged by visual media and nonlinear narratives contrast with qualities of mind encouraged by print media and linear exposition. Both could lead to "intelligence," but to different types of "intelligence." Neil Postman, a proponent of print and the "culture of exposition," argued:

> Almost all of the characteristics we associate with mature discourse were amplified by typography . . . : a sophisticated ability to think conceptually, deductively and sequentially; a high valuation on reason and order; an abhorrence of contradiction; a large capacity for detachment and objectivity; and a tolerance for delayed response. . . . [By contrast] the idea [in visual media] "is to keep everything brief, not to strain the attention of anyone but instead to provide constant stimulation through variety, novelty, action, and movement. [Viewers] are required . . . to pay attention to no concept, no character, and no problem for more than a few seconds at a time. (Postman 1985:63, 105)

Perhaps cultural changes have encouraged mental quickness and short-term memory, while capacities for sustained, deep thinking; critical comparison of arguments; and high-level abstraction remain as uncommon as ever.

5. On standardized tests, the top 1 percent is often used as an indicator of exceptional academic talent, but even this level of distinction is relative. One former president of the University of Chicago, Edward H. Levi, said that intellectual talent worthy of appointment to his faculty would be found in only about 1 in 10,000 students.

6. Some people like to look back on "golden ages" in which the great majority of people showed an active interest in the life of the mind. For the most part, golden ages turn out, on closer inspection, to be rather disappointing. If we look at the education of the entire population in the 1950s—one popular "golden age"—the results are not very reassuring. The schools were more highly tracked than they are today, and minorities, in particular, suffered from very poor educational opportunities (see, e.g., Bracey 1991).

CHAPTER 5

1. As compared to such moral staples of the classroom as honesty, patriotism, and industry, the more strictly intellectual ethos of contemplation, reflection, judgment, and aesthetic appreciation is rare. To the extent that it has been important, it developed mainly among upper-class groups in upper secondary and higher education. The acceptance and especially the persistence of this more intellectualist ethos depends on previous socialization and on continuing reinforcement (Feldman and Newcomb 1969).

2. Indeed, one of the important categorical understandings students learn in school translates quite directly into adult life: the status categories of schooling itself. Children learn that dropouts, high school graduates, community college graduates, and college graduates have distinct statuses in society (Kamens 1981).

3. Perhaps to balance the unfair criticisms of adolescent culture, sociologists have of-

ten gone out of their way to note beneficial effects. In a line of argument that built on Cold War sentiments, some sociologists commended the pluralism of the American high school as complementing the pluralism of American life and explicitly contrasted this pluralism with the potential authoritarianism of a single-status hierarchy based on academics. This argument suggested that the more ways to succeed in school, the more likely a majority of students would end up as confident and well-adjusted adults. Sometimes the images of youth culture were more positive still. During the later 1950s and 1960s, some sociologists provided admiring portraits of the independent, life-embracing, and uncompromising spirit of youth culture. These sociologists interpreted youth culture as a source of socially revitalizing opposition to the life-denying pieties of adult authorities (see, e.g., Freidenberg 1959; Goodman 1960; Flacks 1971).

CHAPTER 6

1. The coming of the credential society was foreseen in the early part of this century by the great German sociologist Max Weber ([1921] 1946): "When we hear from all sides the demand for an introduction of regular curricula and special examinations, the reason behind it is, of course, not a suddenly awakened 'thirst for education' but the desire for [the] monopolization of [positions] by the owners of educational certificates" (p. 241).

2. Although higher educational credentials have become increasingly prevalent, we should recognize that they are not important in all spheres of the job structure. Many people without impressive educational qualifications continue to start successful small businesses (Steinmetz and Wright 1989). Many other businesses are handed down within families (Robinson 1984; Robinson and Garnier 1985). Among small-business owners and farmers, schooling consequently plays a less important role than among other white-collar workers as an investment in the future (Ishida, Muller, and Ridge 1995). Similarly, access to jobs in quite a few skilled trades (e.g., plumber or electrician) is regulated more by family and ethnic networks than by formal educational training structures (see, e.g., Bailey and Waldinger 1991).

3. I am grateful to Michael Hout for sending the General Social Survey tables for the earlier cohort and to Kristopher Proctor for generating the tables for the second cohort. The IQ measure here is based on word recognition. There may be an effect of college graduation itself on word recognition, leading to greater similarity among college graduates of different backgrounds than would be true if the ability measure preceded rather than followed college attendance.

4. In status attainment studies, statistical controls are used to hold constant all differences among variables in the model (i.e., all measured differences among people) except the one under consideration. In thinking about these models people sometimes wonder, what kind of person comes from a high-status family and has high cognitive ability, good grades in school, but low aspirations? But correlations in the population are not so high as to prevent the construction of meaningful partial correlation coefficients. This does not mean that the assumptions and procedures used in this research are completely defensible. A serious problem does sometimes exist with the regression assumption that the variables included in a model are uncorrelated with variables omitted.

5. It is not possible to completely isolate measured "intelligence" from social back-

ground. Even if we accept IQ scores as good measures of intelligence—something that many leading scientists no longer do (see, e.g., Sternberg 1988; Fischer et al. 1996, chaps. 2 and 3)—we find that IQ scores are highly conditioned by the social environment. Families can transmit good nutrition, intellectual stimulation, confidence in test-taking situations, and high levels of comfort with "official" linguistic and cultural codes, or they can transmit the opposite qualities. All these qualities can and do influence results on tests of intelligence and academic aptitude (Sternberg and Grigorenko 1999).

6. Technical difficulties limit the usefulness of more recent data. One potentially useful data set is the National Longitudinal Study of Youth (NLSY), which includes Air Force Qualifying Test scores for men. However, the NLSY has no measure of father's occupation at the highest point in the father's career. The most recent follow-ups of NLSY were conducted of men and women in their mid-30s. Correlations between father's socioeconomic status and children's attainments often become stronger by the time men and women reach the highest point in their careers.

7. Other countries, such as Germany and Hungary, may also show decreasing class inequalities in higher-level educational transitions. Studies are at this point inconclusive. See Erikson and Jonsson (1996:4–5).

CHAPTER 7

1. As specialists in the constitutive influence of social relations, sociologists tend to be skeptical of explanations that focus too much on genetic endowments. But in reality, genetic advantages and disadvantages do figure into the likelihood that people will succeed or fail in school. If we focus only on families in which children's emerging interests are actively supported, we can clearly see that some children have aptitudes for art and computers, others for languages and wordplay. Children know what gives them pleasure, and, by comparing themselves to other children and by hearing the feedback of adults, they soon learn to invest energy and passion in the activities for which they have an aptitude. Researchers continue to disagree about how much intelligence is genetically determined, how much is socially conditioned, and how much is based on interactions between the two. Recent studies of twins raised separately have led to a greater emphasis on genetic factors (Bouchard et al. 1990).

2. Are some societies more prone to racial and ethnic bias than others? Racism is evidently a product of Europe (van den Berghe 1970), but it is certainly not limited to Europe or North America. Historical circumstances seem to matter more than any sociological or political variables. Certainly, both democracies and socialist states have been marked by harsh treatment of minorities, even by instances of genocide. The sometimes brutal treatment of Native Americans by the European settlers in the United States is well known. Socialist regimes sometimes encouraged ethnic hostilities by recruiting elites from one or two dominant ethnic groups, such as the Montenegrins and Croats in the former Yugoslavia and the Russians and Georgians in the former Soviet Union (Echols 1981). Nor does the argument that European societies are particularly biased hold much water, because extreme forms of ethnic hatred are common also among Africans and Asians. Until recently, only Europeans have had the technological and political capacity for genocide.

However, it seems likely that hatred of out-groups is part of the human condition. It is often stimulated by economic competition or cultural resentments, and has often been exploited by politicians for partisan gain.

3. Tracks need not be distinguished in all three ways (i.e., by motivational climate, institutional linkage, and prestige) to show significant net effects. One or two of these distinctions will do. In the industrialized world, the *grandes écoles* in France and the top public universities in Japan have among the strongest direct links to high-status occupations. These are well known as the elite tracks. Nevertheless, the motivational press is intense only in the French case (Suleiman 1978). In Japan, virtually all students treat college as a time for enjoying friends and social life between the competitive wars of secondary school and corporate careers. However, the tight and densely networked links between these prestigious institutions and elite jobs give a large net boost to students, even in the absence of a supportive motivational climate (Cummings 1985).

4. Later selection is not, however, invariably connected to greater chances for lower-status children. Halsey, Heath, and Ridge (1980) showed that the abolition of the "11-plus" examination and the trend toward later selection in Great Britain had little impact on the relative educational chances of working-class youths. Instead, class differences in educational attainment remained "remarkably stable" across men born before and after the major changes in the British system. Those working-class children who entered schooling after the abolition of "11-plus" examination and the tripartite system of secondary education fared no better than those who entered before the "11-plus" examination and the tripartite system was abolished. The unusually strong class divisions in English society, discussed in Chapter 2, may be largely responsible for this result. These divisions have created a strong tendency for working-class children to flee schooling as soon as they reach the minimal school-leaving age. Elsewhere, elimination of early branching has tended to improve the opportunities of working-class youths.

5. The motivational climate in community colleges has been changing in recent years, however. This is largely due to the growing number of low- and middle-income students who cannot afford to begin college at four-year institutions. Many start at community college and save to graduate from a four-year college. Because the community colleges now enroll more of the kinds of students who would at one time have started at four-year colleges, transfer rates have been rising. We see as many as 35 to 40 percent of community college students transferring to four-year colleges today, compared to 20 to 25 percent in the 1990s (Dougherty and Kienzl 2006; Kane and Rouse 1999). Even so, the chances of completing a four-year degree remain higher for otherwise similar students who start at four-year colleges.

6. When credentials are very highly valued on the market (e.g., in the case of medical degrees today), competition for them is also intense. Competition in the context of limited supply raises the expected standards of performance, in most cases, and may further increase the economic value associated with those who ultimately succeed in gaining the credential. This mechanism is one reason why college majors have such different value in the labor market.

CHAPTER 8

1. On the basis of these passages from the irascible Twain (see Chapter 1), the contemplative Rodriguez, and vibrant Alcott, one suspects that the characters who leave strong marks on young minds are tuned to a similar enough emotional key to break through the reserves of pride and uncertainty that are such great staffs of life and such great barriers to learning.

2. It would be wrong to think of the analytical style as invariably superior to the relational style. There is such a thing as too much analysis and not enough "feel" for a context. Asa Hilliard (1976) discusses how a person with an exclusively analytical style would function on a task more suited to a relational style: if asked to learn a dance, the analytical learner is very likely to draw feet on the floor and to break the dance down into steps to learn the dance "piecemeal." For the relational learner, on the other hand, details are likely to be blurred, standards faintly adhered to, or the dance itself may be modified with no real concern for right or wrong so much as "fit" or "harmony" (42).

3. Stevenson and Stigler (1992) point out that the characterizations we sometimes hear of Asian students as docile and deferential do not explain the differences they found. Indeed, the Asian students they studied were lively, engaged, and questioning—not the passive vessels of stereotype. What differed was the organization and culture of classroom life, not the personalities of the children.

4. Some early studies of teacher effectiveness attempted to correlate student achievement with particular teacher behaviors: how often teachers smiled or snapped their fingers or stomped their feet. Not surprisingly, these studies were completely unsuccessful (see Boocock 1972:129–30).

5. These conclusions tell us what kinds of teacher traits will work best with average students in mixed-ability classrooms. To some degree, different kinds of teaching techniques may work best with some kinds of personalities than others. For example, more aloof and autocratic teachers do well with students who are responsive to authority, but they do very poorly with rebellious students. For a discussion of some of these complexities, see Boocock 1972:129–49.

CHAPTER 9

1. Some of the comprehensive school design programs have conducted few scientifically valid evaluations. Many have been evaluated by the designers themselves, and this invariably produces inflated results compared to external evaluations. Only a few rely on randomized assignment to treatment and nontreatment groups. Most focus on simple pre- and post-test designs, or, slightly better, comparison in pre- and post-tests for matched schools, one with the reform program and one without. Occasionally, the demographics of the matched schools are not reported. To calculate the size of treatment effects, researchers have had to impute standard deviations when they are not reported by evaluators (see Borman et al. 2003).

2. The majority of businesses have been involved with schools at only a superficial level. Often consultants will come in for a short time, the company will donate equipment, and executives will deliver motivational talks. Facing the daunting problems of pov-

erty and alienation in inner-city schools, these partnerships often failed to make much difference, and many businesses involved in partnerships have quietly broken off ties after trials of a year or two (Anyon 1997; Deng 1991).

3. Not everyone agrees that small schools are best for students. Watt (2003) notes that the "critical mass" possibilities of larger high schools provide more support and "identity validation" for students who do not "fit in" with the dominant group. However, small schools do not necessarily have to be so small as to contain only one group. Moreover, the problems of friction between cliques may be easier to manage at small schools.

REFERENCES

Abbott, Andrew. 1988. *The System of Professions: An Essay on the Division of Expert Labor.* Chicago: University of Chicago Press.

Adelman, Clifford. 1983. "Devaluation, Diffusion and the College Connection: A Study of High School Transcripts, 1964–1981." Paper prepared for the National Commission on Excellence in Education, U.S. Department of Education.

———. 1999. *Answers in the Toolbox.* Washington, DC: National Center for Educational Statistics, Office of Educational Research and Improvement.

Ainsworth-Darnell, James W., and Douglas B. Downey. 1998. "Assessing the Oppositional Culture Explanation for Racial/Ethnic Differences in School Performance." *American Sociological Review* 63: 536–53.

Alexander, Karl L. 1997. "Public Schools and the Public Good." *Social Forces* 76: 1–31.

Alexander, Karl L., Aaron M. Pallas, and Scott Holupka. 1987. "Consistency and Change in Educational Stratification: Recent Trends Regarding Social Background and College Access." *Research in Social Stratification and Mobility* 6: 161–85.

Alexander, Karl L., Cornelius Riordan, James Fennessey, and Aaron M. Pallas. 1982. "Social Background, Academic Resources, and College Graduation: Recent Evidence from the National Longitudinal Survey." *American Journal of Education* 90: 315–33.

Ali, Anthony, and Augustine Akubue. 1988. "Nigerian Primary Schools and Compliance with Nigerian National Policy on Education: An Evaluation of Continuous Assessment Practices." *Education Review* 12: 625–37.

Allmendinger, Jutta. 1989. "Educational Systems and Labor Market Outcomes." *European Sociological Review* 5: 231–50.

Alrabaa, Sami. 1985. "The Sex Division of Labor in Syrian School Textbooks." *International Review of Education* 31: 335–48.

Amsden, Alice H. 1989. *Asia's Next Giant: South Korea and Late Industrialization.* New York: Oxford University Press.

Anderson, C. Arnold, and Mary Jean Bowman (Eds.). 1965. *Education and Economic Development.* Chicago: Aldine.

Anderson, J. E. 1975. "The Organization of Support and the Management of Self-Help Schools: A Case Study of Kenya." Pp. 363–89 in Godfrey N. Brown and Mervyn

Hiskett (Eds.), *Conflict and Harmony in Education in Tropical Africa*. London: Allen and Unwin.

Anderson-Levitt, Kathryn. (Ed). 2003. *Local Meanings, Global Schooling: Anthropology and World Culture Theory*. New York: Palgrave Macmillan.

Andersson, Bengt-Erik. 1969. *Studies in Adolescent Behavior: Project YG—Youth in Goteberg*. Stockholm: Almqvist and Wiksell.

Angus, David, and Jeffrey Mirel. 1995. "Rhetoric and Reality: The American High School Curriculum, 1945–1990." Pp. 295–328 in Diane Ravitch and Maris A. Vinovskis (Eds.), *Learning from the Past: What History Teaches about School Reform*. Baltimore: Johns Hopkins University Press.

Anyon, Jean. 1979. "Ideology and United States History Textbooks." *Harvard Educational Review* 41: 361–86.

———. 1980. "Social Class and the Hidden Curriculum of Work." *Journal of Education* 162: 67–92.

———. 1997. *Ghetto Schooling: A Political Economy of Urban Educational Reform*. New York: Teachers College Press.

Archbald, Douglas A. 2004. "School Choice, Magnet Schools, and the Liberation Model: An Empirical Study." *Sociology of Education* 77: 283–310.

Archer, Margaret. 1979. *The Social Origins of Educational Systems*. London and Beverly Hills, CA: Sage.

Arnold, Matthew. [1869] 1949. *Culture and Anarchy*. Pp. 469–573. In Lionel Trilling (Ed.), *The Portable Matthew Arnold*. New York: Viking.

Arnove, Robert. 1986. *Education and Revolution in Nicaragua*. New York: Praeger.

Arum, Richard, with Irenee Beattie, Richard Pitt, Jennifer Thompson, and Sandra Way. 2003. *Judging School Discipline: The Crisis of Moral Authority in American Schools*. Cambridge, MA: Harvard University Press.

Arum, Richard B., and Yossi Shavit. 1995. "Secondary Vocational Education and the Transition from School to Work." *Sociology of Education* 68: 187–204.

Asante, Molefi. 1987. *The Afrocentric Idea*. Philadelphia: Temple University Press.

Assal, Adel and Edwin Farrell. 1992. "Attempts to Make Meaning of Terror: Family, Play, and School in Time of Civil War." *Anthropology and Education Quarterly* 23: 275–90.

Attewell, Paul. 2001. "The Winner-Take-All High School: Organizational Adaptations to Educational Stratification." *Sociology of Education* 74: 267–95.

Bailes, Kendall. 1979. *Technology and Society under Lenin and Stalin*. Princeton, NJ: Princeton University Press.

Bailey, Linda. 1995. *Time Use among Teachers: Context Paper for Germany*. Unpublished paper, University of Michigan, Center for Human Growth and Development, Ann Arbor, MI.

Bailey, Thomas, and Roger Waldinger. 1991. "Primary, Secondary, and Enclave Labor Markets: A Training Systems Approach." *American Sociological Review* 56: 432–45.

Baker, David P., Brian Goesling, and Gerald K. LeTendre. 2002. "Socio-economic Status, School Quality, and National Economic Development: A Cross-National Analysis of the 'Heyneman-Loxley Effect' on Mathematics and Science Achievement." *Comparative Education Review* 46: 291–312.

Baker, John R. 1974. *Race*. Oxford: Oxford University Press.

Baker, Therese, and William Velez. 1996. "Access to and Opportunity in Postsecondary Education in the United States: A Review." *Sociology of Education* 69 (extra issue): 82–101.

Ban, Tsunenobu, and William K. Cummings. 1999. "Moral Orientations of Schoolchildren in the United States and Japan." *Comparative Education Review* 43: 64–85.

Barbagli, Marzio. 1982. *Educating for Unemployment: Politics, Labor Markets, and the School System Italy, 1857–1973.* New York: Columbia University Press.

Barber, Benjamin R. 1992. *An Aristocracy of Everyone: The Politics of Education and the Future of America.* New York: Ballantine.

Barr, Rebecca, and Robert Dreeben. 1983. *How Schools Work.* Chicago: University of Chicago Press.

Bartlett, Lesley. 2003. "World Culture or Transnational Project? Competing Educational Projects in Brazil." Pp. 183–200 in Kathryn Anderson-Levitt (Ed.), *Local Meanings, Global Schooling: Anthropology and World Culture Theory.* New York: Palgrave Macmillan.

Bellinger, Robert. 2004. "Engineers' Salaries in Europe below their U.S. Counterparts." *EETimes UK* (September 6): 1–4.

Benavot, Aaron. 2005. *A Global Study of Intended Instructional Time and Official School Curriculum, 1980–2000.* Unpublished paper. United Nations Educational, Scientific, and Cultural Organization, Paris (January).

Benavot, Aaron, and David Kamens. 1989. *The Curricular Content of Primary Education in Developing Countries.* PPR Working Paper No. 237, World Bank, Washington, DC.

Benavot, Aaron, and Phyllis Riddle. 1988. "National Estimates of the Expansion of Mass Education, 1870–1940." *Sociology of Education* 61: 191–210.

Bendix, Reinhard. 1968. "The Extension of Citizenship to the Lower Classes." Pp. 233–56 in Reinhard Bendix et al. (Eds.), *State and Society: A Reader in Comparative Political Sociology.* Boston: Little, Brown.

Bennett, William J. 1993. *The Book of Virtues.* New York: Simon & Schuster.

Berg, Ivar. 1970. *Education and Jobs: The Great Training Robbery.* New York: Praeger.

Berliner, David C. and Bruce J. Biddle. 1995. *The Manufactured Crisis: Myth, Fraud, and the Attack on America's Public Schools.* Reading, MA: Addison-Wesley.

Bernal, Martin. 1987. *Black Athena: The Afroasiatic Roots of Classical Civilization.* New Brunswick, NJ: Rutgers University Press.

Bernstein, Basil. 1961. "Social Class and Linguistic Development: A Theory of Social Learning." Pp. 288–314 in A. H. Halsey, Jean Floud, and C. Arnold Anderson (Eds.), *Education, Economy, and Society.* New York: Free Press.

———. 1971. "On the Classification and Framing of Educational Knowledge." Pp. 47–69 in M. F. D. Young (Ed.), *Knowledge and Control: New Directions in the Sociology of Education.* London: Collier-Macmillan.

———. 1975. *Class, Codes, and Control.* Vol. 3. London: Routledge and Kegan Paul.

Bernstein, Richard. 1994. *Dictatorship of Virtue: Multiculturalism and the Battle for America's Future.* New York: Knopf.

Berthoft, Rowland T. 1971. *An Unsettled People.* New York: Harper and Row.

"The Best Schools in the World." 1991. *Newsweek* 118 (December 2): 50–4.

Biblarz, Timothy J., and Adrian E. Raftery. 1999. "Family Structure, Educational Attainment and Socioeconomic Success: Rethinking the 'Pathology of Matriarchy.'" *American Journal of Sociology* 105: 321–365.

Bidwell, Charles, and Robert Dreeben. 1992. "School Organization and Curriculum." Pp. 345–62 in Philip W. Jackson (Ed.), *Handbook of Research on Curriculum*. New York: Macmillan.

Bills, David B. 2003. "Credentials, Signals, and Screens: Explaining the Relationship between Schooling and Job Assignment." *Review of Educational Research* 73: 441–70.

Blair, Clancy, David Gamson, Steven Thorne, and David P. Baker. 2005. "Rising Mean IQ: Cognitive Demand of Mathematics Education for Young Children, Population Exposure to Formal Schooling, and the Neurobiology of the Prefrontal Cortex." *Intelligence* 33: 93–106.

Blank, Rolf. 1989. *Educational Effects of Magnet High Schools*. Madison, WI: National Center on Effective Secondary Schools.

Blank, Rolf K., Roger E. Levine, and Lauri Steel. 1996. "After 15 Years: Magnet Schools in Urban Education." Pp. 154–72 in Bruce Fuller and Richard F. Elmore (Eds.), *Who Chooses? Who Loses?* New York: Teachers College Press.

Blau, Peter M., and Otis Dudley Duncan. 1967. *The American Occupational Structure*. New York: John Wiley.

Blaug, Mark. 1987. *The Economics of Education and the Education of an Economist*. New York: New York University Press.

Bloch, Marc. 1961. *Feudal Society*. Vol. 1. Chicago: University of Chicago Press.

Block, N. J., and Gerald Dworkin. 1976. "IQ, Heritability, and Inequality." Pp. 410–540 in N. J. Block and Gerald Dworkin (Eds.), *The IQ Controversy*. New York: Random House.

Blossfeld, Hans-Peter. 1992. "Is the German Dual System a Model for a Modern Vocational Training System?" *International Journal of Comparative Sociology* 3: 168–81.

Blossfeld, Hans-Peter, and Yossi Shavit. 1993. *Persisting Barriers: Changes in Educational Opportunities in Thirteen Countries*. Pp. 1–24 in Yossi Shavit and Hans-Peter Blossfeld (Eds.), *Persistent Inequality*. Boulder, CO: Westview.

Blumberg, Rae Lesser. 1984. "A General Theory of Gender Stratification." In Randall Collins (Ed.), *Sociological Theory, 1984*. San Francisco: Jossey-Bass.

Blumer, Herbert. 1969. *Symbolic Interactionism*. New York: Prentice-Hall.

Boocock, Sarane S. 1972. *An Introduction to the Sociology of Learning*. New York: Houghton-Mifflin.

Borman, Geoffrey, Gina M. Hewes, Laura T. Overman, and Shelly Brown. 2003. "Comprehensive School Reform and Achievement: A Meta-Analysis." *Review of Educational Research* 73: 125–230.

Bouchard, Thomas J. et al. 1990. "Sources of Human Psychological Differences: The Minnesota Study of Twins Reared Apart." *Science* 250 (October 12): 223–9.

Boudon, Raymond. 1974. *Education, Opportunity, and Social Inequality*. New York: John Wiley.

———. 1979. "The 1970s in France: A Period of Student Retreat." *Higher Education* 8: 669–81.

Bourdieu, Pierre. 1973. "Cultural Reproduction and Social Reproduction." Pp. 71–112 in Richard Brown (Ed.), *Knowledge, Education, and Cultural Change*. London: Tavistock.

———. 1979. *Outline of a Theory of Practice*. Cambridge, UK: Cambridge University Press.

———. 1984. *Distinction*. Cambridge, MA: Harvard University Press.

———. 1988. *Homo Academicus*. London: Polity.

———. 1996. *The State Nobility: Elite Schools in the Field of Power*. Stanford, CA: Stanford University Press.

Bourdieu, Pierre, and Jean-Claude Passeron. 1977. *Reproduction*. Beverly Hills, CA: Sage.

Bowen, William G., and Derek Bok. 1998. *The Shape of the River: Long-Term Consequences of Considering Race in College and University Admissions*. Princeton, NJ: Princeton University Press.

Bowles, Samuel, and Herbert Gintis. 1976. *Schooling in Capitalist America*. New York: Basic Books.

———. 2005. "Schooling in Capitalist America Revisited." *Sociology of Education* 75: 1–18.

Bracey, Gerald W. 1991. "Why Can't They Be Like We Were?" *Phi Delta Kappan* 73: 104–17.

———. 2003. "NCLB—A Plan for the Destruction of Public Education." Unpublished paper. School of Education, George Mason University.

Bradbury, Katherine, and Jane Katz. 2004. *Wives' Work and Family Income Mobility*. Federal Reserve Bank of Boston Series. Paper No. 04-3.

Brauns, Hildegard, and Susanne Steinmann. 1997. *Educational Reform in France, West Germany, the United Kingdom and Hungary*. Mannheim, Germany: Mannheim Center for European Social Research. Working paper 1/21.

Brint, Steven. 1994. *In an Age of Experts: The Changing Role of Professionals in Politics and Public Life*. Princeton, NJ: Princeton University Press.

———. 2003. "Few Remaining Dreams: Community Colleges Since 1985." *Annals of the American Academy of Political and Social Science* 586 (March): 16–37.

Brint, Steven, Mary F. Contreras, and Michael T. Matthews. 2001. "Socialization Messages in Primary Schools: An Organizational Analysis." *Sociology of Education* 74: 157–80.

Brint, Steven, and Jerome Karabel. 1989. *The Diverted Dream: Community Colleges and the Promise of Educational Opportunity in America, 1900–1980*. New York: Oxford University Press.

Brint, Steven, Mark Riddle, Lori Turk-Bicakci, and Charles S. Levy. 2005. "From the Liberal to the Practical Arts in American Colleges and Universities: Organizational Analysis and Curricular Change." *Journal of Higher Education* 76: 151–80.

Bronfenbrenner, Urie. 1970. *Two Worlds of Childhood: U.S. and U.S.S.R.* New York: Russell Sage.

Brown, David K. 1995. *Degrees of Control: A Sociology of Educational Expansion and Occupational Credentialism*. New York: Teachers College Press.

———. 2001. "The Social Sources of Educational Credentialism: Status Cultures, Labor Markets, and Organizations." *Sociology of Education* (extra issue): 19–34.

Bryk, Anthony S., Valerie E. Lee, and Peter B. Holland. 1993. *Catholic Schools and the Common Good*. Cambridge, MA: Harvard University Press.

Bryk, Anthony S., and Stephen W. Raudenbush. 1988. "Toward a More Appropriate Conceptualization of Research on School Effects: A Three-Level Hierarchical Linear Model." *American Journal of Education* 97: 65–108.

Buchman, Claudia, and Ben Dalton. 2002. "Interpersonal Influences and Educational Aspirations in 12 Countries: The Importance of Institutional Context." *Sociology of Education* 75: 99–122.

Burke, Kenneth. 1969. *A Grammar of Motives*. Berkeley: University of California Press.

Byrne, Eileen M. 1978. *Women and Education*. London: Tavistock.

California Educator. 2002. "Scripted Learning: A Slap in the Face or a Blessing from Above?" *California Educator* 6 (7).

Campbell, Richard T. 1983. "Status Attainment Research: The End of the Beginning or the Beginning of the End?" *Sociology of Education* 58: 47–62.

Capelli, Peter. 1992. "College Students and the Workplace: Assessing Performance to Improve the Fit." *Change* 24 (6) (November/December): 55–61.

Carceles, Gabriel. 1979. "Development of Education in the World: A Summary Statistical Review." *International Review of Education* 25: 147–66.

Carnegie, Andrew. 1889. "Wealth." *North American Review* 148: 653–64.

Carnoy, Martin. 1998. "National Voucher Plans in Chile and Sweden: Did Privatization Reforms Make for Better Education?" *Comparative Education Review* 42: 309–37.

Carnoy, Martin, Rebecca Jacobsen, Lawrence Mishel, and Richard Rothstein. 2005. *The Charter School Dust-Up: Examining the Evidence on Enrollment and Achievement*. Washington, DC and New York: Economic Policy Institute and Teachers College Press.

Carnoy, Martin, Susanna Loeb, and Tiffany L. Smith. 2003. "The Impact of Accountability Practices in Texas High Schools." Pp. 147–74 in Martin Carnoy, Richard Elmore, and Leslie Santee Siskin (Eds.), *The New Accountability: High Schools and High Stakes Testing*. New York: Routledge Falmer.

Carnoy, Martin, and Jeffrey Marshall. 2005. "Cuba's Academic Performance in Comparative Perspective." *Comparative Education Review* 49: 230–61.

Carnoy, Martin, and Joel Samoff. 1990. *Education and Social Transformation in the Third World*. Princeton, NJ: Princeton University Press.

Carson, C. C., R. M. Huelskamp, and T. D. Woodall. 1992. "Perspectives on Education in America." *Journal of Educational Research* 86: 259–310.

Cha, Yun-Kyung. 1992. "The Origins and Expansion of Primary School Curricula, 1800–1920." Pp. 63–73 in John W. Meyer, David H. Kamens, and Aaron Benavot (Eds.), *School Knowledge for the Masses*. London: Falmer.

Chubb, John E., and Terry M. Moe. 1989. *Politics, Markets, and America's Schools*. Washington, DC: Brookings Institution.

Clark, Burton R. 1961. "The 'Cooling Out' Function in Higher Education." Pp. 513–21 in A. H. Halsey (Ed.), *Education, Economy, and Society*. New York: Free Press.

———. 1983. *The Higher Education System: Academic Organization in Cross-National Perspective*. Berkeley: University of California Press.

———. 2004. *Sustaining Change in Universities: Continuities and Case Studies and Concepts*. Berkshire, England: Open University Press.

Clark, Roger. 1992. "Multinational Corporate Investment and Women's Participation in Higher Education in Noncore Nations." *Sociology of Education* 65: 37–47.

Clasen, Donna R., and B. Bradford Brown. 1986. *The Relationship between Adolescent Peer Groups and School Performance*. Unpublished paper presented at the annual meeting of the American Educational Research Association, San Francisco.

Clune, William, and Paula White. 1988. *School-Based Management: Institutional Variation, Implementation, and Issues for Further Research*. New Brunswick, NJ: Center for Policy Research in Education.

Cohen, Elizabeth G. 1984. "Talking and Working Together: Status, Interaction and Learning." Pp. 171–87 in Penelope Peterson and Louise Wilkinson (Eds.), *Instructional Groups in the Classroom: Organization and Processes*. New York: Academic Press.

Cohen, Phyllis C. 1982. *A Calculating People: The Spread of Numeracy in Early America*. Chicago: University of Chicago Press.

Cohen, Rosalie. 1969. "Conceptual Styles, Culture Conflict, and Nonverbal Tests of Intelligence." *American Anthropologist* 71: 828–56.

Coleman, James S. 1961. *The Adolescent Society*. New York: Free Press.

Coleman, James S. et al. 1966. *Equality of Educational Opportunity*. Washington, DC: Government Printing Office.

Coleman, James S., and Thomas Hoffer. 1987. *Public and Private High Schools: The Impact of Communities*. New York: Basic Books.

Coleman, James S., Thomas Hoffer, and Sally Kilgore. 1982. *High School Achievement: Public, Catholic, and Private Schools Compared*. New York: Basic Books.

College Board. 2005. *Advanced Placement Report to the Nation*. Princeton, NJ: The College Board.

Collins, Randall. 1977. "Some Comparative Principles of Educational Stratification." *Harvard Educational Review* 47: 1–27.

———. 1979. *The Credential Society*. New York: Academic Press.

———. 1988. *Theoretical Sociology*. San Diego: Harcourt Brace Jovanovich.

Comer, James P. 1980. *School Power: Implications of an Intervention Project*. New York: Free Press.

Conant, James Bryant. 1938. "The Future of Our Higher Education." *Harper's Magazine* 176 (May): 561–70.

———. 1940. "Education for a Classless Society: The Jeffersonian Tradition." *The Atlantic* 165 (May): 593–602.

Condron, Dennis J., and Vincent J. Roscigno. 2003. "Disparities Within: Unequal Spending and Achievement in an Urban School District." *Sociology of Education* 76: 18–36.

Congressional Budget Office. 1992. *The Use of Grants and Loans to Help Finance Undergraduate Education*. Washington, DC: Congressional Budget Office. CBO Staff Memorandum. Mimeo.

Conley, Dalton. 2004. *The Pecking Order: Which Siblings Succeed and Why*. New York: Pantheon Books.

Connolly, Cyril. [1938] 1973. *Enemies of Promise*. London: Andre Deutsch.

Connor, Walter B. 1979. *Socialism, Politics, and Equality*. New York: Columbia University Press.

Cookson, Peter W., Jr., and Caroline H. Persell. 1985. *Preparing for Power: America's Elite Boarding Schools*. New York: Basic Books.

Costlow, Terry. 2001. "Pay Raises Flat: Engineering Wages Wither, but Managers Top $100,000." *EE Times* (October 23): 1–3.

Cotton, Kathleen. 2001. *New Small Learning Communities: Findings from Recent*

Literature. Washington, DC: U.S. Department of Education, Office of Educational Research and Improvement.

Craig, John E. 1981. "The Expansion of Education." *Review of Research in Education* 9: 151–213.

Crain, Robert L. 1984. *The Quality of American High School Graduates: What Personnel Officers Say and Do about It.* Baltimore: Center for the Social Organization of Schools, Johns Hopkins University. Report No. 354.

Cremin, Lawrence A. (Ed.). 1957. *The Republic and the School: Horace Mann on the Education of Free Men.* New York: Teachers College Press.

———. 1961. *The Transformation of the School.* New York: Vintage.

Cuban, Larry. 1993. *How Teachers Taught: Constancy and Change in American Classrooms, 1880–1990.* 2d ed. New York: Teachers College Press.

Cubberly, Ellwood P. 1922. *A Brief History of Education.* Boston: Houghton-Mifflin.

Cummings, William K. 1985. "Japan." Pp. 131–59 in Burton R. Clark (Ed.), *The School and the University.* Berkeley: University of California Press.

———. 2003. *The Institutions of Education: A Comparative Study of Educational Development in Six Core Nations.* Oxford: Symposium Books. Oxford Studies in Comparative Education.

Darling-Hammond, Linda. 2000. "Reforming Teacher Preparation and Licensing: Debating the Evidence." *Teachers College Record* 102: 28–56.

———. 2004. "Standards, Accountability, and School Reform." *Teachers College Record* 106: 1047–85.

Davies, Scott, and Neil Guppy. 1997. "Fields of Study, College Selectivity, and Student Inequalities in Higher Education." *Social Forces* 75: 1417–38.

Davies, Scott, and Floyd M. Hammack. 2005. "The Channeling of Student Competition in Higher Education: Comparing Canada and the U.S." *Journal of Higher Education* 76: 89–106.

Davies, Scott, Linda Quirke, and Janice Aurini. 2005. *The New Institutionalism Goes to Market: The Challenge of Private Education Organizations.* Unpublished paper. Department of Sociology, McMaster University.

Davis, James A. 1965. *Undergraduate Career Decisions.* Chicago: Aldine.

———. 1982. "Achievement Variables and Class Cultures: Family, Schooling, Job and Forty-Nine Dependent Variables in the Cumulative GSS." *American Sociological Review* 47: 569–86.

Day, Jennifer C., and Eric C. Newburger. 2002. "The Big Payoff: Educational Attainment and Synthetic Estimates of Work-Life Earnings." *Current Population Reports: Special Studies* (July). Washington, DC: U.S. Bureau of the Census. P. 23–210.

de Crevecoeur, Michel-Guillaume-Jean. [J. Hector St. John, pseud.]. [1783] 1912. *Letters of an American Farmer.* New York: E. F. Dutton.

Deer, Cecile. 2002. *Higher Education in England and France since the 1980s.* Oxford: Symposium Books.

Delbanco, Andrew. 1996. "Scholarships for the Rich." *New York Times Magazine* (Sept. 1): 36–39.

de Meulemeester, Jean Luc. 2003. "Convergence of Higher Education Systems in Europe: The English and French Example." *European Educational Research Journal* 2: 628–48.

Deng, Louise. 1991. *Toward the Collaborative Community: The Transformations and Changing Potentials of Business-School Partnerships for Educational Reform.* Unpublished paper, Department of American Studies, Yale University.

Denison, Edward F. 1962. "Education, Economic Growth, and Gaps in Information." *Journal of Political Economy* (suppl.) 70: 124–8.

Department for Education and Skills (DFES). 2004. *Statistical First Release: Participation in Education, Training and Employment by 16–18 Year Olds in England, 2002 and 2003.* London: DFES. (www.dfes.gov.uk)

Desai, Uday. 1991. "Determinants of Educational Performance in India: The Role of Home and Family." *International Review of Education* 37: 245–65.

Devas, Nick. 1997. "Indonesia: What Do We Mean by Decentralization?" *Public Administration and Development* 17: 351–367.

Dewey, John. [1916] 1966. *Democracy and Education.* New York: Free Press.

DFES. *See* Department for Education and Skills.

Diamond, Larry, Juan J. Linz, and Seymour Martin Lipset (Eds.). 1986. *Democracy in Developing Countries.* Boulder, CO: L. Rienner; London: Adamantine.

Dillon, Sam. 2004. "Good Schools or Bad? Conflicting Ratings Leave Parents Baffled." *The New York Times* (Sept. 5): A1 ff.

DiMaggio, Paul J., and John Mohr. 1985. "Cultural Capital, Educational Attainment, and Marital Selection." *American Journal of Sociology* 90: 1231–61.

DiPrete, Thomas A., and David B. Grusky. 1990. "Structure and Trend in the Process of Social Stratification." *American Journal of Sociology* 96: 107–44.

Dobson, Richard B. 1977. "Social Status and Inequality of Access to Higher Education in the USSR." Pp. 254–74 in Jerome Karabel and A. H. Halsey (Eds.), *Power and Inequality in Education.* New York: Oxford University Press.

Dore, Ronald P. 1975. *The Diploma Disease: Education, Qualification, and Development.* Berkeley: University of California Press.

Dougherty, Kevin J. 1994. *The Contradictory College: The Conflicting Origins, Impacts, and Future of the Community College.* Albany: State University of New York Press.

Dougherty, Kevin J., and Gregory S. Kienzl. 2006. "It's Not Enough to Get Through the Open Door: Inequalities by Social Background in Transfer from Community Colleges to Four-Year Colleges." *Teachers College Record* 108: 452–87.

Douglas Commission. 1906. *Report of the Massachusetts Commission on Industrial and Technical Education.* Boston: Commonwealth of Massachusetts.

Downey, Douglas B. 1995. "When Bigger Is Not Better: Family Size, Parental Resources, and Children's Educational Performance." *American Sociological Review* 60: 746–61.

Downey, Douglas B., Paul von Hippel, and Beckett A. Broh. 2004. "Are Schools the Great Equalizer? Cognitive Inequality during the Summer Months and the School Year." *American Sociological Review* 69: 613–35.

Dreeben, Robert. 1968. *On What Is Learned in School.* Reading, MA: Addison-Wesley.

Dreeben, Robert, and Adam Gamoran. 1986. "Race, Instruction, and Learning." *American Sociological Review* 51: 660–9.

Dreze, Jean, and Amartya Sen. 1995. *India: Economic Development and Social Opportunities.* Delhi: Oxford University Press.

DuBois, W. E. B. [1903] 1995. *The Souls of Black Folk.* New York: New American Library.

Durkheim, Emile. [1923] 1961. *Moral Education: A Study in the Theory and Application of the Sociology of Education.* New York: Free Press of Glencoe.

———. [1893] 1964. *The Division of Labor in Society.* Glencoe, IL: The Free Press.

———. [1938] 1977. *The Evolution of Educational Thought.* London: Routledge and Kegan Paul.

Dye, David A., and Martin Reck. 1989. "College Grade Point Average as a Predictor of Adult Success." *Public Personnel Management* 18: 235–41.

Echols, John M. 1981. "Racial and Ethnic Inequality: The Comparative Impact of Socialism." *Comparative Political Studies* 13: 403–44.

Eckstein, Max A., and Harold J. Noah. 1993. *Secondary School Examinations: International Perspectives on Policies and Practice.* New Haven, CT: Yale University Press.

Edmonds, Ronald. 1979. "Effective Schools for the Urban Poor." *Educational Leadership* 38: 15–24.

Edwards, Newton, and Herman G. Richey. 1963. *The School and the American Social Order.* 2d ed. Boston: Houghton-Mifflin.

Elliott, Marta. 1998. "School Finance and Opportunities to Learn: Does Money Well Spent Enhance Students' Achievement?" *Sociology of Education* 71: 223–45.

Elmore, Richard F., and Bruce Fuller. 1996. "Conclusion: Empirical Research on Educational Choice." Pp. 187–200 in Bruce Fuller and Richard F. Elmore (Eds.), *Who Chooses? Who Loses?* New York: Teachers College Press.

Elson, Ruth. 1964. *Guardians of Tradition: American Schoolbooks of the Nineteenth Century.* Lincoln: University of Nebraska Press.

Entwisle, Doris, Karl L. Alexander, and Linda Steffel Olson. 1997. *Children, Schools, and Inequality.* Boulder, CO: Westview Press.

Erickson, Frederick. 1975. "Gatekeeping and the Melting Pot." *Harvard Educational Review* 45: 44–70.

Erikson, Robert, and John H. Goldthorpe. 1992. *The Constant Flux: A Study of Class Mobility in Industrial Society.* Oxford: Clarendon.

Erikson, Robert, and Jan O. Jonsson. 1996. "Explaining Class Inequality in Education: The Swedish Test Case." Pp. 1–65 in Robert Erikson and Jan O. Jonsson (Eds.), *Can Education Be Equalized?* Boulder, CO: Westview.

Eshiwani, G. S. 1985. "Kenya: System of Education." Pp. 2803–10 in T. Neville Postlethwaite and Torsten Husén (Eds.), *International Encyclopedia of Education.* New York: Elsevier.

Etzioni, Amitai. 1968. *The Active Society.* New York: Free Press.

Eurydice. 2002. *Key Data on Education in Europe—2002 Edition.* Brussels: Eurydice.

Fagen, Richard. 1969. *The Transformation of Political Culture in Cuba.* Stanford, CA: Stanford University Press.

Farkas, George. 1993. "Structured Tutoring for At-Risk Children in the Early Years." *Applied Behavioral Science Review* 1: 69–92.

Farkas, Steve, and Jean Johnson. 1996. *Given the Circumstances: Teachers Talk about Public Education Today.* New York: Public Agenda.

Featherman, David L., and Robert M. Hauser. 1978. *Opportunity and Change.* New York: Academic Press.

Featherman, David L., Lancaster Jones, and Robert M. Hauser. 1975. "Assumptions of Mobility Research in the United States: The Case of Occupational Status." *Social Science Research* 4: 329–60.

Feldman, Kenneth, and Theodore M. Newcomb. 1969. *The Impact of College on Students*. San Francisco: Jossey-Bass.

Finkelstein, Martin J., Robert K. Seal, and Jack H. Schuster. 1995. *The American Faculty in Transition: A First Look at the New Academic Generation*. Unpublished manuscript prepared for the National Center for Education Statistics.

Finn, Jeremy D., and Charles M. Achilles. 1990. "Answers and Questions about Class Size: A Statewide Experiment." *American Educational Research Journal* 27: 557–77.

Finn, Jeremy D., Susan B. Gerber, Charles M. Achilles, and Jayne Boyd-Zaharias. 2001. "The Enduring Effects of Small Classes." *Teachers College Record* 103: 145–83.

Fischer, Claude S., Michael Hout, Martin Sanchez Jankowski, Samuel R. Lucas, Ann Swidler, and Kim Voss. 1996. *Inequality by Design*. Princeton, NJ: Princeton University Press.

Fitzgerald, Frances. 1979. *America Revised: History Schoolbooks in the 20th Century*. Boston: Little, Brown.

Fitzpatrick, Sheila. 1979. *Education and Social Mobility in the Soviet Union, 1921–1934*. Cambridge, UK: Cambridge University Press.

Flacks, Richard. 1971. *Youth and Social Change*. Chicago: Markham.

Flinders, David J. 1988. "Teacher Isolation and the New Reform." *Journal of Curriculum Studies* 4: 17–29.

Flynn, James R. 1987. "Massive IQ Gains in 14 Nations: What IQ Tests Really Measure." *Psychological Bulletin* 101: 171–91.

Foster, Philip. 1965. "The Vocational School Fallacy in Development Planning." Pp. 142–66 in C. Arnold Anderson and Mary Jean Bowman (Eds.), *Education and Economic Development*. Chicago: Aldine.

———. 1985. "Africa." Pp. 217–38 in Burton R. Clark (Ed.), *The School and the University*. Berkeley: University of California Press.

Frank, David John, Evan Schofer, and John Charles Torres. 1994. "Rethinking History: Change in the University Curriculum, 1910–90." *Sociology of Education* 67: 231–42.

Freeman, Richard. 1976. *The Overeducated American*. New York: Academic Press.

Freidenberg, Edgar Z. 1959. *The Vanishing Adolescent*. Boston: Beacon.

Friedan, Betty. 1963. *The Feminine Mystique*. New York: Dell.

Fujita, Hidenori. 1986. "A Crisis of Legitimacy in Japanese Education: Meritocracy and Cohesion." *Bulletin of the Faculty of Education, Nagoya University* 32: 117–23.

Fuller, Bruce, and Prema Clarke. 1994. "Raising School Effects While Ignoring Culture: Local Conditions and the Influence of Classroom Tools, Rules, and Pedagogy." *Review of Educational Research* 64: 119–57.

Fuller, Bruce, and Richard Rubinson. 1992. "Does the State Expand Schooling?" Pp. 1–30 in Bruce Fuller and Richard Rubinson (Eds.), *The Political Construction of Education*. New York: Praeger.

Fuller, Bruce, and Conrad W. Snyder, Jr. 1989. "Vocal Teachers, Silent Pupils? Life in Botswana Classrooms." Paper presented at the annual meeting of the Comparative and International Education Society, Boston.

Fuller, Bruce, Lucia Dellaguelo, and Annelie Strath. 1999. "How to Raise Children's Early Literacy: The Influence of Family, Teacher and Classroom in Northeast Brazil." *Comparative Education Review* 43: 1–35.

Gamoran, Adam. 1992. "The Variable Effects of High School Tracking." *American Sociological Review* 57: 812–28.

———. 1996. "Curriculum Standardization and Equality of Opportunity in Scottish Education: 1984–90." *Sociology of Education* 69: 1–21.

Gamoran, Adam, and Robert D. Mare. 1989. "Secondary School Tracking and Educational Inequality: Compensation, Reinforcement, or Neutrality?" *American Journal of Sociology* 94: 1146–83.

Gannicott, Kenneth G., and C. David Throsby. 1992. "Educational Quality in Economic Development: Ten Propositions and an Application to the South Pacific." *International Education Review* 38: 223–39.

GAO. *See* General Accounting Office.

Garms, Walter L., Jr. 1968. "The Correlates of Educational Effort." *Comparative Education Review* 12: 281–99.

Garnier, Maurice, and Michael Hout. 1976. "Inequality of Educational Opportunity in France and the United States." *Social Science Research* 5: 225–46.

Gates, Henry Louis, Jr. 1992. *Loose Canons: Notes on the Culture Wars.* New York: Oxford University Press.

Geiger, H. Kent. 1968. *The Family in Soviet Russia.* Cambridge, MA: Harvard University Press.

General Accounting Office (GAO). 1995. *Restructuring Student Aid Could Reduce Low-Income Dropout Rate.* Washington, DC: General Accounting Office. GAO/HEHS Report 95–48.

Gerson, Kathleen. 1985. *Hard Choices.* Berkeley: University of California Press.

Gibson, Margaret A. 1991. "Ethnicity, Gender, and Social Class: The School Adaptation Patterns of West Indian Youth." Pp. 169–203 in Margaret A. Gibson and John U. Ogbu (Eds.), *Minority Status and Schooling: A Comparative Study of Immigration and Involuntary Minorities.* New York and London: Garland.

Glazer, Nathan. 1997. *We Are All Multiculturalists Now.* Cambridge, MA: Harvard University Press.

Goffman, Erving. 1959. The *Presentation of Self in Everyday Life.* Garden City, NY: Doubleday.

———. 1974. *Frame Analysis: An Essay on the Organization of Experience.* Cambridge, MA: Harvard University Press.

Goldin, Claudia. 1992. *The Meaning of College in the Lives of American Women: The Past 100 Years.* Cambridge, MA: National Bureau of Economic Research. Working Paper No. 4099.

Goldthorpe, John H. 1996. "Problems of Meritocracy." Pp. 255–88 in Robert Erikson and Jan O. Jonsson (Eds.), *Can Education Be Equalized?* Boulder, CO: Westview.

Good, Thomas, and Jere Brophy. 1987. *Looking in Classrooms.* 4th ed. New York: Harper and Row.

Gooden, Andrea R. 1996. *Computers in the Classroom: How Teachers and Students Are Using Technology to Transform Learning.* San Francisco: Jossey-Bass.

Goodlad, John I. 1984. *A Place Called School: Prospects for the Future*. New York: McGraw-Hill.

Goodman, Paul. 1960. *Growing Up Absurd: Problems of Youth in the Organized System*. New York: Random House.

Goodson, Ivor. 1988. *The Making of Curriculum: Collected Essays*. London: Falmer.

Graff, Gerald. 1987. *Professing Literature: An Institutional History*. Chicago: University of Chicago Press.

Graham, Patricia Aljberg. 1992. *S.O.S.: Sustain Our Schools*. New York: Hill and Wang.

———. 1993. "What America Has Expected of Its Schools over the Past Century." *American Journal of Education* 101: 83–98.

Grasso, John, and John Shea. 1979. *Vocational Education and Training: Impact on Youth*. Berkeley, CA: Carnegie Foundation for the Advancement of Teaching.

Gray, John. 1989. *Liberalisms: Essays in Political Philosophy*. London: Routledge.

Green, Sharon Weiner. 1988. *Barron's How to Prepare for the CBEST*. Hauppuage, NY: Barron's Education Series.

Griffin, Gary A. 1985. "The School as a Workplace and the Master Teacher Concept." *Elementary School Journal* 86: 1–16.

Grubb, W. Norton, Laura Goe, and Luis A. Huerta. 2004. "The Unending Search for Equity: California Policy, the 'Improved School Finance' and the Williams Case." *Teachers College Record* 106: 2081–2101.

Grubb, W. Norton, and Marvin Lazerson. 1975. "Rally Round the Workplace: Continuities and Fallacies in Career Education." *Harvard Educational Review* 54: 429–51.

Grusky, David B., and Robert M. Hauser. 1984. "Comparative Social Mobility Revisited: Models of Divergence and Convergence in 16 Countries." *American Sociological Review* 49: 19–38.

Hacker, Andrew. 1990. "Transnational America." *The New York Review of Books* (November 22): 19–24.

Hale-Benson, Janice. 1982. *Black Children: Their Roots, Culture, and Learning Styles*. Provo, UT: Brigham Young University Press.

Hall, Roberta M. 1983. *The College Classroom: A Chilly Climate for Women?* Washington, DC: American Association of University Women. Mimeo.

Halsey, A. H., Anthony Heath, and J. M. Ridge. 1980. *Origins and Destinations*. Oxford: Clarendon.

Hamilton, David, and Associates. 1980. *Notes on the Origin of the Educational Terms Class and Curriculum*. Paper presented at the annual meeting of the American Educational Research Association, Boston.

Hamilton, Stephen F. 1990. *Apprenticeship for Adulthood: Preparing Youth for the Future*. New York: Free Press.

Haney, Walt. 2000. "The Myth of the Texas Miracle in Education." *Education Policy Analysis Archives* 8 (41).

Hannum, Emily. 1999. "Political Change and the Urban-Rural Gap in Basic Education in China, 1949–1990." *Comparative Education Review* 43: 193–211.

———. 2003. "Poverty and Basic Education in Rural China: Villages, Households and Girls' and Boys' Enrollment." *Comparative Education Review* 47: 141–59.

Hanson, E. Mark. 1996. "Educational Change under Autocratic and Democratic Governments: The Case of Argentina." *Comparative Education* 32: 303–17.

Hanushek, Eric A. 1996. "A More Complete Picture of School Resource Policies." *Educational Research* 66: 397–409.

Harbison, Frederick, and Charles A. Myers. 1964. *Education, Manpower, and Economic Growth*. New York: McGraw-Hill.

Hargreaves, Andy. 1993. "Individualism and Individuality: Reinterpreting the Teacher Culture." Pp. 51–76 in Judith W. Little and Milbrey W. McLaughlin (Eds.), *Teachers' Work: Individuals, Colleagues, and Contexts*. New York: Teachers College Press.

Hauser, Robert M. 1992. "The Decline in the College Entry of African-Americans: Findings in Search of an Explanation." Pp. 271–306 in Paul Sniderman et al. (Eds.), *Prejudice, Politics, and Race in America Today*. Stanford, CA: Stanford University Press.

Hauser, Robert M., John Robert Warren, Min-Hsiung Huang, and Wendy Y. Carter. 1996. *Occupational Status, Education, and Social Mobility in the Meritocracy*. CDE Working Paper No. 96-18, Center for Demography and Ecology, University of Wisconsin, Madison, WI.

Haveman, Heather A., and Lisa E. Cohen. 1994. "The Ecological Dynamics of Careers: The Impact of Organizational Founding, Dissolution, and Merger on Job Mobility." *American Journal of Sociology* 100: 104–52.

Heidenheimer, Arnold J. 1973. "The Politics of Public Education, Health, and Welfare in the U.S.A. and Western Europe: How Growth and Reform Potential Have Differed." *British Journal of Political Science* 3: 315–40.

Heidenheimer, Arnold J., Hugh Heclo, and Carolyn T. Adams. 1983. "Education Policy." Pp. 21–51 in Arnold J. Heidenheimer, Hugh Heclo, and Carolyn T. Adams (Eds.), *Comparative Public Policy*. New York: St. Martin's.

HERI. *See* Higher Education Research Institute.

Herrnstein, Richard, and Charles Murray. 1994. *The Bell Curve*. New York: Free Press.

Heyneman, Stephen P. 1993. "Educational Quality and the Crisis of Educational Research." *International Review of Education* 39: 511–7.

Heyneman, Stephen P., and William A. Loxley. 1983. "The Effect of Primary-School Quality on Academic Achievement across Twenty-Nine High- and Low-Income Countries." *American Journal of Sociology* 88: 1162–94.

Heyns, Barbara. 1978. *Summer Learning and the Effects of Schooling*. New York: Academic Press.

Hiebert, James et al. 2003. *Teaching Mathematics in Seven Countries: Results from TIMMS 1999 Video Study*. Washington, DC: National Center for Education Statistics.

Higher Education Research Institute (HERI). 1987. *The American Freshman: Twenty Year Trends, 1966–1985*. Los Angeles: Higher Education Research Institute, Graduate School of Education, University of California, Los Angeles.

———. 2003. *The American Freshman: National Norms for 2002*. Los Angeles: Higher Education Research Institute, Graduate School of Education, University of California Los Angeles.

———. 2005. *The American Freshman: National Norms for 2004*. Los Angeles: Higher Education Research Institute, Graduate School of Education, University of California, Los Angeles.

Hilliard, Asa G. 1976. *Alternatives to IQ Testing: An Approach to the Identification of Gifted Minority Students*. Final report to the California State Department of Education. Sacramento: California State Department of Education.

Hipple, Steven. 2004. "Self-employment in the United States: An Update." *Monthly Labor Review* 127 (7): 13–23.

Hirsch, E. D., Jr. 1987. *Cultural Literacy*. New York: Viking.

Ho, Esther Sui-Chi, and J. Douglas Willms. 1996. "Effect of Parental Involvement in Eighth-Grade Achievement." *Sociology of Education* 69: 126–41.

Hogan, Daniel B. 1979. *The Regulation of Psychotherapists*. Vol. 1. Cambridge, MA: Ballinger.

Hoggart, Richard. 1957. *The Uses of Literacy*. New York: Chatto and Windus.

Holmes, Brian, and Martin MacLean. 1989. *The Curriculum: A Comparative Perspective*. London: Unwin Hyman.

Holt, John. 1964. *How Children Fail*. New York: Pittman.

Hopper, Earl I. 1968. "A Typology for the Classification of Educational Systems." *Sociology* 2: 29–46.

Hopper, Richard (Ed.). 2002. *Constructing Knowledge Societies: New Challenges for Tertiary Education*. New York: World Bank.

Horn, Laura, Laurence K. Kojuku, and C. Dennis Carroll. 2001. *High School Academic Curriculum and the Persistence Path through College*. Washington, DC: National Center for Educational Statistics. NCES 2001-163. August.

Hornberger, Nancy H. 1987. "Schooltime, Classtime, and Academic Learning Time in Rural Highland Puno, Peru." *Anthropology and Education Quarterly* 18: 207–21.

Hout, Michael. 1988. "Expanding Universalism, Less Structural Mobility: The American Occupational Structure in the 1980s." *American Journal of Sociology* 93: 1358–400.

Hout, Michael, and Daniel P. Dohan. 1996. "Two Paths to Educational Opportunity: Class and Educational Selection in Sweden and the United States." Pp. 207–32 in Robert Erikson and Jan O. Jonsson (Eds.), *Can Education Be Equalized?* Boulder, CO: Westview.

Hout, Michael, Adrian E. Raftery, and Eleanor O. Bell. 1993. "Making the Grade: Educational Stratification in the United States, 1925–1989." Pp. 25–49 in Yossi Shavit and Hans-Peter Blossfeld (Eds.), *Persistent Inequality: Changing Inequality in 13 Countries*. Boulder, CO: Westview.

Howard, Ann. 1986. "College Experience and Managerial Performance." *Journal of Applied Psychology* 71: 530–52.

Howard, Suzanne. 1970. *A Comparative Study of Urban and Rural Teacher Roles in a Changing Society, Lebanon*. Unpublished doctoral dissertation. University of Michigan, School of Education.

Hoxby, Caroline M. 2004a. *A Straightforward Comparison of Charter Schools and Regular Public Schools in the United States*. (www.ksg.harvard.edu/faculty/hoxby/papers/hoxbyallcharters.pdf)

———. 2004b. *Achievement in Charter Schools and Regular Public Schools in the United States: Understanding the Differences*. (www.ksg.harvard.edu/pepg/index.htm)

Huber, Joan, and Glenna Spitze. 1983. *Sex Stratification: Children, Housework, and Jobs*. New York: Academic Press.

Huberman, Michael. 1993. "The Model of the Independent Artisan in Teachers' Professional Relations." Pp. 11–50 in Judith W. Little and Milbrey W. McLaughlin (Eds.), *Teachers' Work: Individuals, Colleagues, and Contexts*. New York: Teachers College Press.

Hunter, James Davison. 1991. *Culture Wars: The Struggle to Define America*. New York: Basic Books.

Husén, Torsten. 1965. "A Case Study in Policy-Oriented Research: The Swedish School Reforms." *School Review* 73: 206–25.

———. 1971. "Does Broader Educational Opportunity Mean Lower Standards?" *International Review of Education* 17: 77–89.

———. 1979. "IEA in Retrospect." *Comparative Educational Review* 23: 371–85.

Hyman, Herbert, and Charles Wright. 1979. *Education's Lasting Influence on Values*. Chicago: University of Chicago Press.

Ilchman, Alice Stone, Warren F. Ilchman, and Mary Hale Tolar (Eds.). 2004. *The Lucky Few and the Worthy Many: Scholarship Competitions and the World's Future Leaders*. Bloomington, IN: Indiana University Press.

Ingersoll, Richard M. 2003. *Who Controls Teachers' Work? Power and Accountability in America's Schools*. Cambridge, MA: Harvard University Press.

———. 2005. "The Problem of Under-Qualified Teachers: A Sociological Perspective." *Sociology of Education* 78: 175–8.

Inkeles, Alex. 1979. "National Differences in Scholastic Performance." *Comparative Educational Review* 23: 386–407.

Inkeles, Alex, and Larry J. Sirowy. 1983. "Convergent and Divergent Trends in National Educational Systems." *Social Forces* 62: 303–33.

Ishida, Hiroshi, Walter Muller, and John M. Ridge. 1995. "Class Origin, Class Destination, and Education: A Cross-National Study of Ten Industrial Societies." *American Journal of Sociology* 101: 145–93.

Ishida, Hiroshi, Seymour Spilerman, and Kuo-Hsien Su. 1997. "Educational Credentials and Promotion Chances in Japanese and American Organizations." *American Sociological Review* 62: 866–82.

Jackson, Philip W. 1968. *Life in Classrooms*. Troy, MO; Holt, Rinehart & Winston.

Jackson, Philip W., Robert E. Boorstrom, and David T. Hansen. 1993. *The Moral Life of Schools*. San Francisco: Jossey-Bass.

Jacobs, Jerry A. 1995. "Gender and Academic Specialties: Trends among College Degree Recipients during the 1980s." *Sociology of Education* 68: 81–98.

———. 1996. "Gender Inequality and Higher Education." *Annual Review of Sociology* 22: 153–85.

Jacobson, Matthew F. 1998. *Whiteness of a Different Color: Immigrants and the Alchemy of Race*. Cambridge, MA: Harvard University Press.

Jencks, Christopher, Susan Bartlett, Mary Corcoran, James Crouse, David Eaglesfield, Gregory Jackson, Kent McClelland, Peter Mueser, Michael Olneck, Joseph Schwartz, Sherry Ward, and Jill Williams. 1979. *Who Gets Ahead?* New York: Basic Books.

Jencks, Christopher, James Crouse, and Peter Mueser. 1983. "The Wisconsin Model of Status Attainment: A National Replication with Improved Measures of Ability and Aspiration." *Sociology of Education* 56: 3–19.

Jencks, Christopher, Marshall Smith, Henry Acland, Mary Jo Bane, David Cohen, Herbert Gintis, Barbara Heyns, and Stephen Michelson. 1972. *Inequality*. New York: Harper and Row.

Jessor, Richard, and Shirley L. Jessor. 1977. *Problem Behavior and Psychosocial Development: A Longitudinal Study of Youth*. New York: Academic Press.

Johnson, Sharon. 1985. "The Fourth 'R' Is for Reform." *New York Times Education Survey* (spring): 17–8.

Johnson, Steven. 2005. *Everything Bad Is Good For You: How Today's Popular Culture Is Actually Making Us Smarter*. New York: Riverhead Books/Penguin USA.

Jonsson, Jan O. 1993. "Persisting Inequalities in Sweden." Pp. 101–32 in Yossi Shavit and Hans-Peter Blossfeld (Eds.), *Persistent Inequality*. Boulder, CO: Westview.

Kamens, David. 1981. "Organizational and Institutional Socialization in Education." *Research in the Sociology of Education and Socialization* 2: 111–26.

———. 1992. "Variant Forms: Cases of Countries with Distinct Curricula." Pp. 74–83 in John W. Meyer, David H. Kamens, and Aaron Benavot (Eds.), *School Knowledge for the Masses*. London: Falmer.

Kamens, David H., and Aaron Benavot. 1992. "A Comparative and Historical Analysis of Mathematics and Science Curricula, 1800–1986." Pp. 101–23 in John W. Meyer, David H. Kamens, and Aaron Benavot (Eds.), *School Knowledge for the Masses*. London: Falmer.

———. 2006. "World Models of Secondary Education, 1960–2000." In Aaron Benavot and Cecilia Braslavsky (Eds.), *School Knowledge for Global Citizenship: Comparative and Historical Perspectives on Curricular Contents*. Hong Kong: Springer and Hong Kong University Press.

Kamens, David H., John W. Meyer, and Aaron Benavot. 1996. "Worldwide Patterns in Academic Secondary Education Curricula." *Comparative Education Review* 40: 116–38.

Kanaga, T. 1994. "Japan: System of Education." Pp. 3078–86 in Torsten Husén and T. Neville Postlethwaite (Eds.), *International Encyclopedia of Education*. New York: Elsevier.

Kane, Thomas J., and Cecilia Elena Rouse 1999. "The Community College: Educating Students at the Margin between College and Work." *Journal of Economic Perspectives* 13: 63–84.

Karabel, Jerome. 2005. *The Chosen: The Hidden History of Admission and Exclusion at Harvard, Yale, and Princeton*. Boston: Houghton-Mifflin.

Karen, David. 1991. "The Politics of Class, Race, and Gender: Access to Higher Education in the United States, 1960–1986." *American Journal of Education* 99: 208–37.

———. 2002. "Change in Access to Higher Education in the United States, 1980–1992." *Sociology of Education* 75: 191–210.

Katz, Lawrence, and Kevin M. Murphy. 1992. "Changes in Relative Wages, 1963–1987: Supply and Demand Factors." *Quarterly Journal of Economics* 107: 35–78.

Kaufman, Philip, Martha Naomi Alt, and Christopher D. Chapman. 2001. *Dropout Rates in the United States 2000*. Washington, DC: National Center for Education Statistics.

Kazin, Alfred. 1951. *A Walker in the City*. New York: Grove.

Keddie, Nell. 1971. "Classroom Knowledge." Pp. 133–60 in Michael F. D. Young (Ed.),

Knowledge and Control: New Directions for the Sociology of Knowledge. London: Collier-Macmillan.

Keeves, John P. 1986. "Science Education: The Contribution of IEA Research to a World Perspective." Pp. 19–44 in T. Neville Postlethwaite (Ed.), *International Educational Research: Essays in Honor of Torsten Husén.* Oxford: Pergamon.

Kelley, Jonathan. 1978. "Wealth and Family Background in the Occupational Career: Theory and Cross-Cultural Data." *British Journal of Sociology* 29: 94–109.

Kennedy, Paul. 1996. "The Ends of the Earth: A Journey at the Dawn of the 21st Century." *New York Review of Books* 43 (September): 20–2.

Kerblay, Basile H. 1983. *Modern Soviet Society.* New York: Pantheon.

Kerkhoff, Alan C. 1974. "Stratification Processes and Outcomes in England and the United States." *American Sociological Review* 39: 789–801.

———. 1995. "Institutional Arrangements and Stratification Processes in Industrial Societies." *Annual Review of Sociology* 21: 323–47.

Kerkhoff, Alan C., Richard T. Campbell, and Idee Wingfield-Laird. 1985. "Social Mobility in Great Britain and the United States." *American Journal of Sociology* 91: 281–308.

Kerr, Clark. 1979. "Five Strategies for Education and Their Major Variants." *Comparative Education Review* 23: 171–82.

Kevles, Daniel J. 1995. "E Pluribus Unabomber." *New Yorker* 71 (August 14): 2–4.

Kimball, Bruce. 1986. *Orators and Philosophers: A History of the Idea of Liberal Education.* New York: Teachers College Press.

Kingdom of Cambodia. 1994. *Rebuilding Quality Education and Training in Cambodia.* Phnom Penh: Ministry of Education, Youth and Sport.

Kingston, Paul W., Ryan Hubbard, Brent Lapp, Paul Schroeder, and John Wilson. 2003. "Why Education Matters." *Sociology of Education* 76: 53–70.

Kingston, Paul W., and John C. Smart. 1990. "The Economic Payoff to Prestigious Colleges." Pp. 147–74 in Paul W. Kingston and Lionel S. Lewis (Eds.), *The High-Status Track: Studies in Elite Schools and Stratification.* Albany: State University of New York Press.

Kliebard, Herbert M. 1986. *The Struggle for the American Curriculum.* London: Routledge and Kegan Paul.

———. 1992. "Constructing a History of the American Curriculum." Pp. 157–85 in Philip W. Jackson (Ed.), *Handbook of Research on Curriculum.* New York: Macmillan.

Klitgaard, Robert E. 1985. *Choosing Elites.* New York: Basic Books.

Kohn, Melvin L. 1972. *Class and Conformity.* Homewood, IL: Dorsey.

Kottcamp, Robert B., Eugene F. Provenzo, Jr., and Marilyn M. Cohn. 1986. "Stability and Change in a Profession: Two Decades of Teacher Attitudes, 1964–84." *Phi Delta Kappan* 67: 559–67.

Kozol, Jonathan. 1968. *Death at an Early Age: The Destruction of the Hearts and Minds of Negro Children in the Boston Schools.* New York: Bantam.

———. 1987. *Savage Inequalities: Children in America's Schools.* New York: HarperCollins.

Kramer, Rita. 1991. *Ed School Follies: The Miseducation of America's Teachers.* New York: Free Press.

Kurian, George Thomas. 2001. *The Illustrated Book of World Rankings.* Armonk, NY: M.E. Sharpe.

Labaree, David F. 1988. *The Making of an American High School: The Credentials Market and the Central High School of Philadelphia, 1838–1939.* New Haven, CT: Yale University Press.

Lamont, Michele. 1992. *Men, Money, and Morals.* Chicago: University of Chicago Press.

Lareau, Annette. 1987. "Social Class Differences in Family-School Relationships: The Importance of Cultural Capital." *Sociology of Education* 60: 73–85.

Lasch, Christopher. 1995. *The Revolt of the Elites and the Betrayal of Democracy.* New York: Norton.

Lave, Jean. 1988. *Cognition in Practice: Mind, Mathematics, and Culture in Everyday Life.* Cambridge, UK: Cambridge University Press.

Lee, Valerie E., Robert G. Croninger, and Julia B. Smith. 1996. "Equity and Choice in Detroit." Pp. 70–91 in Bruce Fuller and Richard F. Elmore (Eds.), *Who Chooses? Who Loses?* New York: Teachers College Press.

Lee, Yongsook. 1991. "Koreans in Japan and the United States." Pp. 139–65 in Margaret A. Gibson and John U. Ogbu (Eds.), *Minority Status and Schooling: A Comparative Study of Immigrants and Involuntary Minorities.* New York: Garland.

Leftwich, Adrian. 1995. "Bringing Politics Back In: Towards a Model of the Development State." *Journal of Development Studies* 31: 400–27.

Lehman, Nicholas. 1999. *The Big Test: The Secret History of the American Meritocracy.* New York: Farrar Strauss Giroux.

Lehmann, R. H. 1994. "Germany: System of Education." Pp. 2470–80 in Torsten Husén and T. Neville Postlethwaite (Eds.), *International Encyclopedia of Education.* New York: Elsevier.

Lerner, Daniel. 1958. *The Passing of Traditional Society: Modernizing the Middle East.* Glencoe, IL: Free Press.

Levin, Henry M. 1990. *Building School Capacity for Effective Teacher Empowerment: Applications to Elementary Schools with At-Risk Students.* Paper prepared for the Project on Teacher Empowerment in the Center for Policy Research in Education, Stanford University, Stanford, CA.

Levine, Arthur, and Jeanette Cureton. 1992. "The Quiet Revolution: Eleven Facts about Multiculturalism and the Curriculum." *Change* 24 (January/February): 24–9.

Levy, Daniel C. 1986. *Higher Education and the State in Latin America.* Chicago: University of Chicago Press.

Lewis, Catherine C. 1995. *Educating Hearts and Minds: Reflections on Japanese Preschool and Elementary Education.* Cambridge, UK: Cambridge University Press.

Liaison Committee of the Regents of the University of California and the California State Board of Education. 1955. *A Restudy of the Needs of California in Higher Education.* Sacramento: California State Department of Education.

Liebenow, J. Gus. 1987. "The Military Factor in African Politics: A Twenty-Five Year Perspective." Pp. 126–59 in Gwendolen M. Carter and Patrick O'Meara (Eds.), *African Independence: The First 25 Years.* Bloomington: Indiana University Press.

Lieberman, Ann, and Lynne Miller. 1987. *Teachers, Their World, and Their Work.* Washington, DC: Association for Supervision and Curriculum Development.

Lieberson, Stanley. 1961. "A Societal Theory of Ethnic Relations." *American Sociological Review* 26: 902–10.

———. 1980. *A Piece of the Pie: Black and White Immigrants since 1880*. Berkeley: University of California Press.

Lightfoot, Sarah Lawrence. 1983. *The Good High School: Portraits in Character and Culture*. New York: Basic Books.

Lincoln, Abraham. [1859] 1953. "Address to the Wisconsin State Agricultural Society." Pp. 471–82 in Roy P. Basler and Christian O. Basler (Eds.), *The Collected Works of Abraham Lincoln*. Vol. 3. New Brunswick, NJ: Rutgers University Press.

Lindsay, Paul. 1982. "The Effect of High School Size on Student Participation, Satisfaction and Attendance." *Educational Evaluation and Policy Analysis* 4 (spring): 57–65.

Lipset, Seymour Martin, and Hans Zetterberg. 1956. "A Theory of Social Mobility." *Transactions of the Third World Congress of Sociology* 2: 155–77.

Liu, Xiaofeng Steven, and J. Patrick Meyer. 2005. "Teachers' Perceptions of their Jobs: A Multi-level Analysis of the Teacher Follow-up Survey for 1994–95." *Teachers College Record* 107: 985–1003.

Lockheed, Marlaine E. 1993. "The Condition of Primary Education in Developing Countries." Pp. 20–40 in Henry M. Levin and Marlaine E. Lockheed (Eds.), *Effective Schools in Developing Countries*. London: Falmer.

Lockheed, Marlaine E., Josefina Fonancier, and Leonard J. Bianchi. 1989. *Effective Primary Level Science Teaching in the Philippines*. PPR Working Paper No. WPS 208, World Bank, Washington, DC.

Lockheed, Marlaine E., Adrian Verspoor, and Associates. 1990. *Improving Primary Education in Developing Countries: A Review of Policy Options*. Washington, DC: World Bank.

Lockwood, David. 1956. "Some Remarks on 'The Social System.'" *British Journal of Sociology* 7: 134–46.

London, Howard. 1979. *The Culture of a Community College*. New York: Praeger.

Lortie, Dan C. 1975. *Schoolteacher*. Chicago: University of Chicago Press.

Louis, Karen Seashore, and Helen M. Marks. 1998. "Does Professional Community Affect the Classroom? Teachers' Work and Student Experiences in Restructuring Schools." *American Journal of Education* 106: 532–75.

Loveless, Tom. 2003. *How Well Are American Students Learning?* Washington, DC: Brookings Institution Press.

Lowenthal, Leo. 1957. *Literature and the Image of Man*. Boston: Beacon.

Lucas, Samuel R. 1996. "Selective Attrition in a Newly Hostile Regime: The Case of 1980 Sophomores." *Social Forces* 75: 999–1019.

———. 1999. *Tracking Inequality: Stratification and Mobility in American High Schools*. New York: Teachers College Press.

———. 2001. "Effectively Maintained Inequality: Education Transitions, Track Mobility, and Social Background Effects." *American Journal of Sociology* 106: 1642–90.

MacLeod, Jay. 1987. *Ain't No Makin' It: Leveled Aspirations in a Low-Income Neighborhood*. Boulder, CO: Westview.

Malen, Betty, Rodney T. Ogawa, and Jennifer Kranz. 1990. "What Do We Know about School Based Management? A Case Study of the Literature A Call for Research." Pp. 289–342 in William Clune and John F. Witte (Eds.), *Choice and Control in American Education*. Vol. 2. London: Falmer.

Mann, Dale. 1986. "Can We Help Dropouts? Thinking about the Undoable." Pp. 3–19 in Gary Natriello (Ed.), *School Dropouts: Patterns and Policies*. New York: Teachers College Press.

Mann, Michael. 1986. *The Sources of Social Power*. Vol. 1. Cambridge, England: Cambridge University Press.

Mare, Robert. 1980. "Social Background and School Continuation Decisions." *Journal of the American Statistical Association* 75: 295–305.

Marklund, Sixten. 1994. "Sweden: System of Education." Pp. 5866–73 in Torsten Husén and T. Neville Postlethwaite (Eds.), *International Encyclopedia of Education*. New York: Elsevier.

Marrou, Henri. [1948] 1982. *A History of Education in Antiquity*. Translated by George Lamb. Madison: University of Wisconsin Press.

Martinez, Valerie, Kenneth Godin, and Frank R. Kenerer. 1996. "Public School Choice in San Antonio: Who Chooses and With What Effects?" Pp. 50–69 in Bruce Fuller and Richard F. Elmore (Eds.), *Who Chooses? Who Loses?* New York: Teachers College Press.

Mateju, Petr. 1993. "Who Won and Who Lost in a Socialist Redistribution in Czechoslovakia?" Pp. 251–72 in Yossi Shavit and Hans-Peter Blossfeld (Eds.), *Persisting Inequalities*. Boulder, CO: Westview.

Maurice, Marc, François Sellier, and Jean-Jacques Silvestre. 1986. *The Social Foundations of Industrial Power*. Cambridge, MA: MIT Press.

McConnell, James. 1985. *English Public Schools*. London: Herbert.

McDill, Edward L., Edmund D. Meyer, Jr., and Leo C. Rigby. 1967. "Institutional Effects on the Academic Behavior of High School Students." *Sociology of Education* 40: 181–99.

McKernan, John R., Jr. 1994. *Making the Grade: How a New Youth Apprenticeship System Can Change Our Schools and Save American Jobs*. Boston: Little, Brown.

McPartland, James, and Barbara Schneider. 1996. "Opportunities to Learn and Student Diversity." *Sociology of Education* 69 (extra issue): 66–81.

McPherson, Andrew, and J. Douglas Willms. 1987. "Equalisation and Improvement: Some Effects of Comprehensive Reorganisation in Scotland." *Sociology* 21: 509–39.

Mehan, Hugh. 1993. "Beneath the Skin and between the Ears: A Case Study of the Politics of Representation." Pp. 241–68 in Seth Chaiklin and Jean Lave (Eds.), *Understanding Practice: Perspectives on Activity and Context*. Cambridge, UK: Cambridge University Press.

Meier, Deborah. 1995. *The Power of Their Ideas: Lessons for America from a Small School in Harlem*. Boston: Beacon.

Merry, Michael S. 2005. "Social Exclusion of Muslim Youth in Flemish and French-Speaking Belgian Schools." *Comparative Education Review* 49: 1–22.

Merton, Robert K. [1949] 1968. *Social Theory and Social Structure*. New York: Free Press.

Metz, Mary Haywood. 1993. "Teachers' Ultimate Dependence on Their Students." Pp. 104–36 in Judith W. Little and Milbrey W. McLaughlin (Eds.), *Teachers' Work: Individuals, Colleagues, and Contexts*. New York: Teachers College Press.

MEXT. *See* Ministry of Education, Culture, Sports, Science, and Technology.

Meyer, John W., David H. Kamens, and Aaron Benavot. 1992. *School Knowledge for the Masses*. London: Falmer.

Meyer, John W., Joane Nagel, and Conrad W. Snyder, Jr. 1993. "The Expansion of Mass Education in Botswana: Local and World Society Perspectives." *Comparative Education Review* 37: 454–75.

Meyer, John W., Francisco O. Ramirez, Richard Rubinson, and John Boli-Bennett. 1979. "The World Education Revolution, 1950–1970." Pp. 37–55 in John W. Meyer and Michael T. Hannan (Eds.), *National Development and the World System*. Chicago: University of Chicago Press.

Meyer, John W., Francisco Ramirez, and Yasmin N. Soysal. 1992. "World Expansion of Mass Education, 1870–1980." *Sociology of Education* 65: 128–49.

Meyer John W., and Brian Rowan. 1977. "Institutionalized Organizations: Formal Structure as Myth and Ceremony." *American Journal of Sociology* 83: 340–63.

———. 1978. "The Structure of Educational Organizations." Pp. 78–109 in Marshall Meyer et al. (Eds.), *Environments and Organizations*. San Francisco: Jossey-Bass.

Meyer, John W., David B. Tyack, Joane Nagel, and Audri Gordon. 1979. "Public Education as Nation-Building in America, 1870–1930." *American Journal of Sociology* 85: 591–613.

Michelson, Roslyn Arlin. 1989. "Why Does Jane Read and Write So Well? The Anomaly of Women's Achievement." *Sociology of Education* 62: 47–63.

Miller, L. Scott. 1995. *An American Imperative*. New Haven, CT: Yale University Press.

Mincer, Jacob, and S. Polachek. 1974. "Family Investment in Human Capital: Earnings of Women." *Journal of Political Economy* 82: S76–S111.

Ministère de L'Éducation Nationale. 2005. *Système Éducatif*. Paris: Ministère de L'Éducation Nationale. (www.education.gouv.fr)

Ministry of Education, Culture, Sports, Science, and Technology (MEXT). 1998. *National Curriculum Standards Reform for Kindergarten, Elementary School, Lower and Upper Secondary School and Schools for the Visually Disabled, the Hearing Impaired and the Otherwise Disabled*. Tokyo: MEXT.

Mitra, Georgios, Daniel L. Millrood, and Joshua H. Mateika. 2002. "The Impact of Sleep on Learning and Behaviors in Adolescents." *Teachers College Record* 104: 704–26.

Moeller, Gerald H. 1964. "Bureaucracy and Teachers' Sense of Power." *School Review* 72: 137–57.

Moll, Terence. 1992. "Mickey Mouse Numbers and Inequality Research in Developing Countries." *Journal of Development Studies* 28: 689–704.

Monchalban, A. 1994. "France: System of Education." Pp. 3377–85 in Torsten Husén and T. Neville Postlethwaite (Eds.), *International Encyclopedia of Education*. New York: Elsevier.

Monk-Turner, Elizabeth. 1990. "The Occupational Achievements of Community and Four-Year College Entrants." *American Sociological Review* 55: 719–25.

Moore, Donald R., and Suzanne Davenport. 1990. "School Choice: The New and Improved Sorting Machine." Pp. 187–223 in William L. Boyd and Herbert J. Walberg (Eds.), *Choice in Education: Potential and Problems*. Berkeley, CA: McCutcheon.

Morgan, Stephen L. 2005. *On the Edge of Commitment: Educational Attainment and Race in the United States*. Stanford: Stanford University Press.

Morris, Paul, Gerry McClelland, and Wong Ping Man. 1997. "Explaining Curriculum Change: Social Studies in Hong Kong." *Comparative Education Review* 41: 27–43.

Mortenson, Thomas. 2000. *Public Policy Dilemmas in Higher Educational Opportunity. Postsecondary Education Opportunity: The Mortenson Research Letter.* Mimeo.

———. 2005. *Family Income and Higher Education Opportunity, 1970 to 2003.* Oskaloosa, IA: Postsecondary Education Opportunity. (www.postsecondary.org)

Muller, Walter. 1996. "Class Inequalities in Educational Outcomes: Sweden in Comparative Perspective." Pp. 145–82 in Robert Erikson and Jan O. Jonsson (Eds.), *Can Education Be Equalized?* Boulder, CO: Westview.

Murnane, Richard, John Willett, and Frank Levy. 1995. "The Growing Importance of Cognitive Skills in Wage Determination." *Review of Economics and Statistics* 77: 251–66.

NAEP. *See* National Assessment of Educational Progress.

Nagasawa, Makoto. 2005. "Gender Stratification in Japanese Private Higher Education." *International Higher Education* 40: 10.

National Assessment of Educational Progress (NAEP). 2005. *The Nation's Report Card: America's Charter Schools: Results from the NAEP 2003 Pilot Study.* Washington, DC: National Center for Education Statistics.

National Center for Educational Statistics (NCES). 1985. *High School and Beyond: An Analysis of Course Taking Patterns in Secondary Schools as Related to School Characteristics.* Washington, DC: Government Printing Office.

———. 1994. *Digest of Education Statistics, 1994.* Washington, DC: Government Printing Office.

———. 1996. *Pursuing Excellence: A Study of U.S. Eighth-Grade Mathematics and Science Teaching, Learning, Curriculum, and Achievement in International Context.* Washington, DC: Government Printing Office.

———. 2001a. *Dropout Rates in the United States: 2001.* Washington, DC: NCES.

———. 2001b. *Public School Teachers' Salaries in Upper Secondary Education.* Washington, DC: NCES.

———. 2003. *Digest of Education Statistics 2003.* Washington, DC: NCES.

———. 2004. *The Condition of Education 2004.* Washington, DC: NCES.

———. 2005. *Digest of Education Statistics 2005.* Washington, DC: NCES.

National Commission on Excellence in Education. 1983. *A Nation at Risk.* Washington, DC: Government Printing Office.

NCES. *See* National Center for Educational Statistics.

Neave, Guy R. 1985. "France." Pp. 10–44 in Burton R. Clark (Ed.), *The School and the University.* Berkeley: University of California Press.

Neill, A. S. 1960. *Summerhill: A Radical Approach to Child-Rearing.* New York: Hart.

Newman, Fred M., Robert A. Rutter, and Marshall S. Smith. 1989. "Organizational Factors That Affect Teachers' Sense of Efficacy, Community, and Expectations." *Sociology of Education* 62: 221–38.

Noah, Harold J. 1987. "Reflections." *Comparative Education Review* 31: 137–49.

Nye, Barbara, Larry V. Hedges, and Spyros Konstantopolous. 2000. "Do the Disadvantaged Benefit More from Small Classes? Evidence from the Tennessee Class Size Experiment." *American Journal of Education* 109: 1–26.

Oak Glen School (Oak Glen, California). 1873. *Rules for Teachers.* Mimeo.

Oakes, Jeannie. 1985. *Keeping Track: How Schools Structure Inequality.* New Haven, CT: Yale University Press.

———. 1994. "More Than Misapplied Technology: A Normative and Political Response to Hallinan on Tracking." *Sociology of Education* 67: 84–9.

Oakes, Jeannie, Adam Gamoran, and Reba N. Page. 1992. "Curriculum and Differentiation: Opportunities, Outcomes and Meanings." Pp. 570–608 in Philip W. Jackson (Ed.), *Handbook of Research on Curriculum*. Washington, DC: American Educational Research Association.

Odeotola, Theophilus O. 1982. *Military Regimes and Development: A Comparative Analysis of African States*. London: Allen and Unwin.

OECD. *See* Organization for Economic Cooperation and Development.

Ogbu, John U. 1978. *Minority Education and Caste: The American System in Cross-Cultural Perspective*. New York: Academic Press.

Orfield, Gary. 1994. "Foreword." In Alison Moratz, *Money, Choice, and Equity: Major Investments with Modest Returns*. Cambridge, MA: Harvard Project on School Desegregation.

Organization for Economic Cooperation and Development (OECD). 1996. *Education at a Glance: OECD Indicators*. Paris: OECD.

———. 2000. *Measuring Student Knowledge and Skills: Reading, Mathematical and Scientific Literacy: The PISA Assessment*. Paris: OECD.

———. 2002. *Education at a Glance 2002*. Paris: OECD.

———. 2004. *Education at a Glance: OECD Indicators*. Paris: OECD.

———. 2005. *Education at a Glance: OECD Indicators*. Paris: OECD.

Orwell, George. [1952] 1968. "Such, Such Were the Joys." Pp. 330–69 in Sonia Orwell and Ian Angus (Eds.), *In Front of Your Nose 1945–1950: Collected Essays, Journalism, and Letters of George Orwell*. New York: Harcourt, Brace and World.

Osberg, Lars. 1984. *Economic Inequality in the United States*. Armonk, NY: M. E. Sharpe.

Papert, Seymour. 1993. *The Children's Machine: Rethinking School in the Age of the Computer*. New York: Basic Books.

Parsons, Talcott. 1951. *The Social System*. New York: Free Press.

———. 1959. "The School Class as a Social System: Some of Its Functions in American Society." *Harvard Educational Review* 29: 297–318.

Pascarella, Ernest T., and Patrick T. Terenzini. 1991. *How College Affects Students*. San Francisco: Jossey-Bass.

Pelgrum, Willem J. and Tjeerd Plomp. 1993. *The IEA Study of Computers in Education: Implementation of an Innovation in 21 Education Systems*. Oxford: Pergamon.

Peng, Samuel S. 1977. "Trends in the Entry to Higher Education, 1961–1972." *Educational Researcher* 6 (1): 15–9.

Perrow, Charles. 1986. *Complex Organizations: A Critical Essay*. New York: Random House.

Pfau, Richard F. 1980. *The Comparative Study of Classroom Behaviors*. Comparative Education Review 24: 400–14.

Pfeffer, Jeffrey, and Gerald M. Salancik. 1978. *The External Control of Organizations*. New York: Harper and Row.

Plank, Stephen B., Edward L. McDill, James M. McPartland, and Will J. Jordan. 2001. "Situation and Repertoire: Civility and Incivility, Cursing and Politeness in an Urban High School." *Teachers College Record* 103: 504–24.

Pomponio, Alice, and David F. Lancy. 1986. "A Pen or a Bushknife? School, Work, and Personal Investment in Papua, New Guinea." *Anthropology and Education Quarterly* 17: 40–61.

Pomson, Alex. 2005. "One Classroom at a Time? Teacher Isolation and Community Viewed through the Prism of the Particular." *Teachers College Record* 107: 783–802.

Porter, Rosalie P. 1990. *Forked Tongue: The Politics of Bilingual Education.* New York: Basic Books.

Portes, Alejandro, and Lingxin Hao. 1998. "E Pluribus Unum: Bilingualism and Loss of Language—The Second Generation." *Sociology of Education* 71: 269–95.

Postman, Neil. 1985. *Amusing Ourselves to Death: Public Discourse in the Age of Show Business.* New York: Viking Penguin.

Powell, Arthur G., Eleanor Farrar, and David K. Cohen. 1985. *The Shopping Mall High School: Winners and Losers in the Educational Marketplace.* Boston: Houghton-Mifflin.

Presseisen, Barbara Z., Robert J. Sternberg, Kurt W. Fischer, Catharine C. Knight, and Reuven Feurerstein. 1990. *Learning and Thinking Styles: Classroom Interaction.* Washington, DC: National Education Association.

PROBE Team (Anurada De, Jean Dreze et al.). 1999. *Public Report on Basic Education in India.* New Delhi: Oxford University Press.

Psacharopoulos, George. 1986. "The Planning of Education: Where Do We Stand?" *Comparative Education Review* 30: 560–73.

———. 1987. "To Vocationalize or Not to Vocationalize? That Is the Curricular Question." *International Review of Education* 33: 187–211.

Psacharopoulos, George, and Zafiris Tzannatos. 1992. *Women's Pay in Latin America: Overview and Methodology.* Washington, DC: World Bank.

Public Agenda. 1997. *Getting By: What American Teenagers Really Think about Their Schools.* Washington, DC: Public Agenda. Mimeo.

Rashdall, Hastings. [1895] 1936. The *Universities of Europe in the Middle Ages.* Vol. 1. Oxford: Oxford University Press.

Rau, William, and Ann Durand. 2000. "The Academic Ethic and College Grades: Does Hard Work Help Students to 'Make the Grade'?" *Sociology of Education* 73: 19–38.

Ravitch, Diane. 1983. *The Troubled Crusade: American Education, 1945–1980.* New York: Basic Books.

———. 1985. *The Schools We Deserve.* New York: Basic Books.

———. 1995. *National Standards in American Education.* Washington, DC: Brookings Institution.

Ravitch, Diane, and Chester Finn, Jr. 1987. *What Do Our 17-Year-Olds Know?* New York: Harper and Row.

Renzulli, Linda A. 2005. "Organizational Environments and the Emergence of Charter Schools in the United States." *Sociology of Education* 78: 1–26.

Renzulli, Linda A., and Vincent Roscigno. 2005. "Charter School Policy, Implementation, and Diffusion in the United States." *Sociology of Education* 78: 344–65.

Reskin, Barbara. 1993. "Sex Segregation in the Workplace." *Annual Review of Sociology* 19: 241–70.

Rice, Joseph M. 1893. *The Public School System of the United States.* New York: Century.

Riche, Martha Farnsworth. 1991. "We're All Minorities Now." *American Demographics* 13 (10): 26–34.

Riesman, David, and Ruell Denney. 1951. "Football in America: A Study in Culture Diffusion." *American Quarterly* 3: 309–25.

Ringer, Fritz K. 1969. The *Decline of the German Mandarins: The German Academic Community, 1890–1933*. Cambridge, MA: Harvard University Press.

———. 1979. *Education and Society in Modern Europe*. Bloomington: Indiana University Press.

———. 1992. *Fields of Knowledge: French Academic Culture in Comparative Perspective*. Cambridge, UK: Cambridge University Press.

Rist, Ray C. 1970. "Student Social Class and Teachers' Expectations: The Self-Fulfilling Prophecy in Ghetto Education." *Harvard Educational Review* 40: 411–50.

Robertson, Claire. 1985. "A Growing Dilemma: Women and Change in African Primary Education, 1950–1980." Pp. 17–35 in Gideon Were (Ed.), *Women and Development in Africa*. Nairobi: Gideon S. Were.

Robinson, Robert V. 1984. "Reproducing Class Relations in Industrial Capitalism." *American Sociological Review* 49: 182–96.

Robinson, Robert V., and Maurice Garnier. 1985. "Class Reproduction among Men and Women in France: Reproduction Theory on Its Home Ground." *American Journal of Sociology* 91: 250–80.

Rodriguez, Richard. 1982. *Hunger of Memory*. Boston: David R. Godine.

Rohlen, Thomas P. 1983. *Japan's High Schools*. Berkeley: University of California Press.

Rose, Lowell C., and Alec M. Gallup. 2004. *The 36th Annual Phi Delta Kappa/Gallup Poll on the Public's Attitudes toward the Public Schools*. Bloomington, IN: Phi Delta Kappa, Int.

Rosenbaum, James E. and Amy Binder. 1997. "Do Employers Really Need More Educated Youth?" *Sociology of Education* 70: 68–85.

Rosenbaum, James E., and Takehiko Kariya. 1989. "From High School to Work: Market and Institutional Mechanisms in Japan." *American Journal of Sociology* 94: 1334–65.

Rosenfelt, Deborah S. 1994. "'Definitive' Issues: Women's Studies, Multicultural Education and Curriculum Transformation in Policy and Practice in the United States." *Women's Studies Quarterly* 22: 26–41.

Rosenthal, Robert, and Lenore Jacobsen. 1968. *Pygmalion in the Classroom*. New York: Holt, Rinehart and Winston.

Rothblatt, Sheldon. 1968. *The Revolution of the Dons: Cambridge and Society in Victorian England*. New York: Basic Books.

Rothstein, Richard. 1999. "Linking Poor Performance to Working After School." *New York Times* (October 27): A13.

Rousseau, Jean-Jacques. [1762] 1911. *Émile, or Education*. New York: J. M. Dent.

———. [1754] 1964. "Discourse on the Origins and Foundations of Inequality among Men." Pp. 78–228 in Roger D. Masters (Ed.), *The First and Second Discourses*. New York: St. Martin's.

Rowan, Brian, Robert Miller, Richard Correnti, and Eric Camburn. 2004. "How Comprehensive School Reforms Work." Paper presented at the American Educational Research Association annual meeting. San Francisco (April).

Ruch, Richard S. 2001. *Higher Ed, Inc.: The Rise of the For-Profit University*. Baltimore: Johns Hopkins University Press.

Rumberger, Russell W., and Katherine A. Larson. 1998. "Toward Explaining Differences in Educational Achievement among Mexican American Language Minority Students." *Sociology of Education* 71: 69–93.

Rutter, Michael et al. 1979. *Fifteen Thousand Hours: Secondary Schools and Their Effects on Children*. Cambridge, MA: Harvard University Press.

Sadker, Myra, and David Sadker. 1994. *Failing at Fairness: How America's Schools Cheat Girls*. New York: Scribner.

Schemo, Diana Jean. 2004. "Nation's Charter Schools Lagging Behind, U.S. Test Scores Reveal." *New York Times* (August 17): A1 ff.

Schiefelbein, Ernesto. 1985. "Latin America." Pp. 195–216 in Burton R. Clark (Ed.), *The School and the University*. Berkeley: University of California Press.

Schmitter, Philippe C. 1971. "Military Intervention, Political Competitiveness, and Public Policy in Latin America, 1950–1967." Pp. 425–506 in Morris Janowitz and Jacques van Doorn (Eds.), *On Military Intervention*. Rotterdam: Rotterdam University Press.

Schofer, Evan, and John W. Meyer. 2005. "The Worldwide Expansion of Higher Education in the Twentieth Century." *American Sociological Review* 70: 898–920.

Schultz, Theodore W. 1961. "Investment in Human Capital." *American Economic Review* 51: 1–17.

Scott, Janny, and David Leonhardt. 2005. "Class in America: Shadowy Lines That Still Divide." *New York Times* (May 15): A1 ff.

Sedlak, Michael W., Christopher W. Wheeler, Diane C. Pullin, and Philip A. Cusick. 1986. *Selling Students Short: Classroom Bargains and Academic Reform in the American High School*. New York: Teachers College Press.

Sellar, Walter C., and Robert J. Yeatman. 1931. *1066 and All That: A Memorable History of England*. New York: Dutton.

Selznick, Philip. 1949. *The TVA and the Grass Roots: A Study in the Sociology of Formal Organization*. Berkeley: University of California Press.

———. 1957. *Leadership in Administration: A Sociological Interpretation*. Evanston, IL: Row, Peterson.

Serrano v. Priest, 96 *Cal. Rptr.* 601 (Sept. 20, 1971).

Sewell, William H., Archibald O. Haller, and Alejandro Portes. 1969. "The Educational and Early Occupational Attainment Process." *American Sociological Review* 34: 82–92.

Sewell, William H., and Robert M. Hauser. 1975. *Occupation and Earnings: Achievement in the Early Career*. New York: Academic Press.

Sewell, William H., and Vimal P. Shah. 1967. "Socioeconomic Status, Intelligence, and Attainment of Higher Education." *Sociology of Education* 40: 1–23.

Shah, Saed, and Jefferson Eastmond. 1977. *Primary Education in the Rural Villages of Pakistan, 1976–77*. Islamabad: Ministry of Education.

Sharp, Patricia T., and Randy M. Wood. 1992. "Moral Values: A Study of Selected Third- and Fifth-Grade Reading and Social Studies Textbooks." *Religion and Public Education* 19: 143–53.

Shields, James J. 1992. "Japan." Pp. 321–43 in Peter W. Cookson, Alan R. Sadovnik, and

Susan F. Semel (Eds.), *International Handbook of Educational Reform*. New York: Greenwood.

Shils, Edward A. [1962] 1975. "The Military in the Political Development of the New States." Pp. 483–516 in *Center and Periphery: Essays in Macro-Sociology*. Chicago: University of Chicago Press.

Sikkink, David, and Andrea Mibut. 2000. "Religion and the Politics of Multiculturalism." *Religion and Education* 27 (2): 30–44.

Siskin, Leslie Santee. 2003. "When an Irresistible Force Meets an Immovable Object: Core Lessons about High Schools and Accountability." Pp. 175–94 in Martin Carnoy, Richard Elmore, and Leslie Santee Siskin (Eds.), *The New Accountability: High Schools and High Stakes Testing*. London: Routledge Falmer.

Sizer, Theodore R. 1984. *Horace's Compromise: The Dilemma of the American High School*. Boston: Houghton-Mifflin.

———. 1986. "Rebuilding: First Steps by the Coalition of Essential Schools." *Phi Delta Kappan* 68 (9): 37–42.

Skidmore, Thomas E., and Peter H. Smith. 1989. *Modern Latin America*. New York: Oxford University Press.

Skolverket. 2005. *Upper Secondary Schools*. Stockholm: Skolverket. (www.skolverket.se)

Slavin, Robert E. 1980. "Cooperative Learning." *Review of Educational Research* 50: 315–42.

———. 1994. *Cooperative Learning: Theory, Research, and Practice*. 2d ed. Boston: Allyn and Bacon.

Slavin, Robert E., Nancy L. Karweit, and Nancy A. Madden. 1989. *Effective Programs for Students at Risk*. Boston: Allyn and Bacon.

Slavin, Robert E., Nancy A. Madden, Lawrence J. Dolan, Barbara A. Wasik, Steven M. Ross, and Lana J. Smith. 1994. "'Whenever and Wherever We Choose': The Replication of 'Success for All.'" *Phi Delta Kappan* 75: 639–47.

Slavin, Robert E., Nancy A. Madden, Nancy L. Karweit, Barbara J. Livermon, and Lawrence Dolan. 1990. "Success for All: First-Year Outcomes of a Comprehensive Plan for Reforming Urban Education." *American Educational Research Journal* 27: 255–78.

Slavin, Robert E., and Eileen Oickle. 1981. "Effects of Cooperative Learning Teams on Student Achievement and Race Relations." *Sociology of Education* 54: 174–80.

Smrekar, Claire, James W. Guthrie, Debra E. Owens, and Pearl G. Sims. 2001. *Marching Toward Excellence: Schools' Success and Minority Student Achievement in Department of Defense Schools*. Washington, DC: National Education Goals Panel.

SNES. *See* Syndicat National des Enseignements de Second Degré.

Soares, Joseph A. 1999. *The Decline of Privilege: The Modernization of Oxford University*. Stanford, CA: Stanford University Press.

Somers, Marie-Andree, Patrick J. McEwan, and J. Douglas Willms. 2004. "How Effective Are Private Schools in Latin America?" *Comparative Education Review* 48: 48–69.

Sorenson, Aage. 1970. "Organizational Differentiation of Students and Educational Opportunity." *Sociology of Education* 43: 355–76.

Sorokin, Pitrim A. [1927] 1959. *Social and Cultural Mobility*. Glencoe, IL: Free Press.

Sowell, Thomas. 1981. *Ethnic America: A History*. New York: Basic Books.

———. 1992. *Inside American Education: The Decline, the Deception, the Dogmas.* New York: Free Press.

Soysal, Yasmin N., and David Strong. 1989. "Construction of the First Mass Education Systems in Western Europe." *Sociology of Education* 62: 277–88.

Spence, Michael. 1974. *Market Signalling: Informational Transfer in Hiring and Related Screening.* Cambridge, MA: Harvard University Press.

Squires, Gregory. 1979. *Education and Jobs: The Imbalancing of the Social Machinery.* New Brunswick, NJ: Transaction Books.

Stallmann, H. 1990. "Lehrer und Lehrerbildung in der Bundesrepublik Deutschland und in der Deutschen Demokratischen Republik." In S. Baske (Ed.), *Pedagogische Berufe in der Bundesrepublik Deutschland und in der Deutschen Demokratischen Republik.* Berlin: Duncker & Humblot.

Stambach, Amy. 1998. "'Too Much Studying Makes Me Crazy': School-Related Illnesses on Mount Kilimanjaro." *Comparative Education Review* 42: 497–512.

Stedman, Lawrence C. 1996. "Respecting the Evidence: The Achievement Crisis Remains Real." *Education Policy Analysis Archives* 4 (7).

Steele, Claude. 1997. "A Threat in the Air: How Stereotypes Shape Intellectual Identity and Performance." *The American Psychologist* 52: 613–29.

Steinberg, Laurence, with Bradford Brown and Sanford M. Dornbusch. 1996. *Beyond the Classroom: Why School Reform Has Failed and What Parents Need to Do.* New York: Simon & Schuster.

Steinberg, Stephen. 1981. *The Ethnic Myth.* New York: Atheneum.

Steinmetz, George, and Erik Olin Wright. 1989. "The Fall and Rise of the Petty Bourgeoisie: Changing Patterns of Self-Employment in the Postwar United States." *American Journal of Sociology* 94: 973–1018.

Stepan, Alfred. 1978. *The State and Society: Peru in Comparative Perspective.* Princeton, NJ: Princeton University Press.

Stern, David, Thomas Bailey, and Donna Merritt. 1997. *School-to-Work Policy Insights from Recent International Developments.* Berkeley: National Center for Research in Vocational Education.

Sternberg, Robert J. 1988. *The Triarchic Mind: A New Theory of Human Intelligence.* New York: Viking.

Sternberg, Robert J., and Elena L. Grigorenko. 1999. "Myths in Psychology and Education Regarding the Gene-Environment Debate." *Teachers College Record* 100L: 536–53.

Stevens, Mitchell L. 2001. *Kingdom of Children: Culture and Controversy in the Home Schooling Movement.* Princeton, NJ: Princeton University Press.

Stevenson, David Lee, and David P. Baker. 1991. "State Control of the Curriculum and Classroom Instruction." *Sociology of Education* 64: 1–11.

Stevenson, Harold W., and James W. Stigler. 1992. *The Learning Gap: Why Our Schools Are Failing and What We Can Learn from Japanese and Chinese Education.* New York: Summit.

Stinchcombe, Arthur L. 1959. "Bureaucratic and Craft Administration." *Administrative Sciences Quarterly* 4: 168–87.

———. 1964. *Rebellion in a High School.* Chicago: Quadrangle.

Strauss, Anselm. 1959. *Masks and Mirrors: The Transformation of Identity.* Glencoe, IL: Free Press.

Stromquist, Nelly P. 1989. "Determinants of Educational Participation and Achievement of Women in the Third World: A Review of the Evidence and a Theoretical Critique." *Review of Educational Research* 59: 143–83.

———. 1993. "Sex Equity Legislation in Education: The State as Promoter of Women's Rights." *Review of Educational Research* 63: 379–407.

Suleiman, Ezra N. 1978. *Elites in French Society.* Princeton, NJ: Princeton University Press.

Swedish Institute. 1995. *Upper Secondary and Adult Education in Sweden.* Stockholm: Swedish Institute.

———. 1996. *Compulsory Education in Sweden.* Stockholm: Swedish Institute.

———. 2004. *Higher Education in Sweden.* Stockholm: Swedish Institute. (www.sweden.se)

Syndicat National des Enseignements de Second Degré (SNES). 2004. *Seconde Generale et Technologique.* Paris: SNES. (www.snes.edu)

Szelenyi, Sonja, and Karen Aschaffenburg. 1993. "Inequalities of Opportunity in Hungary." Pp. 273–302 in Yossi Shavit and Hans-Peter Blossfeld (Eds.), *Persisting Inequalities.* Boulder, CO: Westview.

Tauer, Susan M. 1996. *The Mentor-Protégé Relationship and Its Effects on Experienced Teachers.* ERIC Document No. ED 397 004.

Teichler, Ulrich. 1985. "The Federal Republic of Germany." Pp. 45–76 in Burton R. Clark (Ed.), *The School and the University.* Berkeley: University of California Press.

Teodoro, Antonio. 2003. "Paulo Freire, or Pedagogy as the Space and Time of Possibility." *Comparative Education Review* 47: 321–28.

Thompson, Quentin, Julia Tyler, and Peter Howlett. 1995. "Transformation of Higher Education in the United Kingdom." Pp. 279–302 in Susan L. Johnson and Sean C. Rush (Eds.), *Reinventing the University: Managing and Financing Institutions of Higher Education.* New York: John Wiley and Sons.

Thorne, Barrie. 1995. *Gender Play: Girls and Boys in School.* New Brunswick, NJ: Rutgers University Press.

Thurow, Lester. 1973. "Education and Economic Equality." *The Public Interest* 28: 66–81.

Toby, Jackson. 1980. "Crime in American Schools." *The Public Interest* 58: 18–42.

Touré, Sékou. 1965. "Education and Social Progress." Pp. 125–40 in L. Gray Cowan, James O'Connell, and David G. Scanlon (Eds.), *Education and Nation-Building in Africa.* New York: Praeger.

Treiman, Donald J., and Harry B. G. Ganzeboom. 1990. "Cross-National Comparative Status Attainment Research." *Research in Social Stratification and Mobility* 9: 105–27.

Treiman, Donald J., and Patricia A. Roos. 1983. "Sex and Earnings in Industrial Society: A Nine-Nation Comparison." *American Journal of Sociology* 89: 612–50.

Treiman, Donald J., and Kin-Bor Yip. 1988. "Educational and Occupational Attainments in 21 Countries." Pp. 373–94 in Melvin L. Kohn (Ed.), *Cross-National Research in Sociology.* Newbury Park, CA: Sage.

Trow, Martin. 1961. "The Second Transformation of American Secondary Education." *International Journal of Comparative Sociology* 2: 144–66.

Turner, Ralph H. 1960. "Sponsored and Contest Mobility and the School System." *American Sociological Review* 25: 855–67.

Twain, Mark. [1896] 1972. *Life on the Mississippi*. New York: Harper and Row.

Tyack, David. B. 1974. *The One Best System*. Cambridge, MA: Harvard University Press.

———. 1999. "Preserving the Republic by Educating Republicans." Pp. 63–84 in Neil J. Smelser and Jeffrey C. Alexander (Eds.), *Diversity and Its Discontents: Cultural Conflict and Common Ground in Contemporary American Society*. Princeton: Princeton University Press.

Tyack, David B., and Larry Cuban. 1995. *Tinkering toward Utopia: A Century of Public School Reform*. Cambridge, MA: Harvard University Press.

Tyack, David B., and Elisabeth Hansot. 1982. *Managers of Virtue: Public School Leadership in America, 1820–1980*. New York: Basic Books.

Tye, Kenneth A. 1985. *The Junior High School: School in Search of a Mission*. Lanham, MD: University Press of America.

UNCTAD. *See* United Nations Conference on Trade and Development.

UNDP. *See* United Nations Development Project.

UNESCO. *See* United Nations Educational, Scientific, and Cultural Organization.

UNHDP. *See* United Nations Human Development Programme.

UNICEF. *See* United Nations International Children's Emergency Fund.

United Nations Conference on Trade and Development (UNCTAD). 2004. *The Least Developed Countries Report 2004*. New York: UNCTAD.

United Nations Development Project (UNDP). 1994. *Human Development Report 1994*. Delhi: Oxford University Press.

———. 2003. *Human Development Report 2003*. Delhi: Oxford University Press.

———. 2004. *Human Development Report 2004*. Delhi: Oxford University Press.

United Nations Educational, Scientific, and Cultural Organization (UNESCO). 1994. *UNESCO Statistical Yearbook, 1994*. Paris: UNESCO.

———. 2005. *Education for All: Global Monitoring Report*. Paris: UNESCO. (www.efareport.unesco.org)

United Nations Educational, Scientific, and Cultural Organization Institute for Statistics. 2005. *Global Education Digest 2004—Comparing Education Statistics Across the World*. Paris: UNESCO. (www.uis.unesco.org)

United Nations Human Development Programme (UNHDP). 2004. *Human Development Report 2004*. New York: Oxford University Press.

United Nations International Children's Emergency Fund (UNICEF). 2000. *The State of the World's Children 2000*. New York: UNICEF.

United Nations International Conference on Population and Development. 1995. *Population and Development*. New York: United Nations.

United States. Bureau of the Census. 1975. *Historical Statistics of the United States, Colonial Times to 1970, Part 1*. Washington, DC: Government Printing Office.

———. 2001. *Educational Attainment in the United States: March 2001*. Washington, DC: U.S. Census Bureau. (www.census.gov/population)

———. 2003. *Statistical Abstract of the United States, 2003. 123rd edition*. Washington, DC: Government Printing Office.

United States. Department of Education. 1995. *Digest of Education Statistics*. Washington, DC: Government Printing Office.

United States. Office of Education. 1944. *Biennial Survey of Education*. Vol. 2. *Statistics of Higher Education, 1939–40 and 1941–42*. Washington, DC: Department of Health, Education, and Welfare.

Useem, Michael, and Jerome Karabel. 1986. "Pathways to Top Corporate Management." *American Sociological Review* 51: 184–200.

van den Berghe, Pierre L. 1970. *Race and Racism: A Comparative Perspective*. New York: John Wiley.

Veblen, Thorstein. [1918] 1957. *The Higher Learning in America: A Memorandum on the Conduct of Universities by Business Men*. New York: Hill and Wang.

von der Mehden, Fred R. 1969. *Politics of Developing Nations*. 2d ed. Englewood Cliffs, NJ: Prentice Hall.

Waller, Willard. 1932. *The Sociology of Teaching*. New York: John Wiley.

Wallerstein, Immanuel. 1974. *Capitalist Agriculture and the Origins of the European World Economy in the 16th Century*. New York: Academic Press.

Walters, Pamela Barnhouse, David R. James, and Holly J. McCammon. 1997. "Citizenship and Public Schools: Accounting for Racial Inequality in Education in the Pre- and Post-Disenfranchisement South." *American Sociological Review* 62: 34–52.

Warner, W. Lloyd et al. 1944. *Who Shall Be Educated?* New York: Harper and Brothers.

Warner, W. Lloyd, with Marcia Meeker and Kenneth Eells. 1949. *Social Class in America*. Chicago: Science Research Associates.

Watt, Toni Terling. 2003. "Are Small Schools and Private Schools Better for Adolescents' Emotional Adjustment?" *Sociology of Education* 76: 344–67.

Wayne, Andrew J., and Peter Youngs. 2003. "Teacher Characteristics and Student Achievement Gains: A Review." *Review of Educational Research* 73: 89–122.

Weakliem, David, Julia McQuillan, and Tracy Schauer. 1995. "Toward Meritocracy? Changing Social-Class Differences in Intellectual Ability." *Sociology of Education* 68: 271–86.

Weber, Max. [1917] 1946. "The Chinese Literati." Pp. 416–41 in Hans H. Gerth and C. Wright Mills (Eds.), *From Max Weber*. New York: Oxford University Press.

———. [1921] 1946. "Bureaucracy." Pp. 196–244 in Hans H. Gerth and C. Wright Mills (Eds.), *From Max Weber*. New York: Oxford University Press.

———. [1921] 1978. *Economy and Society*. Berkeley: University of California Press.

Wells, Amy Stuart. 1991. "Choice in Education: Examining the Evidence on Equity." *Teachers College Record* 93: 156–73.

———. 1996. "African-American Students' Views of School Choice." Pp. 25–49 in Bruce Fuller and Richard F. Elmore (Eds.), *Who Chooses? Who Loses?* New York: Teachers College Press.

Welter, Rush. 1962. *Popular Education and Democratic Thought in America*. New York: Columbia University Press.

Wenglinsky, Harold. 1997. "How Money Matters: The Effect of School District Spending on Academic Achievement." *Sociology of Education* 70: 221–37.

White, Merry I. 1987. *The Japanese Educational Challenge: A Commitment to Children*. New York: Free Press.

———. 1994. The *Material Child: Coming of Age in Japan and America*. New York: Free Press.

Whitehurst, Gregory J. 2005. *NAEP 2004 Trends in Academic Progress: Three Decades of Student Performance in Reading and Mathematics*. Washington DC: National Center for Education Statistics.

Widner, Jennifer A. 1992. *The Rise of a Party-State in Kenya: From Harambee! to Nyayo!* Berkeley: University of California Press.

Wilkinson, Louise C., and Cora B. Marrett. 1985. *Gender Influence in Classroom Interaction*. Orlando, FL: Academic Press.

Williams, Raymond. 1961. *The Long Revolution*. London: Chatto and Windus.

Willingham, Warren W. 1985. *Success in College: The Role of Personal Qualities and Academic Ability*. New York: College Entrance Examination Board.

Willis, Paul. 1979. *Learning to Labour: How Working Class Kids Get Working Class Jobs*. Westmead, UK: Saxon House.

Willms, J. Douglas, and Frank Echols. 1993. "The Scottish Experience of Parental Choice in Schools." Pp. 49–68 in Edith Rasell and Richard Rothstein (Eds.), *School Choice: Examining the Evidence*. Washington, DC: Economic Policy Institute.

Wilson, William Julius. 1987. *The Truly Disadvantaged: The Inner City, the Underclass, and Public Policy*. Chicago: University of Chicago Press.

Winkler, Donald R. 1990. *Higher Education in Latin America: Issues of Efficiency and Equity*. Discussion Paper 77. Washington, DC: World Bank.

Witte, John F. 1996. "Who Benefits from the Milwaukee Choice Program?" Pp. 118–37 in Bruce Fuller and Richard F. Elmore (Eds.), *Who Chooses? Who Loses?* New York: Teachers College Press.

Witte, John F., Andrea B. Bailey, and Christopher A. Thorn. 1993. *Third-Year Report: Milwaukee Parental Choice Program*. Unpublished manuscript, Department of Political Science, University of Wisconsin, Madison.

Wong, Sandra. 1991. "Evaluating the Context of Textbooks: Public Interest and Professional Authority." *Sociology of Education* 64: 11–8.

World AIDS Conference. 2002. *World AIDS Conference Report*. Barcelona: World AIDS Conference.

World Bank. 1988. *Education in Sub-Saharan Africa: Policies for Adjustment, Revitalization, and Expansion*. Washington, DC: World Bank.

———. 1993. *The East Asian Miracle: Economic Growth and Public Policy*. Washington, DC: World Bank.

———. 2005a. "World Bank Lending for Education, 1963–2003." (www.devdata.worldbank.org/edstats)

———. 2005b. *World Development Indicators 2005*. New York: World Bank.

Wuthnow, Robert. 1996. *Poor Richard's Principle*. Princeton, NJ: Princeton University Press.

Wylie, Laurence. 1974. *Village in the Vaucluse*. 3rd ed. Cambridge, MA: Harvard University Press.

Wyllie, Irvin G. 1954. *The Self-Made Man in America: The Myth of Rags to Riches*. New Brunswick, NJ: Rutgers University Press.

Yair, Gad. 2000. "Educational Battlefields in America: The Tug-of-War over Students' Engagement with Instruction." *Sociology of Education* 73: 247–69.

Young, Michael. 1958. *The Rise of the Meritocracy*. London: Thames and Hudson.

Zeng, Kangmin. 1996. "Prayer, Luck, and Spiritual Strength: The Desecularization of Entrance Examination Systems in East Asia." *Comparative Education Review* 40: 264–79.

Zeng, Kangmin, and Gerald K. LeTendre. 1998. "Adolescent Suicide and Academic Competition in East Asia." *Comparative Education Review* 42: 513–28.

INDEX

Page numbers followed by *n* indicate notes.